graphic

JAVA™

MASTERING THE AWT

D0473417

THE SUNSOFT PRESS
JAVA SERIES

▼ ***Core Java***
Gary Cornell & Cay S. Horstmann

▼ ***Graphic Java***
David Geary & Alan L. McClellan

▼ ***Instant Java***
John A. Pew

▼ ***Java by Example***
Jerry R. Jackson & Alan L. McClellan

▼ ***Just Java***
Peter van der Linden

graphic
JAVA™
MASTERING THE AWT

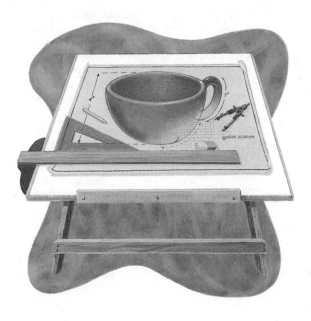

DAVID M. GEARY • ALAN L. MCCLELLAN

SunSoft Press
A Prentice Hall Title

© 1997 Sun Microsystems, Inc.—
Printed in the United States of America.
2550 Garcia Avenue, Mountain View, California
94043-1100 U.S.A.

All rights reserved. This product and related documentation are protected by copyright and distributed under licenses restricting its use, copying, distribution, and decompilation. No part of this product or related documentation may be reproduced in any form by any means without prior written authorization of Sun and its licensors, if any.

RESTRICTED RIGHTS LEGEND: Use, duplication, or disclosure by the United States Government is subject to the restrictions set forth in DFARS 252.227-7013 (c)(1)(ii) and FAR 52.227-19.

The products described may be protected by one or more U.S. patents, foreign patents, or pending applications.

TRADEMARKS—HotJava, Java, Java Developer's Kit, Solaris, SPARC, SunOS, and SunSoft are trademarks of Sun Microsystems, Inc. Café Lite is a trademark of Symantec Corporation. Eiffel is a registered trademark of Interactive Software Engineering. FORTRAN, OS/2, and Smalltalk are registered trademarks of International Business Machines. HP-UX is a trademark of Hewlett-Packard. Macintosh and MacOS are trademarks of Apple Computer, Inc. Netscape and Netscape Navigator are trademarks of Netscape Communications Corporation. NEXTSTEP is a registered trademark of GS Corporation. OSF/1 is a trademark of Open Software Foundation, Inc. Windows 95 and Windows NT are trademarks or registered trademarks of Microsoft Corporation. WinEdit is a trademark of Wilson WindowWare. WinZip is a trademark of Noci Mak Computing.

The publisher offers discounts on this book when ordered in bulk quantities.
For more information, contact Corporate Sales Department, Prentice Hall PTR ,
One Lake Street, Upper Saddle River, NJ 07458. Phone: 800-382-3419; FAX: 201- 236-7141.
E-mail: corpsales@prenhall.com.

Editorial/production supervision: *Patti Guerrieri*
Cover design director: *Jerry Votta*
Cover designer: *Anthony Gemmellaro*
Cover illustration: *Karen Strelecki*
Manufacturing manager: *Alexis R. Heydt*
Acquisitions editor: *Gregory G. Doench*
SunSoft Press publisher: *Rachel Borden*

10 9 8 7 6 5 4 3 2 1

ISBN 0-13-565847-0

SunSoft Press
A Prentice Hall Title

For RoyBoy
David

To Pete and Millie, for all your confidence
Alan

Contents

List of Examples, xvii
List of Tables, xxiii
List of Figures, xxvii
Preface, xxxi
Acknowledgments, xxxix

Part 1 Introducing the Abstract Window Toolkit

Chapter 1
Introduction, 3

The Abstract Window Toolkit, 3

The Graphic Java Toolkit, 3

Peers and Platform Independence, 4

Components—The Foundation of the AWT, 5

Components, Containers and Layout Managers, 6

Components, 7

What a Component Gives You, 9

Containers, 9

Layout Managers, 10

Summary, 10

Chapter 2

Applets and Applications, 13

Java Applets, 13

Using the appletviewer, 13

The Browser Infrastructure, 14

The java.awt.Applet Class, 15

Key java.applet.Applet Methods, 15

java.awt.Component Display Methods, 18

Java Applications, 18

Setting Up an Application, 19

Displaying Applications, 20

Combining Applet and Application Code, 20

Summary, 22

Chapter 3

Graphics, Colors, and Fonts, 25

Manipulating Graphics and Color, 26

Drawing a Rectangle, 27

Overview of DrawnRectangle, 28

Obtaining a Component's Graphics Object, 31

Obtaining a Component's Background Color, 31

Obtaining a Shade of a Color, 32

Filling a Rectangle, 33

gjt.DrawnRectangle Implementation, 34

Drawing an Etched Rectangle, 37

Painting Etched-in and Etched-out Borders, 40

Drawing a 3-D Rectangle, 42

Painting Inset and Raised 3-D Borders, 46

Exercising the Rectangle Classes, 47

Manipulating Fonts, 52

The AWT Font Model, 53

The x,y Origin for Drawing Strings, 53

Overview of gjt.LabelCanvas, 54

Working With FontMetrics in a Program, 55

Obtaining Font Dimensions, 57

Dynamically Positioning a String, 57

Drawing a String in Reverse Video, 59

gjt.LabelCanvas Implementation, 59

Exercising the LabelCanvas, 62

Summary, 65

Chapter 4

Event Handling, 67

The AWT Event Model, 67

Overriding Event Handling Methods, 68

Propagated Events, 69

Event Type Constants, 69

Propagated Events Propagate Outward, 73

Overriding Propagated Event Handlers, 73

Event Modifier Constants, 75

Mouse Button Events, 76

Of Mice and Buttons, 78

Monitoring Mouse Events, 78

Sensing Double Clicking, 81

Action Events, 82

Identifying Components by Label — Just Say No, 85

Custom Component Events, 87

Extending java.awt.Event, 89

Hand-Delivering Events, 91

Summary, 92

Chapter 5

Menus, 95

The Menu Classes, 96

A File Menu, 97

Handling Menu Events, 99

Tear-off Menus, 101

A Menubar Printer, 103

A FrameWithMenuBar Class, 104

    FrameWithMenuBar In Action, 106

Help Menus, 108

Checkbox Menu Items, 111

Cascading Menus, 114

Dynamically Modifying Menus, 116

Summary, 121

Chapter 6

Images, 123

The Image Class and the Image Package, 123

Image Producers and Image Observers, 124

Obtaining and Displaying Images, 125

Differences Between Applets and Applications, 127

Waiting for an Image to Load, 128

Painting Images a Scanline at a Time, 131

    Eliminating the Flash, 132

    Using MediaTracker, 133

Filtering Images, 135

gjt.image.BleachImageFilter, 141

    The Color Model and the Alpha Value of a Pixel, 144

    gjt.image.DissolveFilter, 145

    gjt.image.ImageDissolver, 147

Summary, 153

Chapter 7

Components, Containers, and Layout Managers, 155

The Big Three of the AWT, 156

LayoutManager Responsibilities, 158

Layout Managers and the Good Life, 159

Layout Managers and Container Insets, 161

Peers and Insets, 162

Painting a Container's Components, 163

TenPixelBorder, 163

Layout Managers and Component Preferred Sizes, 166

Standard AWT Layout Managers, 168

Decisions, Decisions—Which Layout Manager to Use?, 169

   The BorderLayout Layout Manager, 170
   The CardLayout Layout Manager, 171
   The FlowLayout Layout Manager, 174
   The GridLayout Layout Manager, 176

The GridBagLayout Layout Manager, 178

   GridBagLayout and GridBagConstraints, 178
   gjt.Box Unit Test, 186

Laying Out Components in Nested Panels, 191

   Communication Among Nested Panels, 196
   GridLabApplet Implementation, 200

Custom Layout Managers, 204

   gjt.BulletinLayout, 204
   gjt.RowLayout, 207
   Exercising the RowLayout Custom Layout Manager, 216
   RowLayoutApplet Implementation, 223
   gjt.ColumnLayout, 225
   Exercising the ColumnLayout Custom Layout Manager, 228

Summary, 232

Part 2   *The Graphic Java Toolkit—Extending the AWT*

Chapter 8

Introducing the Graphic Java Toolkit, 237

Overview of the Graphic Java Toolkit, 238

The GJT Packages, 238
The GJT Classes, 239
Custom Components in the Graphic Java Toolkit, 242
The GJT Utility Classes, 242
Assertions, 242
Packaging Custom Components, 242
Type-Checked Constants, 244
The gjt.Util Class, 246
The GJT test Package, 246

Summary, 249

Chapter 9

Separators and Bargauges, 251

gjt.Separator, 251
Separator Associations and Responsibilities, 252
Exercising the Separator, 258
gjt.Bargauge, 262
Bargauge Associations and Responsibilities, 262
Exercising the Bargauge, 267
Summary, 275

Chapter 10
Borders, 277

gjt.Border, 277
gjt.ThreeDBorder, 282
gjt.EtchedBorder, 283
Exercising Border, 284
Summary, 295

Chapter 11
ImageButton and StateButton, 297

gjt.Image Button, 297
gjt.ImageButton Associations and Responsibilities, 298
Image Button Controllers, 306
   Flexibility, 307
   Hierarchies of Image Button Controllers, 307
   Dynamically Setting Controllers, 308
   Reduced Complexity in ImageButton, 309
   The MouseController Interface, 309
ImageButton Events, 314
Exercising the Image Button and Its Controllers, 315
gjt.StateButton, 322
Exercising the StateButton and Its Controllers, 324
Summary, 327

Chapter 12
Toolbars, 329

Overview of Toolbar, 329
gjt.ImageButtonPanel, 331
   ImageButtonPanel Associations and Responsibilities, 331
gjt.Toolbar Associations and Responsibilities, 336

ImageButtonPanel Mouse Event Controllers, 338
    ImageButtonPanelController, 339
    RadioImageButtonPanelController, 340
ExclusiveImageButtonPanel, 341
Exercising the Toolbar, 342
Summary, 348

Chapter 13
Rubberbanding, 351

The Graphic Java Toolkit Rubberband Package, 352
The Rubberband Base Class, 352
Rubberband Associations and Responsibilities, 353
Painting in XOR Mode, 357
Drawing Rubberband Lines, 358
Drawing Rubberband Rectangles and Ellipses, 359
A Rubberband Panel, 360
Exercising the Rubberband Package, 361
Refactoring the Unit Test, 366
The GJT DrawingPanel Class, 367
Summary, 371

Chapter 14
Dialogs, 373

The AWT Dialog, 373
Dismissing a Dialog, 375
gjt.DialogClient, 376
GJT Dialog Classes, 379
GJTDialog Base Class, 381
gjt.ButtonPanel, 382

gjt.MessageDialog, 383

   The Singleton Pattern and the MessageDialog, 387

gjt.YesNoDialog, 388

gjt.QuestionDialog, 390

gjt.ProgressDialog, 395

Exercising the GJT Dialogs, 397

Summary, 402

Chapter 15
FontDialog, 405

gjt.FontDialog, 406

A Font Panel, 413

Forcing a Container to Lay Out Its Components, 415

The Font Selection Panel, 418

The Font Picker Panel, 419

The Font Buttons Panel, 422

Exercising the gjt.FontDialog, 424

Summary, 428

Chapter 16
Scrollers, 431

Scrollbars, 432

Scrolling With the Graphic Java Toolkit, 435

   gjt.Scroller Layout, 436

gjt.Scroller, 445

gjt.ComponentScroller, 454

gjt.ImageCanvas and gjt.ImageScroller, 457

Exercising the gjt.ImageScroller, 459

Exercising the gjt.ComponentScroller, 463

Summary, 471

Chapter 17
Sprite Animation, 473

The Participants, 473

Sequences and Sprites, 475

  gjt.animation.Sequence, 475
  gjt.animation.Sprite, 480

Playfields and Double Buffering, 488

  gjt.animation.Playfield, 488
  Double Buffering, 493

Collision Detection, 499

  gjt.animation.CollisionArena, 499
  gjt.animation.CollisionDetector, 499
  gjt.animation.SpriteCollisionDetector, 500
  gjt.animation.EdgeCollision, 501

Exercising the gjt.animation Package, 502

  Simple Animation, 503
  Bump Animation, 507
  Two-Sprite Collision, 511

Summary, 515

Part 3   Appendixes

Appendix A
AWT Class Diagrams 519

Appendix B
The Graphic Java CD-ROM, 579

Index, 585

List of Examples

Example 2-1: Starter Applet 16

Example 2-2: Starter Graphical Application. 19

Example 2-3: Combining Applet and Application Code 20

Example 3-1: gjt.DrawnRectangle Source Code. .34

Example 3-2: gjt.EtchedRectangle Class Source Code 38

Example 3-3: gjt.ThreeDRectangle Class Source Code 44

Example 3-4: gjt.test.DrawnRectangleTest Class Source Code. 49

Example 3-5: gjt.LabelCanvas Class Source Code .60

Example 3-6: gjt.test.LabelCanvasTest Class Source Code 63

Example 4-1: MouseSensorApplet Source Code. 76

Example 4-2: EventMonitorApplet Source Code. 78

Example 4-3: DoubleClickApplet Source Code. 81

Example 4-4: ActionApplet Source Code 84

Example 4-5: gjt.SelectionEvent Class Source Code 89

Example 5-1: FileMenuTest Class Source Code. 98

Example 5-2: Expanded FileMenuTest Class Source Code 99

Example 5-3: Improved Event Handling FileMenuTest Class Source
Code. 100

Example 5-4: `MenuBarPrinter` Class Source Code. 103

Example 5-5: `FrameWithMenuBar` Class Source Code 104

Example 5-6: `FileEditMenuTest` Class Source Code 107

Example 5-7: `HelpMenuTest` Class Source Code 110

Example 5-8: `RadioMenu` Class Source Code. 112

Example 5-9: `RadioMenuTest` Class Source Code 113

Example 5-10: `CascadingTest` Class Source Code. 115

Example 5-11: `SelfModifyingMenu` Class Source Code 118

Example 5-12: `SelfModifyingTest` Class Source Code 119

Example 6-1: Simple Applet With an Image 125

Example 6-2: Application With an Image 127

Example 6-3: Image Loading All at Once 128

Example 6-4: Image Loading Smoothly 131

Example 6-5: Image Loading Without Flashing 132

Example 6-6: Image Loading With the `MediaTracker` Class 133

Example 6-7: Image Loading With the `gjt.Util` Class 134

Example 6-8: Bleaching an Image With a Filter 138

Example 6-9: `gjt.image.BleachImageFilter` Class Source Code 142

Example 6-10: `gjt.image.DissolveFilter` Class Source Code. 146

Example 6-11: `gjt.image.ImageDissolver` Class Source Code. 150

Example 7-1: `TenPixelBorder` Class Source Code. 163

Example 7-2: `TenPixelBorderTestApplet` Class Source Code. 165

Example 7-3: `BorderLayoutApplet` Class Source Code. 171

Example 7-4: `CardLayoutApplet` Class Source Code 173

Example 7-5: `FlowLayoutApplet` Class Source Code 175

Example 7-6: `GridLayoutApplet` Class Source Code 177

Example 7-7: `gjt.Box` Class Source Code 181

Example 7-8: `gjt.test.BoxTest` Class Source Code 189

Example 7-9: `GridLabApplet` Class Source Code 201

Example 7-10: `gjt.BulletinLayout` Class Source Code. 205

Example 7-11: `gjt.RowLayout` Class Source Code 213

Example 7-12: `RowLayoutApplet` Class Source Code 223

Example 7-13: `gjt.ColumnLayout` Class Source Code 226

Example 7-14: `ColumnLayoutApplet` Class Source Code 230

Example 9-1: `gjt.Separator` Class Source Code 256

Example 9-2: `gjt.test.SeparatorTest` Class Source Code 259

Example 9-3: `gjt.Bargauge` Class Source Code 265

Example 9-4: `gjt.test.SimpleBargaugeTest` Class Source
Code 269

Example 9-5: `gjt.test.BargaugeTest` Class Source Code 272

Example 10-1: `gjt.Border` Class Source Code . , , , , , , , ...280

Example 10-2: `gjt.ThreeDBorder` Class Source Code 282

Example 10-3: `gjt.EtchedBorder` Class Source Code 283

Example 10-4: `gjt.test.BorderTest` Class Source Code 291

Example 11-1: `gjt.ImageButton` Class Source Code .303

Example 11-2: `gjt.SpringyImageButtonController`Class
Source Code 311

Example 11-3: `gjt.StickyImageButtonController` Class
Source Code 312

Example 11-4: `gjt.ImageButtonEvent` Class Source Code 314

Example 11-5: `gjt.test.ImageButtonTest` Class Source
Code 320

Example 11-6: `gjt.StateButton` Class Source Code .323

Example 11-7: `gjt.StateButtonController` Class Source
Code 324

Example 11-8: `gjt.test.StateButtonTest` Class Source
Code 326

Example 12-1: `gjt.ImageButtonPanel` Class Source Code 334

Example 12-2: `gjt.Toolbar` Class Source Code 337

Example 12-3: `gjt.ImageButtonPanelController` Class
Source Code 339

Example 12-4: `gjt.RadioImageButtonPanelController`
Class Source Code 340

Example 12-5: `gjt.ExclusiveImageButtonPanel` Class Source Code 341

Example 12-6: `gjt.test.ToolbarTest` Class Source Code 346

Example 13-1: `gjt.rubberband.Rubberband` Class Source Code 354

Example 13-2: `gjt.rubberband.RubberbandLine` Class Source Code 358

Example 13-3: `gjt.rubberband.RubberbandRectangle` Class Source Code 359

Example 13-4: `gjt.rubberband.RubberbandEllipse` Class Source Code 359

Example 13-5: `gjt.rubberband.RubberbandPanel` Class Source Code 360

Example 13-6: `gjt.test.RubberbandTest` Class Source Code, Take I 363

Example 13-7: `gjt.DrawingPanel` Class Source Code 367

Example 13-8: `gjt.test.RubberbandTest` Class Source Code 369

Example 14-1: `gjt.test.MessageDialotTest` Class Source Code 378

Example 14-2: `GJTDialog` Class Source Code. 381

Example 14-3: `gjt.ButtonPanel` Class Source Code 382

Example 14-4: `gjt.MessageDialog` Class Source Code 385

Example 14-5: `gjt.YesNoDialog` Class Source Code 389

Example 14-6: `gjt.QuestionDialog` Class Source Code. 392

Example 14-7: `gjt.ProgressDialog` Class Source Code. 396

Example 14-8: `gjt.test.DialogTest` Class Source Code. 399

Example 15-1: `gjt.FontDialog` Class Source Code. 410

Example 15-2: `gjt.test.FontDialogTest` Class Source Code 426

Example 16-1: `gjt.ScrollerLayout` Class Source Code. 442

Example 16-2: `gjt.Scroller` Class Source Code 451

Example 16-3: `gjt.ComponentScroller` Class Source Code 454

Example 16-4: `gjt.ImageCanvas` Class Source Code 457

Example 16-5: `gjt.ImageScroller` Class Source Code. 458

Example 16-6: `gjt.test.ImageScrollerTest` Class Source
Code. 461

Example 16-7: `gjt.test.ComponentScrollerTest` Class
Source Code. 466

Example 17-1: `gjt.animation.Sequence` Class Source
Code 477

Example 17-2: `gjt.animation.Sprite` Class Source Code 484

Example 17-3: `gjt.animation.Playfield` Class Source
Code . . . . , , , , , , , . 490

Example 17-4: `gjt.animation.CollisionArena` Class Source
Code 499

Example 17-5: `gjt.animation.CollisionDetector` Class
Source Code. 500

Example 17-6: `gjt.animation.SpriteCollisionDetector`
Class Source Code 500

Example 17-7: `gjt.animation.EdgeCollisionDetector`
Class Source Code 501

Example 17-8: `gjt.test.SimpleAnimationTest` Class Source
Code 505

Example 17-9: `gjt.test.BumpAnimationTest` Class Source
Code 509

Example 17-10: `gjt.test.TwoDrinkersAnimationTest` Class
Source Code. 513

List of Tables

Table P-1: GJT Package Structure xxxv

Table P-2: Coding Conventions xxxvi

Table P-3: Typographic Conventions xxxvi

Table 1-1: Component Subclasses 7

Table 1-2: Container Subclasses 9

Table 2-1: Commonly Used applet.Applet Methods 16

Table 2-2: Commonly Used awt.Component Methods 18

Table 3-1: gjt.DrawnRectangle Responsibilities 29

Table 3-2: gjt.DrawnRectangle Associations 30

Table 3-3: gjt.EtchedRectangle Responsibilities 38

Table 3-4: gjt.ThreeDRectangle Responsibilities .43

Table 3-5: Java Font Model 52

Table 3-6: gjt.LabelCanvas Responsibilities 56

Table 3-7: gjt.LabelCanvas Associations 56

Table 4-1: Event-Driven Methods Used in Components 68

Table 4-2: java.awt.Event Constants 70

Table 4-3: Propagated Event Handler Convenience Methods 72

Table 4-4: Component Choices When Handling Propagated Events. 74

Table 4-5: Event Handling Guidelines 74

Table 4-6: Event Modifiers 75

Table 4-7: Value of the `what` Argument in the `action()` Method 85

Table 6-1: `java.awt.Image` Methods 124

Table 6-2: Methods That Are Passed an `ImageObserver` 126

Table 6-3: `ImageObserver` Constants 130

Table 6-4: `gjt.image.BleachImageFilter` Responsibilities 141

Table 6-5: `awt.image.ColorModel` Public Abstract Instance
Methods 144

Table 6-6: `gjt.image.DissolveFilter` Responsibilities 145

Table 6-7: `gjt.image.ImageDissolver` Responsibilities 147

Table 7-1: Layout Managers and Preferred/Minimum Sizes 167

Table 7-2: The AWT's Default Layout Manager Classes 168

Table 7-3: `Container` Default Layout Managers 169

Table 7-4: Layout Manager Decision Table 169

Table 7-5: `CardLayout` Stacking Methods 173

Table 7-6: `GridBagConstraints` Instance Variables and Valid
Values 179

Table 7-7: `gjt.Box` Responsibilities 181

Table 7-8: `Component` and `Container` Methods That Invalidate
Containers 200

Table 7-9: `gjt.RowLayout` Responsibilities 210

Table 7-10: `GridLabApplet` and `RowLayoutApplet`
Comparison 218

Table 7-11: `gjt.ColumnLayout` Responsibilities 225

Table 8-1: Graphic Java Toolkit Packages 238

Table 8-2: `gjt` Package Classes 239

Table 8-3: `gjt.animation` Package Classes 241

Table 8-4: `gjt.rubberband` Package Classes 241

Table 8-5: `gjt.test` Package Classes 241

Table 8-6: `gjt.image` Package Classes 241

Table 8-7: `gjt.Assert` Methods 243

Table 8-8: `gjt.Util` Methods 246

Table 9-1: `gjt.Separator` Responsibilities 252

Table 9-2: gjt.Separator Associations 253

Table 9-3: gjt.Bargauge Responsibilities.............................263

Table 9-4: gjt.Bargauge Associations 263

Table 10-1: gjt.Border Responsibilities 279

Table 10-2: gjt.Border Associations.................................279

Table 11-1: gjt.ImageButton Responsibilities 300

Table 11-2: gjt.ImageButton Associations............................301

Table 12-1: gjt.ImageButtonPanel Responsibilities 331

Table 12-2: gjt.ImageButtonPanel Associations.......................332

Table 12-3: gjt.Toolbar Responsibilities.............................336

Table 12-4: gjt.Toolbar Associations................................337

Table 13-1: gjt.rubberband.Rubberband Responsibilities 353

Table 13-2: gjt.rubberband.Rubberband Associations................354

Table 15-1: gjt.FontDialog Responsibilities 407

Table 15-2: gjt.FontDialog Associations 407

Table 16-1: gjt.Scroller Responsibilities.............................445

Table 16-2: gjt.Scroller Associations 445

Table 17-1: gjt.animation.Sequence Responsibilities.................476

Table 17-2: gjt.animation.Sequence Associations 477

Table 17-3: gjt.animation.Sprite Responsibilities 482

Table 17-4: gjt.animation.Sprite Associations.......................483

Table 17-5: gjt.animation.Playfield Responsibilities 489

Table 17-6: gjt.animation.Playfield Associations 489

List of Figures

Figure 1-1: Peers at Work 4

Figure 1-2: AWT Component Class Diagram. 6

Figure 1-3: Java AWT Components 8

Figure 2-1: `Applet`, `Container`, and `LayoutManager` Class
Diagram 15

Figure 2-2: A Starter Applet 17

Figure 2-3: A Java Application 20

Figure 3-1: Rectangles 27

Figure 3-2: Drawn Rectangles. 28

Figure 3-3: Calculating the Inner Bounds of a `DrawnRectangle` 33

Figure 3-4: Etched Rectangles. 37

Figure 3-5: Achieving an Etched Effect 41

Figure 3-6: Three-Dimensional Rectangles. 42

Figure 3-7: `gjt.DrawnRectangle` Unit Test. 48

Figure 3-8: The AWT Font Model 53

Figure 3-9: Drawing Strings With the `drawString()` Method. 53

Figure 3-10: `gjt.LabelCanvas` 55

Figure 3-11: Determining a String's x Location. 58

Figure 3-12: Determining a String's y Location 58

Figure 3-13: Determining a String's x,y Location 59

Figure 3-14: gjt.LabelCanvas Unit Test. 63

Figure 4-1: Action Events 83

Figure 5-1: AWT Menu Classes Diagram 96

Figure 5-2: A File Menu 97

Figure 5-3: A Tear-off Menu 102

Figure 5-4: Motif and Windows 95 Help Menus 109

Figure 5-5: A Checkbox Menu Item 111

Figure 5-6: A Cascading Menu 114

Figure 5-7: A Self-Modifying Menu 117

Figure 6-1: Image Filter Class Diagram 136

Figure 6-2: Bleaching Images. 137

Figure 6-3: Image Filtering Process. 140

Figure 6-4: Dissolving Images 145

Figure 7-1: Container Class Diagram 156

Figure 7-2: Container Extensions Class Diagram 157

Figure 7-3: Container With Insets 161

Figure 7-4: TenPixelBorderTestApplet In Action. 165

Figure 7-5: BorderLayoutApplet in Action 170

Figure 7-6: CardLayout in Action. 172

Figure 7-7: FlowLayout in Action. 175

Figure 7-8: GridLayout in Action. 177

Figure 7-9: An Applet That Uses a GridBagLayout 180

Figure 7-10: A GridBagLayout Applet Resized. 187

Figure 7-11: Nested Panels in an Applet 192

Figure 7-12: Nested Panel Layout Diagram 193

Figure 7-13: Nested Panel Updates. 197

Figure 7-14: FlowLayout Resize Behavior. 208

Figure 7-15: RowLayout at Work. 217

Figure 7-16: RowLayoutApplet Layout Diagram 219

Figure 7-17: ColumnLayout at Work. 229

Figure 8-1: Unit Test Layout Diagram. 248

Figure 9-1: gjt.Separator Class Diagram. 252

Figure 9-2: gjt.Separator Unit Test. 258

Figure 9-3: SeparatorTest Layout Diagram 259

Figure 9-4: gjt.Bargauge Class Diagram 262

Figure 9-5: gjt.Bargauge Class Simple Test 268

Figure 9-6: gjt.Bargauge Unit Test. 270

Figure 9-7: BargaugeTest Layout Diagram 271

Figure 10-1: gjt.Border Class Diagram 278

Figure 10-2: gjt.Border Unit Test 284

Figure 10-3: BorderTest Layout Diagram. 285

Figure 11-1: gjt.ImageButton Class Diagram 298

Figure 11-2: gjt.ImageButtonController Class Diagram 308

Figure 11-3: gjt.ImageButton Unit Test 316

Figure 11-4: ImageButtonTest Layout Diagram. 317

Figure 11-5: gjt.StateButton Unit Test 325

Figure 12-1: gjt.Toolbar Class Diagram 330

Figure 12-2: A Toolbar 330

Figure 12-3: gjt.Toolbar Unit Test 343

Figure 12-4: ToolbarTest Layout Diagram. 344

Figure 13-1: gjt.rubberband Package Diagram 352

Figure 13-2: gjt.rubberband.Rubberband Unit Test 361

Figure 13-3: RubberbandTest Layout Diagram 362

Figure 14-1: AWT Dialog Class Diagram 374

Figure 14-2: MessageDialog Output 377

Figure 14-3: GJT Dialog Class Overview. 379

Figure 14-4: QuestionDialog Applet 380

Figure 14-5: YesNoDialog Applet 380

Figure 14-6: ProgressDialog Applet 381

Figure 14-7: GJT `MessageDialog` Class. 384

Figure 14-8: GJT `YesNoDialog` Class 388

Figure 14-9: GJT `QuestionDialog` Class 391

Figure 14-10: GJT `ProgressDialog` Class 395

Figure 14-11: `DialogTest` Unit Test. 397

Figure 14-12: `DialogTest` Layout Diagram 398

Figure 15-1: `gjt.FontDialog` Class Diagram 406

Figure 15-2: `FontDialog` In Action 408

Figure 15-3: `FontPanel` Layout Diagram 409

Figure 15-4: `FontDialog` With Preview Panel Resized 417

Figure 15-5: `gjt.FontDialog` Unit Test. 425

Figure 16-1: Scrollbar in Windows 95 and Motif 434

Figure 16-2: `gjt.Scroller` Class Diagram 435

Figure 16-3: `ScrollerLayout` Diagram 436

Figure 16-4: `gjt.ComponentScroller` Unit Test 456

Figure 16-5: `gjt.ImageScroller` Unit Test 460

Figure 16-6: `ImageScrollerTest` Layout Diagram. 461

Figure 16-7: `gjt.ComponentScroller` Unit Test 463

Figure 16-8: `ComponentScrollerTest` Layout Diagram 464

Figure 17-1: Animation Package Diagram. 474

Figure 17-2: `Sequence` Class Diagram 475

Figure 17-3: `Sprite` Class Diagram. 481

Figure 17-4: `Playfield` Class Diagram 488

Figure 17-5: Double Buffering in Action 494

Figure 17-6: Simple Animation Unit Test 503

Figure 17-7: Sprite Animation Unit Tests Layout. 505

Figure 17-8: Bump Animation Unit Test 508

Figure 17-9: Two Sprite Collision Animation Unit Test 512

Preface

Programmers working with Java™ typically don't have to write very much code before they're knee-deep in the Abstract Window Toolkit (AWT). And when they're knee-deep, they may start to look around for a helping hand.

In general, the goal of *Graphic Java* is to provide that helping hand. The way we do that is twofold:

- We describe practical use of the AWT, highlighting features, benefits, and *gotchas* and unraveling its mysteries as we go along.

- We describe extending the AWT, focusing on a set of high-level custom components we've developed and packaged as the Graphic Java Toolkit.

We'd like to emphasize use of the Graphic Java Toolkit. In many ways, *Graphic Java* is not just a book with an accompanying CD. It is a *product* with an accompanying book. The Graphic Java Toolkit is a fully developed, fully tested, and fully documented product, and we think you'll find it well worth your while to crack the seal on the book's CD and put that toolkit to use. You'll notice that these aren't *trinket* programs to illustrate a point. They are thoughtfully conceived for real-world utility.

As our subtitle suggests, we aim to help you *master* the AWT. To do that, we divide our book into two parts: exploring the AWT and extending the AWT.

Exploring the AWT

First, in Part 1 of *Graphic Java*, we describe the basics of using the AWT. We'll cover the range of standard classes provided by the AWT and show them in use. This includes:

- Manipulating graphics, colors, and fonts
- Managing events
- Positioning components in the display
- Manipulating images
- Creating menus

To illustrate the AWT in action, we'll draw on several custom components from Graphic Java Toolkit (GJT).

Extending the AWT

Second, in Part 2 of the book, we present the Graphic Java Toolkit. In all, there are over thirty of these custom components. Among these are components such as:

- Image buttons and toolbars
- Separators and bargauges
- Etched and three-dimensional rectangles and borders
- Image and component scrollers
- Rubberbands
- Convenience dialogs

The GJT also includes image filters and a package of classes that develop sprite animations. You are welcome to use and incorporate these into your own program development.

In describing these custom components, we highlight lessons learned and reveal tricks of the trade for those who'll be developing their own custom components. Along the way, we hope to encourage good programming practices, using Java's object-oriented features to develop elegant, maintainable, and readable code. And we try to do these things in practical terms, so that you can see and learn from examples of real programs.

Audience

This book is written for object-oriented programmers working with Java. There are numerous books explaining details of the Java language and how it works vis-a-vis Visual Basic, C, C++, etc. We leave details of how Java works to those books. If you are new to Java, as most people are, you might want one of those books alongside *Graphic Java*.

The Graphic Java Toolkit

The CD that accompanies this book includes:

- All the source code for the Graphic Java Toolkit.

- Unit test applets for all GJT components, including HTML files for unit test applets.

- HTML documentation for all GJT classes

- Numerous image files in .gif format developed by Pixelsite

Virtually all these programs are discussed throughout the book. Feel free to borrow, adapt, or extend these for your own purposes.

The Graphic Java CD Directory Structure

Figure P-1 shows the directory structure on the CD.

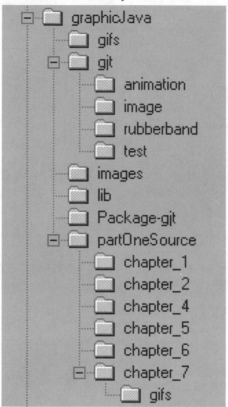

Figure P-1 *Graphic Java* CD Directory Structure

The Graphic Java Toolkit Package Structure

Table P-1 shows the GJT package structure.

Table P-1 GJT Package Structure

Package	Contents
gjt	This package contains the source files for many of the custom components discussed in *Graphic Java*.
gjt.animation	This package contains a set of classes that support sprite animation.
gjt.image	This package contains a set of classes that provide support for image manipulation such as bleaching or dissolving images.
gjt.test	This package contains source code for all the component unit tests discussed in *Graphic Java*.
gjt.rubberband	This package contains a set of classes that support rubberbanding—stretching lines and shapes over a backdrop without affecting the backdrop.

Internet Sources of Information

There are several online sources of information on Java. You can find online guides and tutorials on Sun's home page:

http://java.sun.com/

There is an active net newsgroup dedicated to Java:

comp.lang.java

There is also a mailing list where Java aficionados exchange ideas, questions, and solutions. For information about the mailing list, look on the World Wide Web at:

http://java.sun.com/mail.html

From these newsgroups and web sites, you'll be able to locate countless other resources, tutorials, Frequently-Asked-Questions (FAQs), and online magazines dedicated to Java.

For updates about this book and information about other books in the SunSoft Press Java Series, look on the web at:

http://www.sun.com/smi/ssoftpress/GraphicJava

For some of the coolest looking graphics on the planet, take a look at:

http://www.pixelsight.com:80/PS/pixelsite/pixelsite.html

Conventions Used in This Book

Table P-2 shows the coding conventions used in this book.

Table P-2 Coding Conventions

Convention	Example
Class names have initial capital letters.	`public class LineOfText`
Method names have initial lowercase and the rest of the words have an initial capital letter.	`public int getLength()`
Variable names have initial lowercase and the rest of the words have an initial capital letter.	`private int length` `private int bufferLength`
`static` variables begin with an underscore.	`protected static int _defaultSize = 2;`

Note that, for the most part, we refer to methods without their arguments; however, we include the arguments when the discussion warrants including them.

Table P-3 shows the typographic conventions used in this book.

Table P-3 Typographic Conventions

Typeface or Symbol	Description
CD-Rom (icon)	Indicates that the accompanying code, command, or file is available on the CD that accompanies this book.
`courier`	Indicates a command, file name, class name, method, argument, Java keyword, HTML tag, file content, or code excerpt.
`bold courier`	Indicates a sample command-line entry.
italics	Indicates definitions, emphasis, a book title, or a variable that you should replace with a valid value.

For Mac Users

Although the 1.0.2 version of the JDK is currently available for the Macintosh®, we have found it unreliable and have been unable to thoroughly test all of the applets contained in the book on the Macintosh. While the applets that we did test ran reliably, there were significant setup and configuration problems that we were unable to document for our Mac audience. We will explicitly support the Macintosh in a subsequent edition of *Graphic Java*.

Acknowledgments

We'd like to express our greatest appreciation to all the folks who've helped bring this project together. The good people at Prentice Hall are at the top of that list, headed by Greg Doench and Patti Guerrieri. They have bent over backwards to help put the polish on this book. We'd also like to thank Lisa Iarkowski and Gail Cocker-Bogusz for their help with all the great artwork and Leabe Berman for getting everyone across the country together when we needed to meet.

As always, we count on our conscientious technical reviewers for advice on accuracy and presentation. Of that batch of folks, we'd like to call out the work of Rob Gordon (the only delegate to the Second Luddite Congress to review two Java books), Tom LaStrange (of *twm* fame), and Doreen Collins. Special thanks also to Cay S. Horstmann of San Jose State University for bringing many issues to our attention.

Our immense appreciation goes to Keith Ohlfs of Pixelsite for granting us permission to use all the cool images. Those really provide the spit and polish for the applets. You can see more of Keith's handiwork at:

`http://www.pixelsight.com:80/PS/pixelsite/pixelsite.html`

Mary Lou Nohr, our editor, has done a heroic job helping us meet our deadlines and keeping our copy clean with her always critical eye.

As always, Rachel Borden and John Bortner of SunSoft Press have been there for us whenever we needed them. They're great folks to have on your side.

From the Java inner circle, we want to acknowledge Jerry R. Jackson for his sage advice. Thanks sifu.

Even though we weren't able to make use of his effort, we want to thank Lou Ordorica, Mac wizard, for his help testing applets on the Mac. Next revision, Lou.

Our management staff at SunSoft's Rocky Mountain Technology Center (RMTC) has been very supportive. Those folks include Eric H. Corwin, Director of RMTC, Randy Kalmeta, Dale E. Ferrario, Software Engineering Managers, Lynn Rohrer, Publications Manager, and Beth Papiano, Human Resources Director. This management team has jumped on the Java wave, making RMTC a great place to be.

Special thanks to Ashley Anna Geary, who turned out to be the best tester we have ever encountered. More software developers should have 7 year olds test their software. And while we're on the topic of family members, a big thanks goes to Ian, Drew, and Li McClellan as well. They've been very patient while their dad has been hunched over his computer the past few months. Oh, our wives, Lesa and Julie deserve enormous thanks for backing us up and giving us the time to write this book.

PART ONE

Introducing the Abstract Window Toolkit

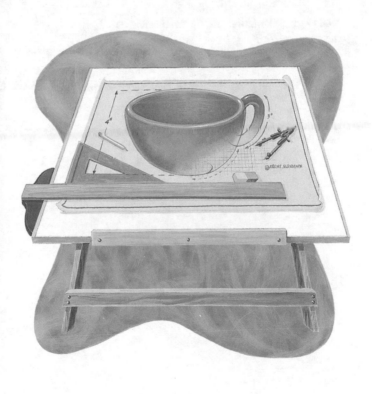

CHAPTER

1

- The Abstract Window Toolkit on page 3

- The Graphic Java Toolkit on page 3

- Peers and Platform Independence on page 4

- Components—The Foundation of the AWT on page 5

- Components, Containers and Layout Managers on page 6

- Summary on page 10

Introduction

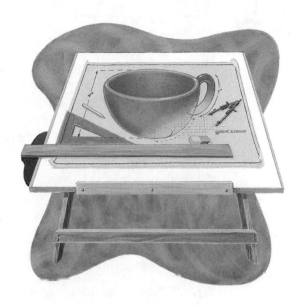

The Abstract Window Toolkit

Anyone writing Java™ applets and graphical applications is going to work with the Abstract Window Toolkit. Commonly referred to as the *AWT*, the Abstract Window Toolkit is part of the freely distributed Java Developer's Kit (JDK). The AWT is composed of a package of classes named java.awt, and it supports everything from creating buttons, menus, and dialog boxes, to complete GUI applications. The AWT classes are platform independent and are primarily used to build graphical user interfaces.

The Graphic Java Toolkit

The Graphic Java Toolkit (we'll refer to it as the *GJT*), is a set of Java packages, each offering custom components that extend the functionality of the AWT. While the AWT provides low-level components such as buttons and scrollbars, the GJT provides higher-level components such as image buttons and a component scroller.

The Graphic Java Toolkit provides more than 35 such components, ranging from image buttons and scrollers to rubberbanding and convenience dialogs. The Graphic Java Toolkit also includes separate packages for sprite animation and image filtering.

We'll refer to components in the Graphic Java Toolkit throughout this book, making general use of them in Part 1, in which we explore the AWT, and focusing specifically on them in Part 2, where we extend the AWT.

Peers and Platform Independence

As the programming interface for applet and graphical application development, the AWT provides a generalized set of classes that can be used without concern for platform-specific windowing issues. This feature is made possible by a set of AWT classes known as *peers*. Peers are native GUI components which are manipulated by the AWT classes. The way peers work and their influence on program development is sometimes confusing, so we'll take a closer look at them here and in subsequent chapters in this book.

The AWT delegates the actual rendering and behavior of menus, panels, labels, buttons, and so on, to the native windowing system. Peers are native, platform-dependent classes. The AWT classes delegate much of their functionality to these native, platform-dependent components. For example, when you use the AWT to create an instance of the Menu class, the Java runtime system creates an instance of a Menu peer. It is the Menu peer that does the real work of displaying and managing the menu behavior. In the case of a Menu, the Solaris™ JDK would create a Motif® Menu peer; the Windows 95™ JDK would create a Windows 95 Menu peer; the Macintosh® JDK would create a Macintosh Menu peer, and so on. Figure 1-1 shows how peers fit into the process of displaying components in native windowing systems.

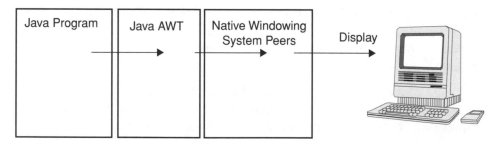

Figure 1-1 Peers at Work
A Java program creates and displays an AWT component, which creates and displays a native component (a peer).

The decision by the Java development team to use a peer approach for portability in the AWT enabled rapid development of a cross-platform window toolkit in the JDK. Using peers obviates the need to reimplement the functionality encapsulated in native windowing components. Additionally, the use of peers enables applets and applications using the AWT to retain the look-and-feel of the native windowing system. (Remember, peers are actually native components.) The Java AWT classes are just wrappers around the peers and delegate functionality to them.

Although using the AWT rarely requires you to deal directly with peers, you might be influenced by their presence. In some ways, the peer approach makes the AWT harder to understand—so much of the implementation is buried in the peers that it is sometimes difficult to trace a sequence of actions by looking through the AWT source. Only the Java designers can implement peers, as doing so requires rebuilding the entire AWT.

Components—The Foundation of the AWT

The AWT is a world of components; approximately half of the classes in the AWT are extensions of the java.awt.Component class. The Component class and its supporting cast are the foundation upon which the AWT is built:

- Component class – An abstract class for GUI components such as menus, buttons, labels, lists, and so on.

- Container – An abstract class that extends Component. Classes derived from Container, most notably Panel, Applet, Window, Dialog, Frame, can *contain* multiple components.

- LayoutManager – An interface that defines methods for positioning and sizing objects within a container. Java defines several default implementations of LayoutManager.

- Graphics class – An abstract class that defines methods for performing graphical operations in a component. Every component has an associated Graphics object.

Figure 1-2 shows a class diagram of the relationships between components, containers, and layout managers.[1]

---

1. Graphic Java contains many class diagrams that show relationships between classes. *AWT Class Diagrams* on page 519 provides an introduction to class diagrams and a complete set of class diagrams for the AWT.

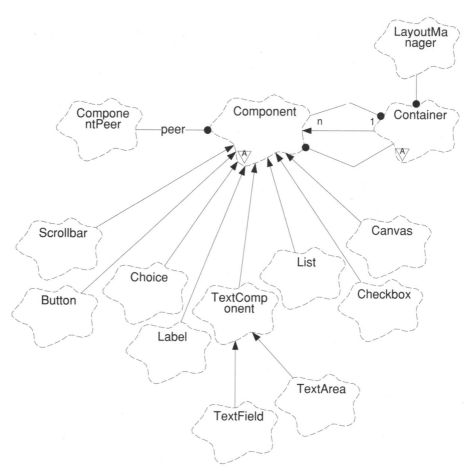

Figure 1-2 AWT Component Class Diagram

Components, Containers and Layout Managers

Component and Container form a simple, yet fundamental relationship of the AWT: containers may contain components. All containers come equipped with a layout manager, which positions and shapes (*lays out*) the container's components. A layout manager's responsibilities are defined by the java.awt.LayoutManager interface.[2] Much of the action that takes place in the AWT occurs between components, containers, and their layout managers.

2. A number of Java books available from Prentice Hall/SunSoft Press discuss Java interfaces.

Components

In Java parlance, user interface controls, such as panels, scrollbars, labéls, text fields, buttons, and so on are generically referred to as *components* because they all extend java.awt.Component. Table 1-1 lists the Java components derived from the Component class.

Table 1-1 Component **Subclasses**

Subclasses	Description
Label	A Component that displays a string.
Button	A textual button that generates an event.
Canvas	A component used for painting graphics.
Checkbox	A button that is essentially a state button. Checkbox provides on/off toggle values.
Choice	A push button that displays a menu.
List	A component that displays a list of selectable items.
Scrollbar	A bar with two arrows and a thumb.
TextComponent	The superclass of TextField and TextArea.
TextArea	A field in which the user can enter keyboard input, as in a scratch pad.
TextField	A field in which the user can enter keyboard input.

Figure 1-3 shows each of the standard Java AWT components.

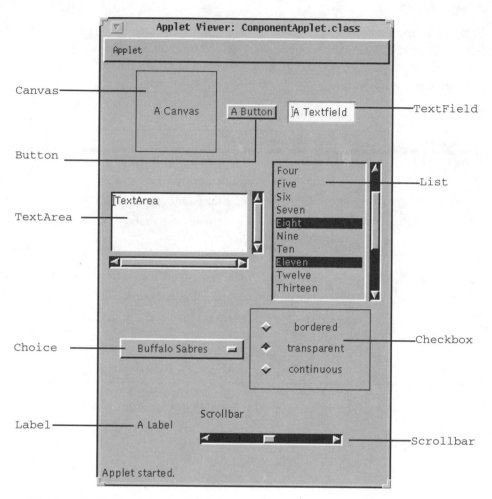

Figure 1-3 Java AWT Components

What a Component Gives You

A host of information is available about each instance of a Component object. For example, a Component has the following affiliated with it:

- Graphics object
- Location
- Size
- Native peer
- Parent container
- Fonts and font dimensions (referred to as font metrics in the AWT)
- Foreground and background colors

A Component can also be displayed or hidden and can report its bounds or whether it contains a given point.

Containers

java.awt.Container class is an abstract class that extends Component. A Container can contain multiple components. Using containers, you can group related components and treat them as a unit. This simplifies an applet's design and is useful in arranging components on the display. Note that the Applet class is a subclass of Panel, which extends Container, so all applets inherit the ability to contain components.

Table 1-2 lists the Java containers derived from the Container class.

Table 1-2 Container **Subclasses**

Subclasses	Description
Applet	An extension of Panel. Applet is the superclass of all applets.
Dialog	A extension of Window that can be modal or non-modal.
FileDialog	A Dialog that allows selection of a file.
Frame	An extension of Window, Frame is the container for an application. A Frame may have a menu bar, but an Applet may not.
Panel	An extension of Container, Panel is a simple container.
Window	An extension of Container, windows have no menu or border. Window is rarely extended directly; it is the superclass of Frame and Dialog.

Layout Managers

Containers merely keep track of the components they contain; they delegate positioning and shaping of their components to a layout manager. The `LayoutManager` interface defines methods for laying out components, and calculating the preferred and minimum sizes of their containers. Java provides five classes that implement the `LayoutManager` interface:

- `BorderLayout` – Lays out North/South/East/West/Center components
- `CardLayout` – Displays one panel at a time from a deck of panels
- `FlowLayout` – Specifies that components flow left to right, top to bottom
- `GridBagLayout` – Imposes constraints on each component in a grid
- `GridLayout` – Lays out components in a simple grid; components are stretched to fill the grid

We're going to talk extensively about layout managers—both about the standard AWT layout managers and about implementing custom layout managers. For now, the important point is to understand at a high level how they fit into the big picture of the AWT and applet development.

Summary

The AWT is a platform-independent windowing toolkit. It relies on *peers*, which are native windowing components that manage the display of applets and applications. Although their presence influences applet and graphical application development, you do not generally need to deal directly with peers.

There are four main classes in the Java Abstract Window Toolkit: the `Component` class, `Container` class, the `Graphics` class, and the `LayoutManager` interface.

Containers contain components, while layout managers position and shape the components contained in a container. These classes and the relationships between them form the foundation of the AWT.

The Graphic Java Toolkit (GJT) provides more than 35 high-level custom components that extend the functionality of the AWT. The GJT provides components such as scrollers, image buttons, separators, and convenience dialogs. The GJT also comes with separate packages for image filtering, rubberbanding, and sprite animation.

Classes from the GJT will serve to illustrate both using and extending the AWT throughout the rest of this book.

CHAPTER 2

- **Java Applets on page 13**

    - Using the appletviewer on page 13

    - The Browser Infrastructure on page 14

    - The java.awt.Applet Class on page 15

    - Key java.applet.Applet Methods on page 15

    - java.awt.Component Display Methods on page 18

- **Java Applications on page 18**

    - Setting Up an Application on page 19

    - Displaying Applications on page 20

- **Combining Applet and Application Code on page 20**

- **Summary on page 22**

Applets and Applications

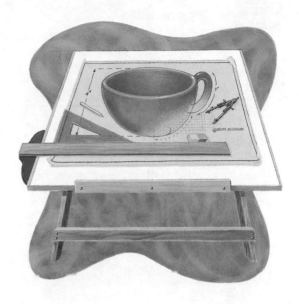

In this chapter, we cover the basics of writing Java applets and graphical applications. We include some simple programs that highlight the key methods used in any applet or graphical application, and we discuss the relationship between an applet and the java.awt package. First, we'll take a look at applets, and then we'll go into some detail about applications, noting differences and implications of each as we go along.

Java Applets

Applets are Java programs that execute within a Java-enabled web browser. Most of the graphical support required for an applet to execute is built in to the browser. The implication for applet programmers is that you don't need to worry about creating a frame for the applet to execute in. Also, applets execute in a secure fashion thanks to the security built in to Java-enabled web browsers, which will not allow an applet to write or modify any files.

Using the appletviewer

Applets are launched by embedding the applet HTML tag in a web page and then viewing that page with a Java-enabled browser or the appletviewer that comes with the Java Development Kit (JDK).

For consistency and ease of illustration, all of the applets in this book are used in the following way:

```
appletviewer applet_name.html
```

In this syntax, *applet_name*.html is a minimal HTML file that can be used as an argument to the appletviewer. The HTML file looks like this:

```
<title>Applet Title</title>
<hr>
<applet code="applet_name.class" width=width height=height>
</applet>
<hr>
```

Each applet on the CD included with this book has a corresponding HTML file that can be used as an argument to appletviewer. Of course, these applets could also be displayed within a Java-enabled web browser, as long as the web page includes the appropriate HTML applet tag to call the applet. The appletviewer ignores all but the applet HTML tag, so it can be used on any HTML file with an applet tag.

The Browser Infrastructure

When applets are executed in a Java-enabled browser, the browser provides a great deal of the infrastructure necessary for an applet's execution. For example, when a web page containing an applet is visited, the browser calls the set of methods required to initialize and start the applet. When the web page containing an applet is no longer displayed, the browser calls methods to terminate the applet's execution.

One point that sometimes confuses programmers new to Java is the absence of a main() statement in the applet code. In applets, main() is unnecessary because control for executing the applet is managed by the browser.

The java.awt.Applet Class

All applets extend `java.applet.Applet` (generically referred to as `Applet`). `Applet` extends `java.awt.Panel`, as illustrated in Figure 2-1. Since `Panel` is an AWT container, it has a default layout manager—a `FlowLayout`, which lays out the applet's components.

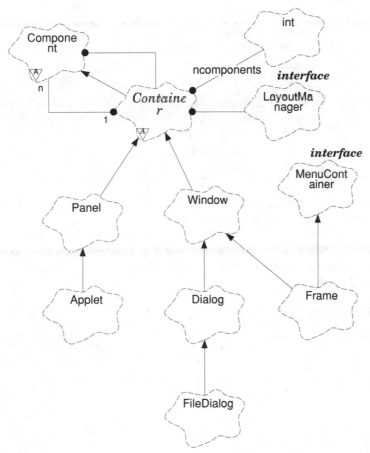

Figure 2-1 `Applet`, `Container`, and `LayoutManager` Class Diagram An `Applet` is a container with a default, `FlowLayout` layout manager.

Key java.applet.Applet Methods

The `Applet` class provides a basic set of methods that define the overall behavior of applets. An applet's execution is controlled by four methods: `init()`, `start()`, `stop()`, and `destroy()`. You don't typically call these methods directly. Rather, they are invoked automatically either by the browser or the `appletviewer`. (Note, however, these methods are commonly overridden in classes that classes that extend `Applet`.) Table 2-1 summarizes their use.

Table 2-1 Commonly Used `applet.Applet` Methods

Common applet.Applet Methods	Description
`init()`	When a document with an applet is opened, the `init()` method is called to initialize the applet.
`start()`	When a document with an applet is opened, the `start()` method is called to start the applet.
`stop()`	When a document with an applet is no longer displayed, the `stop()` method is called. This method is always called before the `destroy()` method is called.
`destroy()`	After the `stop()` method has been called, the `destroy()` method is called to clean up any resources that are being held.

Example 2-1 shows a simple applet and the use of the `init()`, `start()`, `stop()`, and `destroy()` methods; these methods are commonly overridden. Example 2-1 overrides them in lines ❷, ❸, ❹, and ❺ simply to highlight when they are executed. The `start()` method in line ❸ also adds a "Starter" label to the applet every time it is called. Additionally, note that all applets extend the `Applet` class, as in line ❶.

CD-Rom

Example 2-1 Starter Applet

```
import java.appplet.Applet;
import java.awt.Label;

❶ public class StarterApplet extends Applet {
    private Label label;

❷   public void init() {
        System.out.println("Applet.init()");
    }
❸   public void start() {
        System.out.println("Applet.start()");
        label = new Label("Starter");
        add(label);
    }
❹   public void stop() {
        System.out.println("Applet.stop()");
        remove(label);
    }
```

```
❺   public void destroy() {
        System.out.println("Applet.destroy()");
    }
}
```

This applet could be executed by running the `appletviewer` on the following HTML file:

```
<title>Starter Applet</title>
<hr>
<applet code="StarterApplet.class" width=300 height=100>
</applet>
<hr>
```

Figure 2-2 shows the applet window.

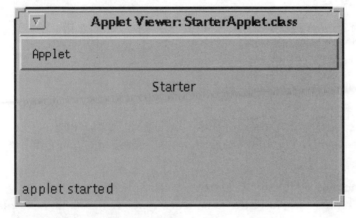

Figure 2-2 A Starter Applet

Running this applet would result with the following output to the screen:

```
Applet.init()
Applet.start()
```

Exiting the applet would result in the following output to the screen:

```
Applet.stop()
Applet.destroy()
```

java.awt.Component Display Methods

The `java.awt.Component` class implements methods to update its display: `paint()`, `repaint()`, and `update()`. Their use, however, sometimes befuddles users. Table 2-2 summarizes how they work.

Table 2-2 Commonly Used `awt.Component` **Methods**

Common awt.Component Methods	Description
`paint()`	Paints the component.
`repaint()`	Schedules a call to the component's `update()` method as soon as possible.
`update()`	Is responsible for redrawing the applet. The default version redraws the background and calls the `paint()` method.

Java Applications

Applications are invoked from the command line and executed by the `java` interpreter. From the developer's point of view, there are primarily two differences between a Java applet and a Java application:

- An application must include a `main()` method.

- If the application requires a window, it must extend the AWT `Frame` class. A Frame is a window in which the application is displayed and, like all containers, comes with a layout manager for positioning and sizing its components.

There is one other notable distinction between a Java application and a Java applet. An application does not have the same security restrictions that an applet does. Whereas an applet cannot write or modify files, an application can perform file I/O. Applications are not constrained by the security restrictions that the Java-enabled browser enforces on applets.

Setting Up an Application

Unlike applets, applications must extend the `Frame` class in order to provide a window in which to run, as in Example 2-2.

Example 2-2 Starter Graphical Application

```
    import java.awt.Event;
❶  import java.awt.Frame;
    import java.awt.Label;

❷  public class StarterApplication extends Frame {
❸     public static void main(String args[]) {
❹         StarterApplication app = new StarterApplication("Starter
              Application");
          app.resize(300,100);
          app.show ();
          System.out.println("StarterApplication.main()");
       }
❺     public StarterApplication(String frameTitle) {
          super(frameTitle);
          add  ("Center", new Label("Starter", Label.CENTER));
       }
❻     public boolean handleEvent(Event event) {
          if(event.id == Event.WINDOW_DESTROY)
              System.exit(0);
          return false;
       }
    }
```

This is a fairly simple application, but it's worth noting exactly how it works since it is different from the applet on page 16 in several ways. The first thing to note is that the application does not import and extend `java.Applet`. Instead, it imports and extends `java.awt.Frame`, in lines ❶ and ❷.

The next important distinction is that the application includes a `main()` method in line ❸. All Java applications require a `main()` method, just like a C or C++ program; `main()` is the first method invoked in an application. This `main()` method creates an instance of a `StarterApplication` (a Frame) in line ❹, which it resizes and shows. Line ❺ is the constructor for the `StarterApplication` class, which initializes a `StarterApplication` instance.

Line ❻ simply sets up a simple event handler for exiting the application.

Displaying Applications

Graphical applications, like all other Java applications, are executed directly by the java interpreter. For example, the compiled application in Example 2-2 is executed in the following manner:

```
java StarterApplication
```

The interpreter would then execute the application, as inFigure 2-3.

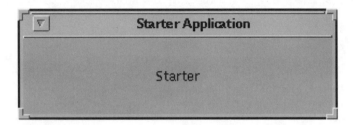

Figure 2-3 A Java Application
The StarterApplication event handling method enables the applet to exit when the user quits the application from the system menu.

Combining Applet and Application Code

There are a number of ways to write a Java program so that it can execute either from within a browser or as a standalone application. One way to do this is to center an Applet within a Frame, as in Example 2-3.

Example 2-3 Combining Applet and Application Code

```
❶ import java.applet.Applet;
   import java.awt.Event;
   import java.awt.Frame;
   import java.awt.Label;

❷ public class StarterCombined extends Applet {
     private Label label;

❸   public static void main(String args[]) {
       StarterCombinedFrame app = new StarterCombinedFrame("Starter
           Application");
```

```
        app.resize(300,100);
        app.show  ();
        System.out.println("StarterCombinedFrame.main()");
    }
    public void init() {
        System.out.println("Applet.init()");
    }
    public void start() {
        System.out.println("Applet.start()");
        label = new Label("Starter");
        add(label);
    }
    public void stop() {
        System.out.println("Applet.stop()");
        remove(label);
    }
    public void destroy() {
        System.out.println("Applet.destroy()");
    }
}

❹ class StarterCombinedFrame extends Frame {
    public StarterCombinedFrame(String frameTitle) {
        super(frameTitle);
❺   StarterCombined applet = new StarterCombined();
        applet.start();
        add  ("Center", applet);
    }
    public boolean handleEvent(Event event) {
        if(event.id == Event.WINDOW_DESTROY)
            System.exit(0);

        return false;
    }
}
```

The import statements starting at line ❶ import the essential classes needed for both an applet and an application. Line ❷ begins the class definition for StarterCombined—the applet class. Putting the main() method (line ❸) in the applet class enables the program to be executed with the same argument, whether it is going to run as an applet or as an application. For example, the following command would execute it as an application:

```
java StarterCombined
```

Using the `appletviewer` program on the following HTML file would execute the program as an applet:

```
<title>Starter Combined Test</title>
<hr>
<applet code="StarterCombined.class" width=300 height=100>
</applet>
<hr>
```

If the program is run as an applet, the `main()` method is completely ignored; instead, the browser or `appletviewer` invokes the `init()` and `start()` methods to start the applet.

Line ❹ begins the definition for `StarterCombinedFrame`—the application class. This class provides the `Frame` for the application to run in. The work starts in line ❺, where a new applet is created and centered in the `Frame`.

Summary

Both applets and applications are executed by the `java` interpreter. Applications must create their own `Frame` in which to display, while applets run in the frame provided by the Java-enabled web browser or `appletviewer`. As a result, applications must handle window destroy events, while an applet's execution is controlled by the browser or `appletviewer`. Applications are free to read and write files, but applets are not permitted to do so.

CHAPTER
3

- Manipulating Graphics and Color on page 26

- Drawing a Rectangle on page 27

    - Obtaining a Component's Graphics Object on page 31

    - Obtaining a Component's Background Color on page 31

    - Obtaining a Shade of a Color on page 32

    - Painting Etched-in and Etched-out Borders on page 40

    - Painting Inset and Raised 3-D Borders on page 46

- Manipulating Fonts on page 52

    - The AWT Font Model on page 53

    - The x,y Origin for Drawing Strings on page 53

    - Obtaining Font Dimensions on page 57

    - Dynamically Positioning a String on page 57

    - Drawing a String in Reverse Video on page 59

- gjt.LabelCanvas Implementation on page 59

- Exercising the LabelCanvas on page 62

- Summary on page 65

Graphics, Colors, and Fonts

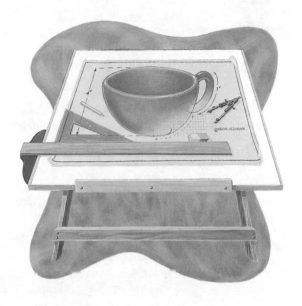

This chapter introduces the Java AWT Graphics class. The Graphics class provides graphical support for components ranging from painting and filling shapes to drawing images and strings to manipulation of graphical regions. AWT programmers are typically involved with the Graphics class before they know it, so this chapter illustrates some of the nuances of using the Graphics class. Additionally, we will introduce the AWT Color, Font, and FontMetrics classes.

This chapter introduces four custom components (DrawnRectangle, EtchedRectangle, ThreeDRectangle, and LabelCanvas) from the Graphic Java Toolkit (GJT). These custom components extend the AWT, but the focus in this chapter is less on extending the AWT and more on the specific use of the Graphics, Color, Font, and FontMetrics classes. Rather than provide arbitrary examples to highlight the use of these AWT classes, we've chosen to discuss custom components from the GJT. (Other custom components in the Graphic Java Toolkit are discussed in *The Graphic Java Toolkit—Extending the AWT*.)

Manipulating Graphics and Color

The `java.awt.Graphics` class is an abstract class that defines a collection of abstract methods for drawing, copying, clipping, filling, and clearing graphical regions in a component. Nearly all applets that use the AWT manipulate a `Graphics` object for at least one graphic service. For example, even simple Hello World applets are quick to use a `Graphics` object to display their clever verbiage:

```
public void paint(Graphics g) {
  g.drawString("Hello Graphic Java World", 75, 100);
}
```

While the AWT contains classes for user interface components such as buttons, menus, dialogs, and so on, it surprisingly does not include anything analogous to purely graphical objects. For example, the AWT does not provide a `Line` class or a `Circle` class. The `Shape` class, the prototypical example of object-oriented case studies[1], is nowhere to be found in the AWT.

Instead of providing purely graphical objects, the AWT employs a simpler (albeit less flexible and extensible) model. Each component comes complete with its own `Graphics` object, through which graphical operations can be performed in the component.

The `Graphics` class is a veritable kitchen sink of graphical operations. Its 40 public methods can be used for drawing strings, filling shapes, drawing images, painting with different colors, and much more. All of the graphical operations performed take place in the `Graphics` object associated component.

If you wanted to draw a line in a component, for example, instead of creating a `Line` object and invoking its `draw()` method, you would obtain the component's `Graphics` object and invoke `Graphics.drawLine()`.

The AWT also includes a `Color` class. For this discussion, we are only interested in using `Color` constants, such as `Color.blue`, `Color.red`, and so on, and in obtaining lighter or darker shades of a color. (The AWT `Color` class is much more interesting when it comes to manipulating `Images`, which we describe in *Images* on page 123.)

To show in greater detail how to manipulate a `Graphics` object, we're going to present a class from the GJT that draws a rectangle. We'll then discuss extensions of that class to illustrate some finer points, such as how to draw etched and three-dimensional lines for the rectangle's border.

---

1.   See Stroustrup, Bjarne. *The C++ Programming Language, section 6.4.2.* Addison-Wesley.

Figure 3-1 shows the various rectangles based on GJT classes we'll present in this chapter.

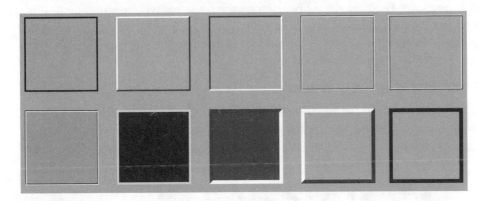

Figure 3-1 Rectangles
The `gjt.*Rectangle` classes in this chapter can be used to draw a variety of rectangles within a component. These classes manipulate a component's `Graphics` object to draw and color a rectangle in a number of different ways.

Drawing a Rectangle

You might have noticed that the AWT does include a `Rectangle` class, which might lead you to believe that we've hoodwinked you in our previous discussion. However, `Rectangle`, `Polygon`, and `Point` classes were added as afterthoughts to the original AWT, and since the original design did not allow for purely graphical objects, these classes wound up without any graphical capabilities. In other words, you cannot draw instances of `awt.Rectangle`, `awt.Polygon`, or `awt.Point`. You can only set and get information about the geometric entity that each represents.

To facilitate examples of a `Graphics` object in action, we'll introduce the handy `gjt.DrawnRectangle`. The `gjt.DrawnRectangle` class is simply a `Rectangle` that can be drawn inside of a component. Instances of `gjt.DrawnRectangle` draw themselves in different line widths and colors and are also able to fill themselves with a color on demand. `gjt.DrawnRectangle` is also the base class for `gjt.EtchedRectangle` and `gjt.ThreeDRectangle`, which we discuss shortly.

It is worthwhile to note that gjt.DrawnRectangle (and the classes that extend it) represent the only custom components in the Graphic Java Toolkit that do not extend the Component class; that is, they extend Rectangle and not Component. This fact has no bearing on the concepts we are stressing in this chapter, but it is interesting to note, for example, that gjt.DrawnRectangle has a public void paint() method that is unrelated to the public void paint(Graphics g) method from the Component class.

Overview of DrawnRectangle

The gjt.DrawnRectangle class paints rectangles with specified line width, line color, and fill color. Figure 3-2 shows two instances of the gjt.DrawnRectangle class with varying parameters.

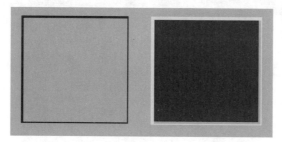

Figure 3-2 Drawn Rectangles
The gjt.DrawnRectangle class provides methods for drawing rectangles with varying line widths and colors.
gjt.DrawnRectangle also includes support for filling and clearing the interior of the rectangle.

The gjt.DrawnRectangle class includes four constructors:

❶ ```
   public DrawnRectangle(Component drawInto) {
       this(drawInto, _defaultThickness, 0, 0, 0, 0);
   }
```
❷ ```
   public DrawnRectangle(Component drawInto, int thick) {
       this(drawInto, thick, 0, 0, 0, 0);
   }
```
❸ ```
   public DrawnRectangle(Component drawInto, int x, int y,
                                            int w, int h) {
       this(drawInto, _defaultThickness, x, y, w, h);
   }
```
❹ ```
   public DrawnRectangle(Component drawInto, int thick,
                         int x, int y, int w, int h) {
```
❺ ```
      Assert.notNull(drawInto);
```
```

```
        Assert.notFalse(thick > 0);

        this.drawInto = drawInto;
        this.thick    = thick;
        reshape(x,y,w,h);
    }
```

All the action that's fit to take place in the AWT takes place inside a `Component`; therefor, `gjt.DrawnRectangle` requires you to pass it a `Component` at construction time. The `Component` passed into the `gjt.DrawnRectangle` constructor is assigned to the aptly named `drawInto` member, which is the `Component` into which the rectangle will be drawn. (The `Assert.notNull` in line ❺ ensures that `gjt.DrawnRectangle` won't accept a null `Component`. Refer to *Introducing the Graphic Java Toolkit* for more information on the Graphic Java Toolkit utility classes.)

The constructors in lines ❶, ❷, and ❸ call a second constructor—the one in line ❹. Using multiple constructors that eventually call just one constructor that does all the work is fairly typical, and we use this technique throughout this book. For example, the statement:

```
        this(drawInto, _defaultThickness, 0, 0, 0, 0);
```

in constructor ❶ actually calls the constructor in line ❹, which sets the `drawInto` component and border thickness and calls the `Rectangle.reshape()` method. If you use the first constructor and just give it a `Component` for an argument, a `gjt.DrawnRectangle` starts at position 0,0, with a width of 0 and a height of 0. You can also call the constructor in line ❹ explicitly and provide a specific x,y starting position, width, and height.

Before looking at the `gjt.DrawnRectangle` code in Example 3-1 on page 34, it's useful to see an overview of its responsibilities (that is, its public methods), as in Table 3-1.

Table 3-1 `gjt.DrawnRectangle` **Responsibilities**

Methods	Description
`Component component()`	Returns the `Component` drawn into.
`int getThickness()`	Returns the line thickness.
`void setThickness(int thick)`	Sets the line thickness.
`void setLineColor(Color lineColor)`	Sets the line color. If not set explicitly, the line color used is three shades darker than the background color of the component being drawn into.

Table 3-1 gjt.DrawnRectangle **Responsibilities (Continued)**

Methods	Description
void setFillColor(Color fillColor)	Sets the color used to fill the rectangle.
void fill()	Fills the inside of the rectangle with the current fill color. (It does not obliterate the border of the rectangle.)
Color getLineColor()	Returns the current line color.
Color getFillColor()	Returns the current fill color.
Rectangle getInnerBounds()	Returns the boundary inside the border of the rectangle.
void paint()	Paints the rectangle inside the associated component.
void clearInterior()	Clears the interior of the rectangle.
void clearExterior()	Erases the lines of the rectangle.
void clear()	Erases the border of the rectangle and clears the rectangle's interior.
String toString()	Returns a String containing information about the DrawnRectangle.
String paramString()	Reports values for specific parameters such as drawn rectangle's color, line thickness, and line color.

The associations (that is, its members) for a gjt.DrawnRectangle are listed inTable 3-2.

Table 3-2 gjt.DrawnRectangle **Associations**

Variable	Description
protected static int _defaultThickness	Defines the default thickness as 2 pixels.
protected Component drawInto	Defines the component to be drawn into.
private int thick;	Line thickness.
private Color lineColor	Line color.
private Color fillColor	Fill color.

Before looking at the gjt.DrawnRectangle class in its entirety, we're going to pull out sections of it to specifically highlight some of its graphical operations and color manipulation, including:

- Obtaining a component's `Graphics` object

- Obtaining a component's background color

- Obtaining a darker or brighter shade of a color

- Filling a rectangle in a component

- Drawing lines in a component

Now let's look at how the `Graphics` object and color are manipulated by the `gjt.DrawnRectangle` class.

Obtaining a Component's Graphics Object

Every component has a `Graphics` object affiliated with it. To manipulate a `Graphics` object first requires obtaining a handle by which to access it. This is accomplished by using the `getGraphics()` method in the `Component` class. In the `DrawnRectangle` class, we obtain a handle on the `Graphics` object affiliated with `drawInto` (a `Component`):

```
Graphics g = drawInto.getGraphics();
```

You'll notice in the `gjt.DrawnRectangle` class that whenever we want to perform graphical operations in the `drawInto` component, we first obtain the `Graphics` object affiliated with `drawInto`. The `Graphics` object can then be manipulated in a variety of ways, as it is in the `gjt.DrawnRectangle` class `paint()`, `clearExterior()`, and `fill()` methods.

Obtaining a Component's Background Color

There's some general utility in being able to find a component's background color. For instance, it is necessary to know the background color in order to erase the component. The `Component.getBackground()` method returns the component's current background color. In the `gjt.DrawnRectangle` class, the `getFillColor()` method invokes the `drawInto` component's `getBackground()` method:

```
public Color getFillColor() {
    if(fillColor == null)
        fillColor = drawInto.getBackground();
    return fillColor;
}
```

If the fill color has not been explicitly set, `getFillColor()` calls the `drawInto` component's `getBackground()` method to obtain the current background color and sets it to the `fillColor` member of the `DrawnRectangle`.

Obtaining a Shade of a Color

The key to obtaining a darker shade of a color is to use the `darker()` method
from the `Color` class. Conversely, there is a corresponding `brighter()` method
also available in the `Color` class. You can obtain incrementally darker or brighter
shades of a color by repeatedly calling either the `darker()` or `brighter()`
methods, respectively. The `gjt.DrawnRectangle.brighter()` method
always returns four shades brighter than the current line color:

```
protected Color brighter() {
    return
    getLineColor().brighter().brighter().brighter().brighter();
}
```

`DrawnRectangle` also implements a `getLineColor()` method, which returns
a darker shade of the background color of the `drawInto` component, if the line
color has not been explicitly set:

```
  public Color getLineColor() {
    if(lineColor == null)
      lineColor =
❶     drawInto.getBackground().darker().darker().darker();
    return lineColor;
  }
```

Line ❶ of `getLineColor()` sets `lineColor` to the background color by
invoking the `getBackground()` method, then darkens the color and sets it.

OO Tip

Provide Defaults, But Let Clients Override

DrawnRectangle provides default values for both line thickness and line color;
however, it also allows clients (and DrawnRectangle extensions) to override
those values. Although it does not always make sense to do so, providing
defaults that clients can override gives them the best of both worlds; they don't
have to deal with such values unless they have a good reason to do so.

Filling a Rectangle

Filling a rectangle relies on the `fillRect()` and `setColor()` methods from the `Graphics` class. Our `gjt.DrawnRectangle` class has a `fill()` method that uses both of these to fill a rectangle with the current fill color:

```
public void fill(Color color) {
   Graphics g = drawInto.getGraphics();

   if(g != null) {
❶     Rectangle r = getInnerBounds();
❷     g.setColor(color);
❸     g.fillRect(r.x, r.y, r.width, r.height);
      setFillColor(color);
   }
}
```

In line ❶, the `fill()` method uses the `gjt.DrawnRectangle` `getInnerBounds()` method, which returns the boundary *inside* the lines drawn for the rectangle, as illustrated in Figure 3-3.

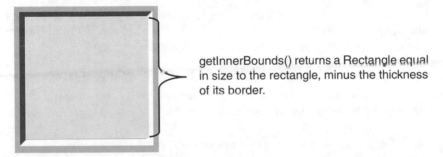

getInnerBounds() returns a Rectangle equal in size to the rectangle, minus the thickness of its border.

Figure 3-3 Calculating the Inner Bounds of a `DrawnRectangle` The `gjt.DrawnRectangle.getInnerBounds()` method creates a new instance of a `Rectangle` with dimensions equal to the area inside its border. (For the sake of illustration, we're using a 3-D rectangle here, even though we haven't discussed it yet. Its broad border lines make it easier to show the inner bounds of the rectangle.)

Once the `fill()` method has obtained the inner bounds of the rectangle, it sets the specified color and fills the rectangle with the `Graphics setColor()` and `fillRect()` methods in lines ❷ and ❸, respectively. The call to `setFillColor()` sets the `DrawnRectangle fillColor` to the color passed into `fill()`.

gjt.DrawnRectangle Implementation

Now let's look at the `gjt.DrawnRectangle` implementation. Several general points are worth highlighting. First, notice that it extends the `Rectangle` class:

```
public class DrawnRectangle extends Rectangle {
```

This means that the size and location for a `gjt.DrawnRectangle` can be set, just like a `java.awt.Rectangle`.

OO Tip

Avoid Public Members

java.awt.Rectangle contains public members for its location and size. Since gjt.DrawnRectangle extends java.awt.Rectangle, a drawn rectangle's location or size may be changed by direct manipulation of its members. If java.awt.Rectangle had made its members private and provided methods to set them, we could override those methods in DrawnRectangle to ensure that a repaint() is invoked whenever the size or location changes. Instead, it is possible for a DrawnRectangle's size and/or location to be out of synch with its graphical representation. It is best to always limit access to members of a class and provide set/get methods instead of making members public.

You'll want to pay particular attention in Example 3-1 to the way this class deals with the `Graphics` object—it's a parameter in several methods—and the `Color` object, both of which we've already mentioned.

Example 3-1 gjt.DrawnRectangle **Source Code**

```
package gjt;

import java.awt.*;

public class DrawnRectangle extends Rectangle {
    protected static int    _defaultThickness = 2;
    protected Component      drawInto;
    private    int           thick;
    private    Color         lineColor, fillColor;

    public DrawnRectangle(Component drawInto) {
        this(drawInto, _defaultThickness, 0, 0, 0, 0);
    }
    public DrawnRectangle(Component drawInto, int thick) {
        this(drawInto, thick, 0, 0, 0, 0);
    }
    public DrawnRectangle(Component drawInto, int x, int y,
```

```
                                   int w, int h) {
        this(drawInto, _defaultThickness, x, y, w, h);
}
public DrawnRectangle(Component drawInto, int thick,
                      int x, int y, int w, int h) {
    Assert.notNull(drawInto);
    Assert.notFalse(thick > 0);

    this.drawInto = drawInto;
    this.thick    = thick;
    reshape(x,y,w,h);
}
public Component component()         {return drawInto;    }
public int  getThickness  ()        {return thick;        }
public void setThickness  (int thick) {this.thick = thick; }

public void setLineColor(Color lineColor) {
    this.lineColor = lineColor;
}
public void setFillColor(Color fillColor) {
    this.fillColor = fillColor;
}
public void fill() {
    fill(getFillColor());
}
public Color getLineColor() {
    if(lineColor == null)
        lineColor =
        drawInto.getBackground().darker().darker().darker();
    return lineColor;
}
public Color getFillColor() {
    if(fillColor == null)
        fillColor = drawInto.getBackground();
    return fillColor;
}
public Rectangle getInnerBounds() {
    return new Rectangle(x+thick, y+thick,
                         width-(thick*2), height-(thick*2));
}
public void paint() {
    Graphics g = drawInto.getGraphics();
    paintFlat(g, getLineColor());
}
private void paintFlat(Graphics g, Color color) {
    if(g != null) {
        g.setColor(color);
        for(int i=0; i < thick; ++i)
```

```java
            g.drawRect(x+i, y+i,
                        width-(i*2)-1, height-(i*2)-1);
        }
    }
    public void clearInterior() {
        fill(drawInto.getBackground());
    }
    public void clearExterior() {
        paintFlat(drawInto.getGraphics(),
                    drawInto.getBackground());
    }
    public void clear() {
        clearExterior();
        clearInterior();
    }
    public void fill(Color color) {
        Graphics g = drawInto.getGraphics();

        if(g != null) {
            Rectangle r = getInnerBounds();
            g.setColor(color);
            g.fillRect(r.x, r.y, r.width, r.height);
            setFillColor(color);
        }
    }
    public String toString() {
        return super.toString() + "[" + paramString() + "]";
    }
    public String paramString() {
        return "color=" + getLineColor() + ",thickness=" +
                thick + ",fillColor=" + getFillColor();
    }
    protected Color brighter() {
    return
    getLineColor().brighter().brighter().brighter().brighter();
    }
}
```

OO Tip

Think Small

Take a look at the implementations of DrawnRectangle.fill() and DrawnRectangle.paint(), and see how long it takes you to figure out what each method does. The DrawnRectangle class has a paltry 1.8 lines of code per method, resulting in two very important benefits: It makes each method easy to understand, and it provides a granularity that reduces bugs and simplifies code extension and modification. For instance, take a look at the implementation of DrawnRectangle.getInnerBounds(). This method reports the bounding box inside of the DrawnRectangle (excluding the border). Since the method is only used in DrawnRectangle.fill(Color), it may seem superfluous to put such a simple calculation in its own method. Realize, however, that derived classes and clients of DrawnRectangle will find innerBounds() very useful, and as DrawnRectangle matures, it may very well find a need for innerBounds() in other methods that materialize down the road.

Drawing an Etched Rectangle

Etched rectangles are useful in a number of contexts in graphical user interfaces. The `gjt.EtchedRectangle` class is an extension of the `DrawnRectangle` class that manipulates line thickness and shading to make it appear as though its border is etched either in or out.

The `gjt.EtchedRectangle` class provides methods for drawing etched-in or etched-out borders. Figure 3-4 shows instances of both an etched-in and etched-out `gjt.EtchedRectangle`.

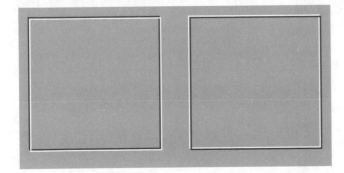

Figure 3-4 Etched Rectangles
The `gjt.EtchedRectangle` class extends `gjt.DrawnRectangle` and overrides `paint()` to draw etched borders.

Table 3-3 lists the responsibilities of a gjt.EtchedRectangle.

Table 3-3 gjt.EtchedRectangle **Responsibilities**

Methods	Description
void etchedIn()	Sets the etching value to Etching.IN.
void etchedOut()	Sets the etching value to Etching.OUT.
boolean isEtchedIn()	Returns true if etched in, false if etched out.
void paint()	Draws an etched border.
void paintEtchedIn()	Calls etchedIn() and passes appropriate color values to paintEtched().
void paintEtchedOut()	Calls etchedOut() and passes appropriate color values to paintEtched().
String paramString()	Reports values for the etched rectangle's line color, thickness, bounds, and whether it is etched in or out.

Example 3-2 shows the code for the gjt.EtchedRectangle class in its entirety; then we highlight specifically how it:

- Paints an etched-in border

- Paints an etched-out border

Note that the paint() method calls appropriately named methods for painting etched in and etched out, depending upon the current state of the gjt.EtchedRectangle. Also, pay attention to the use of the DrawnRectangle.brighter() method, which is used for shading the rectangle borders to create the etched effect. (The Etching and ThreeDBorderStyle classes referenced in this program are simply GJT classes that implement type-safe constants. Refer to *Introducing the Graphic Java Toolkit* for a discussion of the Graphic Java Toolkit utility classes.)

Example 3-2 gjt.EtchedRectangle **Class Source Code**

CD-Rom

```
package gjt;

import java.awt.*;

public class EtchedRectangle extends DrawnRectangle {
  protected static Etching _defaultEtching = Etching.IN;
  private Etching etching;

  public EtchedRectangle(Component drawInto) {
      this(drawInto, _defaultEtching,
          _defaultThickness, 0, 0, 0, 0);
```

```
}
public EtchedRectangle(Component drawInto, int thickness) {
    this(drawInto, _defaultEtching, thickness, 0, 0, 0, 0);
}
public EtchedRectangle(Component drawInto, int x, int y,
                                           int w, int h) {
    this(drawInto, _defaultEtching,
         _defaultThickness, x, y, w, h);
}
public EtchedRectangle(Component drawInto, int thickness,
                                           int x, int y,
                                           int w, int h) {
    this(drawInto, _defaultEtching, thickness, x, y, w, h);
}
public EtchedRectangle(Component drawInto, Etching etching,
                       int thickness, int x, int y,
                       int w, int h) {
    super(drawInto, thickness, x, y, w, h);
    this.etching = etching;
}
public void    etchedIn  () { etching = Etching.IN;         }
public void    etchedOut () { etching = Etching.OUT;        }
public boolean isEtchedIn() { return etching == Etching.IN; }

public void paint() {
    if(etching == Etching.IN) paintEtchedIn();
    else                      paintEtchedOut();
}
public void paintEtchedIn() {
    Graphics g = drawInto.getGraphics();
    if(g != null)
        paintEtched(g, getLineColor(), brighter());

    etchedIn();
}
public void paintEtchedOut() {
    Graphics g = drawInto.getGraphics();
    if(g != null)
        paintEtched(g, brighter(), getLineColor());

    etchedOut();
}
public String paramString() {
    return super.paramString() + "," + etching;
}
private void paintEtched(Graphics g,
                         Color topLeft, Color bottomRight) {
    int  thickness = getThickness();
```

```
int  w = width  - thickness;
int  h = height - thickness;

g.setColor(topLeft);
for(int i=0; i < thickness/2; ++i)
    g.drawRect(x+i, y+i, w, h);

g.setColor(bottomRight);

for(int i=0; i < thickness/2; ++i)
    g.drawRect(x+(thickness/2)+i,
               y+(thickness/2)+i, w, h);
    }
}
```

Painting Etched-in and Etched-out Borders

By default, an instance of gjt.EtchedRectangle paints itself *etched in*. The state of its etching can be changed by calling the etchedIn() and etchedOut() methods; however, only the state is changed and the EtchedRectangle does not repaint itself. To change the state and repaint in one fell swoop, you can use the paintEtchedIn() and paintEtchedOut() methods. For instance, paintEtchedIn() looks like this:

```
    public void paintEtchedIn() {
        Graphics g = drawInto.getGraphics();
        if(g != null)
❶           paintEtched(g, getLineColor(), brighter());

❷       etchedIn();
    }
```

In line ❶, the call to paintEtched() includes parameters for the topLeft color and bottomRight color of the rectangles to be drawn. The call to etchedIn() in line ❷ simply sets the state to Etching.IN.

paintEtchedOut() is a mirror of this. It switches the values of the topLeft and bottomRight arguments to paintEtched() and then sets the state to Etching.OUT.

```
    public void paintEtchedOut() {
        Graphics g = drawInto.getGraphics();
        if(g != null)
            paintEtched(g, brighter(), getLineColor());

        etchedOut();
    }
```

The `paintEtchedIn()` and `paintEtchedOut()` methods rely on the private `paintEtched()` method to draw rectangles and to manipulate the line shading appropriately. This observation leads into the next topic, which is to describe how the `EtchedRectangle paint.Etched()` method achieves its etching effect.

The trick used in `paintEtched()` to create the etching effect is to draw two rectangles, one slightly offset from the other, and then to draw each rectangle's border in slightly different shades. Figure 3-5 shows how this technique is used in the `gjt.EtchedRectangle` class.

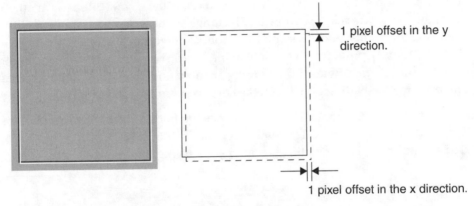

Figure 3-5 Achieving an Etched Effect
The `gjt.EtchedRectangle` achieves its etched effect by drawing two rectangles, one slightly offset from the other, in different shades of the same color.

Here's the `paintEtched()` method that paints either etched-in or etched-out:

```
private void paintEtched(Graphics g,
                         Color topLeft, Color bottomRight) {
    int  thickness = getThickness();
    int  w = width  - thickness;
    int  h = height - thickness;

    g.setColor(topLeft);
    for(int i=0; i < thickness/2; ++i)
        g.drawRect(x+i, y+i, w, h);

    g.setColor(bottomRight);

    for(int i=0; i < thickness/2; ++i)
        g.drawRect(x+(thickness/2)+i,
                   y+(thickness/2)+i, w, h);
}
```

For an etched-in effect, the lines in the first rectangle (line ❶) are drawn in the current line color, and the offset rectangle's lines (line ❷) are drawn in a brighter color. For an etched-out effect, it is just the opposite. The lines in the first rectangle are drawn in a brighter shade and the offset rectangle's lines are drawn in the current line color.

Drawing a 3-D Rectangle

The ability to draw a three-dimensional rectangle is another useful feature in the applet developer's toolkit. Note that we could use the draw3DRect() method from the Graphics class to draw 3-D rectangles, but we want more flexibility in choosing the border thickness and more robust default behavior than draw3DRect() provides. In particular, the Graphics.draw3DRect() method always draws a rectangle whose borders are only one pixel thick, and it creates discernible 3-D shading only when the color is set to lightGray.

The gjt.ThreeDRectangle class provides methods for drawing raised or inset borders, which achieve a 3-D visual effect. Figure 3-6 shows use of ThreeDRectangle to create 3-D borders of varying thickness.

Figure 3-6 Three-Dimensional Rectangles
The gjt.ThreeDRectangle class extends DrawnRectangle and overrides paint() to paint a three-dimensional border.

Table 3-4 lists the responsibilities of a gjt.ThreeDRectangle.

Table 3-4 gjt.ThreeDRectangle **Responsibilities**

Methods	Description
void paint()	Calls either paintRaised() or paintInset(), depending on the current state of the rectangle. This dictates whether the rectangle is drawn raised or inset.
void raise()	Sets the border style to ThreeDBorderStyle.RAISED for the next call to paint().
void inset()	Sets the border style to ThreeDBorderStyle.INSET for the next call to paint().
boolean isRaised()	Returns the current state of the border.
String paramString()	Returns a string of DrawnRectangle parameters.
void paintRaised()	Draws rectangle borders with the top and left lines brighter than the bottom and right lines.
void paintInset()	Draws rectangle borders with the bottom and right lines brighter than the top and left lines.

Example 3-3 shows the source code for the gjt.ThreeDRectangle class. gjt.ThreeDRectangle overrides paint() to paint a 3-D border. We'll first show the entire class and then highlight specifically how it:

- Paints a raised 3-D border
- Paints an inset 3-D border

You'll probably notice that gjt.ThreeDRectangle is very similar to gjt.EtchedRectangle. They are structured similarly, and both override paint() to produce etching and three-dimensional effects.

Example 3-3 gjt.ThreeDRectangle **Class Source Code**

```java
package gjt;

import java.awt.*;

public class ThreeDRectangle extends DrawnRectangle {
  protected static ThreeDBorderStyle _defaultState =
                                    ThreeDBorderStyle.RAISED;
  private ThreeDBorderStyle state;

  public ThreeDRectangle(Component drawInto) {
      this(drawInto, _defaultState,
          _defaultThickness, 0, 0, 0, 0);
  }
  public ThreeDRectangle(Component drawInto, int thickness) {
      this(drawInto, _defaultState, thickness, 0, 0, 0, 0);
  }
  public ThreeDRectangle(Component drawInto,
                      int x, int y, int w, int h) {
      this(drawInto,
          _defaultState, _defaultThickness, x, y, w, h);
  }
  public ThreeDRectangle(Component drawInto, int thickness,
                                      int x, int y,
                                      int w, int h) {
      this(drawInto, _defaultState, thickness, x, y, w, h);
  }
  public ThreeDRectangle(Component drawInto,
                      ThreeDBorderStyle state,
                      int thickness, int x, int y,
                      int w, int h) {
      super(drawInto, thickness, x, y, w, h);
      this.state = state;
  }
  public void paint() {
      if(state == ThreeDBorderStyle.RAISED) paintRaised();
      else                                  paintInset ();
  }
  public void raise() { state = ThreeDBorderStyle.RAISED; }
  public void inset() { state = ThreeDBorderStyle.INSET;  }

  public boolean isRaised() {
      return state == ThreeDBorderStyle.RAISED;
  }
  public String paramString() {
      return super.paramString() + "," + state;
  }
```

```java
public void paintRaised() {
    Graphics g = drawInto.getGraphics();

    if(g != null) {
        raise                  ();
        drawTopLeftLines     (g, brighter());
        drawBottomRightLines(g, getLineColor());
    }
}
public void paintInset() {
    Graphics g = drawInto.getGraphics();

    if(g != null) {
        inset                  ();
        drawTopLeftLines     (g, getLineColor());
        drawBottomRightLines(g, brighter());
    }
}
private void drawTopLeftLines(Graphics g, Color color) {
    int thick = getThickness();
    g.setColor(color);

    for(int i=0; i < thick; ++i) {
        g.drawLine(x+i, y+i,   x + width-(i+1), y+i);
        g.drawLine(x+i, y+i+1, x+i, y + height-(i+1));
    }
}
private void drawBottomRightLines(Graphics g, Color color) {
    int thick = getThickness();
    g.setColor(color);

    for(int i=1; i <= thick; ++i) {
        g.drawLine(x+i-1, y + height-i,
                   x + width-i, y + height-i);
        g.drawLine(x + width-i, y+i-1,
                   x + width-i, y + height-i);
    }
}
}
```

Painting Inset and Raised 3-D Borders

Painting the rectangle borders inset or raised to produce a 3-D effect is another shadowing trick. In the gjt.ThreeDRectangle class, two methods implement the painting of raised and inset 3-D borders: paintRaised() and paintInset(). Here's how they work:

```
public void paintRaised() {
    Graphics g = drawInto.getGraphics();

    if(g != null) {
        raise();
        drawTopLeftLines     (g, brighter());
        drawBottomRightLines(g, getLineColor());
    }
}
public void paintInset() {
    Graphics g = drawInto.getGraphics();

    if(g != null) {
        inset();
        drawTopLeftLines     (g, getLineColor());
        drawBottomRightLines(g, brighter());
    }
}
```

Since the 3-D effect is achieved by painting different shades for the top left and bottom right sides of the rectangle, we need a more specific utility than Graphics.drawRect(). As a result, paintRaised() and paintInset() both invoke drawTopLeftLines() and drawBottomRightLines(), passing each the appropriate shade of the current line color.

drawTopLeftLines() and drawBottomRightLines() draw individual lines that converge at a 45 degree angle in the corners. Both employ the Graphics drawLine() method, as follows:

```
    private void drawTopLeftLines(Graphics g, Color color) {
        int thick = getThickness();
        g.setColor(color);

❶       for(int i=0; i < thick; ++i) {
            g.drawLine(x+i, y+i,   x + width-(i+1), y+i);
            g.drawLine(x+i, y+i+1, x+i, y + height-(i+1));
        }
    }
    private void drawBottomRightLines(Graphics g, Color color) {
        int thick = getThickness();
        g.setColor(color);
```

```
❷        for(int i=1; i <= thick; ++i) {
            g.drawLine(x+i-1, y + height-i,
                        x + width-i, y + height-i);
            g.drawLine(x + width-i, y+i-1,
                        x + width-i, y + height-i);
        }
    }
```

The AWT currently allows drawing lines only one pixel thick. The loops in lines ❶ and ❷ draw lines whose thickness is equal to the current thickness of the `ThreeDRectangle`.

Notice that both `paintRaised()` and `paintInset()` are somewhat paranoid that the `Graphics` object returned from `drawInto.getGraphics()` may turn out to be null. They both include this check:

```
if(g != null) {
```

This may lead you to wonder if you, too, need to check that a `Graphics` object obtained from `Component.getGraphics()` is valid. The answer is, of course, yes and no.

The answer in this case resides in the fact that our custom component is not an extension of `Component`. Remember that `DrawnRectangle` is merely a `Rectangle`. Recall that the `Component void paint(Graphics)` method is invoked by the AWT machinery when it is time for the `Component` to paint itself (recall our discussion of `paint()` in *Drawing a Rectangle* on page 27). Since `gjt.DrawnRectangle` is not a `Component` (it extends the graphically challenged `Rectangle`), its `paint()` method must be called manually. While we know that the AWT would never give us a null `Graphics` object when invoking `paint(Graphics)`, the same cannot be said for `DrawnRectangle.paint()`, since it needs to be invoked manually.

The moral is this: extensions of `java.awt.Component` are assured that a valid `Graphics` object is passed to methods that are invoked by the AWT machinery, while classes that do not extend `java.awt.Component` should always check the validity of `Graphics` objects passed to their methods.

Exercising the Rectangle Classes

All of the Graphic Java Toolkit custom components include unit tests. This is really a topic for *The Graphic Java Toolkit—Extending the AWT,* in which we talk more about the rationale for unit tests and how the unit tests are structured. Since we're introducing custom components in this chapter to highlight use of AWT

Graphics and Color objects, we'll include the unit test here as well. For now, just be aware that the unit test extends UnitTest and overrides its title() and centerPanel() methods.

You've already seen the output from the DrawnRectangleTest class to illustrate all the types of borders and rectangles you can draw with the *Rectangle classes. Figure 3-7 shows this output again for completeness. A color picture of Figure 3-7 is included in the color inserts section of the book that better illustrates the shading and coloring of the rectangles.

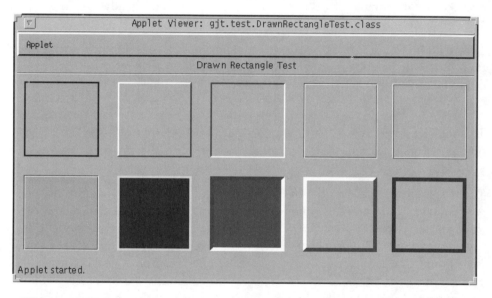

Figure 3-7 gjt.DrawnRectangle Unit Test

The unit test code is in Example 3-4 on page 49. The interesting aspect of the unit test is the DrawnRectangleTestPanel class, which extends Panel. DrawnRectangleTestPanel creates new instances of DrawnRectangle, EtchedRectangle, and ThreeDRectangle. All of the rectangles are passed a reference to the DrawnRectangleTestPanel instance, which is the component being drawn into. DrawnRectangleTestPanel.paint() then paints and fills the rectangles.

As you look through the unit test, pay attention to use of color constants. The `Color` class provides a set of constants that can be used to set the color of your choice. The complete list of color constants is:

- `Color.black`
- `Color.blue`
- `Color.cyan`
- `Color.darkGray`
- `Color.gray`
- `Color.green`
- `Color.lightGray`
- `Color.magenta`
- `Color.orange`
- `Color.pink`
- `Color.red`
- `Color.white`
- `Color.yellow`

Also notice that `DrawnRectangleTest` overrides `Component.mouseDown()` in order to print information about the `gjt.DrawnRectangle` in which the mouse down event occurred. The `gjt.DrawnRectangle` is passed to a shorthand method for printing information about the `gjt.DrawnRectangle` in question.

Example 3-4 shows the code for the unit test.

Example 3-4 `gjt.test.DrawnRectangleTest` **Class Source Code**

```
package gjt.test;

import java.awt.*;
import gjt.DrawnRectangle;
import gjt.EtchedRectangle;
import gjt.ThreeDRectangle;

public class DrawnRectangleTest extends UnitTest {
  public String title() { return "Drawn Rectangle Test";   }
  public Panel centerPanel() {
     return new DrawnRectangleTestPanel();
  }
```

```
    }

    class DrawnRectangleTestPanel extends Panel {
      private DrawnRectangle  drawnFilledOrange,
                              drawnFilledBlue, drawnBlue;
      private EtchedRectangle etchedOut,
                              etchedIn, etchedFilledCyan;
      private ThreeDRectangle thinRaised,
                              thinInset, thickRaised, thickInset;

      public DrawnRectangleTestPanel() {
          drawnFilledOrange =
              new DrawnRectangle (this, 10,  10,  100, 100);
          drawnFilledBlue =
              new DrawnRectangle (this, 135, 135, 100, 100);
          drawnBlue =
              new DrawnRectangle (this, 505, 135, 100, 100);
          etchedFilledCyan =
              new EtchedRectangle(this, 10,  135, 100, 100);

          etchedIn = new EtchedRectangle(this, 385, 10, 100, 100);
          etchedOut= new EtchedRectangle(this, 505, 10, 100, 100);

          thinRaised =
              new ThreeDRectangle(this, 135, 10,  100, 100);
          thinInset  =
              new ThreeDRectangle(this, 260, 10,  100, 100);
          thickRaised =
              new ThreeDRectangle(this, 385, 135, 100, 100);
          thickInset =
              new ThreeDRectangle(this, 260, 135, 100, 100);

          drawnFilledOrange.setLineColor(Color.black);

          drawnFilledBlue.setLineColor(Color.yellow);
          drawnFilledBlue.setThickness(3);

          drawnBlue.setLineColor(Color.blue);
          drawnBlue.setThickness(5);

          thickRaised.setThickness(5);
          thickInset.setThickness (5);
      }

      public void paint(Graphics g) {
          drawnFilledOrange.paint();
          drawnFilledOrange.fill (Color.orange);
```

```
        drawnFilledBlue.paint   ();
        drawnFilledBlue.fill    (Color.blue);

        drawnBlue.paint          ();

        etchedIn.paintEtchedIn   ();
        etchedOut.paintEtchedOut();

        etchedFilledCyan.paintEtchedIn();
        etchedFilledCyan.fill(Color.cyan);

        thinRaised.paintRaised   ();
        thinInset.paintInset     ();

        thickRaised.paintRaised ();

        thickInset.paintInset   ();
        thickInset.fill          (Color.red);
    }
    public boolean mouseDown(Event event, int x, int y) {
        if(drawnFilledOrange.inside(x,y))
            show(drawnFilledOrange);

        if(drawnFilledBlue.inside(x,y))     show(drawnFilledBlue);
        if(drawnBlue.inside(x,y))           show(drawnBlue);
        if(etchedIn.inside(x,y))            show(etchedIn);
        if(etchedOut.inside(x,y))           show(etchedOut);
        if(etchedFilledCyan.inside(x,y))    show(etchedFilledCyan);
        if(thinRaised.inside(x,y))          show(thinRaised);
        if(thickRaised.inside(x,y))         show(thickRaised);
        if(thinInset.inside(x,y))           show(thinInset);
        if(thickInset.inside(x,y))          show(thickInset);

        return true;
    }
    private void show(DrawnRectangle drawnRectangle) {
        System.out.println(drawnRectangle);
    }
}
```

Manipulating Fonts

The AWT includes two classes that support font manipulation: the aptly named `Font` class and the `FontMetrics` class. The `Font` class provides a basic set of fonts and font styles. Remember that Java is platform independent, so fonts such as Helvetica, Times Roman, and so on are always mapped to an available font on the native platform. Table 3-5 shows font mappings from Java to the respective supported platforms.

Table 3-5 Java Font Model

Java Font [1]	Maps to Windows Font...	Maps to X Window™ Font...	Maps to Macintosh Font...
Courier	Courier New	adobe-courier	Courier
Dialog	MS Sans Serif	b&h-lucida	Geneva
DialogInput	MS Sans Serif	b&h-lucidatypewriter	Geneva
Helvetica	Arial	adobe-helvetica	Helvetica
TimesRoman	Times New Roman	adobe-times	Times Roman
Symbol	WingDings	itc-zapfdingbats	Symbol

1. The default font is misc-fixed on X Windows, Arial on Windows 95, and Geneva on Macintosh.

The `Font` class defines font styles in terms of these constants:

- `Font.PLAIN`
- `Font.BOLD`
- `Font.ITALIC`
- `Font.BOLD + Font.ITALIC`

The AWT Font Model

The AWT font model is similar to the one used in the X Window System. Figure 3-8 shows how font height, ascent, descent and leading are calculated in the AWT.

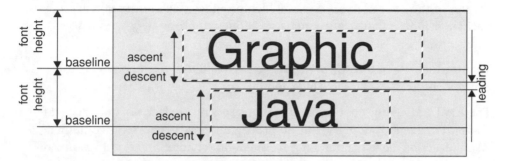

Figure 3-8 The AWT Font Model
The font height is the distance between one baseline and another. The ascent is measured from the baseline to the top of the characters, and the descent is measured from the baseline to the bottom of the characters. The leading is the distance from the descent of one line to the ascent of the next line of text.

The x,y Origin for Drawing Strings

You may remember our use of the Graphics drawRect() method in the gjt.EtchedRectangle class earlier in the chapter. The location passed to drawRect() represents the upper left-hand corner of the rectangle. In contrast, the location passed to the Graphics drawString() method represents the baseline of the characters. Figure 3-9 illustrates how these methods differ.

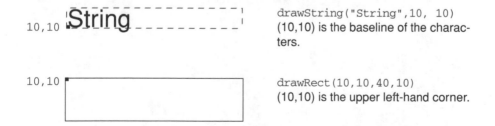

Figure 3-9 Drawing Strings With the drawString() Method
The drawString() method uses the baseline as the point of origin. The drawRect() method uses the upper left-hand corner as the point of origin.

Overview of gjt.LabelCanvas

The Graphic Java Toolkit includes a FontDialog class that enables selecting fonts and changing a font's point size, so we'll defer a detailed discussion of the Font class to our chapter on *FontDialog* on page 405. For now, we'll focus more on the use of the FontMetrics class, which provides size information about a particular font so that strings can be positioned appropriately within a Component.

To introduce use of the FontMetrics class, we'll describe another custom component from the Graphic Java Toolkit—gjt.LabelCanvas.

The AWT Label does not respond to mouse events. In fact, not only does it fail to respond to events, but it also fails to propagate those events to its container. [2] (We'll describe the event handling model in our chapter on *Event Handling* on page 67.) As a result, not only are labels themselves unresponsive to a mouse down event, for instance, but the Container in which they reside will never see the event. This makes it problematic to create labels that can be selected. At first glance, you might think of extending Label itself to add selection behavior. However, since a Label does not sense a mouse down, extending Label leads to a dead end. Instead, we'll create a custom component that extends Canvas and displays a string that can be selected and deselected.

2. Actually, this is not strictly a problem with the Label class; it is a bug in the current AWT.

Working With FontMetrics in a Program

The gjt.LabelCanvas class will help illustrate some nuances of the FontMetrics class. In particular, it will show how to obtain a handle on a font's FontMetrics and show some detail about positioning strings within a Component. Figure 3-10 shows the LabelCanvas class in action.

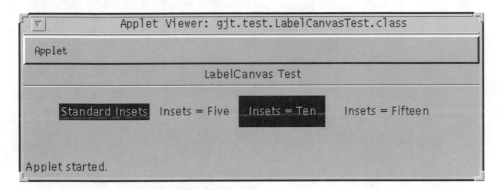

Figure 3-10 gjt.LabelCanvas
This figure shows the gjt.LabelCanvas in use. A LabelCanvas can be selected and deselected. The LabelCanvas generates selection events when it is selected or deselected.

When a gjt.LabelCanvas is selected or deselected, it delivers a SelectionEvent to its container. For the unit test, the container of the LabelCanvas simply prints information about the selection event:

```
LabelCanvas Standard Insets selected
LabelCanvas Insets = Five selected
LabelCanvas Insets = Ten selected
LabelCanvas Insets = Ten deselected
LabelCanvas Insets = Fifteen selected
LabelCanvas Insets = Fifteen deselected
```

Table 3-6 and Table 3-7 list the LabelCanvas class responsibilities and associations, respectively.

Table 3-6 gjt.LabelCanvas **Responsibilities**

Methods	Description
void paint(Graphics g)	Overrides Component paint(). Paints the string according to the selection state.
void setInsets(Insets insets)	Sets insets for a LabelCanvas.
Dimension minimumSize()	Overrides Component minimumSize(). Returns preferredSize().
String getLabel()	Returns the string representing the label.
boolean isSelected()	Returns state of the selection.
void select()	Sets selection state to true, and repaints.
void deselect()	Sets selection state to false, and repaints.
void resize(int w, int h)	Overrides Component resize(). This is a precautionary measure.
void reshape(int x, int y, int w, int h)	Overrides Component reshape(). Centers the string in the canvas.
Dimension preferredSize()	Overrides Component preferredSize(). Sets preferred size large enough to accommodate the string, plus the size of the insets.
boolean mouseDown(Event event, int x, int y)	Overrides Component mouseDown(). Controls selection.

Table 3-7 gjt.LabelCanvas **Associations**

Variables	Description
String label	The string displayed in the canvas.
boolean selected	Tracks the state of the selection.
Insets insets	Is set as if we're using a container.
Point labelLoc	Specifies the x,y point at which the string should be drawn.

With this overview of how LabelCanvas works, let's highlight several ways in which it makes use of the FontMetrics class. For those who prefer to see the whole kit and caboodle, we'll also show you the gjt.LabelCanvas code in its entirety.

Obtaining Font Dimensions

Just as every component has a Graphics object affiliated with it, every Graphics object has a FontMetrics object affiliated with it. The Graphics.getFontMetrics() method returns information about font dimensions.

Accessing a component's FontMetrics is accomplished by obtaining a reference to the component's Graphics object and calling getFontMetrics():

```
Graphics g = getGraphics();
FontMetrics fm = g.getFontMetrics();
```

Dynamically Positioning a String

When it is resized, gjt.LabelCanvas uses its labelLocation() method to recalculate the string's position:

```
public void reshape(int x, int y, int w, int h) {
    super.reshape(x, y, w, h);
    labelLoc = labelLocation(getGraphics());
}
```

After the essential call to super.reshape() is made, the labelLoc position is calculated, based on the size of the string:

```
    private Point labelLocation(Graphics g) {
        Dimension   size = size();
❶       FontMetrics fm   = g.getFontMetrics();
❷       int x = (size.width/2) - (fm.stringWidth(label)/2);
❸       int y = (size.height/2) + (fm.getAscent()/2);
❹       return new Point(x,y);
    }
```

As you can see, several of the FontMetrics methods are at work here. (For a list of FontMetrics methods, refer to *AWT Class Diagrams* on page 519.) After obtaining the FontMetrics object in line ❶, we use the font width, ascent, and leading to determine the x,y location for drawing the string. First, in line ❷, we determine the x location by subtracting half the width of the component (that is, the Canvas) by the half the width of the label, as illustrated in Figure 3-11.

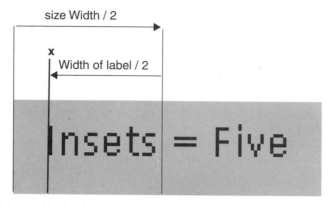

x = (size.width/2) - (fm.stringWidth(label)/2);

Figure 3-11 Determining a String's x Location

Then, in line ❸ (page 57), we determine the y location as in Figure 3-12. As you look at Figure 3-12, remember that the location passed to `Graphics.drawString()` represents the *baseline* of the string's characters.

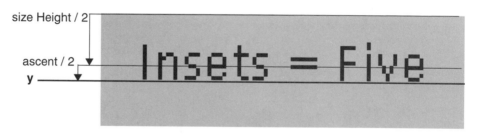

y = (size.height/2) + (fm.getAscent()/2);

Figure 3-12 Determining a String's y Location

Note that we can't just divide the height of the component by 2 to center the string in the vertical direction. While that is the center of the `Canvas`, it will not result in a centered string. We must adjust according to the font ascent to determine the string's baseline.

The `point` returned in line ❹ (page 57) represents the x,y location necessary for drawing a string (refer to page 53). Figure 3-13 shows our final x,y location.

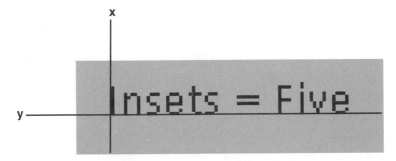

Figure 3-13 Determining a String's x,y Location

Now, based on the `point` returned by `LabelCanvas.labelLocation()`, the `LabelCanvas` can reposition the label's text string appropriately after the canvas has been resized:

```
g.drawString(label, labelLoc.x, labelLoc.y);
```

Drawing a String in Reverse Video

One of the characteristics of a `gjt.LabelCanvas` is that it draws the selected string in reverse video. This is accomplished by a protected method called `paintSelected()`, which works like this:

```
protected void paintSelected(Graphics g) {
    Point labelLoc = labelLocation(g);

    g.setColor(getForeground());
    g.fillRect(0,0,size().width,size().height);
    g.setColor(getBackground());
    g.drawString(label, labelLoc.x, labelLoc.y);
}
```

Armed with the information supplied by the `labelLocation()` method, which establishes our drawing position, we simply fill the canvas with the foreground color and draw the string in the background color.

gjt.LabelCanvas Implementation

Now that we've seen some of the particulars of dealing with `FontMetrics` in the `LabelCanvas` class, let's look at the code in its entirety in Example 3-5. There are a couple of items to pay attention to as you look through the code. For example, notice how we override the `Component.preferredSize()` method:

```
    public Dimension preferredSize() {
❶    FontMetrics fm = getFontMetrics(getFont());
    return new Dimension(
❷    insets.left + fm.stringWidth(string) + insets.right,
❸    insets.top  + fm.getHeight() + insets.bottom);
    }
```

Essentially, we obtain the `FontMetrics` in line ❶ and then calculate a preferred size based on the size of the string and the `insets` settings. The `insets` value specifies the *inside* margins of a container. We'll describe insets in detail in our chapter on *Components, Containers, and Layout Managers* [3]. The default `insets` value for `LabelCanvas` is 2 for the top, bottom, left, and right edges of the canvas. The result is that the horizontal preferred size is equal to the width of the string, plus the left and right insets, as calculated in line ❷. The vertical preferred size is equal to font height plus the top and bottom insets, as calculated in line ❸.

You might also pay attention to how the `mouseDown()` method ends up setting the `selected` variable. The point to make is that when `selected` is `true`, our overridden `paint()` method calls `paintSelected()` to invert the foreground and background colors of the `LabelCanvas`, as we describe on page 59. (We'll go into much more detail concerning overriding `Component.mouseDown()` in our chapter on *Event Handling*.)

Example 3-5 `gjt.LabelCanvas` **Class Source Code**

```
package gjt;

import java.awt.*;

public class LabelCanvas extends Canvas {
   private String   label;
   private boolean  selected  = false;
   private Insets   insets    = new Insets(2,2,2,2);
   private Point    labelLoc = new Point(0,0);

   public LabelCanvas(String label) {
       this.label = label;
   }
   public void paint(Graphics g) {
       if(selected == true) paintSelected(g);
       else
           g.drawString(label, labelLoc.x, labelLoc.y);
```

3.   Our use of insets here is somewhat different than that described in Chapter 7. Layout managers do not position components inside of a container's insets; here, insets are used to compute the overall size of the `LabelCanvas`.

```java
}
public void setInsets(Insets insets) {
    this.insets = insets;
    repaint();
}
public Dimension minimumSize() {
    return preferredSize();
}

public String  getLabel  () { return label;                   }
public boolean isSelected() { return selected;                }
public void    select     () { selected = true;  repaint(); }
public void    deselect   () { selected = false; repaint(); }

public void resize(int w, int h) {
    reshape(location().x, location().y, w, h);
}
public void reshape(int x, int y, int w, int h) {
    super.reshape(x, y, w, h);
    labelLoc = labelLocation(getGraphics());
}
public Dimension preferredSize() {
    FontMetrics fm = getFontMetrics(getFont());
        return new Dimension(
                insets.left + fm.stringWidth(label) +
                insets.right,
                insets.top  + fm.getHeight() +
                insets.bottom);
}
public boolean mouseDown(Event event, int x, int y) {
    if(selected) deselect();
    else         select  ();

    int eventType = isSelected() ?
                SelectionEvent.SELECT :
                SelectionEvent.DESELECT;

    Event newEvent = new SelectionEvent(this,
                                        event,
                                        eventType);
    deliverEvent(newEvent);
    return false;
}
protected void paintSelected(Graphics g) {
    Point labelLoc = labelLocation(g);

    g.setColor(getForeground());
    g.fillRect(0,0,size().width,size().height);
```

```
        g.setColor(getBackground());
        g.drawString(label, labelLoc.x, labelLoc.y);
    }
    protected String paramString() {
        return super.paramString() + ",text=" + label;
    }
    private Point labelLocation(Graphics g) {
        Dimension   size = size();
        FontMetrics fm   = g.getFontMetrics();
        int x = (size.width/2) - (fm.stringWidth(label)/2);
        int y = (size.height/2) + (fm.getAscent()/2);
        return new Point(x,y);
    }
}
```

Exercising the LabelCanvas

Now that you've seen some details about using the FontMetrics class and had
a chance to look at the gjt.LabelCanvas code, let's see the LabelCanvas in
action. First of all, look at Figure 3-10, which shows our unit test implementation
of the gjt.LabelCanvas class.

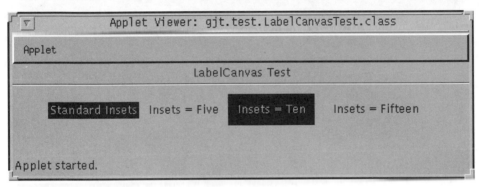

Figure 3-14 `gjt.LabelCanvas` Unit Test
The bottom picture shows selected `gjt.LabelCanvas` instances.

Example 3-6 shows the unit test code that puts the `gjt.LabelCanvas` to work. Notice that each instance of `gjt.LabelCanvas` is constructed with different insets. Also notice the overridden `Component.handleEvent()` method. We will discuss event handling in detail in *Event Handling* on page 67.

Example 3-6 `gjt.test.LabelCanvasTest` **Class Source Code**

```
package gjt.test;

import java.applet.Applet;
import java.awt.Event;
import java.awt.Panel;
import java.awt.Insets;
import java.awt.Graphics;
import gjt.LabelCanvas;
import gjt.SelectionEvent;
import gjt.Util;
```

```
public class LabelCanvasTest extends UnitTest {
  public String title() { return "LabelCanvas Test"; }
  public Panel centerPanel() {
      return new LabelCanvasTestPanel(this);
  }
}

class LabelCanvasTestPanel extends Panel {
  Applet applet;
  public LabelCanvasTestPanel(Applet applet) {
      this.applet = applet;
      LabelCanvas standard =
          new LabelCanvas("Standard Insets");
      LabelCanvas insetFive =
          new LabelCanvas("Insets = Five");
      LabelCanvas insetTen =
          new LabelCanvas("Insets = Ten");
      LabelCanvas insetFifteen =
          new LabelCanvas("Insets = Fifteen");

      insetFive.setInsets    (new Insets(5,5,5,5));
      insetTen.setInsets     (new Insets(10,10,10,10));
      insetFifteen.setInsets(new Insets(15,15,15,15));

      add(standard);
      add(insetFive);
      add(insetTen);
      add(insetFifteen);
  }
  public boolean handleEvent(Event event) {
      if(event instanceof SelectionEvent) {
          LabelCanvas canvas = (LabelCanvas)event.target;

          if(event.id == SelectionEvent.SELECT)
              System.out.println("LabelCanvas " +
                                  canvas.getLabel() +
                                  " selected");
          else
              System.out.println("LabelCanvas " +
                                  canvas.getLabel() +
                                  " deselected");
      }
      return false;
  }
}
```

Summary

This chapter covers the basics of using the Graphics, Color, and FontMetrics classes in the Java AWT. In particular, we have illustrated how to obtain a component's Graphics object, how to draw lines and rectangles, and how to fill rectangles. The Graphic Java Toolkit custom components described in this chapter also illustrate how to obtain brighter or darker shades of a color, along with the use of color constants. Lastly, we've introduced the AWT font model, and presented another GJT custom component (gjt.LabelCanvas) to illustrate the use of the java.awt.FontMetrics class. There are other corners of the Graphics, Color, Font, and FontMetrics classes worth exploring, and we do that in later chapters that focus on custom components. Particularly, the *FontDialog* chapter illustrates manipulation of font styles and sizes, while the *Sprite Animation* chapter covers more advanced usage of the Graphics class.

CHAPTER
4

- The AWT Event Model on page 67

- Event Modifier Constants on page 75

- Mouse Button Events on page 76

- Of Mice and Buttons on page 78

- Monitoring Mouse Events on page 78

- Sensing Double Clicking on page 81

- Action Events on page 82

- Identifying Components by Label — Just Say No on page 85

- Custom Component Events on page 87

  - Extending java.awt.Event on page 89

  - Hand-Delivering Events on page 91

- Summary on page 92

Event Handling

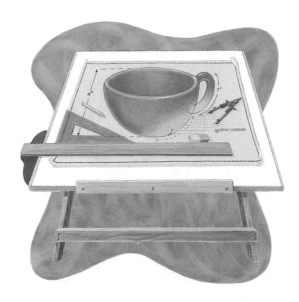

Modern graphical user interfaces are typically event driven, meaning they spend much of their time idling, waiting for an event to occur; when an event occurs, an event handler responds to the event. Applets and applications developed using the AWT are no different, so in this chapter, we introduce event handling in AWT components and offer advice on a variety of points, including when to override event handling methods and when to handle an event or pass it on. We also introduce several applets to illustrate event handling techniques, such as sensing double clicks, managing action events, and generating and delivering events to custom components.

The AWT Event Model

As is the case with nearly all object-oriented user interface toolkits, the AWT is event driven. Actually, since the AWT uses a peer approach, the underlying event subsystem is native to the platform on which an applet or application is running. So, for instance, if an applet is executed under Motif, it uses the X Window event handling system. Our focus, however, is not on the underlying native event system but on the AWT layer through which we respond to events.

Overriding Event Handling Methods

Essentially, AWT event handling is a pretty simple proposition: when an event occurs inside a component, a method of that component is invoked. If you want the component to respond to an event, you simply override the appropriate method. For instance, a component's `void resize(int w, int h)` method is invoked when the component is resized. If you wanted to take some action when a resize event occurs, you would override `resize()` and take care of business. There are a number of component methods which, like `resize()`, are called in response to some event. Table 4-1 shows a partial list of such methods.

Table 4-1 Event-Driven Methods Used in Components

Method	Event
Methods You Frequently Override in Components	
`void resize(int w, int h)`	Component has been resized.
`void reshape(int x, int y, int w, int h)`	Component resized and moved.
`void paint(Graphics g)`	Component needs to be painted.
`void update(Graphics g)`	By default erase, then repaint.
`void addNotify()`	Peer created.
Methods You Infrequently Override in Components	
`void move(int x, int y)`	Component moved to x,y location.
`void layout()`	Component needs to be laid out.
`void validate()`	If invalid, lay out.

It is common to override the first group of methods in Table 4-1 when developing custom components. The methods in the second group in the table represent more obscure events, such as when a component needs to be laid out (we will discuss layout managers in detail in *Components, Containers, and Layout Managers*). It is rarely necessary to override the methods associated with these events. Of course, by overriding any of the methods in Table 4-1, you are rewriting what the component does by default. As a result, you will often see event handler methods that call the superclass version before adding embellishments:

```
public addNotify() {   // Default version creates the peer object.
  super.addNotify();   // Peer is created only after this call.
  // Now we are guaranteed that things like the Component's
  // Graphics are available, since the peer has been created
}
```

Propagated Events

The events discussed above occur in a component and are handled (or ignored) by the component in which the event occurred. Such events are of concern only to the component in which they occurred.

A second group of events is referred to as *propagated* events; whenever a propagated event occurs in a component, the component's handleEvent(Event) method is invoked. The component's handleEvent() method may choose to propagate the event to its container or handle the event entirely on its own.

Note the distinction between propagated events and the events listed in Table 4-1. Propagated events are always handled by a component's handleEvent() method, which is passed a java.awt.Event. Propagated events may be propagated to the component's container; if so, the container's handleEvent() method is invoked and the java.awt.Event is passed along.

Since propagated events involve a java.awt.Event, they are generically referred to as AWT events. The rest of this chapter will only be concerned with such events.

Event Type Constants

Every java.awt.Event has an id field whose value indicates the type of event that has occurred. Typically, the first thing a component's handleEvent() method does is to check the event's id field to determine the type of event. For instance, a handleEvent() method concerned with mouse events might look something like this:

```
public boolean handleEvent(Event event) {
  if(event.id == Event.MOUSE_DOWN) {
    // react to mouse down
    return true; // event fully handled, do not propagate
  }
  else if(event.id == Event.MOUSE_UP) {
    // react to mouse up
    return true; // event fully handled, do not propagate
  }
```

```
  // let superclass handle event and decide to propagate
  return super.handleEvent(event);
}
```

Notice that this example returns `true` if the event is a mouse up or mouse down event, signifying that we have fully handled the event and therefore do not wish to propagate the event to our container. If the event is not a mouse up or mouse down, we give the superclass a chance to handle the event. If we were to return `false`, the event would be propagated directly to the component's container and the superclass would never have a chance to handle the event. Therefore, it is always a good idea to have overridden `handleEvent()` methods return `super.handleEvent(event)` if they have not fully handled the event, instead of propagating the event directly to the component's container.

AWT Tip

Avoid Returning false From a handleEvent() Method

Returning false from a handleEvent() method propagates the event to the component's container without giving the component's superclass a chance to process the event. Therefore, it is a good idea to avoid returning false from a handleEvent() method. Instead, if a class has not fully handled a particular event, it should always give its superclass a chance to process the event and let the superclass decide whether to propagate the event to the component's container. Even if you know that your superclass is not interested in a particular type of event, there are no guarantees that the superclass will not be modified in the future to process an event that you are not interested in.

Table 4-2 shows the complete list of `java.awt.Event` type constants.

Table 4-2 `java.awt.Event` **Constants**

Event Constants
Window Event Constants
WINDOW_DESTROY
WINDOW_EXPOSE
WINDOW_ICONIFY
WINDOW_DEICONIFY
WINDOW_MOVED
Keyboard Event Constants
KEY_PRESS
KEY_RELEASE
KEY_ACTION

Table 4-2 `java.awt.Event` **Constants (Continued)**

Event Constants
`KEY_ACTION_RELEASE`
Mouse Event Constants
`MOUSE_DOWN, MOUSE_UP`
`MOUSE_MOVE`
`MOUSE_ENTER, MOUSE_EXIT`
`MOUSE_DRAG`
Scrollbar Event Constants
`SCROLL_LINE_UP, SCROLL_LINE_DOWN`
`SCROLL_PAGE_UP, SCROLL_PAGE_DOWN`
`SCROLL_ABSOLUTE`
List Event Constants
`LIST_SELECT, LIST_DESELECT`
Action Event Constants
`ACTION_EVENT`
`LOAD_FILE`
`SAVE_FILE`
`GOT_FOCUS, LOST_FOCUS`

Propagated Event Handler Methods

Checking against the `id` field of an event to decipher the type of event in overridden `handleEvent()` methods is rather ugly and requires keeping track of all the event constants listed in Table 4-2, which is not very object-oriented[1]. As a result, `java.awt.Component` implements a `handleEvent()` method that deciphers the type of event and invokes one of a number of convenience methods. Table 4-3 lists all of the convenience methods that are invoked by `java.awt.Component.handleEvent()`.

---

1. See Meyer, Bertrand. *Object Oriented Software Construction,* section 10.2.2. Prentice Hall.

Table 4-3 Propagated Event Handler Convenience Methods

Method	Event
boolean action (Event, Object)	An action event.
boolean mouseUp (Event,int,int)	Mouse up.
boolean mouseDown (Event,int,int)	Mouse down.
boolean mouseDrag (Event,int,int)	Mouse drag.
boolean mouseMove (Event,int,int)	Mouse move.
boolean mouseEnter (Event,int,int)	Mouse entered component.
boolean mouseExit (Event,int,int)	Mouse exited component.
boolean keyUp (Event,int)	Key up.
boolean keyDown (Event,int)	Key down.
boolean gotFocus (Event,Object)	Component has focus.
boolean lostFocus (Event,Object)	Component lost focus.

When handling propagated events, you can choose to do one of the following:

- Override handleEvent() and check against the id field of the event to determine the type of event

- Override one of the convenience methods listed in Table 4-3

Let's take a look at the implementation of Component.handleEvent(Event) in order to see exactly how the convenience methods are invoked:

```
public boolean handleEvent(Event evt) {
  switch (evt.id) {
    case Event.MOUSE_ENTER:
        return mouseEnter(evt, evt.x, evt.y);

    case Event.MOUSE_EXIT:
        return mouseExit(evt, evt.x, evt.y);

    case Event.MOUSE_MOVE:
        return mouseMove(evt, evt.x, evt.y);

    case Event.MOUSE_DOWN:
        return mouseDown(evt, evt.x, evt.y);

    case Event.MOUSE_DRAG:
        return mouseDrag(evt, evt.x, evt.y);

    case Event.MOUSE_UP:
        return mouseUp(evt, evt.x, evt.y);
```

```
    case Event.KEY_PRESS:
    case Event.KEY_ACTION:
        return keyDown(evt, evt.key);

    case Event.KEY_RELEASE:
    case Event.KEY_ACTION_RELEASE:
        return keyUp(evt, evt.key);

    case Event.ACTION_EVENT:
        return action(evt, evt.arg);
    case Event.GOT_FOCUS:
        return gotFocus(evt, evt.arg);
    case Event.LOST_FOCUS:
        return lostFocus(evt, evt.arg);
  }
  return false;
}
```

`java.awt.Component.handleEvent(Event)` simply deciphers the type of event and then invokes a convenience method. All of the convenience methods are implemented in `Component` as *no-ops*; they exist solely for you to override them and give them some teeth.

Propagated Events Propagate Outward

Applets often have a fairly complex nested layout in which various extensions of `Panel` are nested within one another and positioned according to the container's layout manager. Indeed, this is the core of AWT development—an art that we explore throughout this book.

Events are propagated from the component in which the event occurred to the outermost container. However, any component along the chain of containers can halt the propagation of the event if its `handleEvent()` method completely handles the event and returns `true`.

Overriding Propagated Event Handlers

As we discussed previously, methods that handle a propagated event return a `boolean` value, which indicates whether the event was handled or not. A `true` return value indicates that the event has been handled and should not be propagated to the component's container. A `false` return value signals that the event has not been handled completely and should be forwarded to the component's container. Table 4-4 summarizes the choices a component has when confronted with a propagated event.

Table 4-4 Component Choices When Handling Propagated Events

A Component Can Do This With a Propagated Event...	Then `handleEvent()`...
Propagate event to its container.	Returns `false`.
Not propagate event to its container.	Returns `true`.
Let superclass handle and decide to propagate.	Returns `super.handleEvent(event)`.

Whether you override `handleEvent()` or override one of the convenience methods listed in Table 4-3 on page 72, you must decide the manner in which you will return from the propagated event handler. In either case, if you have completely handled the event, then you can just return `true`, signifying the event is completely handled and should not be propagated. If you have not completely handled the event, then there are two guidelines to follow, as listed in Table 4-5.

Table 4-5 Event Handling Guidelines

If You Have Not Completely Handled the Event and You Have...	Then...
Overridden `handleEvent()`.	Call `super.handleEvent(event)` and let the superclass determine whether or not to propagate the event.
Overridden one of the convenience methods in Table 4-3.	Return `false` and propagate the event to the component's container.

Let's look at the rationale for these guidelines. First, as we've already mentioned in the *AWT Tip* on page 70, it's preferable when using `handleEvent()` to leave the decision to propagate the event to the superclass's `handleEvent()`. It is just good practice to give the superclass a chance to handle the event.

However, this doesn't work so neatly with the convenience methods. Consider, for instance, the consequences of returning `super.handleEvent(event)` from one of the convenience methods. If you were to override `mouseDown()`, for example, and return `super.handleEvent()`, you might wind up in an infinite loop. If none of your superclasses override `handleEvent()`, you will invoke `Component.handleEvent()`, which detects the mouse down event and invokes mouseDown(), putting you right back where you started. As a rule of thumb, when overriding the convenience methods, it is best to propagate the event directly to the container.

AWT Tip

Propagate Unhandled Events From Event Handler Convenience Methods

Event handler convenience methods such as mouseDown() should never return super.handleEvent(event) but should instead directly propagate unhandled events to their container. By default, Component.handleEvent(Event) deciphers the event type and invokes a convenience method, which will result in an infinite loop if super.handleEvent(event) is invoked from the convenience method to begin with.

To highlight AWT event handling in action, we will provide a series of small applets in the rest of this chapter that illustrate various features and nuances of the AWT event handling model.

Event Modifier Constants

In addition to an id field, each java.awt.Event also contains a modifier field that provides additional information about the event. For example, you might want to know which key or which mouse button triggered an event. The Event class defines a handful of constants that provide such information. Table 4-6 lists the modifier constants. We'll show how to use these later in this chapter, but it's useful to have them handy for reference.

Table 4-6 Event Modifiers

Event Modifier Constant	Type	Meaning
ALT_MASK	Keyboard	ALT key is down.
ALT_MASK	Mouse Button	Button 2 is pressed.
CTRL_MASK	Keyboard	CONTROL key is down.
DOWN	Function Key	DOWN key is pressed.
END	Function Key	END key is pressed.
F1 - F12	Function Key	FUNCTION key 1 – 12 is pressed.
HOME	Function Key	HOME key is pressed.
LEFT	Function Key	LEFT key is pressed.
META_MASK	Keyboard	META key is down.
META_MASK	Mouse Button	Button 3 is pressed.

Table 4-6 Event Modifiers (Continued)

Event Modifier Constant	Type	Meaning
PGDOWN	Function Key	PAGE DOWN key is pressed.
PGUP	Function Key	PAGE UP key is pressed.
RIGHT	Function Key	RIGHT key is pressed.
SHIFT_MASK	Keyboard	SHIFT key or caps lock is down.
UP	Function Key	UP key is pressed.

Mouse Button Events

To illustrate handling mouse button events, we'll describe a MouseSensorApplet. The MouseSensorApplet uses a BorderLayout layout manager and places an instance of a MouseSensorCanvas in the center of the applet. Remember that an applet is an extension of Container, so components can be added to an applet. (Since most of the applets in this chapter simply place a blank canvas inside an applet, we won't show pictures of them unless there's something to illustrate.) The MouseSensorCanvas class overrides the mouseDown(), mouseUp(), and mouseDrag() convenience methods from java.awt.Component. It also implements a whichMouseButton() method to print the mouse button that initiated the event. Example 4-1 shows the implementation for MouseSensorApplet.

Example 4-1 MouseSensorApplet **Source Code**

```
import java.applet.Applet;
import java.awt.*;

public class MouseSensorApplet extends Applet {
  public void init() {
      setLayout(new BorderLayout());
      add("Center", new MouseSensorCanvas());
  }
}

class MouseSensorCanvas extends Canvas {
  public boolean mouseDown(Event event, int x, int y) {
      System.out.println(whichMouseButton(event) + ":  Down");
      return true;
  }
  public boolean mouseUp(Event event, int x, int y) {
      System.out.println(whichMouseButton(event) + ":  Up");
      return true;
  }
  public boolean mouseDrag(Event event, int x, int y) {
```

```
        System.out.println(whichMouseButton(event) + ":  Drag");
        return true;
    }
    private String whichMouseButton(Event event) {
        String s = new String("Mouse Button 1");

        if((event.modifiers & Event.META_MASK) != 0)
            s = "Mouse Button 2";
        else if((event.modifiers & Event.ALT_MASK) != 0)
            s = "Mouse Button 3";

        return s;
    }
}
```

Notice that each of our convenience methods (mouseUp(), mouseDown() and
mouseDrag()) prints information about the event, with the help of
whichMouseButton(). These methods return true, indicating that the event is
fully handled and should not be propagated to the container, which in this case is
the applet.

The whichMouseButton() method does the work of distinguishing between
the different mouse buttons:

```
    private String whichMouseButton(Event event) {
        String s = new String("Mouse Button 1");

❶       if((event.modifiers & Event.META_MASK) != 0)
            s = "Mouse Button 2";
❷       else if((event.modifiers & Event.ALT_MASK) != 0)
            s = "Mouse Button 3";

        return s;
    }
```

In order to detect mouse button 2 and 3, this method simply uses a logical AND to
combine the modifiers field of the event with the AWT Event class constants,
ALT_MASK and META_MASK in lines ❶ and ❷.

Note that we could have overridden handleEvent() and checked the id field
of the event in order to sense mouse button events, but we have chosen to
override convenience methods instead.

NOTE: In the JDK 1.0.2 release, there is a bug in the Windows 95 version of the
AWT in which a mouse up with button 1 is detected as a mouse up with button 2. [2]

Of Mice and Buttons

Different platforms typically use different types of mice. Macintosh systems normally use a one-button mouse, PC's a two- or three-button mouse, and SPARC® systems a three-button mouse. Java deals with these differences by assuming that all mice have one button. For example, the AWT distinguishes only one mouse up event. Correspondingly, there is only one method (mouseUp()) to account for this. There's no mouseUp1(), mouseUp2(), mouseUp3() to account for the different mouse buttons that might initiate an event. This is also the case for mouse events such as a mouse down or mouse drag. In effect, the AWT is developed for the lowest common denominator.

As we've seen in the whichMouseButton() method above, the mechanism employed to determine which mouse button triggered an event is to look at the event's modifier field. If the modifier field ORed with the Event.META_MASK is non-zero, then we know that mouse button 2 initiated the event, while an ALT_MASK represents mouse button 3. Therefore, on a system with a one-button mouse, mouse button 2 can be simulated by holding down the Meta key when clicking the mouse, while mouse button 3 can be simulated by holding down the Alt key.

Monitoring Mouse Events

In the next applet, we'll illustrate monitoring mouse events such as the mouse moving, entering, and exiting an applet. This particular applet—called EventMonitorApplet—also monitors mouse up and down events and prints information about each event. EventMonitorApplet extends the Applet class (as do all applets). It includes an EventPrinter class that checks to see if an event is a mouse event, and if so, its print() method prints which mouse event occurred. The EventMonitorApplet includes an instance of EventPrinter that is both public and static. It is public because both EventMonitor and EventPrinter classes use it. It is static because only one EventPrinter is required. Note that this applet is set up just like the MouseSensorApplet. It creates an applet, sets its layout to BorderLayout, and then positions an instance of a class that extends Canvas in the center of the applet. Example 4-2 shows the EventMonitorApplet in its entirety.

Example 4-2 EventMonitorApplet **Source Code**

2.   Note to all those left-handers out there: We generically refer to mouse buttons 1, 2, and 3 rather than left, middle, and right. Mouse button 1 represents the primary mouse button.

```
import java.applet.Applet;
import java.awt.*;

public class EventMonitorApplet extends Applet {
  public static EventPrinter printer = new EventPrinter();

  public void init() {
      setLayout(new BorderLayout());
      add("Center", new EventMonitor());
  }
  public boolean handleEvent(Event event) {
      System.out.print("APPLET:   ");
      printer.print(event);
      System.out.println();
      return true;
  }
}


class EventMonitor extends Canvas {
  public boolean handleEvent(Event event) {
      System.out.print("CANVAS:   ");
      EventMonitorApplet.printer.print(event);
      System.out.println();
      return true;
  }
}

class EventPrinter {
  public void print(Event event) {
      String s = null;

      if(event.id == Event.MOUSE_DOWN)        s = "Mouse Down";
      else if(event.id == Event.MOUSE_UP)     s = "Mouse Up";
      else if(event.id == Event.MOUSE_DRAG)   s = "Mouse Drag";
      else if(event.id == Event.MOUSE_MOVE)   s = "Mouse Move";
      else if(event.id == Event.MOUSE_EXIT)   s = "Mouse Exit";
      else if(event.id == Event.MOUSE_ENTER)  s = "Mouse Enter";

      if(s != null)
          System.out.print(s);
      else
          System.out.print(event.id);
  }
}
```

The EventMonitor class, which extends Canvas, expands to fill the entire applet. (The fact that the EventMonitor canvas expands to consume the entire applet area is the by-product of adding it centered in a BorderLayout. We'll talk more about BorderLayout and layout managers in general in *Components, Containers, and Layout Managers* on page 155.)

EventMonitorApplet and EventMonitor both override the handleEvent() method, causing two things to occur when a mouse action takes place:

- Calls System.out.print to print APPLET: or CANVAS:, respectively
- Calls the print() method in the EventPrinter class to print the mouse event that occurred (e.g., MOUSE_UP, MOUSE_DOWN)

So, when dragging the mouse over the applet, you'll see output similar to this:

```
APPLET:   Mouse Enter
CANVAS:   Mouse Enter
CANVAS:   Mouse Move
CANVAS:   Mouse Move
CANVAS:   Mouse Move
CANVAS:   Mouse Down
CANVAS:   Mouse Up
CANVAS:   Mouse Move
CANVAS:   Mouse Move
CANVAS:   Mouse Exit
APPLET:   Mouse Exit
```

The EventMonitorApplet illustrates that events are propagated from the component in which the event occurred to outermost container. Our containment strategy here is easy to expose: We have a Canvas (EventMonitor) contained inside an Applet (EventMonitorApplet). Both of them have overridden boolean handleEvent(Event), ready to deal with whatever events come their way.

Of course, the return value of the EventMonitor handleEvent() method determines whether EventMonitorApplet sees events that were generated in EventMonitor. In the previous output, the only events that EventMonitorApplet sees are mouse enter and mouse exit events; all the rest are effectively gobbled up by EventMonitor. (Note that there is a bug under Windows 95 that results in some events being propagated up to the EventMonitorApplet, even though they are never explicitly propagated).

If, for instance, the `EventMonitor handleEvent()` method returned `false`, then events would be passed to the container's (`EventMonitorApplet`) `handleEvent()` method. The applet output would change to look something like this:

```
APPLET:   Mouse Enter
CANVAS:   Mouse Enter
APPLET:   Mouse Enter
CANVAS:   Mouse Move
APPLET:   Mouse Move
CANVAS:   Mouse Down
APPLET:   Mouse Down
CANVAS:   Mouse Up
APPLET:   Mouse Up
CANVAS:   Mouse Down
APPLET:   Mouse Down
CANVAS:   Mouse Up
APPLET:   Mouse Up
CANVAS:   Mouse Move
APPLET:   Mouse Move
CANVAS:   Mouse Exit
APPLET:   Mouse Exit
APPLET:   Mouse Exit
```

Sensing Double Clicking

Sensing that the mouse has been *double-clicked* requires use of the `Event` `clickCount` field. To illustrate this, we've written the `DoubleClickApplet` program, which is set up like the previous event applets in this chapter. Example 4-3 shows the `DoubleClickApplet` code.

Example 4-3 `DoubleClickApplet` **Source Code**

```java
import java.applet.Applet;
import java.awt.*;

public class DoubleClickApplet extends Applet {
  public void init() {
      setLayout(new BorderLayout());
      add("Center", new DoubleClickCanvas());
  }
}
```

```
class DoubleClickCanvas extends Canvas {
  public boolean mouseDown(Event event, int x, int y) {
     if(event.clickCount == 2)
         System.out.println("Double click");
     return true;
  }
}
```

The overridden mouseDown() method simply checks to see if the Event clickCount field equals 2. If so, mouseDown() informs us that a double click has occurred. Regardless of whether a double click has occurred or not, mouseDown() returns true because our simple-minded applet is not prepared to deal with a propagated event.

There's an interesting aside here. Note that the location of the cursor seems to have no bearing upon whether or not clickCount is advanced. If you click the mouse at one location and then hastily move to another location and click again, it will register as a double click. This may lead one to the AWT source in search of an algorithm for advancing the clickCount; we do have the AWT source, after all. It may be hard to believe at first, but clickCount is not set anywhere other than at construction time, when it is set to zero; who, then, is responsible for advancing clickCount? The answer lies in the component's peer—the unseen laborer that implements much of the functionality of the AWT. Unless we have the source for the peers, which we do not, then we have no way of ever knowing the exact criterion for advancing clickCount.

Action Events

Action events are those activated by one of the following subclasses of Component:

- Button
- Checkbox
- TextField
- Choice

These events are the result of specific button, checkbox, or choice selections, or are generated from a return in a textfield, as illustrated in Figure 4-1.

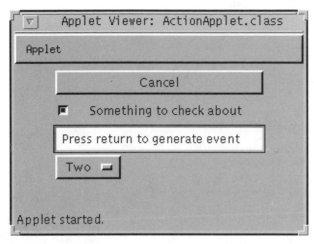

Figure 4-1 Action Events
Action events are events generated by using the mouse to select choice items, checkboxes, or buttons or by entering a carriage return in a textfield.

The `ActionApplet` creates each of these AWT components. The unique characteristic of these AWT components is that *only* `Button`, `Checkbox`, `TextField`, and `Choice` components generate events that are routed through the `Component action()` method. (In contrast, an event in any other component would never result in a call to the `Component action()` method.)

One thing you'll notice in the `ActionApplet` is that instead of putting a `Canvas` in the applet as with the other applets in this chapter, it places a `Panel` in the applet. We need to use a `Panel` here because a `Panel` is a `Container`, and we need to put our components (the button, checkbox, text field, and choice) into a container. (We could have used a `Panel` in the previous applets; however, we cannot use a `Canvas` for this applet because `Canvas` is *not* a `Container`.) Also, for the sake of variety, we use the default layout manager, `FlowLayout`, in this applet. This behaves exactly as in the previous applets, which used `BorderLayout`. Now, let's look at the `ActionApplet` in Example 4-4 and then describe what the `action()` method is doing.

Example 4-4 ActionApplet **Source Code**

```java
import java.applet.Applet;
import java.awt.*;

public class ActionApplet extends Applet {
  public void init() {
      add(new ActionPanel());
  }
}

class ActionPanel extends Panel {
  Button    button    = new Button("Cancel");
  Checkbox  checkbox  = new Checkbox(
                               "Something to check about");
  TextField textfield = new TextField(25);
  Choice    choice    = new Choice();

  public ActionPanel() {
      choice.addItem("One");
      choice.addItem("Two");
      choice.addItem("Three");
      choice.addItem("Four");

      setLayout(new GridLayout(0,1));
      add(button);
      add(checkbox);
      add(textfield);
      add(choice);
  }
  public boolean action(Event event, Object what) {
      if(event.target instanceof Button)
          System.out.print("Button:   ");
      if(event.target instanceof Choice)
          System.out.print("Choice:   ");
      if(event.target instanceof TextField)
          System.out.print("TextField:   ");
      if(event.target instanceof Checkbox)
          System.out.print("Checkbox:   ");

      System.out.println(what.getClass().getName() +
                         "= " + what);
      return true;
  }
}
```

The `action()` method is passed an `event` and an object we have named `what`. This second argument differs according to the type of component that triggered the event. For example, if `event` is from an instance of `Button`, then `what` will be a `String` containing the label of the button. Table 4-7 shows how the value of the `what` argument is set, based on the component that generates the `event`.

Table 4-7 Value of the `what` Argument in the `action()` Method

If the `event` Is From an Instance of...	Then the `what` Is Set to a...
`Button`	`String` with the text of label of the button.
`Checkbox`	`Boolean` value, which is `true` if the checkbox is checked and `false` if it isn't checked.
`TextField`	`String` that represents the text in the text field.
`Choice`	`String` that represents the text displayed in the choice.

For example, output from the `ActionApplet` program looks like this:

```
Button:   java.lang.String= Cancel
Checkbox:   java.lang.Boolean= true
TextField:   java.lang.String= Press return to generate event
Choice:   java.lang.String= Two
```

As the output suggests, a `TextField` generates an action event *only* after a carriage return. (The 1.0.2 version of the AWT provides no mechanism for being notified when a character other than a carriage return is typed into a textfield.)

Action events for a `Button`, `CheckBox`, or `Choice` are generated when each is selected with the mouse.

Identifying Components by Label — Just Say No

It is standard AWT practice to check against the labels of certain components (in particular, buttons) to determine the component with which an event is associated. For instance, the following applet displays three buttons and uses the labels of the buttons to determine which one triggered an action event:

```
import java.applet.Applet;
import java.awt.*;

public class ButtonActionApplet extends Applet {
  public void init() {
```

```
        Button buttonOne    = new Button("Button One");
        Button buttonTwo    = new Button("Button Two");
        Button buttonThree = new Button("Button Three");

        add(buttonOne);
        add(buttonTwo);
        add(buttonThree);
    }
    public boolean action(Event event, Object what) {
        if(what.equals("Button One"))
            System.out.println("Button One");
        if(what.equals("Button Two"))
            System.out.println("Button Two");
        if(what.equals("Button Three"))
            System.out.println("Button Three");

        return true;
    }
}
```

While this applet produces the desired effect, namely, it prints the identity of the button activated, it is fraught with difficulties. First of all, the labels of the buttons may very well change over time, causing modification of the action() method each and every time a button has its label changed. This is not a consideration for a toy applet like the one above; however, in the real world it may be unacceptable for a complex applet or application to keep button label strings in synch with event handling methods. Furthermore, identifying components by their labels has serious implications for internationalization [3].

A much better approach is to identify components by reference, instead of their labels, as depicted by the revised applet below:

```
import java.applet.Applet;
import java.awt.*;

public class ButtonActionByRefApplet extends Applet {
    private Button buttonOne    = new Button("Button One");
    private Button buttonTwo    = new Button("Button Two");
    private Button buttonThree = new Button("Button Three");

    public void init() {
        add(buttonOne);
        add(buttonTwo);
        add(buttonThree);
    }
```

3. A future version of Java will support internationalization.

```
public boolean action(Event event, Object what) {
    if(event.target == buttonOne)
        System.out.println(buttonOne.getLabel());
    if(event.target == buttonTwo)
        System.out.println(buttonTwo.getLabel());
    if(event.target == buttonThree)
        System.out.println(buttonThree.getLabel());

    return true;
  }
}
```

Notice that we have moved the declarations for the buttons from being local to init() to private members of the class. Second, in the action() method, we check the target of the event against the button references to identify which button triggered the action event.

This approach ensures that the applet continues to function properly even if we change the labels of the buttons. Note also that we get the label from the buttons themselves to print out the buttons' identity, instead of hardcoding the button labels in the action() method.

AWT Tip

Identify Components By Reference, Not By Their Labels

It is standard AWT practice to identify components by their labels when handling certain events. This has some serious implications for maintaining applets and applications, since the methods that identify components must be kept in synch with the component's labels. Additionally, identifying components by their labels will present difficulties once Java implements internationalization. A better approach is to identify components by reference.

Custom Component Events

Every java.awt.Event has an id field that identifies the type of the event. The id field is used to decipher the kind of event that has occurred. For instance, a handleEvent() method for a component containing an AWT List might look something like this:

```
public boolean handleEvent(Event event) {
   .
   .
   .
   if(event.id == LIST_SELECT) {
      // react to list selection
   }
   else if(event.id == LIST_DESELECT) {
      // react to list deselection
   }
   .
   .
   .
}
```

As we have discussed previously, java.awt.Event defines a number of constants to identify different types of events that may occur within AWT components, as shown in Table 4-2 on page 70.

While this list of constants is sufficient for events as far as standard AWT components are concerned, they are of no use for events that occur in custom components. For instance, consider the Graphic Java Toolkit's LabelCanvas, which is essentially a string that can be selected and deselected. Obviously, none of the defined constants for event types in java.awt.Event correspond to a gjt.LabelCanvas select or deselect event.

How then, do you go about generating an event for a custom component? One possibility is to use an existing constant that approximates your needs. For instance, LIST_SELECT is a selection event; we could use LIST_SELECT to identify a LabelCanvas selection. However, this alternative is less than desirable, especially if we have a container that contains both an AWT List and a GJT LabelCanvas.

Another possibility is to define your own constants, in this case, to signify LabelCanvas select or deselect events. In the LabelCanvas class, we could define two constants:

```
public class LabelCanvas {
   public static final int LABELCANVAS_SELECT = 701;
   public static final int LABELCANVAS_DESELECT = 702;
   .
   .
   .
}
```

The drawback to this approach is that we must be certain that the values chosen for the constants do not have any counterparts in the java.awt.Event class. Of course, as you might guess from our odd-looking values, 701 and 702 are poor choices indeed, for they are the same as LIST_SELECT and LIST_DESELECT. Using these values for gjt.LabelCanvas select and deselect events would result in handleEvent() methods that could not properly distinguish between AWT List selections and GJT LabelCanvas selections.

Your inclination at this point may be to go snooping around the java.awt.Event source in order to come up with a unique constant. However, doing so has two serious drawbacks. First of all, you would be relying upon the implementation of java.awt.Event instead of its interface, which violates the spirit of object-oriented development [4]. Second, ensuring that a value is currently used as an event id for a standard AWT event does not ensure that the value is not being used in some other custom component or that it will not be used in the future.

Defining constants to represent custom component events is too problematic. The best solution for managing custom component events is to extend the java.awt.Event class. This enables clients to check against the type of event in order to determine the kind of event that has occurred.

Extending java.awt.Event

The Graphic Java Toolkit contains a SelectionEvent class in Example 4-5, which extends java.awt.Event.

Example 4-5 gjt.SelectionEvent **Class Source Code**

```
public class SelectionEvent extends Event {
    public static final int SELECT   = 1;
    public static final int DESELECT = 2;

    private int eventType;

    public SelectionEvent(Object target,
                          Event  event,
                          int    type) {
        super(target, event.when, event.id, event.x, event.y,
              event.key,  event.modifiers, event.arg);

        Assert.notFalse(type == SELECT || type == DESELECT);
```

---

4. See Cox, Brad, *Object Oriented Programming An Evolutionary Approach*, page 49–52. Addison-Wesley.

```
            eventType = type;
            id = -1;
    }
    public boolean isSelected() {
            return eventType == SELECT;
    }
    protected String paramString() {
            String typeString = new String();

            if(eventType == SelectionEvent.SELECT)
                typeString = "SELECT";
            else if(eventType == SelectionEvent.DESELECT)
                typeString = "DESELECT";

            return super.paramString() + typeString;
    }
}
```

Since a select or deselect event is typically the result of a standard AWT event such as a mouse down, a gjt.SelectionEvent is constructed with a java.awt.Event, along with the target of the selection and an integer value that must be either SELECT or DESELECT. The constructor assigns the id field of the event to -1[5] and assigns eventType to either SELECT or DESELECT.

A container that contains a gjt.LabelCanvas would implement its handleEvent() method something like this:

```
public boolean handleEvent(Event event) {
        if(event instanceof SelectionEvent) {
            SelectionEvent sevent = (SelectionEvent)event;

            if(sevent.isSelected()) {
                // do something for selection
            }
            else {
                // do something for deselection
            }
        }
}
```

Since gjt.SelectionEvent is a class, we use the instanceof operator to find out if the event in question is a gjt.SelectionEvent. If so, we invoke SelectionEvent.isSelected() to determine if the event was a SELECT event and then take appropriate action.

---

5.   Yes, we are counting on one value, namely, -1 as not being used as the value for id fields for other events. All custom events in the GJT use -1 for the id field.

Hand-Delivering Events

Standard AWT events are delivered for us. That is, we simply have to check for
the type of event we are interested in when we override handleEvent().
Obviously, an event such as a gjt.SelectionEvent is never going to be
generated and delivered to our handleEvent() methods by the underlying
AWT infrastructure.

Custom components, therefore, must create and hand-deliver their own events.
For instance, gjt.LabelCanvas overrides mouseDown() to create a
gjt.SelectionEvent(), which it hand-delivers:

```
public boolean mouseDown(Event event, int x, int y) {
  if(selected) deselect();
  else     select ();
  int eventType = isSelected() ?
               SelectionEvent.SELECT :
               SelectionEvent.DESELECT;

    Event newEvent = new SelectionEvent(this, event,
                                        eventType);
    deliverEvent(newEvent);

  return true;
}
```

The first thing gjt.LabelCanvas.mouseDown() does is to toggle the selected
state of the LabelCanvas. After that business is taken care of, a new
SelectionEvent is created, to which the LabelCanvas itself is passed as the
target, along with the mouse down event. Finally, the event is hand-delivered by
using the deliverEvent() method from the java.awt.Event class.

java.awt.Event.deliverEvent() delivers the event to itself, which at first
glance may seem a rather odd thing to do. However, since the LabelCanvas
class itself does not override handleEvent(), the event is handled by
Component.handleEvent(). The default action taken by
java.awt.Event.handleEvent() is to ignore the event, since its id field is
equal to -1[6], and return false, signifying that the event was not fully handled;
therefore, it is propagated to the LabelCanvas container, which is exactly our
desired result.

6.   Note that we had to reassign the id field, or Component.handleEvent() would
     invoke mouseDown(), and we would go into an infinite loop.

For completeness, let's take a look at the `handleEvent()` method defined in the `gjt.LabelCanvas` unit test [7], which handles instances of `gjt.SelectionEvent` and prints them out:

```
public boolean handleEvent(Event event) {
    if(event instanceof SelectionEvent) {
        SelectionEvent sevent = (SelectionEvent)event;
        LabelCanvas     canvas = (LabelCanvas)event.target;

        if(sevent.isSelected())
            System.out.println("LabelCanvas "   +
                                canvas.getLabel() +
                                " selected");
        else
            System.out.println("LabelCanvas "   +
                                canvas.getLabel() +
                                " deselected");
        return true;
    }
    return super.handleEvent(event);
}
```

The Graphic Java Toolkit also defines events for image buttons. The `gjt.ImageButton` class generates an `ImageButtonEvents` when it is armed, disarmed, or activated, which it delivers to itself (its container) in a manner similar to `LabelCanvas`.

Summary

All applets involving the AWT are event driven. The applets display their components and wait patiently for some event to take place. There's a special group of event handling methods, generically referred to as propagated event handlers because they either handle an event or propagate it up to the container in which the component is displayed. A propagated event handler returns a `boolean true` to indicate the event has been completely handled and should not be propagated up to its container. It returns `false` to indicate the event is being propagated up to the container and should be handled there. Propagated events always work their way from the innermost component to the outermost container. We've seen that overridden `handleEvent()` methods should never return `false` and directly propagate events to their containers but should instead return `super.handleEvent(event)` to give their superclass a crack at the event and decide whether or not to propagate the event. Additionally, we have seen that

7.   Each custom component in the GJT comes complete with a unit test. We discuss unit tests in *Introducing the Graphic Java Toolkit*.

overridden convenience methods, such as mouseDown() should not return super.handleEvent() because doing so may very well result in an infinite loop.

The AWT Button, Checkbox, TextField, and Choice components are unique in that they generate events that are routed through a Component action() method. This method takes an Event argument and an Object argument. The latter is set according to the type of Component that generated the event.

While it is standard AWT practice to check against the label of certain components to identify the component with which an event is associated, we have advised you to check against object references rather than labels.

Finally, we have seen how to subclass java.awt.Event, generate events from custom components and hand-deliver such events to a custom component's container.

CHAPTER 5

- The Menu Classes on page 96

- A File Menu on page 97

- Handling Menu Events on page 99

- Tear-off Menus on page 101

- A Menubar Printer on page 103

- A FrameWithMenuBar Class on page 104

- Help Menus on page 108

- Checkbox Menu Items on page 111

- Cascading Menus on page 114

- Dynamically Modifying Menus on page 116

- Summary on page 121

Menus

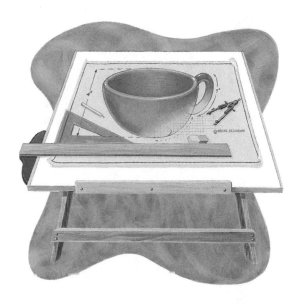

Release 1.0.2 of the AWT only supports menus that reside in a menubar. Furthermore, a menubar may only be attached to a `Frame`. As a result, this chapter pertains strictly to applications and is not pertinent to applets [1]. The next release of the AWT will support pop-up menus, which are not attached to a menubar and thus are relevant to applets. A subsequent edition of Graphic Java will provide coverage of AWT pop-up menus.

It is interesting to note that it is possible to create a pop-up menu class that extends `Window` and uses AWT graphics primitives to paint the pop-up. However, such a pop-up menu loses the native look and feel of menus because it is drawn by hand and not by a menu peer. Additionally, since the AWT will soon include pop-up menus that will be implemented with peers (and retain native platform look-and-feel), it is a considerable waste of effort to implement your own pop-up menu class unless you simply cannot live without pop-up menus of some sort until the AWT provides them.

---

1.   An applet's frame is the browser or the `appletviewer` window, to which it is not possible to attach a menubar.

Note that all of the examples in this chapter are applications and therefore must be run through the `java` interpreter directly instead of employing `appletviewer` or a browser to invoke the `java` interpreter for you. For instance, to run the `FileMenuTest` application, which we'll discuss shortly, you will need to execute the following command:

```
java FileMenuTest
```

The Menu Classes

Figure 5-1 shows the relationships between the AWT's menu classes.

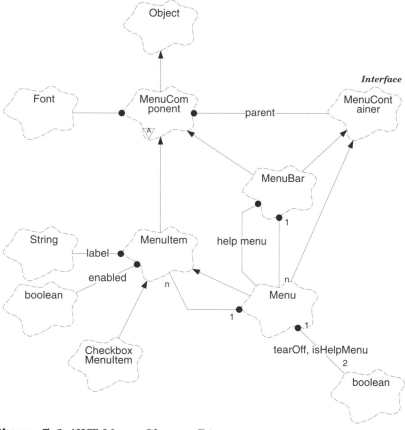

Figure 5-1 AWT Menu Classes Diagram

We will be concerned with three classes when dealing with menus: MenuBar, Menu, and MenuItem. The first thing to note from the class diagram is that each of these classes extends MenuComponent; a MenuComponent is simply something that can be displayed in a menu. Second, notice that Menu and Menubar both implement MenuContainer, meaning they may both contain instances of MenuComponent. Finally, note that Menu extends MenuItem; this enables us to create cascading menus, as we shall soon discover.

Notice that none of the menu classes extends java.awt.Component. Although this may seem insignificant, consider that since menu items are not components, we may not paint or draw strings inside of a menu. This makes it impossible to render owner-drawn menus [2] in the current AWT.

A File Menu

Let's start off with a simple example that creates the file menu in Figure 5-2.

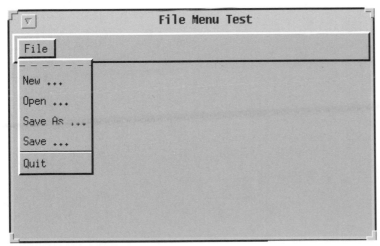

Figure 5-2 A File Menu

Most applications that provide a menubar have a file menu as the leftmost menu in their menubar, and most provide the menu items we have added to our example. Implementing such a menu is straightforward, as illustrated in Example 5-1.

2. Owner-drawn menus are menus into which a client may draw something.

Example 5-1 `FileMenuTest` **Class Source Code**

```java
import java.awt.*;

public class FileMenuTest extends Frame {
    private MenuBar mbar;
    private MenuItem quitItem;

    public static void main(String args[]) {
        FileMenuTest test = new FileMenuTest("File Menu Test");
        test.reshape(300,300,300,100);
        test.show();
    }
    public FileMenuTest(String s) {
        super(s);

        MenuBar mbar    = new MenuBar();
        Menu    fileMenu = new Menu("File", true);

        fileMenu.add("New ...");
        fileMenu.add("Open ...");
        fileMenu.add("Save As ...");
        fileMenu.add("Save ...");
        fileMenu.addSeparator();
        fileMenu.add("Quit");

        mbar.add(fileMenu);
        setMenuBar (mbar);
    }
    public boolean handleEvent(Event event) {
        if(event.id == Event.WINDOW_DESTROY)
            System.exit(0);

        return false;
    }
}
```

This version of the `FileMenuTest` class extends `Frame` and provides a `main()` method, signifying that we are developing an application, not an applet. (See *Applets and Applications* on page 13 for a discussion of developing applets versus applications.) The `FileMenuTest` constructor takes a string, which is immediately passed to the superclass' (`Frame`) constructor. The string passed to the `Frame` constructor will be used as the title of the window.

The `FileMenuTest` constructor creates a `MenuBar` and a `Menu`. The string passed to the `Menu` constructor is the menu's title and will be displayed in the menubar.

Adding menu items to a menu is accomplished by invoking the `Menu.add()` method and passing in the string that will be used for the menu item.

After creating the menubar and the menu, `FileMenuTest` adds the menu to the menubar and then calls `Frame.setMenuBar()` to set the frame's menubar.

Handling Menu Events

Menubars and menus take care of displaying themselves, but attaching behavior to menu items is something you must handle yourself. The first order of business is to identify which menu item has been selected, and then to go about implementing the functionality associated with the menu item. Example 5-2 expands `FileMenuTest` to print the label of the item selected and to quit the application when the "Quit" item is selected.

Example 5-2 Expanded `FileMenuTest` Class Source Code

```
import java.awt.*;

public class FileMenuTest extends Frame {
  private MenuBar mbar;

  public static void main(String args[]) {
      FileMenuTest test = new FileMenuTest("File Menu Test");
      test.reshape(300,300,100,100);
      test.show();
  }
  public FileMenuTest(String s) {
      super(s);

      MenuBar mbar     = new MenuBar();
      Menu    fileMenu = new Menu("File", true);

      fileMenu.add("New ...");
      fileMenu.add("Open ...");
      fileMenu.add("Save As ...");
      fileMenu.add("Save ...");
      fileMenu.addSeparator();
      fileMenu.add("Quit");

      mbar.add(fileMenu);
      setMenuBar (mbar);
  }
  public boolean handleEvent(Event event) {
      if(event.id == Event.WINDOW_DESTROY)
          System.exit(0);
```

```
❶   if(event.target instanceof MenuItem) {
            MenuItem item = (MenuItem)event.target;

            System.out.println(item.getLabel());

❷   if(item.getLabel().equals("Quit"))
                System.exit(0);
        }
        return false;
    }
}
```

The overridden `handleEvent()` method checks to see if the target of the event is an instance of `MenuItem` on line ❶. If so, we simply print the label of the menu item activated by invoking `MenuItem.getLabel()`. On line ❷, we check to see if the label of the menu item is "Quit." If so, we exit the application.

You may have noticed that we are going against our own advice offered in our *Event Handling* chapter on page 67. In that chapter we advise you to check against object references instead of relying upon the object's label, when checking for the quit menu item.

Here is a revised version of `FileMenuTest` that does the right thing, checking for the quit menu item against an object reference and not against the quit menu item's label.

Example 5-3 Improved Event Handling `FileMenuTest` **Class Source Code**

```
import java.awt.*;

public class FileMenuTest extends Frame {
    private MenuBar mbar;
    private MenuItem quitItem;

    public static void main(String args[]) {
        FileMenuTest test = new FileMenuTest("File Menu Test");
        test.reshape(300,300,300,100);
        test.show();
    }
    public FileMenuTest(String s) {
        super(s);
```

```
        MenuBar  mbar       = new MenuBar();
❶       Menu      fileMenu = new Menu("File", true);

        fileMenu.add("New ...");
        fileMenu.add("Open ...");
        fileMenu.add("Save As ...");
        fileMenu.add("Save ...");
        fileMenu.addSeparator();
        fileMenu.add(quitItem = new MenuItem("Quit"));

❷       mbar.add(fileMenu);
        setMenuBar (mbar);
     }
     public boolean handleEvent(Event event) {
         if(event.id == Event.WINDOW DESTROY)
             System.exit(0);

         if(event.target instanceof MenuItem) {
             MenuItem item = (MenuItem)event.target;

             System.out.println(item.getLabel());

             if(item == quitItem)
                 System.exit(0);
         }
         return false;
     }
}
```

Line ❶ creates a new instance of menu, which we highlight here because we want to reference that line in our section on tear-off menus. Notice that in line ❷, we are using a different version of Menu.add()—one that takes a MenuItem instead of a string. It is interesting to note that Menu.add(MenuItem) returns the menu item it is passed in, while Menu.add(String) returns void, even though it obviously results in a MenuItem being created.

Tear-off Menus

Tear-off menus are implemented under Motif and are menus that, as their name indicates, may be torn off and placed aside for quick access. Tear-off menus have a perforated line at the top of the menu. Once torn off, they can be placed in their own window, as illustrated in Figure 5-3.

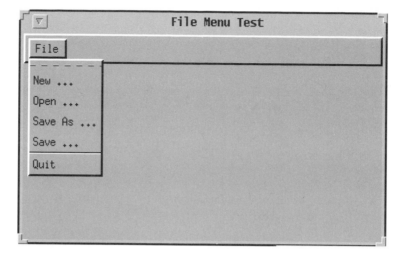

Figure 5-3 A Tear-off Menu
The top picture shows the perforated tear-off menu. The bottom
picture shows the menu after being *torn off*.

A Menu provides a constructor that allows you to specify whether you want the
menu being constructed to be a tear-off menu. We invoke this constructor in line
❶ of Example 5-3, passing true as the second argument. Doing so indicates that
the menu should be of the tear-off variety.

The AWT 1.0.2 does not support tear-off menus under Windows 95, so passing
true as a second argument to the Menu constructor is currently an exercise in
futility under Windows 95.

A Menubar Printer

In order to illustrate the relationships between menus, menubars, and menu items, we'll present a simple class in Example 5-4 that walks you through all the menus in a menubar and prints information about each item.

Example 5-4 MenuBarPrinter **Class Source Code**

```java
import java.awt.Menu;
import java.awt.MenuItem;
import java.awt.MenuBar;

public class MenuBarPrinter {
  static public void print(MenuBar menubar) {
      int      numMenus = menubar.countMenus();
      Menu     nextMenu;
      MenuItem nextItem;

      System.out.println();
      System.out.println("MenuBar has "          +
                          menubar.countMenus() +
                          " menus");
      System.out.println();

      for(int i=0; i < numMenus; ++i) {
          nextMenu = menubar.getMenu(i);
          System.out.println(nextMenu);

          int numItems = nextMenu.countItems();

          for(int j=0; j < numItems; ++j) {
              nextItem = nextMenu.getItem(j);
              System.out.println(nextItem);
          }
          System.out.println();
      }
  }
}
```

The MenuBarPrinter class contains a lone static method, which is passed a MenuBar and prints information about each menu in the menubar. Notice that we use MenuBar.countMenus(), MenuBar.getMenu(), Menu.countItems(), and Menu.getItem() to traverse through all of the menu items contained in each menu in the menubar.

A FrameWithMenuBar Class

Applications containing a menubar typically do the following things:

1. Create a menubar

2. Add menus to the menubar

3. Set the frame's menubar

4. Handle menu item events

In good object-oriented fashion, we will encapsulate these tasks in a base class illustrated in Example 5-5. You can extend this class whenever you need a frame with a menubar.

OO Tip

Encapsulate Common Functionality in Base Classes

Encapsulating common functionality in a base class is one of the tenets of object-oriented development; it increases reuse and reduces reimplementing similar functionality in more than one class. Often such code is not identified until two or more classes have reimplemented the same functionality. In such cases, it is well worth your while to *refactor* the code in question and push the similar functionality up into a base class.

Example 5-5 FrameWithMenuBar **Class Source Code**

```java
import java.awt.*;

public abstract class FrameWithMenuBar extends Frame {
    private MenuBar        mbar     = new MenuBar();
    private MenuBarPrinter printer;

    public abstract void createMenus(MenuBar menuBar);

    public FrameWithMenuBar(String s) {
        super(s);

        createMenus(mbar);
        setMenuBar (mbar);
    }
    public boolean handleEvent(Event event) {
        if(event.id == Event.WINDOW_DESTROY) {
            aboutToBeDestroyed();
            System.exit(0);
        }
        if(event.target instanceof MenuItem)
            return handleMenuEvent((MenuItem)event.target);
```

```
            return super.handleEvent(event);
    }
❶   public void printMenus() {
        if(printer == null)
            printer = new MenuBarPrinter();

        printer.print(mbar);
    }
❷   public boolean handleMenuEvent(MenuItem item) {
        showMenuItem(item);
        return true;
    }
❸   protected void aboutToBeDestroyed() {
    }
    private void showMenuItem(MenuItem item) {
        Menu menu = (Menu)item.getParent();
        System.out.println(menu.getLabel() +
                             ":  "          +
                           item.getLabel());

    }
}
```

Each `FrameWithMenuBar` comes complete with a `MenuBar` and
`MenuBarPrinter` reference. `FrameWithMenuBar` leaves one abstract method
for extensions to implement:

```
void createMenus(MenuBar)
```

Extensions simply create the menus they wish to attach to the menubar and then
add them to the menubar passed in to `createMenus()`.

`FrameWithMenuBar` also takes care of the drudgery involved with handling a
window destroy event. Before exiting the application, the
`aboutToBeDestroyed()` method (line ❸) is invoked, which
`FrameWithMenuBar` implements as a no-op. Classes that extend
`FrameWithMenuBar` may override `aboutToBeDestroyed()` if they have
unfinished business to take care of before the application is exited.

Note that `aboutToBeDestroyed()` is a protected method. We chose to make
`aboutToBeDestroyed()` protected instead of public to ensure that no hooligan
developers run around directly invoking `aboutToBeDestroyed()`. Limiting
the access of `aboutToBeDestroyed()` to extensions of `FrameWithMenuBar`
ensures that the method will only be invoked when the frame is actually about to
be destroyed.[3]

Additionally, FrameWithMenuBar detects events that have occurred involving a MenuItem; such events result in a call to handleMenuEvent() in line ❷, which by default prints information about the menu item in question. Extensions of FrameWithMenuBar will almost invariably override handleMenuEvent() to do something more meaningful than printing the menu item's label.

Finally, each FrameWithMenuBar comes with a printMenus() method that prints information about all of the menus in the menubar. Notice that we use a technique known in object-oriented circles as *lazy instantiation* for creating the MenuBarPrinter. The printMenus() method checks to see if the MenuBarPrinter instance is null. If so, it creates the MenuBarPrinter. This technique ensures that the MenuBarPrinter only gets created the first time it is needed.

OO Tip

Employ Lazy Instantiation for Rarely Used Class Members

FrameWithMenuBar comes with the capability to print out the label for each menu in its menubar. While this capability may at times be beneficial, in all honesty it will probably be used sparingly. In such cases, it is a good idea to employ lazy instantiation, where an object is not created until it is needed for the first time. The Graphic Java Toolkit implements lazy instantiation in several classes, which we shall see in *The Graphic Java Toolkit—Extending the AWT*.

FrameWithMenuBar In Action

To illustrate extending FrameWithMenuBar, we present a FileEditMenuTest application in Example 5-6. This extension of FrameWithMenuBar attaches both a file and an edit menu to its menubar.

---

3. Actually, the aboutToBeDestroyed() method is accessible by extensions of FrameWithMenuBar *and* other classes in the same package. We are somewhat wary of using Java's private protected, which provides the same access as the C++ definition of protected, as we are unsure of private protected's future.

Example 5-6 `FileEditMenuTest` **Class Source Code**

```java
import java.awt.*;

public class FileEditMenuTest extends FrameWithMenuBar {
  private MenuItem quitItem;

  public static void main(String args[]) {
      FileEditMenuTest test =
          new FileEditMenuTest("FileEdit Menu Test");

      test.reshape(300,300,300,100);
      test.show();
  }
  public FileEditMenuTest(String s) {
      super(s);
  }
  public void createMenus(MenuBar mbar) {
      mbar.add(createFileMenu());
      mbar.add(createEditMenu());
  }
  private Menu createFileMenu() {
      Menu fileMenu = new Menu("File");

      fileMenu.add("New ...");
      fileMenu.add("Open ...");
      fileMenu.add("Save As ...");
      fileMenu.add("Save ...");
      fileMenu.addSeparator();
      fileMenu.add(quitItem = new MenuItem("Quit"));

      return fileMenu;
  }
  private Menu createEditMenu() {
      Menu editMenu = new Menu("Edit");

      editMenu.add("Cut");
      editMenu.add("Copy");
      editMenu.add("Paste");

      return editMenu;
  }
  public boolean handleMenuEvent(MenuItem item) {
      if(item == quitItem)
          System.exit(0);

      return super.handleMenuEvent(item);
  }
}
```

We override the required `createMenus()` method in order to add a file menu and an edit menu to the menubar passed in. Note that `FrameWithMenuBar` takes care of creating the menubar and attaching it to the frame, leaving us to take care of business specific to `FileEditMenuTest`, namely, creation of the file and edit menus and adding them to the menubar.

The overridden `handleMenuEvent()` is only concerned with catching activation of the quit menu item, which it responds to by exiting the application. Otherwise, we are perfectly happy in this example with the default behavior provided by the superclass (`FrameWithMenuBar`) version of `handleMenuEvent()`, which simply prints out the menu item's label.

In the remaining examples in this chapter, we will subclass `FrameWithMenuBar` when creating and using AWT menus.

Help Menus

The AWT provides support for a help menu. A help menu is created and added to a menubar just like any other menu. Help menus, however, need to be identified by invoking `MenuBar.setHelpMenu()`, which ensures that the help menu is the rightmost menu in the menubar, regardless of when it was added to the menubar.

Help menus under Motif are right-justified in the menubar itself, while help menus under Windows 95 are simply placed to the right of the other menus in the menubar, as illustrated in Figure 5-4.

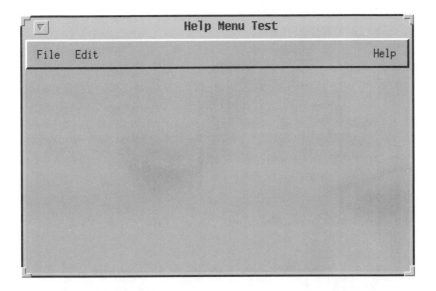

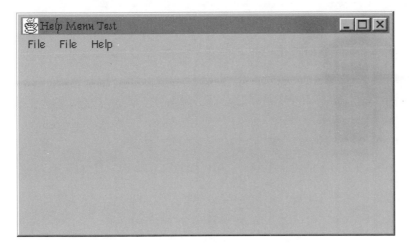

Figure 5-4 Motif and Windows 95 Help Menus
Motif help menus are right-justified in the menubar itself, as in
the top picture. WIndows 95 help menus are placed to the right of
the other menus, as in the bottom picture.

Example 5-7 shows an implementation of a help menu.

Example 5-7 HelpMenuTest **Class Source Code**

```java
import java.awt.*;
import java.util.Vector;

public class HelpTest extends FrameWithMenuBar {
  private MenuItem quitItem;

  public static void main(String args[]) {
     HelpTest frame = new HelpTest("Help Menu Test");
     frame.reshape(300,300,300,100);
     frame.show();
  }
  public HelpTest(String s) {
     super(s);
  }
  public void createMenus(MenuBar mbar) {
     Menu helpMenu = createHelpMenu();

     mbar.add(helpMenu);
     mbar.add(createFileMenu());
     mbar.add(createEditMenu());

     mbar.setHelpMenu(helpMenu);
  }
  public boolean handleMenuEvent(MenuItem item) {
     if(item == quitItem)
         System.exit(0);

     return super.handleMenuEvent(item);
  }
  private Menu createFileMenu() {
     Menu fileMenu = new Menu("File");
     fileMenu.add(quitItem = new MenuItem("Quit"));
     return fileMenu;
  }
  private Menu createEditMenu() {
     Menu editMenu = new Menu("File");

     editMenu.add("Cut");
     editMenu.add("Copy");
     editMenu.add("Paste");

     return editMenu;
  }
  private Menu createHelpMenu() {
     Menu helpMenu = new Menu("Help");
```

❶

```
        helpMenu.add("Overview ...");
        helpMenu.add("Topics ...");
        helpMenu.add("About ...");

        return helpMenu;
    }
}
```

Once again, thanks to `FrameWithMenuBar`, we are only concerned with creating menus, adding them to the menubar, and reacting to menu events.

Notice that ,normally, menus added to a menubar appear in the menubar in the order in which they are added. However, using `MenuBar.setHelpMenu()` as in line ❶ causes the help menu to be the rightmost menu in the menubar, regardless of when it is added to the menubar. We purposely added the help menu to the menubar first in line ❶ to illustrate this point.

Checkbox Menu Items

The AWT provides a `CheckboxMenuItem` class. A `CheckboxMenuItem` is a menu item that toggles between checked and unchecked when activated. In fact, we've already seen this in our tear-off menu example. Figure 5-5 shows the `CheckboxMenuItem` class at work.

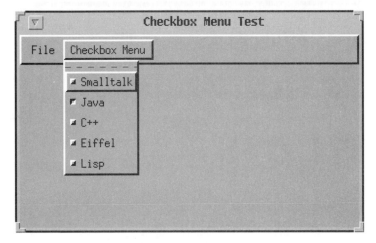

Figure 5-5 A Checkbox Menu Item
Activated menu items toggle between checked or unchecked.

A `CheckboxMenuItem` is often used in a menu that exhibits radio button behavior. That is, when one of the menu items is checked, the other items in the menu are all unchecked, so that only one checkbox menu item is checked at a time.

It is a simple matter to extend `Menu` and provide a `RadioMenu` class that adds `CheckboxMenuItem` items (only) and implements the mutually exclusive selection behavior. Example 5-8 shows the `RadioMenu` implementation.

Example 5-8 RadioMenu **Class Source Code**

CD-Rom

```java
import gjt.Assert;

import java.awt.Menu;
import java.awt.MenuItem;
import java.awt.CheckboxMenuItem;

public class RadioMenu extends Menu {
    public RadioMenu(String s, boolean tearOff) {
        super(s, tearOff);
    }
❶  public void add(String s) {
        add(new CheckboxMenuItem(s));
    }
❷  public MenuItem add(MenuItem item) {
        Assert.notFalse(item instanceof CheckboxMenuItem);
        return super.add(item);
    }
❸  public void selectItem(MenuItem item) {
        CheckboxMenuItem nextItem;
        int              numItems = countItems();

        for(int i=0; i < numItems; ++i) {
            if(item != getItem(i)) {
                nextItem = (CheckboxMenuItem)getItem(i);
                nextItem.setState(false);
            }
        }
    }
}
```

RadioMenu overrides `add(String)` in line ❶ to ensure that the item being added to it is a `CheckboxMenuItem`. Additionally, `RadioMenu` overrides `add(MenuItem)` in line ❷, where it asserts that the item passed in is a `CheckboxMenuItem`. (We discuss the Graphic Java Toolkit's `Assert` class in our *Introducing the Graphic Java Toolkit*.)

RadioMenu.selectItem() in line ❸ goes through each of its menu items and sets its state to false (unchecked), except for the item that was activated. This ensures that only one item at a time is checked.

RadioMenuTest in Example 5-9 illustrates the use of RadioMenu.

Example 5-9 RadioMenuTest **Class Source Code**

```
import java.awt.*;

public class RadioMenuTest extends FrameWithMenuBar {
  private RadioMenu radioMenu;
  private MenuItem  quitItem;

  public static void main(String args[]) {
      RadioMenuTest test =
          new RadioMenuTest("FileEdit Menu Test");

      test.reshape(300,300,300,100);
      test.show();
  }
  public RadioMenuTest(String s) {
      super(s);
  }
  public void createMenus(MenuBar mbar) {
      mbar.add(createFileMenu());
      mbar.add(createRadioMenu());
  }
  private Menu createFileMenu() {
      Menu fileMenu = new Menu("File");
      fileMenu.add(quitItem = new MenuItem("Quit"));
      return fileMenu;
  }
  private Menu createRadioMenu() {
      radioMenu = new RadioMenu("Radio Menu", true);

      radioMenu.add("Smalltalk");
      radioMenu.add("Java");
      radioMenu.add("C++");
      radioMenu.add("Eiffel");
      radioMenu.add("Lisp");

      return radioMenu;
  }
  public boolean handleMenuEvent(MenuItem item) {
      if(item == quitItem)
          System.exit(0);
      else
```

```
        radioMenu.selectItem(item);

    return super.handleMenuEvent(item);
  }
}
```

Notice that `RadioMenuTest` calls `RadioMenu.selectItem()` to ensure the mutually exclusive behavior of the menu.

Cascading Menus

As we previously alluded to, cascading menus are possible with the AWT by virtue of the fact that `Menu` extends `MenuItem`. As we have seen, `Menu.add(MenuItem)` adds a menu item to a menu. Since a `Menu` is a `MenuItem`, the `Menu.add(MenuItem)` method is perfectly happy to take a `Menu` as an argument, which it dutifully adds to itself.

Figure 5-6 shows the cascading menu created by Example 5-10.

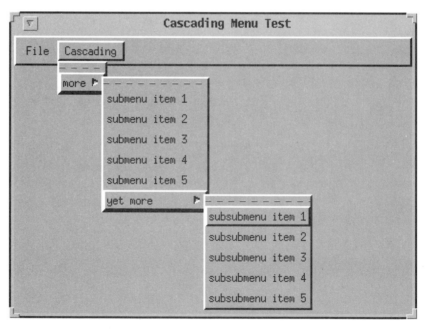

Figure 5-6 A Cascading Menu

Example 5-10 shows the code that produces this style of menu.

Example 5-10 CascadingTest Class Source Code

```java
import java.awt.*;

public class CascadingTest extends FrameWithMenuBar {
  private MenuItem quitItem;

  public static void main(String args[]) {
      CascadingTest test =
          new CascadingTest("Cascading Menu Test");

      test.reshape(300,300,300,100);
      test.show();
  }
  public CascadingTest(String s) {
      super(s);
  }
  public void createMenus(MenuBar mbar) {
      mbar.add(createFileMenu());
      mbar.add(createCascadingMenu());
  }
  private Menu createFileMenu() {
      Menu fileMenu = new Menu("File");
      fileMenu.add(quitItem = new MenuItem("Quit"));
      return fileMenu;
  }
  private Menu createCascadingMenu() {
      Menu cascading  = new Menu("Cascading", true);
      Menu submenu    = new Menu("more", true);
      Menu subsubmenu = new Menu("yet more", true);

      submenu.add("submenu item 1");
      submenu.add("submenu item 2");
      submenu.add("submenu item 3");
      submenu.add("submenu item 4");
      submenu.add("submenu item 5");

      subsubmenu.add("subsubmenu item 1");
      subsubmenu.add("subsubmenu item 2");
      subsubmenu.add("subsubmenu item 3");
      subsubmenu.add("subsubmenu item 4");
      subsubmenu.add("subsubmenu item 5");

      submenu.add(subsubmenu);
      cascading.add(submenu);

      return cascading;
  }
```

❶

```
public boolean handleMenuEvent(MenuItem item) {
    if(item == quitItem)
        System.exit(0);

    return super.handleMenuEvent(item);
  }
}
```

The `createCascadingMenu()` method in line ❶ creates three menus:

- cascading
- submenu
- subsubmenu

subsubmenu is added to submenu, and submenu is added to cascading. Notice that a Menu is aware of the fact that we are adding a Menu instead of a MenuItem, and it does the right thing, which in this case is to create a MenuItem with a pull-right arrow on the far right edge of the menu item that represents the added menu.

Dynamically Modifying Menus

So far, we have mostly modified menus before they are created, by adding items to them. Sometimes it is necessary to modify a menu after it is created, which is supported by the AWT.

The SelfModifyingMenu class illustrated in Figure 5-7 contains an item that is either enabled and disabled by an item above it. This class also contains two menu items for adding an item and removing the last item added to the menu.

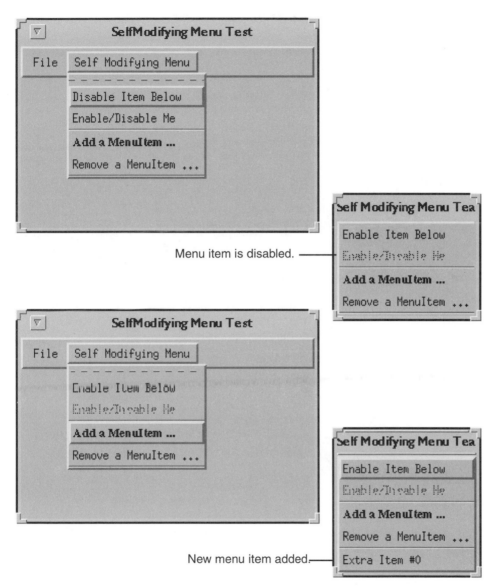

Menu item is disabled.

New menu item added.

Figure 5-7 A Self-Modifying Menu
The top pair of pictures show the Enable/Disable item grayed-out. The bottom pair of pictures show a menu item added to the menu. This menu uses tear-off menus, which we've used to show the different states of the self-modifying menu.

Example 5-11 shows the code that achieves this effect.

Example 5-11 SelfModifyingMenu **Class Source Code**

```
import java.awt.*;

class SelfModifyingMenu extends Menu {
    private Vector newItems = new Vector();
    private MenuItem toggleItem, enablerItem,  addItem, removeItem;

    public SelfModifyingMenu() {
        super("Self Modifying Menu", true);
        add(enablerItem = new MenuItem("Disable Item Below"));
        add(toggleItem = new MenuItem("Enable/Disable Me"));
        addSeparator();
        add(addItem = new MenuItem("Add a MenuItem ..."));
        add(removeItem = new MenuItem("Remove a MenuItem ..."));
        addItem.setFont(new Font("TimesRoman", Font.BOLD, 12));
        addSeparator();
    }
    public boolean handleMenuEvent(MenuItem item) {
        if(item == enablerItem) {
            toggleItem();
            if(toggleItem.isEnabled())
                        enablerItem.setLabel("Disable Item Below");
            else        enablerItem.setLabel("Enable Item Below");
        }
        else if(item == addItem) addItem();
        else if(item == removeItem) removeLastItem();
        return true;
    }
    public void addItem() {
        MenuItem newItem = new MenuItem("Extra Item #" +
                            newItems.size());
        add(newItem);
        newItems.addElement(newItem);
    }
    public void removeLastItem() {
        if(newItems.size() == 0)
            System.out.println("Hey, nothing to remove!");
        else {
            MenuItem removeMe = (MenuItem)newItems.lastElement();
            remove(removeMe);
            newItems.removeElement(removeMe);
        }
    }
    public void toggleItem() {
        if(toggleItem.isEnabled())
            toggleItem.disable();
        else toggleItem.enable();
    }
}
```

❶
❷
❸
❹

There are a couple of points of interest here. First, note in line ❶ that the
enablerItem ("Disable Item Below") should update its label to be in
synch with the item it is enabling/disabling. The calls to MenuItem.setLabel()
in lines ❷ and ❸ do not cause the menu item's label to update. This is a bug in the
1.0.2 version of the AWT.

Second, while setting the addItem font in line ❹ works just fine under Motif, it
has no effect under Windows 95. This is another 1.0.2 AWT bug.

For the most part, however, the SelfModifyingMenu works as advertised.
Example 5-12 is an application that exercises our SelfModifyingMenu.

Example 5-12 SelfModifyingTest **Class Source Code**

```
import java.awt.*;
import java.util.Vector;

public class SelfModifyingTest extends FrameWithMenuBar {
  private SelfModifyingMenu selfModifyingMenu;
  private MenuItem quitItem;

  public static void main(String args[]) {
      Frame frame =
          new SelfModifyingTest("SelfModifying Menu Test");

      frame.reshape(100,100,300,100);
      frame.show();
  }
  public SelfModifyingTest(String s) {
      super(s);
  }
  public void createMenus(MenuBar mbar) {
      mbar.add(createFileMenu());
      mbar.add(selfModifyingMenu = new SelfModifyingMenu());
  }
  private Menu createFileMenu() {
      Menu fileMenu = new Menu("File");
      fileMenu.add(quitItem = new MenuItem("Quit"));
      return fileMenu;
  }
  public boolean handleMenuEvent(MenuItem item) {
      if(item.getLabel().equals("Quit"))
          System.exit(0);
      else
          return selfModifyingMenu.handleMenuEvent(item);

      return true;
  }
}
```

```java
class SelfModifyingMenu extends Menu {
  private Vector    newItems = new Vector();
  private MenuItem toggleItem, enablerItem,
                   addItem, removeItem;

  public SelfModifyingMenu() {
      super("Self Modifying Menu", true);

      add(enablerItem = new MenuItem("Disable Item Below"));
      add(toggleItem  = new MenuItem("Enable/Disable Me"));
      addSeparator();

      add(addItem     = new MenuItem("Add a MenuItem ..."));
      add(removeItem = new MenuItem("Remove a MenuItem ..."));
      addItem.setFont(new Font("TimesRoman", Font.BOLD, 12));
      addSeparator();
  }
   public boolean handleMenuEvent(MenuItem item) {
      if(item == enablerItem) {
          toggleItem();

          if(toggleItem.isEnabled())
              enablerItem.setLabel("Disable Item Below");
          else
              enablerItem.setLabel("Enable Item Below");
      }
      else if(item == addItem)    addItem();
      else if(item == removeItem) removeLastItem();

      return true;
  }
  public void addItem() {
      MenuItem newItem =
          new MenuItem("Extra Item #" + newItems.size());

      add(newItem);
      newItems.addElement(newItem);
  }
  public void removeLastItem() {
      if(newItems.size() == 0)
          System.out.println("Hey, nothing to remove!");
      else {
          MenuItem removeMe =
              (MenuItem)newItems.lastElement();

          remove(removeMe);
          newItems.removeElement(removeMe);
      }
```

```
    }
    public void toggleItem() {
        if(toggleItem.isEnabled()) toggleItem.disable();
        else                       toggleItem.enable();
    }
}
```

Summary

The 1.0.2 version of the AWT supports menus that reside in menubars only; subsequent versions of the AWT will include pop-up menus that can be displayed over any component. The AWT menu classes do not extend `java.awt.Component` and therefore cannot be drawn in directly. This means that it is currently impossible to create owner-drawn menus with the AWT.

Menubars and menus are easy to create and display in the AWT; however, there is a certain amount of drudgery that every application with a menubar must implement. We have encapsulated that drudgery in a `FrameWithMenuBar` class that is extended by most of the example applications in this chapter. We have also presented a general-utility class, `MenuBarPrinter`, that prints each menu and menu item contained in a menubar.

Tear-off menus are supported by the AWT. A menu is designated as a tear-off menu at construction time by passing an additional boolean argument to a `Menu` constructor; a `true` value indicates that the menu is to be a tear-off, while a `false` value indicates that the menu is not a tear-off. Tear-off menus do not tear off under Windows 95.

The AWT supports help menus, which are like ordinary menus in every respect except that they are always the rightmost menu in the menubar. Under Motif, the help menu is right-justified in the menubar itself. Under Windows 95, the menu is simply the rightmost menu in the menubar.

The AWT also supports checkbox menu items, and we have presented a general purpose class—`RadioMenu`—which provides checkbox menu items that are mutually exclusive, ensuring that only one of its items is checked at any given time.

We have also explored implementing cascading menus and menus that can be modified dynamically. Since `Menu` extends `MenuItem`, a `Menu` can be added as an item to another menu. Menus can have their items enabled or disabled after their creation, and items can be added to or removed from a menu after construction.

Currently, setting a menu item's font does not work under Windows 95, and setting a menu item's label after construction does not work under either Motif or Windows 95.

CHAPTER

6

- The Image Class and the Image Package on page 123

- Image Producers and Image Observers on page 124

- Obtaining and Displaying Images on page 125

- Differences Between Applets and Applications on page 127

- Waiting for an Image to Load on page 128

- Painting Images a Scanline at a Time on page 131

  - Eliminating the Flash on page 132

  - Using MediaTracker on page 133

- Filtering Images on page 135

- gjt.image.BleachImageFilter on page 141

  - The Color Model and the Alpha Value of a Pixel on page 144

  - gjt.image.DissolveFilter on page 145

  - gjt.image.ImageDissolver on page 147

- Summary on page 153

Images

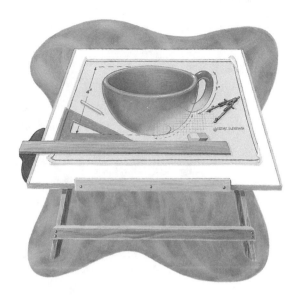

There are two major topics of discussion concerning images and the AWT: obtaining and displaying images, and manipulating images. We will discuss each topic in this chapter, and we will subsequently encounter a good deal of real-life use of images in the chapters that describe the Graphic Java Toolkit custom components.

We will begin by introducing some applets and applications that show various display characteristics and nuances of displaying images. Then we'll introduce a couple of GJT custom components that show how to filter images.

In order to make the most out of this chapter, you will want to run the applets discussed. Some paint images a line at time, some paint all at once, some have an annoying flash, and some are nice and smooth—all characteristics we can't really capture in static screen snapshots.

The Image Class and the Image Package

The AWT provides a `java.awt.Image` class. References to `java.awt.Image` are passed to methods of other AWT objects for displaying and manipulating images. For instance, images can be displayed in a component by invoking `Graphics.drawImage(Image, int, int, ImageObserver)`.

`java.awt.Image` is an abstract class that simply defines methods that provide information about an image. Table 6-1 lists the abstract methods that `java.awt.Image` defines.

Table 6-1 `java.awt.Image` **Methods**

Method
`public abstract int getWidth(ImageObserver observer);`
`public abstract int getHeight(ImageObserver observer);`
`public abstract ImageProducer getSource();`
`public abstract Graphics getGraphics();`
`public abstract Object getProperty(String name,` `                       ImageObserver observer);`
`public abstract void flush();`

Nearly all of the infrastructure for creating and manipulating images resides in the `java.awt.image` *package* (not to be confused with the `java.awt.Image` *class*). The `java.awt.image` package defines interfaces for producing and obtaining an image, along with classes for filtering and manipulating images. While the `java.awt.Image` class provides a reference to an image, it is actually the `java.awt.image` package that undertakes all of the grunt work associated with obtaining and manipulating images.

Image Producers and Image Observers

If you've ever visited a web site containing a number of images, you're aware that it takes some time to download those images, especially over a network. As a result, much of the image-related work in the AWT, such as loading and drawing an image is handled asynchronously. The sender and receiver of asynchronous image transactions are defined by two AWT interfaces: `java.awt.image.ImageProducer` and `java.awt.image.ImageObserver`.

An `ImageProducer` is responsible for producing the bits of an image and for passing them along to an `ImageObserver`. An `ImageProducer` notifies an `ImageObserver` of its progress by invoking the only method defined by the `ImageObserver` interface: `imageUpdate()`.

Implementors of `ImageObserver` are ubiquitous in the AWT, mainly because `Component` implements `ImageObserver`. Every component, therefore, is an `ImageObserver` that can choose to be updated on the progress a given `ImageProducer` is making in loading an image.

Understanding that image-related tasks happen asynchronously and understanding the relationship between ImageProducer and ImageObserver are key to understanding image manipulation in the AWT. In the rest of this chapter, we illustrate these concepts through a number of applets.

Obtaining and Displaying Images

Let's begin by taking a look at a very simple applet, Example 6-1, that obtains an image and displays it in a canvas. Notice that we do a couple things in this applet solely for the sake of illustration; we print the codebase—the URL defining the location of the applet—and we print the dimensions of the Image object's width and height in the showImageSize() method.

Example 6-1 Simple Applet With an Image

```java
import java.net.URL;
import java.applet.Applet;
import java.awt.Graphics;
import java.awt.Image;

public class ImageTestAppletSimple extends Applet {
  private Image im;

  public void init() {
      URL codebase = getCodeBase();
      System.out.println(codebase);
❶    im = getImage(codebase, "saint.gif");
      showImageSize();
  }
  public void paint(Graphics g) {
❷    g.drawImage(im,0,0,this);
  }
  private void showImageSize() {
      System.out.print  ("Image width=" + im.getWidth(this));
      System.out.println(" height=" + im.getHeight(this));
  }
}
```

The method we're most interested in is the Applet.getImage() method called in line ❶, which returns an Image. To illustrate the asynchronous behavior of loading an image, we call showImageSize() immediately after getImage() returns the Image im. If you run the applet, you'll see that showImageSize() prints the following for the width and height of the image:

```
Image width=-1 height=-1
```

Although your first thought may be that this is an extremely small image, the rather odd-looking values for width and height indicate that although getImage() has returned an Image, the bits that define the image are not yet loaded. Image.getWidth() and Image.getHeight() return -1 until the image is fully loaded.

When you run the applet, you can see the image being loaded chunks of pixels at time, from top to bottom. That's because the Graphics.drawImage() method (line ❷) also runs asynchronously. Let's take a closer look at that call:

```
g.drawImage(im,0,0,this);
```

Graphics.drawImage() is passed an:

- Image (im)

- x,y coordinate (0,0) (the upper left-hand corner of the image)

- ImageObserver object (this)

We're most interested in the last argument: this, of course, is the applet itself. If we trace its lineage, we see that Applet extends Component and Component implements ImageObserver. Classes like Applet that need to deal with images asynchronously implement the ImageObserver interface. The ImageObserver interface defines a collection of constants and one method, imageUpdate(), for use by classes that want to deal with images. ImageObserver.imageUpdate() is defined as:

```
public boolean imageUpdate(Image img, int infoflags,
    int x, int y, int width, int height);
```

All asynchronous methods dealing with images take an ImageObserver as an argument. Table 6-2 lists these methods.

Table 6-2 Methods That Are Passed an ImageObserver

Method
boolean Component.prepareImage(Image image,   ImageObserver observer)
boolean Component.prepareImage(Image image, int width, int height,   ImageObserver observer)
int Component.checkImage(Image image, ImageObserver observer)
int Component.checkImage(Image image, int width, int height,   ImageObserver observer)
boolean Graphics.drawImage(Image img, int x, int y,   ImageObserver observer);

Table 6-2 Methods That Are Passed an `ImageObserver` **(Continued)**

Method

`boolean Graphics.drawImage(Image img, int x, int y,`
`                           int width, int height,`
`                           ImageObserver observer);`

`public boolean Graphics.drawImage(Image img, int x, int y,`
`                           Color bgcolor,`
`                           ImageObserver observer);`

`public boolean Grahics.drawImage(Image img, int x, int y,`
`                           int width, int height,`
`                           Color bgcolor,`
`                           ImageObserver observer);`

`public int Image.getWidth(ImageObserver observer);`
`public int Image.getHeight(ImageObserver observer);`

`public boolean Toolkit.prepareImage(Image image, int width,`
`                           int height,`
`                           ImageObserver observer);`

`public int Toolkit.checkImage(Image image, int width, int height,` `                           ImageObserver observer);`
`public Image Toolkit.createImage(ImageProducer producer);`

Differences Between Applets and Applications

Applets provide built-in support for obtaining images: namely, the
`Applet.getImage()` method. A Java application, however, does not extend
`Applet`, so you need to write an application that is going to incorporate images a
little differently than you do an applet. Example 6-2 illustrates how an application
obtains and displays an image.

Example 6-2 Application With an Image

```
import java.net.URL;
import java.applet.Applet;
import java.awt.*;

public class ImageTestApplication extends Frame {
  static public void main(String args[]) {
      ImageTestApplication app = new ImageTestApplication();
  }
  public ImageTestApplication() {
      super("Image Test");
      im = Toolkit.getDefaultToolkit().getImage("saint.gif");
      reshape(100, 100, 220, 330);
      show   ();
```

❶

```
        }
    public void paint(Graphics g) {
        g.drawImage(im,0,0,this);
    }
    public boolean handleEvent(Event event) {
        if(event.id == Event.WINDOW_DESTROY)
            System.exit(0);

        return false;
    }
}
```

The application obtains an `Image` in line ❶. Instead of calling
`Applet.getImage()`, the application calls the `getImage()` method from the
`Toolkit` class. We first call the static `getDefaultToolkit()`, which returns
the default `Toolkit` for the platform the application is running on, and then we
invoke the toolkit's `getImage()` method. Note that the `Toolkit.getImage()`
method is overloaded to take either a `URL` or a `String` as an argument.

Waiting for an Image to Load

As we noted above, both the applet and application we have presented so far load
their image in chunks, from the top of the image to the bottom, due to the
asynchronous nature of image loading. A more aesthetically pleasing approach is
to wait for the image to load completely before displaying it. There are a number
of ways in which to accomplish this; one way is to implement `imageUpdate()`,
which keeps us informed as to the progress of the loading of the image in
question.

The applet in Example 6-3 is almost exactly like the one in Example 6-1 on
page 125, except that it implements `ImageObserver.imageUpdate()`.

Example 6-3 Image Loading All at Once

```
import java.net.URL;
import java.applet.Applet;
import java.awt.Graphics;
import java.awt.Image;

public class ImageTestAppletWithUpdate extends Applet {
    private Image im;

    public void init() {
        URL codebase = getCodeBase();
        System.out.println(codebase);
        im = getImage(codebase, "saint.gif");
```
❶

```
      showImageSize();
   }
   public void paint(Graphics g) {
     g.drawImage(im,0,0,this);
   }
   public boolean imageUpdate(Image image, int flags,
                              int x, int y, int w, int h)
   {
       System.out.println("imageUpdate():  x=" + x + ", y=" +
                          y + "  w=" + w + ",h=" + h);
       if((flags & ALLBITS) != 0)
           repaint();

       return true;
   }
   private void showImageSize() {
       System.out.print  ("Image width=" + im.getWidth(this));
       System.out.println(" height=" + im.getHeight(this));
   }
}
```

Our implementation of `imageUpdate()` prints the x, y, width, and height of each row of pixels as they are passed in. If you run the applet, you'll see printed output something like this:

```
Image width=-1 height=-1
imageUpdate():  x=0, y=0   w=217,h=321
imageUpdate():  x=0, y=0   w=217,h=1
imageUpdate():  x=0, y=1   w=217,h=1
imageUpdate():  x=0, y=2   w=217,h=1
imageUpdate():  x=0, y=3   w=217,h=1
imageUpdate():  x=0, y=4   w=217,h=1
```

As we previously pointed out, as soon as the image is returned by `getImage()` in line ❶, `showImageSize()` prints:

```
Image width=-1 height=-1
```

Of course, the mystery associated with this applet is who is invoking our applet's `imageUpdate()` method. Every `Image` has an associated `ImageProducer`, which, as we've alluded to before, provides the actual bits for the image. As soon as the call to `getImage()` is made on line ❶, the `ImageProducer` for the `Image` `im` begins to load the image, and our applet goes on to bigger and better things. As the image is being loaded, the `ImageProducer` associated with `im` calls our applet's `imageUpdate()` method every time it obtains a new scanline. As is usually the case, we are not actually interested in doing anything with each scanline as it is handed to us, other than to print out some statistics that illustrate the asynchronous nature of image loading.

Note that our applet's implementation of imageUpdate() uses the ImageObserver constant ALLBITS in line ❷ to determine when the Image is completely loaded. Once the flags OR'd with ALLBITS are non-zero, we know that all bits for the image have been loaded. Once the image has been completely loaded, we call repaint(), and this time, since the image is ready and waiting to be displayed, it is blasted into the applet in one fell swoop.

The ImageObserver defines several constants besides ALLBITS, as shown in Table 6-3.

Table 6-3 ImageObserver **Constants**

Constant	Indicates...
ABORT	The imageUpdate() was aborted.
ALLBITS	All bits have been loaded into the Image.
ERROR	An error occurred during an imageUpdate().
FRAMEBITS	Another complete frame of a multi-frame Image is available.
HEIGHT	The height of the Image is available.
PROPERTIES	The Image's properties are available.
SOMEBITS	More pixels are available for a scaled variation of the Image.
WIDTH	The width of the Image is available.

While the applet above displays its image all at once, it takes some time for the image to load (especially with us printing out statistics from imageUpdate()). Additionally, the larger the image is, the longer it will take for the image to load. If you have a web page, for instance, with a number of large images, the delay incurred by waiting for each image to load may be unacceptable. In such a case, you may wish to paint each scanline of the image as it becomes available. Our next applet does exactly that.

Painting Images a Scanline at a Time

The next applet, Example 6-4, is a variation of the one we just looked at. Instead of calling repaint() after all the bits have been loaded into the Image object, this applet calls repaint() in line ❶ every time imageUpdate() is called.

Example 6-4 Image Loading Smoothly

```java
import java.net.URL;
import java.applet.Applet;
import java.awt.Graphics;
import java.awt.Image;

public class ImageTestAppletWithDynamicUpdate extends Applet {
  private Image im;

  public void init() {
      URL codebase = getCodeBase();
      System.out.println(codebase);
      im = getImage(codebase, "saint.gif");
      showImageSize();
  }
  public void paint(Graphics g) {
    g.drawImage(im,0,0,this);
  }
  public boolean imageUpdate(Image image, int flags,
                             int x, int y, int w, int h)
  {
      System.out.println("imageUpdate(): x=" + x + ", y=" +
                            y + "  w=" + w + ",h=" + h);
      repaint();
      return true;
  }
  private void showImageSize() {
      System.out.print  ("Image width=" + im.getWidth(this));
      System.out.println(" height=" + im.getHeight(this));
  }
}
```

This applet, as advertised, paints each scanline as it becomes available. However, we have incurred a horrible penalty for keeping users informed as to the progress of our image loading: the image flashes as it is being drawn. Our next applet employs a simple mechanism to smoothly display each scanline without any flashing.

Eliminating the Flash

The culprit of the annoying flashing is the applet's update() method. Recall from our *Applets and Applications* chapter that a call to a component's repaint() method results in the component's update() method being called as soon as possible. Therefore, when we call repaint() in line ❶ of Example 6-4, a call to update() is scheduled. The default implementation of Component.update() is to erase the entire background of the component and invoke the component's paint() method. Therefore, each time a scanline is available, we invoke repaint(), resulting in a call to update(), which erases the background and then invokes paint(). Our implementation of paint() draws as much of the image as is currently available. All of this erasing and repainting results in the flashing which we seek to eliminate.

The simple solution, illustrated by Example 6-5, is to override update() to call paint() directly. This eliminates the constant erasure of the applet's background and results in the image being displayed in a smooth fashion.

Example 6-5 Image Loading Without Flashing

CD-Rom

```java
import java.net.URL;
import java.applet.Applet;
import java.awt.Graphics;
import java.awt.Image;

public class ImageTestAppletWithSmoothDynamicUpdate
                                    extends Applet {
    private Image im;

    public void init() {
        URL codebase = getCodeBase();
        System.out.println(codebase);
        im = getImage(codebase, "saint.gif");
        showImageSize();
    }
    public void paint(Graphics g) {
      g.drawImage(im,0,0,this);
    }
    public boolean imageUpdate(Image image, int flags,
                            int x, int y, int w, int h)
    {
        System.out.println("imageUpdate():  x=" + x + ", y=" +
                            y + "   w=" + w + ",h=" + h);
        repaint();
        return true;
    }
```

```
    public void update(Graphics g) {
        paint(g);
    }
    private void showImageSize() {
        System.out.print  ("Image width=" + im.getWidth(this));
        System.out.println(" height=" + im.getHeight(this));
    }
}
```

Of course, it still takes awhile for the image to paint, mostly due to the fact that we are still doggedly printing out statistics for each scanline. You may wish to modify the applet so that it does not print out statistics each time a scanline is available; you will notice a considerable increase in speed by doing so.

Using *MediaTracker*

The MediaTracker class provides a more convenient way than we've illustrated thus far to manage the asynchronous loading of an Image object. Essentially, a MediaTracker object can *track* or monitor the loading of an Image. Let's look at the applet in Example 6-6.

Example 6-6 Image Loading With the MediaTracker **Class**

```
import java.net.URL;
import java.applet.Applet;
import java.awt.Graphics;
import java.awt.Image;
import java.awt.MediaTracker;

public class ImageTestAppletWithMediaTracker extends Applet {
  private Image im;

  public void init() {
      URL codebase = getCodeBase();
      System.out.println(codebase);

❶    MediaTracker tracker = new MediaTracker(this);

      im = getImage(codebase, "saint.gif");

❷    tracker.addImage(im, 0);
❸    try { tracker.waitForID(0); }
      catch(InterruptedException e) { }

      showImageSize();
  }
  public void paint(Graphics g) {
    g.drawImage(im,0,0,this);
```

```
    }
    private void showImageSize() {
        System.out.print  ("Image width=" + im.getWidth(this));
        System.out.println(" height=" + im.getHeight(this));
    }
}
```

Using `MediaTracker` is a simple, three-step process:

1. Create an instance of it, as we've done in line ❶.

2. Use `MediaTracker.addImage()` to specify the image that needs to be tracked, as we've done in line ❷.

3. Create a `try/catch` block as we do in line ❸. The `try` block waits for the image associated with ID to fully load. The `MediaTracker waitForID()` method may throw an `InterruptedException`, so it's necessary to implement a `catch` block. In our case, we catch it but don't do anything with it, which is typically the case in practice.

If you wish to wait for images to load entirely before displaying them, employing an instance of `MediaTracker` is probably the way to go. Using `MediaTracker` means you need not override `imageUpdate()` and go through the trouble of ORing the correct constant with the flags variable passed in.

However, using `MediaTracker` requires you to follow the three steps outlined above. The Graphic Java Toolkit encapsulates the steps involved in using `MediaTracker` in the `gjt.Util.waitForImage()` method. This reduces waiting for an image to one simple statement, no overriding methods or fooling around with ORing bits, or implementing `try/catch` blocks. Example 6-7 illustrates use of `gjt.Util.waitForImage()`.

Example 6-7 Image Loading With the `gjt.Util` Class

```
import java.net.URL;
import java.applet.Applet;
import java.awt.Graphics;
import java.awt.Image;

import gjt.Util;

public class ImageTestAppletWithGJTUtil extends Applet {
  private Image im;

  public void init() {
      URL codebase = getCodeBase();
      System.out.println(codebase);
```

```
            im = getImage(codebase, "saint.gif");
❶           Util.waitForImage(this, im);
            showImageSize();
    }
    public void paint(Graphics g) {
        g.drawImage(im,0,0,this);
    }
    private void showImageSize() {
            System.out.print  ("Image width=" + im.getWidth(this));
            System.out.println(" height=" + im.getHeight(this));
    }
}
```

Implementation of the Graphic Java Toolkit `Util.waitForImage()` method invoked in line ❶ above is straightforward:

```
public static void waitForImage(Component component,
                                Image image){
   MediaTracker tracker = new MediaTracker(component);
   try {
      tracker.addImage(image, 0);
      tracker.waitForID(0);
   }
   catch(InterruptedException e) { Assert.notNull(null); }
}
```

As you can see, `gjt.Util.waitForImage()` simply encapsulates the steps involved in using `MediaTracker`, which we would otherwise have to reimplement for each image we wish to load in this fashion.

Filtering Images

Thus far, we've shown you how to obtain and display images and highlighted some features of the AWT (and the GJT) along the way. There will be times, however, when you will need to manipulate images in a more sophisticated fashion. The `java.awt.image` package provides the infrastructure for filtering images, furthermore the GJT provides two image filters:

- `gjt.image.BleachImageFilter`
- `gjt.image.DissolveFilter`

The former sets the degree of transparency for each color in an image, while the latter increases the brightness of each color in an image. The class diagram in Figure 6-1 illustrates the `java.awt.image` classes involved in filtering images and also shows where the GJT filters fit in.

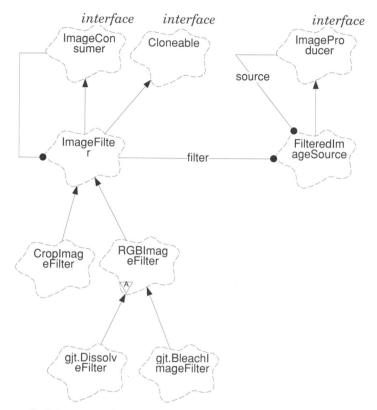

Figure 6-1 Image Filter Class Diagram
A FilteredImageSource is an ImageProducer that runs the bits of
an image supplied by another ImageProducer through an
ImageFilter, and produces a filtered version of the original image.

The GJT filters extend `RGBImageFilter`— an abstract filter that leaves the actual
filtering of pixels to extensions but provides the infrastructure for delivering one
pixel at a time from an image. We'll first take a look at how the
`gjt.image.BleachImageFilter` is used and implemented, and then we'll
take a look at the `gjt.DissolveImageFilter`.

To begin, look at Figure 6-2. It shows the effect of running an image through the
`gjt.image.BleachImageFilter`. The image on the left is the original image,
and the image on the right is the image produced after the original image is run
through the `gjt.image.BleachImageFilter`.

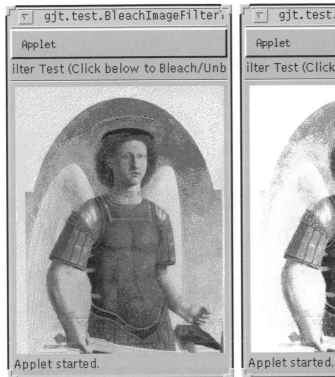

Figure 6-2 Bleaching Images

To illustrate the `gjt.image.BleachImageFilter` in action, we'll look at Example 6-8, which is the unit test for this filter.

After you've looked through Example 6-8, we'll highlight some of the dynamics of passing an image through a filter. Then we'll look specifically at the inner workings of the `gjt.image.BleachImageFilter`.

Example 6-8 Bleaching an Image With a Filter

CD-Rom

```
package gjt.test;

import java.applet.Applet;
import java.awt.*;
❶ import java.awt.image.FilteredImageSource;

import gjt.Util;
import gjt.image.BleachImageFilter;

public class BleachImageFilterTest extends UnitTest {
  public String title() {
      return "BleachImageFilter Test " +
              "(Click below to Bleach/Unbleach Picture)";
  }
  public Panel centerPanel() {
      return new BleachImageFilterTestPanel(this);
  }
}

class BleachImageFilterTestPanel extends Panel {
  BleachImageFilterTestCanvas canvas;

  public BleachImageFilterTestPanel(Applet applet) {
      add(canvas = new BleachImageFilterTestCanvas(applet));
  }
  public boolean mouseDown(Event event, int x, int y) {
      canvas.toggleBleaching();
      canvas.repaint();
      return true;
  }
}

class BleachImageFilterTestCanvas extends Canvas {
❷   private Image            im;
❸   private Image            bleached;
    private BleachImageFilter filter;
    private boolean           showingBleached = false;

  public BleachImageFilterTestCanvas(Applet applet) {
      int     bp;
      String bleachPercent =
              applet.getParameter("bleachPercent");

      if(bleachPercent != null)
          bp = new Integer(bleachPercent).intValue();
      else
```

```
           bp = 50;

        im = applet.getImage(applet.getCodeBase(),
                           "gifs/saint.gif");
        Util.waitForImage(this, im);

❹      FilteredImageSource source =
           new FilteredImageSource(im.getSource(),
                                   new BleachImageFilter(bp));

❺      bleached = createImage(source);
❻      Util.waitForImage(this, bleached);

        showImageSize();
   }
   public Dimension preferredSize() {
        return new Dimension(im.getWidth(this),
                             im.getHeight(this));
   }
❼  public void paint(Graphics g) {
        if(showingBleached) g.drawImage(bleached,0,0,this);
        else                g.drawImage(im,      0,0,this);
   }
   public void toggleBleaching() {
        showingBleached = showingBleached ? false : true;
   }
   private void showImageSize() {
        System.out.print  ("Image width-" + im.getWidth(this));
        System.out.println(" height=" + im.getHeight(this));
   }
  }
```

The first thing to note about this applet is that in line ❶, we import
FilteredImageSource from the java.awt.image package. The
FilteredImageSource class implements the ImageProducer interface. As
we'll see in line ❹, it is constructed with an ImageProducer and an
ImageFilter.

Line ❷ declares im, which is the original, unbleached image, while in line ❸ we
declare bleached, which is the bleached version of the original image.

Line ❹ creates a new instance of FilteredImageSource, which is used to filter
the original image and produce a bleached version of the image.
FilteredImageSource is an ImageProducer that produces a filtered version
of an image. A FilteredImageSource is constructed with an ImageProducer,
which supplies the bits of the original image, and an ImageFilter, which not
surprisingly, filters the image supplied by the ImageProducer. Note that in this

particular case, we obtain the ImageProducer from the original image. Remember that each image has an `ImageProducer` that can produce the bits for its associated image. `FilteredImageSource` prods the image producer it was passed in its constructor to cough up the bits of the original image and then runs those bits through the image filter that was also supplied to its constructor. Finally, since `FilteredImageSource` is an image producer itself, it can be passed to `Applet.createImage(ImageProducer)`—as is done on line ❺—to produce the filtered version of the original image.

In line ❺, we create a new, filtered image and assign it to `bleached`. The `Component.createImage()` method takes an `ImageProducer` for an argument. The `createImage()` method knows how to obtain the bits of an image from the specified `ImageProducer` argument. Figure 6-3 sketches how this transaction of events takes place.

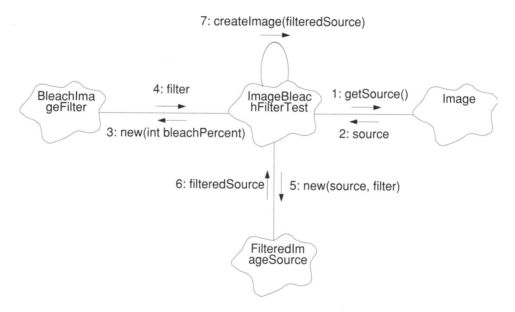

Figure 6-3 Image Filtering Process
The `ImageBleachFilterTest` applet obtains the `ImageProducer` for the original image, creates a `BleachImageFilter`, and then uses the `ImageProducer` and the `BleachImageFilter` to construct a `FilteredImageSource`. Finally, the `FilteredImageSource` is passed to `Applet.createImage()`, which returns a filtered version of the original image.

Of course, all of this happens asynchronously, so in line ❻ we use the
waitForID() method from the gjt.Util class, to wait for the bleached version
of the original image to be fully loaded.

In line ❼, we override the paint() method to enable toggling between the
standard and bleached images.

gjt.image.BleachImageFilter

Now that we've seen how a FilteredImageSource is used to produce a
filtered version of an image, we will reveal the implementation of
BleachImageFilter. There are a couple of important items to note about
gjt.image.BleachImageFilter as you look through its implementation. For
example, notice that it extends RGBImageFilter; it is standard AWT practice to
extend RGBImageFilter for filtering images. Doing so requires overriding its
only abstract method: filterRGB(), which is passed one pixel at a time for
filtering.

Also, note the use of canFilterIndexColorModel (a boolean instance variable
of RGBImageFilter) in the gjt.image.BleachImageFilter constructor.
When canFilterIndexColorModel is set to false, the filterRGB()
method is called to filter every pixel in an image. (The default behavior of an
RGBImageFilter is to convert each pixel in the image, one at a time.) When
canFilterIndexColorModel is set to true, as in
gjt.image.BleachImageFilter, the filterRGB() method is passed one
pixel for each *color* in the ColorModel. Setting canFilterIndexColorModel
to true allows the BleachImageFilter to filter by color and avoids the
overhead of calling filterRGB() for every pixel in an image. Before we look at
the implementation of gjt.image.BleachImageFilter, take a look at
Table 6-4.

Table 6-4 gjt.image.BleachImageFilter **Responsibilities**

Methods	Description
int percent()	Defines the extent to which an image will be bleached.
void percent(int percent)	Sets bleaching percent.
int filterRGB(int x, int y, int rgb)	Brightens each color in the image.

Example 6-9 shows the gjt.image.BleachImageFilter implementation.

Example 6-9 `gjt.image.BleachImageFilter` **Class Source Code**

CD-Rom

```java
package gjt.image;

import java.awt.image.*;
import gjt.Assert;

public class BleachImageFilter extends RGBImageFilter {
  private int percent;

  public BleachImageFilter(int percent) {
      Assert.notFalse(percent >= 0 && percent <= 100);
      this.percent = percent;
      canFilterIndexColorModel = true;
  }
  public int  percent()             { return percent;   }
  public void percent(int percent) { percent = percent; }

  public int filterRGB(int x, int y, int rgb) {
❶     DirectColorModel cm =
          (DirectColorModel)ColorModel.getRGBdefault();

❷     int    alpha = cm.getAlpha(rgb);
      int    red   = cm.getRed(rgb);
      int    green = cm.getGreen(rgb);
      int    blue  = cm.getBlue (rgb);
      double percentMultiplier = (double)percent/100;

❸     red   = Math.min((int)
              (red + (red * percentMultiplier)), 255);
      green = Math.min((int)
              (green + (green * percentMultiplier)), 255);
      blue  = Math.min((int)
              (blue  + (blue  * percentMultiplier)), 255);

❹     alpha = alpha << 24;
      red   = red   << 16;
      green = green << 8;

❺     return alpha | red | green | blue;
  }
}
```

The BleachImageFilter constructor sets canFilterIndexColorModel to true. As we mentioned previously, this means that BleachImageFilter.filterRGB() will only be called as many times as there are colors in the ColorModel, instead of for every pixel in the image. Filters that modify colors independent of the position of pixels in the image should do likewise to avoid a great deal of unnecessary overhead.

Of course, filterRGB() is where all of the action takes place. On line ❶, we obtain the default RGB color model, which we put to work on line ❷ to extract the alpha, red, green, and blue components of the pixel (rgb) passed in, which is a color model's only raison d'etre. The red, green, blue, and alpha values for a pixel always fall between 0 and 255; the higher the number, the brighter the color.

Starting on line ❸, we set each value to the minimum of (original value + original value * percent/100) and 255. For instance, if the original value of the red component were 150 and our percent was 50, we would set the red component to 150 + (150 * 50/100), which turns out to be 225. However, if the red component were 250, we would set the red component to 255, because 250 + (250 * 50/250) turns out to be 300, which is greater than the maximum allowed value of 255.

Finally, on line ❹, we shift the alpha, red, and green bits in order to place them in the correct location bitwise. The alpha component of a color occupies bits 25–32, the red component occupies bits 17–24, and the green component occupies bits 9–16. The blue component of a pixel occupies bits 1–8, so there is no need to shift the blue component. On line ❺, we reconstruct a pixel value from the shifted components, by ORing them. The reconstructed pixel value is then returned from the filterRGB() method. Remember, the job of filterRGB() is to take a pixel value, convert it however it sees fit, and then return the modified pixel value. Since BleachImageFiliter.filterRGB() gets invoked for every color in the image's color model, each color is brightened by the percentage specified by the percent member of the BleachImageFilter.

Notice that BleachImageFilter does not modify the alpha component of the pixel value; the alpha component controls the transparency (or opacity, depending upon your point of view) of a pixel. The gjt.image.DissolveFilter, which we will discuss shortly, controls the transparency of an image and thus manipulates the alpha value of each pixel in the color model. This leaves the red, blue, and green components untouched. But we are getting ahead of ourselves.

The Color Model and the Alpha Value of a Pixel

In case our brief discussion of the `ColorModel` class and the alpha value of a pixel left you wanting more, we will cover both in a bit more detail before diving into the `gjt.image.DissolveFilter`.

Each pixel in an image has an RGB color value. The alpha, red, green, and blue components of a pixel can be accessed by the invoking the methods defined by `awt.image.ColorModel`, which are described in Table 6-5.

Table 6-5 `awt.image.ColorModel` **Public Abstract Instance Methods**

Abstract Methods	Description
int getAlpha(int pixel)	Returns the opacity for a color in a pixel.
int getRed(int pixel)	Returns the integer value for red.
int getBlue(int pixel)	Returns the integer value for blue.
int getGreen(int pixel)	Returns the integer value for green.
int getPixelSize()	Returns pixel size.
int getRGB(int pixel)	Returns the integer RGB value.

Besides having a red, green, and blue value, each pixel value also includes an *alpha* value. The alpha value represents the transparency of a color and, like its red, green, and blue counterparts, is an integer whose value is always between 0 and 255. An alpha value of 0 means the color is completely transparent, and an alpha value of 255 means the color is completely opaque. You can see the effect of modifying an image's alpha value in Figure 6-4.

Figure 6-4 Dissolving Images
The gjt.image.ImageDissolver in action.

gjt.image.DissolveFilter

The gjt.image.DissolveFilter sets the level of transparency for each color
in an image. Table 6-6 lists the DissolveFilter public instance methods,
followed by the implementation of gjt.image.DissolveFilter in
Example 6-10.

Table 6-6 gjt.image.DissolveFilter **Responsibilities**

Methods	Description
void setOpacity(int opacity)	Sets the opacity for a color.
int filterRGB(int x, int y, int rgb)	Returns the RGB value.

Example 6-10 `gjt.image.DissolveFilter` **Class Source Code**

CD-Rom

```
package gjt.image;

import java.awt.image.*
import gjt.Assert;

public class DissolveFilter extends RGBImageFilter {
 private int opacity;

    public DissolveFilter() {
        this(0);
    }
    public DissolveFilter(int opacity) {
        canFilterIndexColorModel = true;
        setOpacity(opacity);
    }
    public void setOpacity(int opacity) {
        Assert.notFalse(opacity >= 0 && opacity <= 255);
        this.opacity = opacity;
    }
    public int filterRGB(int x, int y, int rgb) {
        DirectColorModel cm =
            (DirectColorModel)ColorModel.getRGBdefault();
❶      int alpha = cm.getAlpha(rgb);
        int red   = cm.getRed  (rgb);
        int green = cm.getGreen(rgb);
        int blue  = cm.getBlue (rgb);

❷      alpha = opacity;

❸      return alpha << 24 | red << 16 | green << 8 | blue;
    }
 }
```

Note the similarity between the implementations of `DissolveFilter` and `BleachImageFilter`. Both classes override `java.awt.image.RGBImageFilter`, and both implement the required `filterRGB()`. Additionally, both set `canFilterColorIndexModel` to true and both extract the alpha, red, green, and blue components of each pixel passed into `filterRGB()`.

While `BleachImageFilter` manipulates the red, green, and blue components of each pixel passed into `filterRGB()` and leaves the alpha component untouched, `DissolveFilter` does the inverse, letting the red, green, and blue components pass through untouched, modifying only the alpha value. `DissolveFilter` sets the alpha value for each color in the image to its `opacity`.

gjt.image.ImageDissolver

Now that we've seen how `gjt.image.DissolveFilter` manipulates the alpha value of each color in an image, let's look at `gjt.image.ImageDissolver`, which uses `DissolveFilter` for the practical purpose of fading an image in or out.

Table 6-7 lists the `ImageDissolver` responsibilities.

Table 6-7 `gjt.image.ImageDissolver` **Responsibilities**

Methods	Description
`void fadeIn(int x, int y)`	Fades in the image.
`void fadeOut(int x, int y)`	Fades out the image.

`gjt.image.ImageDissolver` creates an array of images of varying transparency, from totally translucent to totally opaque, with the assistance of a `gjt.image.DissolveFilter`. The `fadeIn()` and `fadeOut()` methods cycle through the array of images and display each image in a `Component` that is passed to the `ImageDissolver` constructor. `fadeIn()` cycles through the array from the totally transparent image to the totally opaque image, while `fadeOut()` cycles through the array in reverse order.

Example 6-11 on page 150 shows the `gjt.image.ImageDissolver` class in its entirety. However, it is a fairly complicated class, so we'll guide you through some of the highlights before showing you the entire class.

One of the first things to point out is that the `ImageDissolver` contains two `Image` objects: one for the image to be drawn on-screen and one for the image to be drawn off-screen. This is our first exposure to double buffering, which warrants a short introduction.

Double buffering is a technique for smoothly drawing a series of images. Each image is first drawn in an off-screen buffer and then copied, or *blitted* [1], to an area on-screen. Double buffering eliminates the flicker associated with drawing a series of images and is discussed in more detail in *Sprite Animation* on page 473. `ImageDissolver` employs double buffering for a flicker-free fading effect.

After declaring the on-screen and off-screen images, we declare an array of images to hold the images created by `gjt.image.DissolveFilter`:

---

1. *Blit* is a term derived from the phrase bit block transfer. A block transfer is sometimes referred to as a BLT (not to be confused with the sandwich), so *blit* is short for a Bit BLT.

```
Image      image, offscreen;
Image[]    dissolvedImages;
```

ImageDissolver has two constructors:

```
    public ImageDissolver(Component comp, Image image) {
        this(comp, image, _defaultNumImages, _defaultPause);
    }
    public ImageDissolver(Component comp, Image im,
❶                         int numImages, int pause) {
        this.image      = im;
        this.comp       = comp;
        this.numImages  = numImages;
        dissolvedImages = new Image[numImages];
        pauseInterval   = pause;

❷       Util.waitForImage(comp, im);
❸       dissolvedImages = createImages(image, numImages, comp);
    }
```

Note that both constructors take a Component, which is the component into which the images will be drawn. Also, the second constructor in line ❶ takes a pause value, which is used to control the rate at which the images are faded in and out. Line ❷ makes use of the waitForImage() method from the gjt.Util class to ensure that the image passed in is fully loaded. (Recall from *Using MediaTracker* on page 133 that this method encapsulates the MediaTracker capability for waiting for the asynchronous loading of an image to complete.)

On line ❸, the constructor calls createImages(). This is where gjt.image.ImageDissolver creates an array of images with varying degrees of transparency:

```
    static public Image[] createImages(Image image,
                                        int numImages,
                                        Component component) {
        Image         images[] = new Image[numImages];
        MediaTracker  tracker  = new MediaTracker(component);

        DissolveFilter      filter;
        FilteredImageSource fis;

        for(int i=0; i < numImages; ++i) {
❶           filter = new DissolveFilter((255/(numImages-1))*i);
❷           fis    = new FilteredImageSource(image.getSource(),
                                             filter);

            images[i] = component.createImage(fis);
❸           tracker.addImage(images[i], i);
```

```
        }
❸       try { tracker.waitForAll(); }
        catch(InterruptedException e) { }

        return images;
    }
```

CreateImages() is passed the original image, the number of images to be produced, and the component into which the images will be drawn. On line **❶**, a DissolveFilter is created with a specified opacity. Notice that when i is 0, the opacity passed to the filter's constructor is (255/ (numImages-1)) * i, which turns out to be zero, no matter what numImages is. When i is equal to numImages-1, the opacity turns out to be (255 / (numImages-1)) * (numImages-1), or 255. Therefore, createImages() creates an array of numImages images, whose transparency varies from totally transparent (alpha value of 0) to totally opaque (alpha value of 255). The images in between have varying degrees of transparency.

On line **❸**, we add each image created to an instance of MediaTracker (tracker), and then on line **❹**, we have tracker wait for all the images in the array to be fully loaded. Finally, we return the array of images created.

Next, let's look at one of the gjt.image.ImageDissolver public fadeIn() method:

```
    public void fadeIn(int x, int y) {
        if(offscreen == null)
❶           offscreen = comp.createImage(image.getWidth(comp),
                                          image.getHeight(comp));

❷       Graphics offg  = offscreen.getGraphics();
❸       Graphics compg = comp.getGraphics();

        if(offg != null && compg != null) {
❹           clearComponent(compg, x, y);
            for(int i=0; i < numImages; ++i) {
                blitImage(compg, offg, x, y, i);
                pause      ();
            }
            blitOpaqueImage(compg, offg, x, y);
        }
    }
```

In line **❶**, createImage() creates the off-screen image, if it has not been created previously, that has the same width and height as each image in the array of images to be displayed.

Lines ❷ and ❸ obtain the `Graphics` object for the off-screen and on-screen images, respectively. Then in line ❹, the work of fading in an array of images begins. The first order of business for `fadeIn()` is to erase the region of the component into which the images will be drawn, which is exactly what `clearComponent()` does. Then `fadeIn()` cycles through the array of images, blitting each image into the component at the specified location. Each pass through the loop is accompanied by a call to `pause()`, which pauses for the amount of time in milliseconds specified by the `pauseInterval` member.

The `blitImage()` method first draws an image from the array into the off-screen buffer and then copies the image into the component at the specified offset.

```
      private void blitImage(Graphics compg, Graphics offg,
                             int x, int y, int index) {
❶          offg.drawImage (dissolvedImages[index], 0, 0, comp);
❷          compg.drawImage(offscreen,              x, y, comp);
      }
```

In line ❶, we use the `Graphics` object of the off-screen image to draw an image from the `Image` array into the off-screen image. In line ❷, the image is blitted from the off-screen image into the component.

Now we are ready to present the `gjt.image.ImageDissolver` class in its entirety in Example 6-11. You might pay special attention to the `pause()` method, which simply causes the current thread to sleep for the time specified in `pauseInterval` (in milliseconds).

Example 6-11 `gjt.image.ImageDissolver` **Class Source Code**

```
package gjt.image;

import java.awt.*;
import java.awt.image.*;
import gjt.Util;

public class ImageDissolver {
  private static int _defaultNumImages = 10,
                     _defaultPause = 50;
  Component comp;
  int       numImages, pauseInterval;
  Image     image, offscreen;
  Image[]   dissolvedImages;

  static public Image[] createImages(Image image,
                                      int numImages,
                                      Component component) {
        Image         images[] = new Image[numImages];
```

```
        MediaTracker tracker  = new MediaTracker(component);

        DissolveFilter       filter;
        FilteredImageSource fis;

        for(int i=0; i < (numImages-1); ++i) {
            filter = new DissolveFilter((255/(numImages-1))*i);
            fis    = new FilteredImageSource(image.getSource(),
                                             filter);


            images[i] = component.createImage(fis);
            tracker.addImage(images[i], i);
        }
        try { tracker.waitForAll(); }
        catch(InterruptedException e) { }

        images[numImages-1] = image;
        return images;
    }

    public ImageDissolver(Component comp, Image image) {
        this(comp, image, _defaultNumImages, _defaultPause);
    }
    public ImageDissolver(Component comp, Image im,
                          int numImages, int pause) {
        this.image      = im;
        this.comp       = comp;
        this.numImages  = numImages;
        dissolvedImages = new Image[numImages];
        pauseInterval   = pause;

        Util.waitForImage(comp, im);
        dissolvedImages = createImages(image, numImages, comp);
    }
    public void fadeIn(int x, int y) {
        if(offscreen == null)
            offscreen = comp.createImage(image.getWidth(comp),
                                         image.getHeight(comp));

        Graphics offg  = offscreen.getGraphics();
        Graphics compg = comp.getGraphics();

        if(offg != null && compg != null) {
            clearComponent(compg, x, y);
            for(int i=0; i < numImages; ++i) {
                blitImage(compg, offg, x, y, i);
                pause     ();
```

```
                }
                blitOpaqueImage(compg, offg, x, y);
            }
        }
    public void fadeOut(int x, int y) {
        if(offscreen == null)
            offscreen = comp.createImage(image.getWidth(comp),
                                    image.getHeight(comp));

        Graphics offg  = offscreen.getGraphics();
        Graphics compg = comp.getGraphics();

        if(offg != null && compg != null) {
            blitOpaqueImage(compg, offg, x, y);
            for(int i=numImages-1; i >= 0; --i) {
                clearOffscreen();
                blitImage     (compg, offg, x, y, i);
                pause         ();
            }
        }
    }
    private void blitImage(Graphics compg, Graphics offg,
                          int x, int y, int index) {
        offg.drawImage (dissolvedImages[index], 0, 0, comp);
        compg.drawImage(offscreen,               x, y, comp);
    }
    private void blitOpaqueImage(Graphics compg, Graphics offg,
                               int x, int y) {
        offg.drawImage(image, 0, 0, comp);
        compg.drawImage(offscreen, x, y, comp);
    }
    private void clearComponent(Graphics compg, int x, int y) {
        clearOffscreen();
        compg.drawImage(offscreen, x, y, comp);
    }
    private void clearOffscreen() {
        Graphics offg = offscreen.getGraphics();

        offg.setColor(comp.getBackground());
        offg.fillRect(0, 0,
                image.getWidth(comp), image.getHeight(comp));
    }
    private void pause() {
        try { Thread.currentThread().sleep(pauseInterval); }
        catch(InterruptedException e) { }
    }
}
```

Summary

There are two major areas of concern when incorporating images into applets. One is the basic task of obtaining and displaying images. The other is the task of manipulating images.

This chapter has covered the basics of obtaining and displaying images, including the distinction between `ImageProducer` and `ImageObserver`, and loading images a scanline at a time or all at once. We have also discussed elimination of flashing when painting an image a scanline at a time, along with the use of `MediaTracker` for waiting for images to load. Additionally, we have introduced image filtering and double buffering and presented two GJT image filters: `gjt.image.BleachImageFilter` and `gjt.image.DissolveFilter`. We have also presented a GJT custom component that can be used to fade an image in or out of a `java.awt.Component`.

CHAPTER
7

- **The Big Three of the AWT on page 156**

- **LayoutManager Responsibilities on page 158**

- **Layout Managers and the Good Life on page 159**

- **Layout Managers and Container Insets on page 161**

- **Peers and Insets on page 162**

- **Painting a Container's Components on page 163**

- **TenPixelBorder on page 163**

- **Layout Managers and Component Preferred Sizes on page 166**

- **Standard AWT Layout Managers on page 168**

- **Decisions, Decisions—Which Layout Manager to Use? on page 169**

- **The GridBagLayout Layout Manager on page 178**

- **Laying Out Components in Nested Panels on page 191**

- **Custom Layout Managers on page 204**

- **Summary on page 232**

Components, Containers, and Layout Managers

Perhaps the most fundamental relationship in the entire AWT is the relationship between components, containers, and layout managers. Understanding how the three relate to one another is paramount to developing non-trivial applets and applications using the AWT. As a result, we will spend a good deal of effort to illustrate not only the relationships between components, containers, and layout managers, but also the standard AWT layout managers and implementing custom layout managers.

No matter how thorough we are in this chapter, we realize that readers are not going to become layout manager gurus without significant exposure to using and implementing layout managers in the real world. When we cover custom components from the Graphic Java Toolkit in *The Graphic Java Toolkit—Extending the AWT*, we'll be dealing with a different layout situation in nearly every chapter, which will lead us to a number of insights concerning layout managers and their relationships with components and containers.

The Big Three of the AWT

To really get your teeth into the AWT, you're going to have to deal with components, containers, and layout managers in a fairly sophisticated fashion. This means you're going to have to be sensitive to the nuances of their relationship to one another. Primarily, you need to know where one stops working for you and where another starts.

A component contained in a container is quite likely to be subjected to a life of stretching, squashing, and being moved about. Although you might suspect the component's container of dishing out such punishment, containers are spatially challenged; they delegate the laying out of their components to a layout manager. A container's layout manager is the sole force behind positioning and shaping the components contained in its associated container.

Figure 7-2 shows a class diagram for `java.awt.Container`.

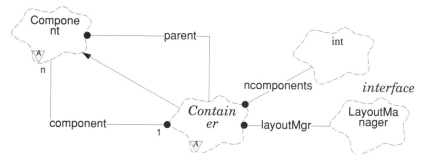

Figure 7-1 Container Class Diagram

Containers are simply components that can contain other components. They don't actually *do* anything with the components they contain; they just keep track of them.

The AWT provides a handful of classes that extend `Container`, as illustrated in Figure 7-2.

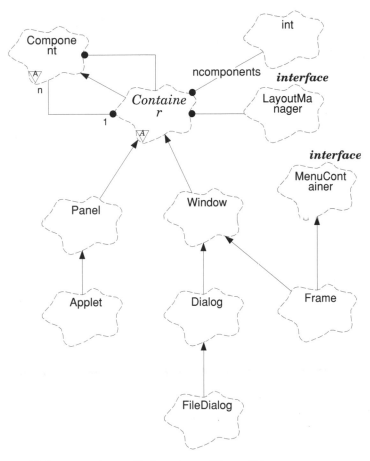

Figure 7-2 `Container` Extensions Class Diagram

Each container has access to a `LayoutManager` that is responsible for positioning and shaping the components contained in the container. When an event occurs that causes a container to lay out its components (such as resizing a window), the container's layout manager is called upon to lay out the components that reside in the container.

Essentially, then, containers farm out the job of laying out their components to a layout manager. Different layout managers implement different algorithms for laying out components; containers are free to choose the layout algorithm of their choice by employing the appropriate layout manager. This technique of defining a family of algorithms and encapsulating each one in a class is known as the *strategy pattern.*[1] (The strategy pattern has a number of benefits that we will explore in more detail when we look at separating event handling from components in our *Image Button* chapter.)

LayoutManager Responsibilities

`LayoutManager` is an interface that requires classes that implement it to define the following methods [2]:

```
void        addLayoutComponent (String name, Component comp);
void        removeLayoutComponent (Component comp);
Dimension   preferredLayoutSize (Container parent);
Dimension   minimumLayoutSize (Container parent);
void        layoutContainer (Container parent);
```

Layout managers are responsible for:

• Calculating the preferred and minimum sizes for a container

• Laying out the components contained in a container

It's important to note that while each container has exactly one layout manager, a single layout manager may wind up working for more than container. Therefore, when a layout manager has to perform some work for a container, it must be passed a reference to the container requesting its services. In fact, if you look at `Panel.java`, you will see that a `java.awt.Panel`, by default, shares a single and presumably overworked `FlowLayout`:

```
public class Panel extends Container {
   final static LayoutManager panelLayout = new FlowLayout();
      .
      .
      .
   public Panel() {
      setLayout(panelLayout);
   }
```

---

1. See Gamma, Helm, Johnson, Vlissides. *Design Patterns*, p. 315. Addison-Wesley.
2. Contrary to popular misconception, an implementor of an interface does not *have* to implement all the methods defined in the interface; however, classes that claim to implement an interface but do not actually implement all of its methods are abstract classes. See the discussion of `ImageButtonPanelController` in *Toolbars* on page 329.

Since `panelLayout` is a static member, there is only one `panelLayout` for all instances of `Panel`. When a `Panel` equipped with its default layout manager is laid out, a reference to the `Panel` is passed to the `layoutContainer(Container)` method of the `static panelLayout` instance, which obliges by laying out the components in yet another `Panel`.

Layout Managers and the Good Life

The previous discussion may lead you to the conclusion that layout managers have a very difficult lot in life and are required to dutifully lay out the components of many different containers. While this is true for some layout managers, there is another entirely different type of layout manager that lives the good life, working for only one container that contains a strictly defined set of components.

From our perspective, a layout manager lives the good life when it works for one and only one container. `BorderLayout` is a layout manager that knows how to live. It works for one container, and it keeps track of a finite set of components to be laid out within that container. At most, it lays out five components—identified by "North," "South," "East," "West," and "Center"—in its container.

`FlowLayout`, on the other hand, does not keep track of specific components, such as a north or south component. Instead, it lays out all of the components it finds in the container it is currently laying out.

The layout manager's implementation of two methods of the `LayoutManager` interface determines whether it works for one container or is resigned to toil for a potential army of containers:

```
void addLayoutComponent (String name, Component comp);
void removeLayoutComponent(Component comp);
```

Layout managers that have been relegated to working for many components typically provide *no-op* implementations of these two methods. For instance, `FlowLayout` implements them as follows:

```
public void addLayoutComponent(String name, Component comp) { }
public void removeLayoutComponent(Component comp) { }
```

To understand the reasoning behind these *no-op* implementations, let's take a look at how a layout manager's addLayoutComponent() is invoked. In Container.java, we find:

```
public synchronized Component add(String name, Component comp) {
    // ...
    if (layoutMgr != null) {
        layoutMgr.addLayoutComponent(name, comp);
    }
    // ...
}
```

Whenever a named component is added to a container, it invokes its layout manager's addLayoutComponent(String,Component) method. Layout managers that live the good life take note and retain a reference to both the component and its name, whereas the other layout managers do nothing.

When it comes time to actually lay out components, layout managers living the good life simply lay out the named components that they are keeping track of. Other layout managers cycle through all of the components contained in the container being laid out and lay out each of them in succession.

BorderLayout.layoutContainer(Container), for instance, lays out only the components that have been added to it through its addLayoutComponent(String,Component) method. As you might suspect, BorderLayout lays out its "North" component in the north, its "South" component in the south, and so on.

FlowLayout.layoutContainer(Container), on the other hand, cycles through each component contained in the container and lays it out within the container. FlowLayout lays out components from left to right and top to bottom within the container.

Meaningful implementations of addLayoutComponent() and removeLayoutComponent() mean that the layout manager itself is keeping track of a finite number of clearly defined components for the only container it ever deals with. No-op implementations of the two methods indicate that the layout manager is on call to lay out any container with an unknown number of components.

Layout Managers and Container Insets

Every container has a set of *insets* associated with it. These are the container's top, bottom, left, and right inside margins, defined in pixels, as illustrated in Figure 7-3.

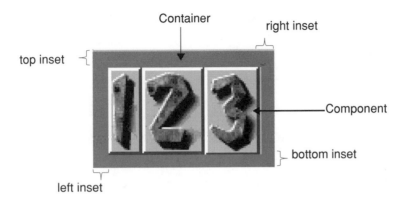

Figure 7-3 Container With Insets
Layout managers are careful not to lay out components inside the container's insets.

A container's insets values are important because layout managers are careful not to place components anywhere inside a container's insets[3].

`java.awt.Container` defines the following `insets()` method that provides access to a container's insets:

```
Insets Container.insets()
```

`Container`, however, does not define a separate method for setting its insets. If you want to set a container's insets, you must extend a class derived from `Container` and overwrite the `insets()` method, like so:

```
public Insets insets() {
   return new Insets(10,10,10,10);
}
```

---

3.   We speak only for the standard AWT layout managers. It is up to implementors of custom components to respect the insets of a container.

Notice that `Container.insets()` is a little off-kilter with the rest of the AWT; most parameters of AWT classes have both a get and a set method, meaning you can query and/or change the parameter at runtime without having to extend a class to change a parameter. This is not the case with a container's insets; a container must override `insets()` in order to change its insets. This relegates setting a container's insets to a per-class basis instead of a per-object basis.

AWT Tip

Frame Insets Are Unique...

If you are writing a Java application, as opposed to an applet, be aware that a Frame object's insets, by default, include the height of the menu bar, if the frame is so equipped. This knowledge comes in handy if you accidentally draw into a frame underneath its menu bar. While layout managers will not place components inside a container's insets, there is nothing to stop you from performing graphical operations inside a containers insets.

Peers and Insets

You might be curious to know what the default insets are for each extension of `java.awt.Container`. Let's track this down by looking at `Insets Container.inset()`:

```
public Insets insets() {
  ContainerPeer peer = (ContainerPeer)this.peer;
  return (peer != null) ? peer.insets() : new Insets(0, 0, 0, 0);
}
```

If a container does not override `insets()`, then its peer supplies the value; otherwise, an `Inset` with zero for all margins is returned. Now, if we look at `ContainerPeer.java` to find out the value a container's peer returns for insets, we see this:

```
public interface ContainerPeer extends ComponentPeer {
  Insets insets();
}
```

Now we've hit a dead end, as is always the case when trying to track down peer behavior, because all peers are defined in terms of interfaces.

The reason we cannot find out a default value for insets is because there isn't one. Each container's peer is given leeway to return whatever insets make sense for the platform on which the peer resides, and therefore there is no cross-platform default for the insets of a `Container`. The peer approach—using native peer components—retains look-and-feel across platforms, and this is one of the trade-offs with which we must deal as a consequence.

We'll explore in more depth exactly how layout managers deal with a container's insets when we discuss developing custom layout managers later on in this chapter.

Painting a Container's Components

Containers do not have to explicitly paint the components they contain; a container's components are painted (or drawn, if you will) automatically. Custom components that extend `Container` only need to override their `paint(Graphics)` method if they need to perform some graphical operations above and beyond painting the components they contain.

TenPixelBorder

It's about time that we presented some code that illustrates the concepts we've discussed up to this point. We'll start with the `TenPixelBorder` class, which illustrates many of the topics we have covered so far. `TenPixelBorder` is a simple class, so we'll show you the code in Example 7-1 and then highlight the essentials of how it works.

Example 7-1 `TenPixelBorder` **Class Source Code**

```
import java.awt.*;

public class TenPixelBorder extends Panel {
  public TenPixelBorder(Component borderMe) {
      setLayout(new BorderLayout());
      add("Center", borderMe);
  }
  public Insets insets() {
      return new Insets(10,10,10,10);
  }
  public void paint(Graphics g) {
      Dimension mySize  = size();
      Insets    myInsets = insets();
```

```
        g.setColor(Color.gray);

        // Top Inset area
        g.fillRect(0,0,mySize.width,myInsets.top);

        // Left Inset area
        g.fillRect(0,0,myInsets.left,mySize.height);

        // Right Inset area
        g.fillRect(mySize.width - myInsets.right,0,
                   myInsets.right,mySize.height);

        // Bottom Inset area
        g.fillRect(0,mySize.height - myInsets.bottom,
                   mySize.width,mySize.height);
    }
}
```

TenPixelBorder extends Panel, thereby inheriting the ability to contain components. An instance of TenPixelBorder must be constructed with a Component (borderMe), which it adds to itself. Notice that TenPixelBorder sets its layout manager to an instance of BorderLayout and adds borderMe as the center component. The result is that borderMe is reshaped to fill the entire space taken up by TenPixelBorder, minus the space taken up by the insets specified by the overridden TenPixelBorder.insets() method [4].

Finally, TenPixelBorder overrides paint(Graphics) and fills the regions specified by the insets with a gray color. Remember that the components contained by TenPixelBorder, namely borderMe, will be painted automatically, so the overridden TenPixelBorder.paint(Graphics) is only concerned with painting the border. Additionally, while the BorderLayout will ensure that borderMe does not encroach upon the area specified by TenPixelBorder.insets(), TenPixelBorder is free to draw into the area specified by its insets. Let's look at TenPixelBorderTestApplet in Figure 7-4. This is a simple applet that exercises an instance of TenPixelBorder.

---

4.   Center components fill the available space that is not occupied by the north, south, east, and west components laid out by a BorderLayout. Since borderMe is the only component within TenPixelBorder, it fills the entire area of the panel.

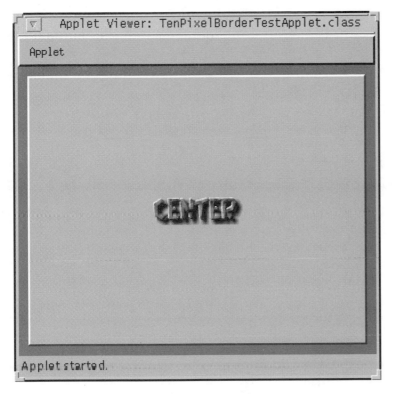

Figure 7-4 TenPixelBorderTestApplet In Action

Example 7-2 shows the TenPixelBorderTestApplet.

Example 7-2 TenPixelBorderTestApplet **Class Source Code**

```
import java.applet.Applet;
import java.awt.*;
import gjt.ImageButton;

public class TenPixelBorderTestApplet extends Applet {
  public void init() {
      Image image = getImage(getCodeBase(),"gifs/center.gif");

      ImageButton    button = new ImageButton   (image);
      TenPixelBorder border = new TenPixelBorder(button);

      setLayout(new BorderLayout());
      add("Center", border);
  }
}
```

The `TenPixelBorderTestApplet` passes a `gjt.ImageButton` to the
`TenPixelBorder` constructor. Although we have not yet discussed the GJT
image buttons, they significantly spruce up our examples throughout this chapter,
and their use is simple enough to be easily understood. For now it is enough to
know that a `gjt.ImageButton` is a custom component that can be added to a
`Container`, just like any other component.

Also, note that `TenPixelBorderTestApplet` centers an instance of
`TenPixelBorder`. Since our applet has not defined any insets, the
`TenPixelBorder` fills all the available space in the applet.

Layout Managers and Component Preferred Sizes

Components implement two very important methods that affect their interactions
with layout managers:

```
// Component methods
public   Dimension preferredSize();
public   Dimension minimumSize();
```

As their names suggest, `preferredSize()` returns the preferred size of the
component; `minimumSize()` returns the minimum size a component can
tolerate. [5]

Layout managers are tasked with figuring out the preferred and minimum sizes
for a container by implementing the following methods from the
`LayoutManager` interface:

```
//LayoutManager methods
Dimension preferredLayoutSize(Container)
Dimension minimumLayoutSize (Container)
```

Such methods typically cycle through all of the container's components and
fashion preferred and minimum sizes for the container by taking into account
each component's preferred and minimum sizes.

Layout managers, of course, are also responsible for laying out their container's
components. They do this by implementing the `layoutContainer()` method:

```
void layoutContainer(Container)
```

5.   A component's minimum size is ignored most of the time.

While some layout managers completely ignore the preferred size of the components they lay out, others are infinitely receptive to each and every component's plea for a preferred size. Still other layout managers will pay attention to only half of a component's preferred size. BorderLayout, for instance, will respect a north component's preferred height, but stretches the component to fill its container horizontally, thereby ignoring the component's preferred width. Table 7-1 shows a list of the standard AWT layout managers and their attitudes toward a component's preferred and minimum sizes.

Table 7-1 Layout Managers and Preferred/Minimum Sizes

Layout Manager	Respects Component's Preferred/Minimum Size Like This...
BorderLayout	North and south components: Respects preferred height, ignores preferred width. East and west components: Respects preferred width, ignores preferred height. Center component: Ignores both preferred width and height.
FlowLayout	Respects preferred width and height.
CardLayout	Ignores preferred width and height.
GridLayout	Ignores preferred width and height.
GridBagLayout	Varies depending on GridBagConstraints for the component. (We cover GridBagConstraints in *GridBagLayout and GridBagConstraints* on page 178)

AWT Tip

Override preferredSize() and minimumSize() When Extending Canvas

When you create custom components that extend Canvas, always override preferredSize() and minimumSize(). By default, the preferred size for a Canvas is (0,0). If your Canvas resides in a container whose layout manager honors preferredWidth and preferredHeight, you'll never see the Canvas displayed if you neglect to override preferredSize(). Failing to override these methods may lead you on a long debugging session in order to figure out why your component is not appearing on the screen.

Standard AWT Layout Managers

The AWT comes with five standard layout managers, as shown in Table 7-2.

Table 7-2 The AWT's Default Layout Manager Classes

Classes That Implement LayoutManager	Description
BorderLayout	Lays out the components around the sides and in the center of the container in north, east, west, south, and center positions. Gaps between components can be specified. BorderLayout is the default layout manager for Window, Dialog and Frame containers.
CardLayout	Displays one component at a time from a *deck* of components. The user can swap different components in and out.
FlowLayout	Displays components left to right, top to bottom. FlowLayout is the default layout manager for applets.
GridBagLayout	Arranges components both vertically and horizontally, using an elaborate set of constraints to determine how much space is allocated to each component and how it should be placed relative to previous components.
GridLayout	Lays out components in a grid, with each component stretched to fill the grid. Horizontal and vertical gaps between components can be specified.

The designers of the AWT hit a home run with the concept of layout managers (we'll look at why it's such a hit when we discuss benefits of the strategy pattern in the *ImageButton and StateButton* chapter). They also did a decent job of supplying a set of default layout managers, which are sufficient to handle probably 90 percent of all your layout needs.

The five layout managers in Table 7-2 provide a range of capabilities, from BorderLayout, a simple layout manager that is useful in an infinite variety of layouts, to the behemoth GridBagLayout, a very complex layout manager that can lay out nearly anything you can imagine.

The AWT classes that extend `Container` each have a default layout manager.
`BorderLayout` is by far the most frequently used layout manager within the
AWT. As Table 7-3 shows, it is the default layout manager for most of the AWT
classes that extend `Container`.

Table 7-3 `Container` **Default Layout Managers**

Container **Extension**	**Default Layout Manager**
Panel	FlowLayout
Window	BorderLayout
Dialog	BorderLayout
Frame	BorderLayout

Decisions, Decisions—Which Layout Manager to Use?

Programmers new to the AWT may be confused about when to use the AWT's
standard layout managers. In fact, that's largely the result of practice, trial, and
error. However, Table 7-4 presents some high-level guidelines that you might find
useful.

Table 7-4 Layout Manager Decision Table

Layout Manager	Use When...	An Example Is...
BorderLayout	A container divides its components into regions: north and south, or east and west. A single component needs to fill the entire area of the container it resides in.	gjt.UnitTest, TenPixelBorder.
CardLayout	You want to be able to swap different panels in or out.	A set of panels that presents itself as a stack of tabbed folders.
FlowLayout	A container's components fill the container from left to right, top to bottom.	Fixed-size containers that lay out their components in rows or columns.
GridLayout	A container divides its components into a grid.	A calendar or spreadsheet.
GridBagLayout	A container has complicated layout needs.	Input forms, such as a container that has components for name, address, zip code, etc.

The BorderLayout Layout Manager

Once you've worked on a few nested layouts, you'll come to appreciate the neat ability of BorderLayout to lay out components into regions. Nearly every nested layout has a BorderLayout lurking somewhere inside. (In the Graphic Java Toolkit, we will find immediate use for a BorderLayout for laying out a UnitTest.) Figure 7-4 shows an applet that uses BorderLayout.

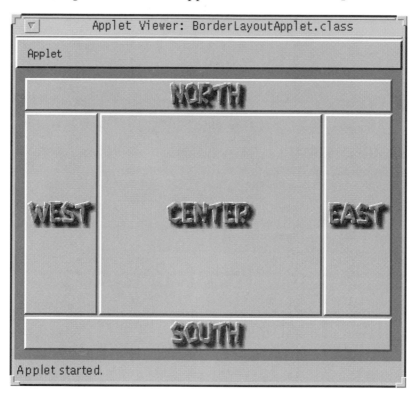

Figure 7-5 BorderLayoutApplet in Action

Example 7-3 shows the implementation of the BorderLayoutApplet class. BorderLayoutApplet is very similar to TenPixelBorderTestApplet, except that it adds five image buttons, one for each of the compass points and center. BorderLayout stretches the north and south components horizontally so that the components span the entire width of the container in which they reside, while sizing them vertically according to their preferred height. The east and west components are stretched vertically so that they span the entire height of the container in which they reside; they are sized horizontally according to their preferred width. The Center component gets whatever space is left over, regardless of its preferred size.

Example 7-3 BorderLayoutApplet **Class Source Code**

```java
import java.net.URL;
import java.applet.Applet;
import java.awt.*;
import gjt.ImageButton;

public class BorderLayoutApplet extends Applet {
  private ImageButton north, south, east, west, center;

  public void init() {
      URL             cb       = getCodeBase();
      Panel           buttonPanel = new Panel();
      TenPixelBorder  border   = new TenPixelBorder(buttonPanel);

      north  = new ImageButton(getImage(cb,"gifs/north.gif"));
      east   = new ImageButton(getImage(cb,"gifs/east.gif"));
      west   = new ImageButton(getImage(cb,"gifs/west.gif"));
      center = new ImageButton(getImage(cb,"gifs/center.gif"));
      south  = new ImageButton(getImage(cb,"gifs/south.gif"));

      buttonPanel.setLayout(new BorderLayout(2,2));
      buttonPanel.add("North",  north);
      buttonPanel.add("South",  south);
      buttonPanel.add("East",   east);
      buttonPanel.add("West",   west);
      buttonPanel.add("Center", center);

      setLayout(new BorderLayout());
      add("Center", border);
  }
}
```

The CardLayout Layout Manager

CardLayout keeps track of a deck, if you will, of components. From this deck, it can display or *deal* any one container at a time. Although it is nowhere near as versatile as the other AWT layout managers, it is nonetheless quite useful. (The GJT has two custom components that use the services of a CardLayout.) Figure 7-6 shows sample output from our CardLayout applet.

Figure 7-6 CardLayout in Action
These pictures show four panels displayed by
CardLayoutApplet.

Example 7-4 show the `CardLayoutApplet` code. Notice as you look through the code that `CardLayout` is unique among layout managers in that it has methods you can call directly to control which component is displayed. In the overridden `mouseUp()` method, we invoke one of those methods: `CardLayout.next(Component)`. Table 7-5 lists the methods implemented by `CardLayout` (in addition to those defined in `LayoutManager`) that allow clients to control which component is currently displayed.

Table 7-5 CardLayout **Stacking Methods**

Method
public void first(Container parent)
public void next(Container parent)
public void previous(Container parent)
public void last(Container parent)
public void show(Container parent,String name)

Example 7-4 CardLayoutApplet **Class Source Code**

```
import java.applet.Applet;
import java.net.URL;
import java.awt.*;
import gjt.ImageButton;

public class CardLayoutApplet extends Applet {
  private ImageButton tiny, small, med, lrg;
  private Panel        cardPanel   = new Panel(),
                       tinyPanel   = new Panel(),
                       smallPanel  = new Panel(),
                       MediumPanel = new Panel(),
                       LargePanel  = new Panel();
  private CardLayout   card        = new CardLayout();

  public void init() {
     TenPixelBorder border   = new TenPixelBorder(cardPanel);
     URL            cb = getCodeBase();

     cardPanel.setLayout(card);
```

```
        tinyPanel.setLayout   (new BorderLayout());
        smallPanel.setLayout  (new BorderLayout());
        MediumPanel.setLayout (new BorderLayout());
        LargePanel.setLayout  (new BorderLayout());

        tiny  = new ImageButton(getImage(cb,"gifs/gjTiny.gif"));
        small = new ImageButton(getImage(cb,"gifs/gjSmall.gif"));
        med   = new ImageButton(getImage(cb,"gifs/gjMedium.gif"));
        lrg   = new ImageButton(getImage(cb,"gifs/gjLarge.gif"));

        tinyPanel.add   ("Center", tiny);
        smallPanel.add  ("Center", small);
        MediumPanel.add ("Center", med);
        LargePanel.add  ("Center", lrg);

        cardPanel.add("tiny",  tinyPanel);
        cardPanel.add("small", smallPanel);
        cardPanel.add("med",   MediumPanel);
        cardPanel.add("lrg",   LargePanel);

        setLayout(new BorderLayout());
        add("Center", border);
    }
    public boolean mouseUp(Event event, int x, int y) {
        card.next(cardPanel);
        return true;
    }
}
```

The FlowLayout Layout Manager

FlowLayout simply shoves in components, left to right, top to bottom. Like
BorderLayout, it is a basic layout that is handy in a variety of layout situations.
Figure 7-7 shows how FlowLayout positions components when a window has
been resized.

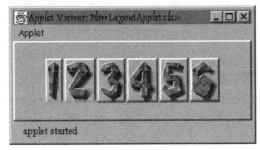

Figure 7-7 FlowLayout in Action

Example 7-5 shows the FlowLayoutApplet code.

Example 7-5 FlowLayoutApplet **Class Source Code**

```java
import java.net.URL;
import java.applet.Applet;
import java.awt.*;
import gjt.ImageButton;

public class FlowLayoutApplet extends Applet {
    private ImageButton one, two, three, four, five, six;
```

```
public void init() {
    URL            cb = getCodeBase();
    Panel          panel   = new Panel();
    TenPixelBorder border  = new TenPixelBorder(panel);

    one   = new ImageButton(getImage(cb, "gifs/one.gif"));
    two   = new ImageButton(getImage(cb, "gifs/two.gif"));
    three = new ImageButton(getImage(cb, "gifs/three.gif"));
    four  = new ImageButton(getImage(cb, "gifs/four.gif"));
    five  = new ImageButton(getImage(cb, "gifs/five.gif"));
    six   = new ImageButton(getImage(cb, "gifs/six.gif"));

    panel.setLayout(new FlowLayout());
    panel.add(one);
    panel.add(five);
    panel.add(two);
    panel.add(three);
    panel.add(four);
    panel.add(five);
    panel.add(six);

    setLayout(new BorderLayout());
    add("Center", border);
    }
}
```

FlowLayout is handy when you have a fixed-size component and you wish to lay out components in either a row or a column.

The GridLayout Layout Manager

GridLayout, as you might guess, lays out components in a grid; clients can set the gap between components and the number of rows and columns at construction time (and *only* at construction time). GridLayout is obviously useful when you want to lay out components in applets such as spreadsheets or calendars. Figure 7-8 shows output from an applet with ImageButton components positioned by GridLayout.

Figure 7-8 GridLayout in Action

Example 7-6 shows the GridLayoutApplet code. Notice that the applet explicitly sets the number of rows and columns in the call to the GridLayout constructor. The applet also sets the horizontal and vertical gaps between the components (image buttons) to ten pixels.

Example 7-6 GridLayoutApplet **Class Source Code**

```
import java.net.URL;
import java.applet.Applet;
import java.awt.*;
import gjt.ImageButton;
import gjt.StickyImageButtonController;

public class GridLayoutApplet extends Applet {
  private ImageButton one, two, three, four, five, six,
                      seven, eight, nine, ten;

  public void init() {
      URL            cb   = getCodeBase();
      Panel          buttonPanel = new Panel();
      TenPixelBorder border = new TenPixelBorder(buttonPanel);
```

```
one   = new ImageButton(getImage(cb, "gifs/one.gif"));
two   = new ImageButton(getImage(cb, "gifs/two.gif"));
three = new ImageButton(getImage(cb, "gifs/three.gif"));
four  = new ImageButton(getImage(cb, "gifs/four.gif"));
five  = new ImageButton(getImage(cb, "gifs/five.gif"));
six   = new ImageButton(getImage(cb, "gifs/six.gif"));
seven = new ImageButton(getImage(cb, "gifs/seven.gif"));
eight = new ImageButton(getImage(cb, "gifs/eight.gif"));
nine  = new ImageButton(getImage(cb, "gifs/nine.gif"));
ten   = new ImageButton(getImage(cb, "gifs/ten.gif"));

buttonPanel.setLayout(new GridLayout(3,2,10,10));
buttonPanel.add(one);
buttonPanel.add(two);
buttonPanel.add(three);
buttonPanel.add(four);
buttonPanel.add(five);
buttonPanel.add(six);
buttonPanel.add(seven);
buttonPanel.add(eight);
buttonPanel.add(nine);
buttonPanel.add(ten);

setLayout(new BorderLayout());
add("Center", border);
    }
}
```

The GridBagLayout Layout Manager

Like GridLayout, the GridBagLayout layout manager positions components in a grid. Unlike GridLayout, in which you explicitly specify the number of rows and columns in the grid, GridBaglayout implicitly determines the number of rows and columns.

GridBagLayout is capable of handling nearly any layout situation; however, it is one of the most complex and difficult classes in the AWT to use. Users are often put off by its complexity, but it's an extremely useful layout manager. For that reason, we'll spend some time demystifying GridBagLayout.

GridBagLayout and GridBagConstraints

GridBagLayout allows its clients to specify many parameters concerning exactly how each component is positioned within its grid cell; this involves the assistance of another class: GridBagConstraints.

GridBagLayout is unique among the other AWT layout managers in this regard. Using the other layout managers only requires you to call setLayout() to set the layout manager and then add components to the container. Using

GridBaglayout requires you to set the *constraints* for each of the components to be laid out. Think of constraints as guidelines for the layout manager to use in positioning each component in a *grid cell*. GridBagLayout uses these constraints as it implicitly determines the number of rows and columns necessary to position and size its components.

GridBagConstraints provides a variety of instance variables and constants used by GridBagLayout in positioning and sizing a component within a container. Table 7-6 shows these variables and constant values.

Table 7-6 GridBagConstraints **Instance Variables and Valid Values**

Instance Variable	Default Value	Valid Values	Specifies...
anchor	CENTER	CENTER EAST NORTH NORTHEAST NORTHWEST SOUTH SOUTHEAST SOUTHWEST WEST	Where to anchor a component in its grid when the component is smaller than its grid cells.
fill	NONE	BOTH HORIZONTAL NONE VERTICAL	Direction in which component should fill extra space.
gridx gridy	RELATIVE	RELATIVE or integer values representing x,y position in the grid.	Grid position of the component.
gridwidth gridheight	1 1	RELATIVE REMAINDER or integer values representing the width and height in the grid.	Width and height of the component in grid cells.
ipadx ipady	0	Integer values representing number of pixels.	Space to be added on each side of the component.
insets	insets(0,0, 0,0);	Values specified in a call to the insets() method.	Margins to be added to the inside edge of a container.
weightx weighty	0	Integer values representing number of grid cells.	How extra space is consumed by the component's grid cell.

To illustrate use of `GridBagLayout` and `GridBagConstraints`, let's take a look at an example. Figure 7-9 shows an applet that uses a `GridBagLayout` to lay out its components.

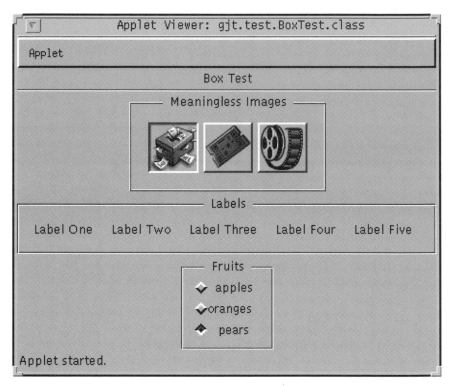

Figure 7-9 An Applet That Uses a `GridBagLayout`
The `gjt.Box` unit test shows the `GridBagLayout` positioning three separate boxes within a container. Each box also uses an instance of `GridBagLayout` to position and size components within the box.

The Graphic Java Toolkit `Box` implementation is almost entirely an exercise in the usage of `GridBagLayout`, so we'll discuss its implementation here. UI toolkits frequently have something similar to the `gjt.Box` class to group a logical collection of widgets that perform a related function. (Various windowing systems refer to classes that serve this function by other names. For instance, Motif calls this a Frame.)

Table 7-7 shows the responsibilities for the gjt.Box class.

Table 7-7 gjt.Box **Responsibilities**

Methods	Description
void etchedIn()	Sets the etching value to Etching.IN.
void etchedOut()	Sets the etching value to Etching.OUT.
void paint(Graphics g)	Paints the etched border and title string.
void resize(int w, int h)	Resizes the box according to the new dimensions.
void reshape(int x, int y, int w, int h)	Positions the box and reshapes it according to the new size and location.

The gjt.Box implementation is simple, so we'll show it here and then highlight its use of GridBagLayout. Notice in Example 7-7 that the gjt.Box class extends Panel. A gjt.Box has two constructors, each taking a Component as an argument. Also, when you're looking through the code, note that gjt.Box overrides the paint() method in order to paint an etched rectangle.

Example 7-7 gjt.Box **Class Source Code**

```
package gjt;

import java.awt.*;

public class Box extends Panel {
  private EtchedRectangle box = new EtchedRectangle(this);
  private Label          titleLabel;

  public Box(Component surrounded, String title) {
      this(surrounded, new Label(title, Label.CENTER));
  }
  public Box(Component surrounded, Label label) {
      Assert.notNull(surrounded);
      Assert.notNull(label);

      titleLabel = label;

      GridBagLayout      gbl = new GridBagLayout();
      GridBagConstraints gbc = new GridBagConstraints();

      setLayout(gbl);
      gbc.gridwidth = GridBagConstraints.REMAINDER;
      gbc.anchor    = GridBagConstraints.NORTH;
      gbl.setConstraints(titleLabel, gbc);
```

```
        add(titleLabel);

        gbc.insets  = new Insets(0,10,10,10);
        gbc.anchor  = GridBagConstraints.CENTER;
        gbc.weighty = 1.0;
        gbc.weightx = 1.0;
        gbc.fill    = GridBagConstraints.BOTH;
        gbl.setConstraints(surrounded,gbc);
        add(surrounded);
    }
    public void etchedIn ()            { box.etchedIn (); }
    public void etchedOut()            { box.etchedOut(); }
    public void paint     (Graphics g) { box.paint();     }

    public void resize(int w, int h) {
        reshape(location().x, location().y, w, h);
    }
    public void reshape(int x, int y, int w, int h) {
        super.reshape(x,y,w,h);

        FontMetrics fm   = titleLabel.getFontMetrics(
                                titleLabel.getFont());
        int         top  = insets().top + fm.getAscent();
        Dimension   size = size();

        box.reshape(0, top, size.width-1, size.height-top-1);
    }
    protected String paramString() {
        return super.paramString() + ",etching=" +
        (box.isEtchedIn() ? Etching.IN : Etching.OUT) +
        ",title=" + titleLabel;
    }
}
```

The second of the `gjt.Box` constructors has the code pertinent to
`GridBagLayout`, including our first use of `GridBagConstraints`. Having
seen Table 7-6, let's look at the `gjt.Box` constructor again and make some sense
of it:

```
    public Box(Component surrounded, Label label) {
        Assert.notNull(surrounded);
        Assert.notNull(label);

        titleLabel = label;

❶       GridBagLayout      gbl = new GridBagLayout();
❷       GridBagConstraints gbc = new GridBagConstraints();
```

```
❸          setLayout(gbl);
           gbc.gridwidth = GridBagConstraints.REMAINDER;
           gbc.anchor    = GridBagConstraints.NORTH;
           gbl.setConstraints(titleLabel, gbc);
           add(titleLabel);

           gbc.insets  = new Insets(0,10,10,10);
           gbc.anchor  = GridBagConstraints.CENTER;
           gbc.weighty = 1.0;
           gbc.weightx = 1.0;
           gbc.fill    = GridBagConstraints.BOTH;
           gbl.setConstraints(surrounded,gbc);
           add(surrounded);
       }
```

In lines ❶ and ❷, we create instances of GridBagLayout and
GridBagConstraints, respectively. The setLayout() call in line ❸ then sets
the GridBagLayout as the layout manager for the Box. The remaining lines set
GridBagConstraints instance variables for the layout manager to use. We'll
talk about each of the remaining lines in this constructor in smaller units to
more completely illustrate how they work.

First, let's look at the line that sets the gridwidth to be used in laying out the
Label component:

```
gbc.gridwidth = GridBagConstraints.REMAINDER;
```

gridwidth is often specified as REMAINDER. This indicates that this component
owns the remainder of the space available in the row, which means that the
component will be the last in its row [6]. The next component added to the
container will be positioned in the next row. In the case of the gjt.Box class, we
want the titleLabel grid cell to take up the remaining space in its row. Setting
gridwidth to REMAINDER ensures that the next component is positioned below
it.

The next setting specifies the anchor location of the titleLabel:

```
gbc.anchor    = GridBagConstraints.NORTH;
```

This ensures that when a box is resized, the titleLabel component stays
positioned in the north (that's the *constraint* placed on its anchor). You can anchor
a component to any of the compass points or in the center of the component's grid
cell. Specifying North as the anchor point centers the component in its grid cell:

---

6.   Similarly, a value of REMAINDER for gridheight indicates that the component is
     the last component in its *column*.

NORTHWEST and NORTHEAST left-justify and right-justify the component, respectively. (Refer to Table 7-6 on page 179 for a list of constraints and their valid values.)

Next, we set the constraints and add titleLabel to the container. The call to setConstraints() is where GridBagLayout is passed the GridBagConstraints values we've set.

```
gbl.setConstraints(titleLabel, c);
add(titleLabel);
```

So far, here's what we've set with GridBagConstraints:

- gridwidth to REMAINDER, ensuring the next component will be positioned below the current component

- anchor position to NORTH

The call to setConstraints() makes those constraints available to the layout manager. At this point, the layout manager is capable of positioning the label centered in the north position, like this:

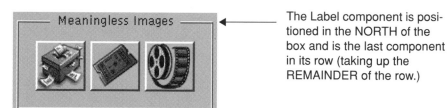

The Label component is positioned in the NORTH of the box and is the last component in its row (taking up the REMAINDER of the row.)

The next set of GridBagConstraints values establishes constraints for the next component. First, the GridBagConstraint.insets member is set to the newly created Insets. The integer arguments to the Insets() method specify the top, left, bottom, and right insets, in that order.

```
gbc.insets  = new Insets(0,10,10,10);
```

AWT Tip

GridBagConstraints Insets Are Different From Container Insets

Whereas insets values for a Container represent the inside border of the container, GridBagConstraints insets values represent a margin around the outside of a component. To reiterate, Container insets define margins around the inside of the container, while GridBagLayout insets define margins around the outside of the component. This is evident in the Box class; the GridBagConstraints insets are assigned to the component, not its container.

Next, the `anchor` position is set to the CENTER of the container. (Note that up to this point, `gridwidth` is still set to REMAINDER and `anchor` is still set to NORTH.) We modify the `anchor` because we want the title to be positioned in the north but the component to be centered in the box:

```
gbc.anchor  = GridBagConstraints.CENTER;
```

The `weight.x` and `weight.y` values are set to 1.0, meaning that the component will consume 100 percent of the available space when the container is enlarged:

```
gbc.weighty = 1.0;
gbc.weightx = 1.0;
```

The constructor then sets the `fill` variable to BOTH:

```
gbc.fill    = GridBagConstraints.BOTH;
```

This means that the `surrounded` component will fill in both directions. If the box is enlarged, this component will fill the entire box horizontally and vertically, minus the area specified by the insets. No matter what the size of the box, the component inside the box always has a margin between it and the inside border of the container. The component is always 20 pixels less in width than the box and 10 pixels less in height than the box. (Because the component is centered in the box, we don't need to put an inset space on the top.) Any component placed in a box will always have these inset margins, which look like this:

Insets(0,10,10,10)

10 pixel inset on the left.

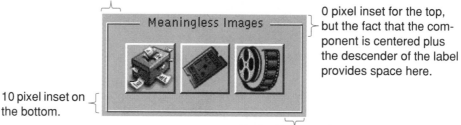

0 pixel inset for the top, but the fact that the component is centered plus the descender of the label provides space here.

10 pixel inset on the bottom.

10 pixel inset on the right.

The constraint values are set for the (surrounded) component by virtue of the call to setConstraints()

```
gbl.setConstraints(surrounded,c);
add(surrounded);
```

Notice that we're still using the same instance of GridBagConstraints previously used. For every call to setConstraints(), GridBagLayout makes copies of the GridBagConstraints variable values; therefore, we can reuse the same GridBagConstraints to specify constraints for multiple components. We can continue modifying variables in the same GridBagConstraints object without affecting the titleLabel positioning we've already established.

gjt.Box Unit Test

Each component in the Graphic Java Toolkit has a unit test. We've already seen the applet that exercises the gjt.Box class on page 180. It just so happens that the BoxTest applet also uses GridBagLayout in order to position three boxes (named iconbox, labelbox, and checkboxbox) in the container. Let's take a look at the unit test for gjt.Box in Figure 7-10 and see how the three boxes are positioned and sized when the applet is resized.

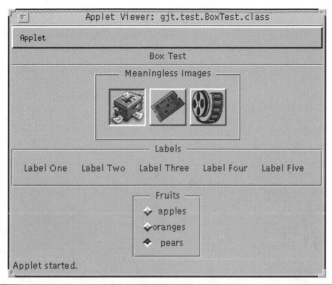

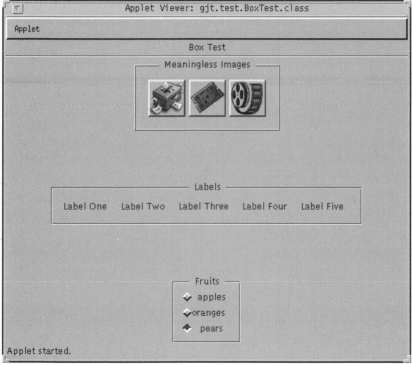

Figure 7-10 A GridBagLayout Applet Resized
The BoxTest applet shows how the layout manager positions the
boxes when the window is resized.

When the applet is resized, the three boxes remain centered horizontally and hold their respective anchor positions vertically. No matter how the applet is resized, the three boxes are always centered horizontally. In the vertical direction, the iconbox stays in the north, the checkboxbox stays in the south, and the labelbox stays centered. Using GridBagLayout, we achieve this layout effect in only a few lines of code (which emphasizes the power of this most maligned of the AWT layout managers). Here's the set of GridBagConstraints parameters that defines this behavior:

```
        GridBagLayout        gbl = new GridBagLayout();
        GridBagConstraints gbc = new GridBagConstraints();

        setLayout(gbl);
        gbc.anchor     = GridBagConstraints.NORTH;
❶       gbc.gridwidth = GridBagConstraints.REMAINDER;
❷       gbc.weighty    = 0.50;
        gbl.setConstraints(iconbox,   gbc);
        add(iconbox);
        gbl.setConstraints(labelbox, gbc);
        add(labelbox);

❸       gbc.anchor     = GridBagConstraints.SOUTH;
❹       gbc.weighty    = 0;
        gbl.setConstraints(checkboxbox, gbc);
        add(checkboxbox);
    }
```

Notice that just like the gjt.Box, gjt.test.BoxTest creates an instance of GridBagLayout and an instance of GridBagConstraints. It also sets a series of constraints and calls setConstraints() for each component so that GridBagLayout has access to those constraint values.

Both iconbox and labelbox use exactly the same constraints. Setting their gridwidth to REMAINDER in line ❶ ensures that the next component added is positioned below the previous component. This results in the labelbox being positioned below the iconbox.

Again, note that GridBagLayout copies constraints so that the same constraints object can be used for more than one component.

The weighty 0.50 setting in line ❷ controls vertical space taken up by the grid cells when the container is resized. It causes the *grid cell* to take up half of the extra space in the vertical direction. Note that the boxes themselves do not take up half of the extra space, but the grid cells in which they reside get the extra space

AWT Tip

Don't Confuse Resizing the Grid Cell With Resizing the Component

There's a common misconception that when GridBagLayout repositions components after the container has been resized, the component is resized to fill available space, as set in the weightx and weighty constraints. The components themselves do not resize to consume that extra space; the grid cells in which the components reside do. (You can see this behavior by running the BoxTest applet and resizing it.) In order to get the component itself to consume the extra space, set GridBagConstraints.fill to BOTH.

Lines ❸ and ❹ set the constraints for the checkbox. It is anchored to the south, so when the window is resized, it will always be positioned in the south. Its weighty is 0.0, so there will never be any extra space beneath it.

Now that we've covered the specific layout portion of the gjt.test.BoxTest, let's look at the entire class in Example 7-8. Notice that this class uses two other classes from the Graphic Java Toolkit: gjt.ExclusiveImageButtonPanel and gjt.Orientation. You'll also notice that gjt.test.BoxTest extends our standard UnitTest class, which provides a steady framework for printing a title at the top and displaying a component in the Panel below the title.

Example 7-8 gjt.test.BoxTest **Class Source Code**

```
package gjt.test;

import java.applet.Applet;
import java.awt.*;
import gjt.Box;
import gjt.ExclusiveImageButtonPanel;
import gjt.Orientation;

public class BoxTest extends UnitTest {
  public String title() {
      return "Box Test";
  }
  public Panel centerPanel() {
      return new BoxTestPanel(this);
  }
}

class BoxTestPanel extends Panel {
  private Applet applet;
  private Box     iconbox, labelbox, checkboxbox;
  private Panel  panelInLabelbox    = new Panel();
```

```java
        private Panel   panelInCheckboxbox = new Panel();
        private ExclusiveImageButtonPanel panelInIconbox;

    public BoxTestPanel(Applet applet) {
        GridBagLayout       gbl = new GridBagLayout();
        GridBagConstraints gbc = new GridBagConstraints();

        this.applet     = applet;
        panelInIconbox = new ExclusiveImageButtonPanel(
                            Orientation.HORIZONTAL);

        populateIconPanel     ();
        populateLabelPanel     ();
        populateCheckboxPanel();

        iconbox     = new Box(panelInIconbox,
                            "Meaningless Images");
        labelbox     = new Box(panelInLabelbox,     "Labels");
        checkboxbox = new Box(panelInCheckboxbox, "Fruits");
        iconbox.etchedOut();

        setLayout(gbl);
        gbc.anchor     = GridBagConstraints.NORTH;
        gbc.gridwidth = GridBagConstraints.REMAINDER;
        gbc.weighty     = 0.50;
        gbl.setConstraints(iconbox,  gbc);
        add(iconbox);
        gbl.setConstraints(labelbox, gbc);
        add(labelbox);

        gbc.anchor     = GridBagConstraints.SOUTH;
        gbc.weighty     = 0;
        gbl.setConstraints(panelInCheckboxbox, gbc);
        add(checkboxbox);
    }
    private void populateIconPanel() {
        Image ballot, film, ticket;

        ballot  = applet.getImage(applet.getCodeBase(),
                            "gifs/ballot_box.gif");
        ticket  = applet.getImage(applet.getCodeBase(),
                            "gifs/movie_ticket.gif");
        film     = applet.getImage(applet.getCodeBase(),
                            "gifs/filmstrip.gif");

        panelInIconbox.add(ballot);
        panelInIconbox.add(ticket);
        panelInIconbox.add(film);
    }
```

```
    private void populateLabelPanel() {
        panelInLabelbox.add(new Label("Label One"));
        panelInLabelbox.add(new Label("Label Two"));
        panelInLabelbox.add(new Label("Label Three"));
        panelInLabelbox.add(new Label("Label Four"));
        panelInLabelbox.add(new Label("Label Five"));
    }
    private void populateCheckboxPanel() {
        CheckboxGroup group = new CheckboxGroup();

        panelInCheckboxbox.setLayout(new GridLayout(3,0));
        panelInCheckboxbox.add(new Checkbox("apples",
                                    group, false));
        panelInCheckboxbox.add(new Checkbox("oranges",
                                    group, false));
        panelInCheckboxbox.add(new Checkbox("pears",
                                    group, true));

    }
}
```

Laying Out Components in Nested Panels

A `Container` can contain components, and, fortunately for all involved, the
AWT designers chose to make `Container` an extension of `Component`. What
this means, of course, is that containers can contain not only components, but also
other containers, since a `Container` is a `Component`. (This is an implementation
of a design pattern known as *composite*. [7])

This crucial ability—to nest containers inside of one another—is a necessity if we
are to design screens of much complexity for use in applets. Attempting to lay out
a complicated screenful of containers with a single layout manager is usually an
exercise in futility, no matter which layout manager you choose for the job.

Although we can give you some guidelines to follow, designing nested panels is
something that is best learned by experimenting with different layout managers
and layout situations. In *The Graphic Java Toolkit—Extending the AWT*, we will
explore designing nested panels in nearly every chapter; for now we'll take a look
at a single contrived example—an applet that allows you to vary the settings of a
`GridLayout`.

`GridLabApplet` displays a grid of `gjt.ImageButton` objects. This applet
includes controls for setting the number of rows and columns and for setting the
vertical and horizontal gaps between those buttons. Figure 7-11 shows a picture of
`GridLabApplet` in action.

7.   See.Gamma, Helm, Johnson, Vlissides. *Design Patterns*, p. 163. Addison-Wesley

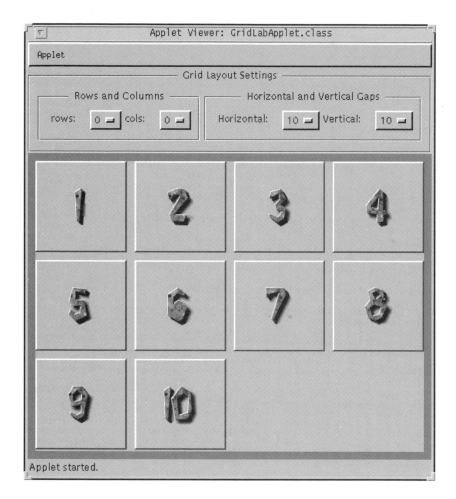

Figure 7-11 Nested Panels in an Applet
The GridLabApplet includes several layers of panels.

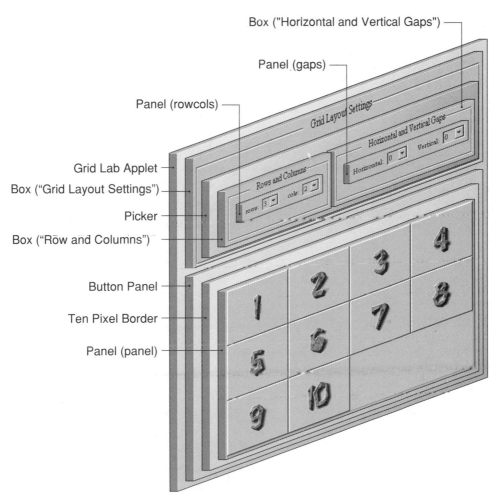

Figure 7-12 Nested Panel Layout Diagram

This applet is layered a little bit like an onion with its multiple layers, so we'll refer both to the diagram above and to appropriate sections of the GridLabApplet code to describe how the applet is assembled.

GridLabApplet sets its layout manager to a BorderLayout. The north component is a gjt.Box from the Graphic Java Toolkit. In the code, the north component is set like this:

```
add("North",  new Box(picker, "Grid Layout Settings"));
```

The gjt.Box, which uses GridBagLayout, surrounds a Panel component named Picker. The constructor for the Picker class creates two more instances of Panel, one for the Row/Column and one for the Horizontal/Vertical gaps.

```
public Picker(ButtonPanel buttonPanel) {
   Panel rowCols = new Panel();
   Panel gaps    = new Panel();
      .
      .
      .
❶  add(new Box(rowCols, "Rows and Columns"));
❷  add(new Box(gaps,    "Horizontal and Vertical Gaps"));
```

The rowCols and gaps panels are added to the Picker panel, but first they're wrapped in boxes, in lines ❶ and ❷. (Recall that a gjt.Box essentially *surrounds* a component, which in this example is an instance of Panel.)

All of this results in the components in the "Grid Layout Settings" Box being laid out like so:

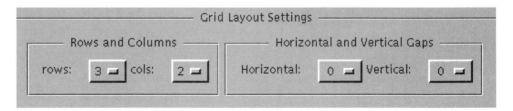

Now, in the center of the `GridLabApplet`, we add a `Button Panel`:

```
add("Center", buttonPanel);
```

The `ButtonPanel` class creates an instance of `Panel` and an instance of `TenPixelBorder`:

```
private Panel          panel  = new Panel();
private TenPixelBorder border = new TenPixelBorder(panel);
```

As we have discussed previously, `TenPixelBorder` employs a `BorderLayout` to center the component it is passed and draws a gray border ten pixels thick around the component.

The `panel` passed to the `border` is the one that holds the buttons that will be positioned in a grid. First, several `gjt.ImageButton` variables are declared:

```
private ImageButton   one, two, three, four, five,
                      six, seven, eight, nine, ten;
```

The `ButtonPanel` constructor then creates instances of `gjt.ImageButton`, adds them to the `panel`, and sets the layout manager for the `panel` to an instance of `GridLayout`:

```
public ButtonPanel(Applet applet) {
    URL cb = applet.getCodeBase();

    one   = new ImageButton(applet.getImage(
                              cb, "gifs/one.gif"));
    two   = new ImageButton(applet.getImage(
                              cb, "gifs/two.gif"));
    three = new ImageButton(applet.getImage(
                              cb, "gifs/three.gif"));
        .
        .
        .
    panel.setLayout(new GridLayout(3,2));
    panel.add(one);   panel.add(two);   panel.add(three);
    panel.add(four);  panel.add(five);  panel.add(six);
    panel.add(seven); panel.add(eight); panel.add(nine);
    panel.add(ten);

    setLayout(new BorderLayout());
    add        ("Center", border);
}
```

Notice that at the end of this constructor we add `border`, which is our
`TenPixelBorder` instance, to the center of the `ButtonPanel`. The
`ButtonPanel` is centered beneath the north component and looks like this:

Communication Among Nested Panels

In applets with multiple nested panels, actions that occur in one panel may
require a layout manager to reposition and resize components in other panels.
That's certainly true in our `GridLabApplet`. When a user selects from the "Rows
and Columns" or "Gaps" `Choice` components, the `ButtonPanel` needs to
update accordingly. For example, look at the buttons in Figure 7-13.

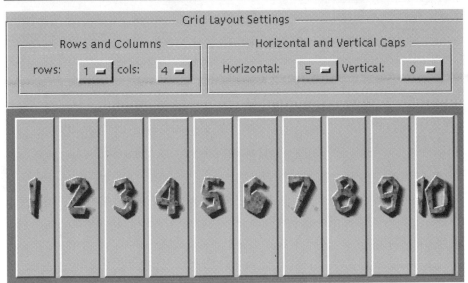

Figure 7-13 Nested Panel Updates

The ButtonPanel updates when selections are made in the Picker panel. In this case, the bottom picture shows the ButtonPanel updated with one row specified and a horizontal gap of 5. (Note that once the number of rows has been set, the columns button value does not update because GridLayout does not provide any means for determining its settings.)

To force `ButtonPanel` to lay out its components, we have to do a few things. First of all, we have to make sure that if a choice is selected, the `Picker` panel has access to the `ButtonPanel`. To accomplish that, we pass in an instance of `ButtonPanel` in the `Picker` constructor:

```
public Picker(ButtonPanel buttonPanel) {
```

Also, we need to make sense of the selection that was made. That happens in the applet's `action()` method:

```
public boolean action(Event event, Object what) {
    int numRows=0, numCols=0, hgap=0, vgap=0;

    numRows =
    (new Integer(rowChoice.getSelectedItem())).intValue();
    numCols =
    (new Integer(colChoice.getSelectedItem())).intValue();
    hgap    =
    (new Integer(hchoice.getSelectedItem())).intValue();
    vgap    =
    (new Integer(vchoice.getSelectedItem())).intValue();

    buttonPanel.updateLayout(numRows, numCols, hgap, vgap);
    return true;
}
```

The `action()` method extracts integer values from the four `Choice` objects it contains, like so:

```
hgap    =
(new Integer(hchoice.getSelectedItem())).intValue();
```

In this line,

- The `getSelectedItem()` from the `Choice` class returns a character string.

- The `Integer` class takes a `String` as an argument and constructs an `Integer` object.

- The `Integer` `intValue()` method returns the primitive data type integer value (as opposed to an `Integer` object).

- The integer value is then assigned to one of the four respective variables for rows, columns, horizontal gap, and vertical gap.

Once we've extracted the integer values, we pass them to the `ButtonPanel` `updateLayout()` method:

```
public void updateLayout(int rows, int cols,
                         int hgap, int vgap) {
```

```
        try {
❶          panel.setLayout(new GridLayout(rows,cols,hgap,vgap));
❷          border.validate();
        }
        catch(IllegalArgumentException e) {
            MessageDialog d = MessageDialog.getMessageDialog(
              Util.getFrame(this),
              (DialogClient)this,
              "Error",
              "Row: 0  Col: 0 is an illegal combination");

            d.pack();
            d.show();
        }
    }
```

There are a few things in particular to point out about updateLayout(). In line ❶, note that it creates a new GridLayout with the parameters we've extracted from the selections in the Picker panel. Creating a new GridLayout is required because you're not allowed to change the number of rows and columns in a GridLayout after construction. When the new GridLayout is set as the ButtonPanel layout manager, the previous GridLayout is discarded and cleaned up by the Java garbage collector.[8]

We should point out an important side effect from calling setLayout() (line ❶) for a Panel: it *invalidates* the panel. A panel is considered invalid anytime it has been changed and needs to be laid out again.

In line ❷, we call the validate() method for the border, which is the parent container of panel. The Container.validate() method checks whether the components contained in the container are valid or invalid. If any of them are invalid, their layout() method is invoked.

By calling setLayout(), we implicitly invalidate panel. By invoking validate() for the border (which is the panel container), we force panel to be laid out. Doing so reshapes and redisplays all of the components it contains.

Note that there are number of Component and Container methods that implicitly invalidate a container—the Component methods invalidate the component's container. These are listed in Table 7-8.

8.   A number of Java books available from Prentice Hall/SunSoft Press discuss Java garbage collection.

Table 7-8 Component **and** Container **Methods That Invalidate Containers**

Methods
void Component.show()
void Component.hide()
void Component.reshape(int x, int y, int width, int height)
Component Container.add(Component, int pos)
Component Container.remove(Component, int pos)
void Container.setLayout(LayoutManager mg)

A container can be invalidated *explicitly* by invoking the invalidate() method.

AWT Tip

Forcing a Container To Be Laid Out

Sometimes it is necessary to force a container to be laid out (we will see another example of this in the *FontDialog* chapter). In order to force a layout, the container in question must be invalidated. A container can be invalidated either explicitly by calling the invalidate() method or implicitly by calling one of the methods in Table 7-8. After the container is invalidated, invoking validate() on the Container (or the Container's parent) results in the container being laid out.

GridLabApplet Implementation

Now let's look through the entire code for the GridLabApplet in Example 7-9. Although the main focus in this applet is how it's composed of nested panels and how it employs layout managers in the respective panels, also note that it uses a few of the custom components from the Graphic Java Toolkit, including the gjt.Box, gjt.MessageDialog, gjt.DialogClient, gjt.ImageButton, and the gjt.Util classes. As you look through the code, refer to Figure 7-11 on page 192 and the two primary panels. One is called Picker; it is the north component of the applet and contains gjt.Box, Panel, Label, and Choice components. The other is called ButtonPanel; it is centered beneath Picker and contains a TenPixelBorder which (ultimately) contains the image buttons displayed in a grid.

Example 7-9 GridLabApplet **Class Source Code**

```java
import java.applet.Applet;
import java.net.URL;
import java.awt.*;
import gjt.Box;
import gjt.DialogClient;
import gjt.ImageButton;
import gjt.MessageDialog;
import gjt.Util;

public class GridLabApplet extends Applet {
  public void init() {
      ButtonPanel buttonPanel = new ButtonPanel(this);
      Picker        picker     = new Picker(buttonPanel);

      setLayout(new BorderLayout());
      add("North",  new Box(picker, "Grid Layout Settings"));
      add("Center", buttonPanel);
  }
}

class ButtonPanel extends Panel implements DialogClient {
  private ImageButton     one, two, three, four, five,
                          six, seven, eight, nine, ten;

  private Panel          panel  = new Panel();
  private TenPixelBorder border = new TenPixelBorder(panel);

  public ButtonPanel(Applet applet) {
      URL cb = applet.getCodeBase();

      one   = new ImageButton(applet.getImage(
                              cb, "gifs/one.gif"));
      two   = new ImageButton(applet.getImage(
                              cb, "gifs/two.gif"));
      three = new ImageButton(applet.getImage(
                              cb, "gifs/three.gif"));
      four  = new ImageButton(applet.getImage(
                              cb, "gifs/four.gif"));
      five  = new ImageButton(applet.getImage(
                              cb, "gifs/five.gif"));
      six   = new ImageButton(applet.getImage(
                              cb, "gifs/six.gif"));
      seven = new ImageButton(applet.getImage(
                              cb, "gifs/seven.gif"));
      eight = new ImageButton(applet.getImage(
                              cb, "gifs/eight.gif"));
```

```
        nine  = new ImageButton(applet.getImage(
                                  cb, "gifs/nine.gif"));
        ten   = new ImageButton(applet.getImage(
                                  cb, "gifs/ten.gif"));

        panel.setLayout(new GridLayout(3,2));
        panel.add(one);   panel.add(two);   panel.add(three);
        panel.add(four);  panel.add(five);  panel.add(six);
        panel.add(seven); panel.add(eight); panel.add(nine);
        panel.add(ten);

        setLayout(new BorderLayout());
        add       ("Center", border);
   }
   public void updateLayout(int rows, int cols,
                            int hgap, int vgap) {
  try {
        panel.setLayout(new GridLayout(rows,cols,hgap,vgap));
        border.validate();
     }
     catch(IllegalArgumentException e) {
        MessageDialog d = MessageDialog.getMessageDialog(
           Util.getFrame(this),
           (DialogClient)this,
           "Error",
           "Row: 0  Col: 0 is an illegal combination");

        d.pack();
        d.show();
     }
  }
  public void dialogDismissed(Dialog d) { }
}

class Picker extends Panel {
  private Label  hgapLabel = new Label("Horizontal:");
  private Label  vgapLabel = new Label("Vertical:");
  private Label  rowLabel  = new Label("rows:");
  private Label  colLabel  = new Label("cols:");

  private Choice hchoice   = new Choice();
  private Choice vchoice   = new Choice();
  private Choice rowChoice = new Choice();
  private Choice colChoice = new Choice();

  private ButtonPanel buttonPanel;

  public Picker(ButtonPanel buttonPanel) {
```

```
        Panel rowCols = new Panel();
        Panel gaps    = new Panel();

        this.buttonPanel = buttonPanel;
        hchoice.addItem("0");
        hchoice.addItem("5");
        hchoice.addItem("10");
        hchoice.addItem("15");
        hchoice.addItem("20");

        vchoice.addItem("0");
        vchoice.addItem("5");
        vchoice.addItem("10");
        vchoice.addItem("15");
        vchoice.addItem("20");

        rowChoice.addItem("0");
        rowChoice.addItem("1");
        rowChoice.addItem("2");
        rowChoice.addItem("3");
        rowChoice.addItem("4");
        rowChoice.addItem("5");
        rowChoice.select (3);

        colChoice.addItem("0");
        colChoice.addItem("1");
        colChoice.addItem("2");
        colChoice.addItem("3");
        colChoice.addItem("4");
        colChoice.addItem("5");
        colChoice.select (2);

        rowCols.add(rowLabel);
        rowCols.add(rowChoice);
        rowCols.add(colLabel);
        rowCols.add(colChoice);

        gaps.add(hgapLabel);
        gaps.add(hchoice);
        gaps.add(vgapLabel);
        gaps.add(vchoice);

        add(new Box(rowCols, "Rows and Columns"));
        add(new Box(gaps,    "Horizontal and Vertical Gaps"));
}
public boolean action(Event event, Object what) {
        int numRows=0, numCols=0, hgap=0, vgap=0;
```

```
    numRows =
    (new Integer(rowChoice.getSelectedItem())).intValue();
    numCols =
    (new Integer(colChoice.getSelectedItem())).intValue();
    hgap    =
    (new Integer(hchoice.getSelectedItem())).intValue();
    vgap    =
    (new Integer(vchoice.getSelectedItem())).intValue();

    buttonPanel.updateLayout(numRows, numCols, hgap, vgap);
    return true;
  }
}
```

Custom Layout Managers

Although the AWT's standard layout managers are well equipped to handle most layout situations, there comes a time when they just won't do. You will also find that for certain types of layouts, it is simpler to use a custom layout manager that deals with an exact type of layout than it is to use one of the AWT's layout managers, even though one of them may suffice.

A custom layout manager involves implementing the LayoutManager interface, which is defined as:

```
void addLayoutComponent (String name, Component comp);
void removeLayoutComponent(Component comp);
Dimension preferredLayoutSize (Container parent);
Dimension minimumLayoutSize (Container parent);
void layoutContainer (Container parent);
```

We've discussed each of these methods in detail earlier in this chapter, so instead of rehashing the responsibilities of each method, let's take a look at some custom layout managers that implement them.

gjt.BulletinLayout

Upon hearing of layout managers, newcomers to the AWT often have an overwhelming compulsion to simply set their container's layout manager to null and explicitly position and size the components displayed in their container.

Almost without exception, such a strategy is ill-fated. A container with a null layout manager will not be able to cope with resize events. As soon as this discovery is made, the next step is to override resize() to reposition and reshape the components laid out in the container. Once things have degenerated to this point, all of the benefits of the strategy pattern (see the *ImageButton and StateButton* chapter for more discussion of the strategy pattern) go down the tubes. The algorithm for laying out components becomes hardcoded in the container, and therefore the container cannot easily change its layout strategy. Furthermore, once the layout strategy is hardcoded into the container, it is not available for others to use.

Usually, such object-oriented backsliding is prompted by the need for a simple layout strategy that merely moves components to their specified location and reshapes them to their preferred size. The Graphic Java Toolkit encapsulates such a strategy in a simple layout manager: the `gjt.BulletinLayout`, which lays out components as though they were on a bulletin board—components are positioned according to their location and reshaped according to their preferred size.

`gjt.BulletinLayout` is a simple custom layout manager that will serve as our first foray into implementing custom layout managers. Example 7-10 shows its implementation. Notice that `BulletinLayout` implements `addLayoutComponent()` and `removeLayoutComponent()` as no-ops, which indicates that it does not keep track of a finite set of components to lay out. Instead, it lays out all the components it finds in the container it is currently laying out.

Also note that `BulletinLayout` implements `preferredLayoutSize()` and `minimumLayoutSize()` to simply return the union of all the preferred and minimum sizes for all the visible components. These two methods invoke a number of container methods, such as `insets()`, `countComponents()`, and `getComponent()`, that are routinely used by layout managers.

`BulletinLayout` implements the required `layoutContainer()`, which operates on all visible components and reshapes them so that they reside at their specified location and are resized according to their preferred sizes.

Example 7-10 `gjt.BulletinLayout` **Class Source Code**

```
package gjt;

import java.awt.*;

public class BulletinLayout implements LayoutManager {
  public BulletinLayout() {
  }
  public void addLayoutComponent(String name, Component comp) {
  }
  public void removeLayoutComponent(Component comp) {
  }
  public Dimension preferredLayoutSize(Container target) {
```

CD-Rom

```
            Insets    insets      = target.insets();
            Dimension dim         = new Dimension(0,0);
            int       ncomponents = target.countComponents();
            Component comp;
            Dimension d;
            Rectangle preferredBounds = new Rectangle(0,0);
            Rectangle compPreferredBounds;

            for (int i = 0 ; i < ncomponents ; i++) {
                comp = target.getComponent(i);

                if(comp.isVisible()) {
                    d = comp.preferredSize();
                    compPreferredBounds =
                        new Rectangle(comp.location());
                    compPreferredBounds.width  = d.width;
                    compPreferredBounds.height = d.height;

                    preferredBounds =
                        preferredBounds.union(compPreferredBounds);
                }
            }
            dim.width  += insets.left + insets.right;
            dim.height += insets.top + insets.bottom;

            return dim;
        }
    public Dimension minimumLayoutSize(Container target) {
            Insets    insets      = target.insets();
            Dimension dim         = new Dimension(0,0);
            int       ncomponents = target.countComponents();
            Component comp;
            Dimension d;
            Rectangle minimumBounds = new Rectangle(0,0);
            Rectangle compMinimumBounds;

            for (int i = 0 ; i < ncomponents ; i++) {
                comp = target.getComponent(i);

                if(comp.isVisible()) {
                    d = comp.minimumSize();
                    compMinimumBounds =
                        new Rectangle(comp.location());
                    compMinimumBounds.width  = d.width;
                    compMinimumBounds.height = d.height;
```

```
            minimumBounds =
                minimumBounds.union(compMinimumBounds);
        }
    }
    dim.width   += insets.left + insets.right;
    dim.height  += insets.top + insets.bottom;

    return dim;
}
public void layoutContainer(Container target) {
    Insets      insets       = target.insets();
    int         ncomponents = target.countComponents();
    Component comp;
    Dimension ps;
    Point loc;

    for (int i = 0 ; i < ncomponents ; i++) {
        comp = target.getComponent(i);

        if(comp.isVisible()) {
            ps  = comp.preferredSize();
            loc = comp.location();

            comp.reshape(insets.left + loc.x,
                         insets.top + loc.y,
                         ps.width, ps.height);
        }
    }
}
}
}
```

gjt.RowLayout

You might wonder why we need custom layout managers at all. After all, we've shown that the standard AWT layout managers are fairly comprehensive in what they can do and that the GridBagLayout layout manager is powerful enough to lay out almost anything. However, there are occasions when its simpler and more straightforward to encapsulate some layout functionality in a custom layout manager than it is to commit to memory the constraints necessary to manipulate GridBagLayout. In fact, our GridLabApplet offers a case in point. Look at Figure 7-14 and notice what happens to the Picker when the applet is resized horizontally to about half its starting size.

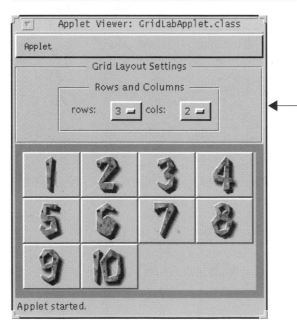

When resized to be smaller, FlowLayout places the "Gaps" box below the "Rows and Columns" panel where it is no longer visible.

Figure 7-14 `FlowLayout` Resize Behavior

The `Picker` panel does not have a layout manager explicitly set, so it is using the default layout manager for `Panel`, which is `FlowLayout`. From the output in Figure 7-14, it appears that `FlowLayout` is unable to position the "Gaps" box appropriately. Actually, `FlowLayout` has positioned it, but you can't see it. When the applet is resized small enough that there's no longer enough room to place another component to the right of the previous one, `FlowLayout` places the next component in the next row. In `GridLabApplet`, this is causing the "Gaps" box to be hidden, because `FlowLayout` doesn't care if the `Picker` panel is tall enough to display the "Gaps" box it has placed below the "Rows and Columns" box.

We want the buttons in the boxes displayed so that we can see them, even if both boxes don't entirely fit in the panel, so here's a case where the default layout manager is insufficient for the behavior we want. And although we could probably use `GridBagLayout` to accomplish the desired behavior, we want a more general purpose solution that won't require us to deal with a variety of constraints each and every time we want to employ it.

Additionally, there are times when you just want to lay out components in a row or column and be guaranteed that the components will stay aligned in their row or column, no matter what kind of resizing adversity comes their way. The Graphic Java Toolkit provides two such layout managers: `gjt.RowLayout` and `gjt.ColumnLayout`. We'll discuss their implementations and show their accompanying unit tests so that you can see them in action.

The `gjt.RowLayout` layout manager is useful for components such as toolbars that might contain image buttons displayed in a row. With `gjt.RowLayout`, the container with the image buttons is sure to *visibly* display all the image buttons when the container is reduced in size (unlike `FlowLayout` in the `GridLabApplet` in Figure 7-14.)

As its name suggests, `gjt.RowLayout` lays out components in a row. At construction time, a user of `gjt.RowLayout` can specify both the horizontal orientation and vertical orientation of the components to be positioned and sized, and a gap between components can also be set.

To start off, take a look at Table 7-9, which shows the responsibilities of the `gjt.RowLayout` class. You'll notice that these are the standard five methods that must be defined by any class that implements `LayoutManager`.

Table 7-9 gjt.RowLayout **Responsibilities**

Methods	Description
void addLayoutComponent(String name, Component comp)	Is a *no-op* implementation.
void removedLayoutComponent(Component comp)	Is a *no-op* implementation.
Dimension preferredLayoutSize(Container targert)	Returns the preferred container height and width for the layout manager.
Dimension minimumLayoutSize(Container targert)	Returns the minimum container height and width for the layout manager.
void layoutContainer(Container target)	Positions components in a container.

If you recall from our discussion in the section *Layout Managers and the Good Life* on page 159, the fact that this layout manager does not define an implementation for addLayoutComponent() and removeLayoutComponent() suggests that gjt.RowLayout does *not* live the good life. No-op implementations of these methods indicate that the layout manager is on call to lay out any container and an unknown number of components.

gjt.RowLayout is a fairly involved layout manager, so before looking at the entire source code for it, we'll highlight some details about its implementation. As described in Table 7-9, the gjt.RowLayout addLayoutComponent() and removeLayoutComponent() are no-op methods, so the implementations of the other methods from the LayoutManager interface reveal exactly how gjt.RowLayout works. We'll start with preferredLayoutSize():

```
    public Dimension preferredLayoutSize(Container target) {
❶        Insets     insets      = target.insets();
❷        Dimension  dim         = new Dimension(0,0);
         int        ncomponents = target.countComponents();
❸        Component  comp;
❹        Dimension  d;
```

preferredLayoutSize() returns the preferred width and height of the container passed in. Let's quickly go through some of these initial settings. Line ❶ obtains the insets for the container that gjt.RowLayout is going to lay out. In line ❷, the preferredLayoutSize() return value is initialized to 0,0. The Component in line ❸ is a reference to the next component to be positioned and sized in the container. The Dimension d variable in line ❹ is used to hold the preferred size of each component in the container.

Next, `preferredLayoutSize()` loops through the components in the container and calculates the return value.

```
        for (int i = 0 ; i < ncomponents ; i++) {
            comp = target.getComponent(i);

            if(comp.isVisible()) {
❶              d = comp.preferredSize();

❷              dim.width  += d.width;
❸              dim.height  = Math.max(d.height, dim.height);

❹              if(i > 0) dim.width += gap;
            }
        }
❺       dim.width  += insets.left + insets.right;
❻       dim.height += insets.top + insets.bottom;

        return dim;
    }
```

The `for` loop cycles through every component in the container. If the `component` is visible, then the component's `preferredSize()` is assigned to `d` in line ❶. As the method loops through each component in the container, the component's preferred width is added to `dim.width` in line ❷. The preferred width of the container will be equal to the sum of the widths of all visible components plus the gaps between them.

The `dim.height` calculated in line ❸ is going to end up being the maximum height of the tallest component in the row of components.

Line ❹ accounts for the gap between components. `i` is 0 the first time through the loop, so the gap is not added until the second time through the loop.

Line ❺ adds the left and right insets of the container to the preferred width and line ❻ adds the top and bottom insets of the container to the preferred height. This results in the final preferred width and height for a container using `gjt.RowLayout`.

The `minimumLayoutSize()` implementation is calculated exactly like the `preferredLayoutSize()` except that `Dimension d` holds the minimum size of each component in the container instead of the preferred size:

```
    d = comp.minimumSize();
```

Note that this method of looping through the container's components and doing some calculations is typically the way preferredLayoutSize() and minimumLayoutSize() are implemented. The algorithms for each method are often mirror images of each other, with the exception of gathering either the preferred or minimum size of the component, respectively.

(Rather than duplicate the algorithm for preferredLayoutSize() and minimumLayoutSize(), we could have coded the algorithm in a third method and passed a boolean value to determine whether we were calculating the preferred or minimum size. However, for the sake of illustration and because custom layout managers are often implemented with two distinct, but very similar methods, we've chosen to be a little redundant.)

The layoutContainer() method implementation defines exactly how components in a container are going to be positioned and sized. It calculates the positions where the container starts positioning its components. Here's how it works:

```
public void layoutContainer(Container target) {
    Insets    insets       = target.insets();
    int       ncomponents  = target.countComponents();
    int       top          = 0;
    int       left         = insets.left;
    Dimension tps          = target.preferredSize();
    Dimension targetSize   = target.size();
    Component comp;
    Dimension ps;

❶   if(horizontalOrientation == Orientation.CENTER)
        left = left + (targetSize.width/2) - (tps.width/2);
❷   if(horizontalOrientation == Orientation.RIGHT)
        left = left + targetSize.width - tps.width;

    for (int i = 0 ; i < ncomponents ; i++) {
        comp = target.getComponent(i);

        if(comp.isVisible()) {
            ps  = comp.preferredSize();

❸           if(verticalOrientation == Orientation.CENTER)
                top = (targetSize.height/2) - (ps.height/2);
❹           else if(verticalOrientation == Orientation.TOP)
                top = insets.top;
❺           else if(
                verticalOrientation == Orientation.BOTTOM)
                top = targetSize.height -
```

```
                        ps.height - insets.bottom;

❻              comp.reshape(left,top,ps.width,ps.height);
❼              left += ps.width + gap;
            }
        }
    }
```

Lines ❶ and ❷ set the left edge according to the horizontal orientation. If the orientation is CENTER, the left edge is set to half of the container's width, minus half of the container's preferred size. Remember that the preferred size of the container, calculated in the `preferredLayoutSize()` is just large enough to hold all the components. If the horizontal orientation is RIGHT, then the left edge is set to the width of the container minus the preferred width.

Then, `layoutContainer()` cycles through all of the components in the container and assesses the vertical orientation in lines ❸, ❹, and ❺.

Note that the `reshape()` call in line ❻ uses the left and top we've just calculated and also uses the component's preferred height and width. As a result, `RowLayout` will not stretch or shrink any component to any size other than the component's preferred height and width.

Line ❼ modifies the `left` value, placing it at the left edge of the next component so the loop can cycle through and position it appropriately.

Now, let's take a look at the `gjt.RowLayout` code in Example 7-11. Notice that a `gjt.RowLayout` has four constructors that take a variety of orientation and gap settings. As is our practice, the first three constructors call the fourth one, which does the work:

Example 7-11 `gjt.RowLayout` **Class Source Code**

```
package gjt;

import java.awt.*;

public class RowLayout implements LayoutManager {
  static private int _defaultGap = 5;

  private int gap;
  private Orientation verticalOrientation;
  private Orientation horizontalOrientation;

  public RowLayout() {
      this(Orientation.CENTER,
          Orientation.CENTER, _defaultGap);
```

```
    }
    public RowLayout(int gap) {
        this(Orientation.CENTER, Orientation.CENTER, gap);
    }
    public RowLayout(Orientation horizontalOrient,
                     Orientation verticalOrient) {
        this(horizontalOrient, verticalOrient, _defaultGap);
    }
    public RowLayout(Orientation horizontalOrient,
                     Orientation verticalOrient, int gap) {
        Assert.notFalse(gap >= 0);
        Assert.notFalse(
            horizontalOrient == Orientation.LEFT    ||
            horizontalOrient == Orientation.CENTER ||
            horizontalOrient == Orientation.RIGHT);
        Assert.notFalse(
            verticalOrient   == Orientation.TOP     ||
            verticalOrient   == Orientation.CENTER ||
            verticalOrient   == Orientation.BOTTOM);

        this.gap                  = gap;
        this.verticalOrientation  = verticalOrient;
        this.horizontalOrientation = horizontalOrient;
    }

    public void addLayoutComponent(String name, Component comp) {
    }
    public void removeLayoutComponent(Component comp) {
    }

    public Dimension preferredLayoutSize(Container target) {
        Insets     insets      = target.insets();
        Dimension dim          = new Dimension(0,0);
        int        ncomponents = target.countComponents();
        Component comp;
        Dimension d;

        for (int i = 0 ; i < ncomponents ; i++) {
            comp = target.getComponent(i);

            if(comp.isVisible()) {
                d = comp.preferredSize();

                dim.width  += d.width;
                dim.height = Math.max(d.height, dim.height);

                if(i > 0) dim.width += gap;
            }
```

```
        }
        dim.width  += insets.left + insets.right;
        dim.height += insets.top + insets.bottom;

        return dim;
    }
    public Dimension minimumLayoutSize(Container target) {
        Insets     insets     = target.insets();
        Dimension dim         = new Dimension(0,0);
        int        ncomponents = target.countComponents();
        Component comp;
        Dimension d;

        for (int i = 0 ; i < ncomponents ; i++) {
            comp = target.getComponent(i);

            if(comp.isVisible()) {
                d = comp.minimumSize();

                dim.width  += d.width;
                dim.height = Math.max(d.height, dim.height);

                if(i > 0) dim.width += gap;
            }
        }
        dim.width  += insets.left + insets.right;
        dim.height += insets.top + insets.bottom;

        return dim;
    }
    public void layoutContainer(Container target) {
        Insets     insets     = target.insets();
        int        ncomponents = target.countComponents();
        int        top        = 0;
        int        left       = insets.left;
        Dimension tps          = target.preferredSize();
        Dimension targetSize   = target.size();
        Component comp;
        Dimension ps;

        if(horizontalOrientation == Orientation.CENTER)
            left = left + (targetSize.width/2) - (tps.width/2);
        if(horizontalOrientation == Orientation.RIGHT)
            left = left + targetSize.width - tps.width;

        for (int i = 0 ; i < ncomponents ; i++) {
            comp = target.getComponent(i);
```

```
        if(comp.isVisible()) {
            ps   = comp.preferredSize();

            if(verticalOrientation == Orientation.CENTER)
                top = (targetSize.height/2) - (ps.height/2);
            else if(verticalOrientation == Orientation.TOP)
                top = insets.top;
            else if(
                verticalOrientation == Orientation.BOTTOM)
                top = targetSize.height -
                        ps.height - insets.bottom;

            comp.reshape(left,top,ps.width,ps.height);
            left += ps.width + gap;
        }
    }
  }
}
```

Exercising the RowLayout Custom Layout Manager

Now that we've seen the implementation of the gjt.RowLayout, let's see it in action. For an idea of how gjt.RowLayout works, take a look at Figure 7-15, which shows the RowLayoutApplet.

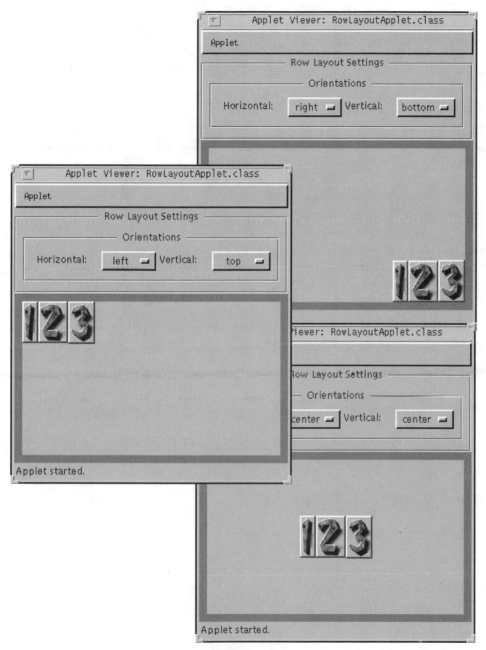

Figure 7-15 RowLayout at Work
This sequence of pictures shows a sample of RowLayout
positioning image buttons in a row, with various orientation
settings.

You may have noticed that there are several parallels between RowLayoutApplet and GridLabApplet, which we explored earlier in this chapter. If you followed that discussion, then you'll quickly see what's going on in RowLayoutApplet. Table 7-10 summarizes the similarities between the two applets.

Table 7-10 GridLabApplet **and** RowLayoutApplet **Comparison**

GridLabApplet **Panels**	RowLayoutApplet **Panels**	**Position**
ButtonPanel	RowButtonPanel	North
Picker	RowPicker	Center

Besides the panel construction and layout, also notice that just as GridLabApplet has action() and updateLayout() methods to communicate among panels, RowLayout has action() and updateOrientations() to communicate among panels. Also, just as GridLabApplet has a ButtonPanel and Picker Panel, RowLayoutApplet has RowButtonPanel and RowPicker.

To illustrate how panels are layered in the RowLayoutApplet, take a look at Figure 7-16 before we go through the code.

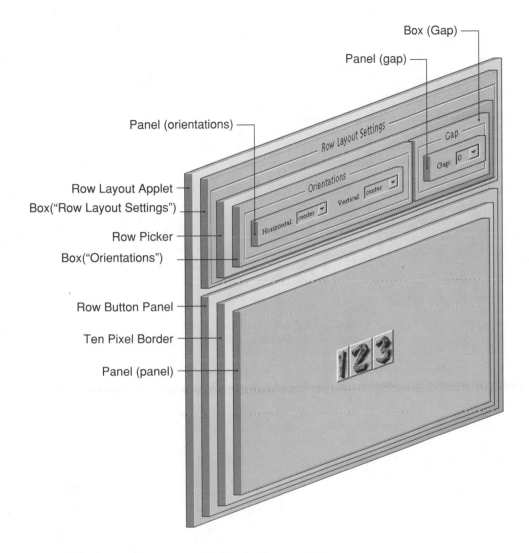

Figure 7-16 RowLayoutApplet Layout Diagram

Now, let's take a look at some of the unique characteristics of
RowLayoutApplet, starting with its init() method, where two panels are
positioned with an instance of BorderLayout. One panel is in the north and one
is in the center:

```
public void init() {
    setLayout(new BorderLayout());
    add("Center", buttonPanel = new RowButtonPanel(this));
```

```
      add("North", new Box(new RowPicker(buttonPanel),  Box("Gap")
                               "Row Layout Settings"));
   }
```

The `RowPicker` is a bit more complex than the `RowButtonPanel`, so we'll look at it first. The `RowPicker` in the north is defined like this:

```
   class RowPicker extends Panel {
❶    private Label   horientLabel = new Label("Horizontal:");
     private Label   vorientLabel = new Label("Vertical:");
     private Label   gapLabel     = new Label("Gap:");

❷    private Choice hchoice   = new Choice();
     private Choice vchoice   = new Choice();
     private Choice gapChoice = new Choice();

     private RowButtonPanel buttonPanel;

❸    public RowPicker(RowButtonPanel buttonPanel) {
❹        Panel orientations = new Panel();
❺        Panel gap          = new Panel();

         this.buttonPanel = buttonPanel;
         hchoice.addItem("left");
         hchoice.addItem("center");
         hchoice.addItem("right");
         hchoice.select(1);

         vchoice.addItem("top");
         vchoice.addItem("center");
         vchoice.addItem("bottom");
         vchoice.select(1);

         gapChoice.addItem("0");
         gapChoice.addItem("5");
         gapChoice.addItem("10");
         gapChoice.addItem("15");
         gapChoice.addItem("20");

         orientations.add(horientLabel);
         orientations.add(hchoice);
         orientations.add(vorientLabel);
         orientations.add(vchoice);

         gap.add(gapLabel);
         gap.add(gapChoice);

❻        add(new Box(orientations, "Orientations"));
```

```
❼        add(new Box(gap,              "Gap"));
    }
```

The statements in lines ❶ and ❷ create the Label and Choice components. The RowPicker constructor in line ❸ takes a buttonPanel. RowPicker maintains a reference to the RowButtonPanel instance in order to update it when the choice values are modified.

Two panels are created to hold the Label and Choice components in lines ❹ and ❺. These panels will each be enclosed in a gjt.Box, which we do in lines ❻ and ❼.

Next, let's look at RowButtonPanel. The RowButtonPanel in the center component in Figure 7-16 on page 219. It is defined like this:

```
    class RowButtonPanel extends Panel implements DialogClient {
        private ImageButton    one, two, three;
        private Panel          panel  = new Panel();
❶       private TenPixelBorder border = new TenPixelBorder(panel);
        private TenPixelBorder border = new TenPixelBorder(panel);

        public RowButtonPanel(Applet applet) {
            URL cb = applet.getCodeBase();

❷           one   = new ImageButton(applet.getImage(codeBase,
                                                 "gifs/one.gif"));
            two   = new ImageButton(applet.getImage(cb,
                                                 "gifs/two.gif"));
            three = new ImageButton(applet.getImage(cb,
                                                 "gifs/three.gif"));

❸           panel.setLayout(new RowLayout(0));
            panel.add(one);
            panel.add(two);
            panel.add(three);

❹           setLayout(new BorderLayout());
            add      ("Center", border);
        }
    }
```

Note that the RowButtonPanel constructed in line ❶ is a panel built in to a TenPixelBorder. The statements in line ❷ create the gjt.ImageButton objects we're going to lay out, and in line ❸ we set the layout to be managed by an instance of gjt.RowLayout. The setLayout() in line ❹ sets the buttonPanel layout manager to be an instance of BorderLayout, which will center the border.

So what we have here is three `ImageButton` objects being laid out by `RowLayout` inside a panel inside a border being laid out by `BorderLayout`. Clear as mud? Refer back to Figure 7-16 on page 219 and that should help.

We haven't mentioned it yet, but `RowLayoutApplet` provides for both horizontal and vertical orientations in the `Choice` components. A user can mix and match these and `RowLayout` will position the image buttons accordingly. The `action()` and `updateOrientations()` method manage this in `RowLayoutApplet`. Here's the `action()` method:

```
        public boolean action(Event event, Object what) {
            String horient, vorient;
            int    gap;

            horient = hchoice.getSelectedItem();
            vorient = vchoice.getSelectedItem();
❶           gap     =
            (new Integer(gapChoice.getSelectedItem())).intValue();

❷           buttonPanel.updateOrientations(
                        Orientation.fromString(horient),
                        Orientation.fromString(vorient), gap);

            return true;
        }
```

The `action()` method handles the gap in line ❶ in the same way the `GridLabApplet` calculated the number of rows and columns. However, In `GridLabApplet`, we only needed to extract an integer from the `Choice` selected. In the `RowLayoutApplet action()` method, we need to take the incoming string ("left," "center," "right," "top," or "bottom") and convert it to an orientation constant such as `Orientation.LEFT`, `Orientation.CENTER`, and so on. To do this, we use the `fromString()` method from the Graphic Java Toolkit `Orientation` class, as in line ❷. (The `gjt.Orientation` class is discussed in the *Custom Components* chapter). `Orientation.fromString()` returns an appropriate `Orientation` constant.

The `updateOrientations()` method then takes those orientation values and uses them to create and set the new `RowLayout`:

```
        public void updateOrientations(Orientation horient,
                                       Orientation vorient,
                                       int gap) {
            panel.setLayout(new RowLayout(horient, vorient, gap));
            border.validate();
        }
```

Remember that the call to `setLayout()` invalidates the panel, and the call to `border.validate()` results in the `panel` being laid out.

RowLayoutApplet Implementation

Now let's look through the `RowLayoutApplet` class in Example 7-12. As you look through the code, particularly note the use of `RowButtonPanel` and `RowPicker`. You may also want to refer to the 3-D layout diagram in Figure 7-16 on page 219.

Example 7-12 `RowLayoutApplet` **Class Source Code**

```
import java.applet.Applet;
import java.net.URL;
import java.awt.*;
import gjt.*;

public class RowLayoutApplet extends Applet {
  private RowButtonPanel buttonPanel;

  public void init() {
      setLayout(new BorderLayout());
      add("Center", buttonPanel = new RowButtonPanel(this));
      add("North", new Box(new RowPicker(buttonPanel),
                       "Row Layout Settings"));
  }
}

class RowButtonPanel extends Panel implements DialogClient {
  private ImageButton     one, two, three;
  private Panel           panel  = new Panel();
  private TenPixelBorder border = new TenPixelBorder(panel);

  public RowButtonPanel(Applet applet) {
      URL cb = applet.getCodeBase();

      one   = new ImageButton(applet.getImage(cb,
                                  "gifs/one.gif"));
      two   = new ImageButton(applet.getImage(cb,
                                  "gifs/two.gif"));
      three = new ImageButton(applet.getImage(cb,
                                  "gifs/three.gif"));

      panel.setLayout(new RowLayout(0));
      panel.add(one);
      panel.add(two);
      panel.add(three);
```

```
            setLayout(new BorderLayout());
            add      ("Center", border);
        }

        public void updateOrientations(Orientation horient,
                                       Orientation vorient,
                                       int gap) {
            panel.setLayout(new RowLayout(horient, vorient, gap));
            border.validate();
        }
        public void dialogDismissed(Dialog d) { }
    }

class RowPicker extends Panel {
    private Label   horientLabel = new Label("Horizontal:");
    private Label   vorientLabel = new Label("Vertical:");
    private Label   gapLabel     = new Label("Gap:");

    private Choice hchoice    = new Choice();
    private Choice vchoice    = new Choice();
    private Choice gapChoice = new Choice();

    private RowButtonPanel buttonPanel;

    public RowPicker(RowButtonPanel buttonPanel) {
        Panel orientations = new Panel();
        Panel gap          = new Panel();

        this.buttonPanel = buttonPanel;
        hchoice.addItem("left");
        hchoice.addItem("center");
        hchoice.addItem("right");
        hchoice.select(1);

        vchoice.addItem("top");
        vchoice.addItem("center");
        vchoice.addItem("bottom");
        vchoice.select(1);

        gapChoice.addItem("0");
        gapChoice.addItem("5");
        gapChoice.addItem("10");
        gapChoice.addItem("15");
        gapChoice.addItem("20");

        orientations.add(horientLabel);
        orientations.add(hchoice);
        orientations.add(vorientLabel);
```

```
        orientations.add(vchoice);

        gap.add(gapLabel);
        gap.add(gapChoice);

        add(new Box(orientations,  "Orientations"));
        add(new Box(gap,           "Gap"));
    }
    public boolean action(Event event, Object what) {
        String horient, vorient;
        int    gap;

        horient = hchoice.getSelectedItem();
        vorient = vchoice.getSelectedItem();
        gap     =
        (new Integer(gapChoice.getSelectedItem())).intValue();

        buttonPanel.updateOrientations(
                    Orientation.fromString(horient),
                    Orientation.fromString(vorient), gap);

        return true;
    }
}
```

gjt.ColumnLayout

The ColumnLayout layout manager is another custom layout manager in the Graphic Java Toolkit. It is very similar in design and capability to the RowLayout layout manager, except that it positions components in columns instead of rows. You'll notice in Table 7-11 that, like all custom layout managers, ColumnLayout implements the standard LayoutManager methods.

Table 7-11 gjt.ColumnLayout **Responsibilities**

Methods	Description
void addLayoutComponent(String name, Component comp)	Is a no-op implementation.
void removedLayoutComponent(Component comp)	Is a no-op implementation.
Dimension preferredLayoutSize(Container targert)	Returns the preferred container height and width for the layout manager.
Dimension minimumLayoutSize(Container targert)	Returns the minimum container height and width for the layout manager.
void layoutContainer(Container target)	Positions components in a container.

Since `ColumnLayout` is so close to the `RowLayout` custom layout manager, we won't discuss its implementation. We include it here for completeness. Example 7-13 shows the `ColumnLayout` code.

Example 7-13 gjt.`ColumnLayout` **Class Source Code**

```java
package gjt;

import java.awt.*;

public class ColumnLayout implements LayoutManager {
  static private int _defaultGap = 5;

  private int         gap;
  private Orientation horizontalOrientation;
  private Orientation verticalOrientation;

  public ColumnLayout() {
      this(Orientation.CENTER,
          Orientation.CENTER, _defaultGap);
  }
  public ColumnLayout(int gap) {
      this(Orientation.CENTER, Orientation.CENTER, gap);
  }
  public ColumnLayout(Orientation horizontalOrient,
                      Orientation verticalOrient) {
      this(horizontalOrient, verticalOrient, _defaultGap);
  }
  public ColumnLayout(Orientation horizontalOrient,
                      Orientation verticalOrient, int gap) {
      Assert.notFalse(gap >= 0);
      Assert.notFalse(
          horizontalOrient == Orientation.LEFT   ||
          horizontalOrient == Orientation.CENTER ||
          horizontalOrient == Orientation.RIGHT);
      Assert.notFalse(
          verticalOrient   == Orientation.TOP    ||
          verticalOrient   == Orientation.CENTER ||
          verticalOrient   == Orientation.BOTTOM);

      this.gap                 = gap;
      this.verticalOrientation   = verticalOrient;
      this.horizontalOrientation = horizontalOrient;
  }

  public void addLayoutComponent(String name,
                                 Component comp) {
  }
```

```
public void removeLayoutComponent(Component comp) {
}

public Dimension preferredLayoutSize(Container target) {
    Insets      insets      = target.insets();
    Dimension dim           = new Dimension(0,0);
    int          ncomponents = target.countComponents();
    Component comp;
    Dimension d;

    for (int i = 0 ; i < ncomponents ; i++) {
        comp = target.getComponent(i);

        if(comp.isVisible()) {
            d = comp.preferredSize();
            if(i > 0)
                dim.height += gap;

            dim.height += d.height;
            dim.width  = Math.max(d.width, dim.width);
        }
    }
    dim.width  += insets.left + insets.right;
    dim.height += insets.top  + insets.bottom;
    return dim;
}
public Dimension minimumLayoutSize(Container target) {
    Insets      insets      = target.insets();
    Dimension dim           = new Dimension(0,0);
    int          ncomponents = target.countComponents();
    Component comp;
    Dimension d;

    for (int i = 0 ; i < ncomponents ; i++) {
        comp = target.getComponent(i);

        if(comp.isVisible()) {
            d = comp.minimumSize();

            dim.width  = Math.max(d.width, dim.width);
            dim.height += d.height;

            if(i > 0) dim.height += gap;
        }
    }
    dim.width  += insets.left + insets.right;
    dim.height += insets.top  + insets.bottom;
```

```
            return dim;
        }
    public void layoutContainer(Container target) {
        Insets    insets       = target.insets();
        int       top          = insets.top;
        int       left         = 0;
        int       ncomponents   = target.countComponents();
        Dimension preferredSize = target.preferredSize();
        Dimension targetSize    = target.size();
        Component comp;
        Dimension ps;

        if(verticalOrientation == Orientation.CENTER)
            top += (targetSize.height/2) -
                    (preferredSize.height/2);
        else if(verticalOrientation == Orientation.BOTTOM)
            top = targetSize.height - preferredSize.height +
                    insets.top;

        for (int i = 0 ; i < ncomponents ; i++) {
            comp = target.getComponent(i);
            left = insets.left;

            if(comp.isVisible()) {
                ps = comp.preferredSize();

                if(horizontalOrientation == Orientation.CENTER)
                    left = (targetSize.width/2) - (ps.width/2);
                else if(
                  horizontalOrientation == Orientation.RIGHT) {
                    left = targetSize.width - ps.width -
                            insets.right;
                }
                comp.reshape(left,top,ps.width,ps.height);
                top += ps.height + gap;
            }
        }
    }
  }
}
```

Exercising the ColumnLayout Custom Layout Manager

Figure 7-17 shows sample the ColumnLayoutApplet. As you can see, the
ColumnLayout layout manager positions components in column format
according to the orientations specified in the Choice selections in the top panel of
the applet.

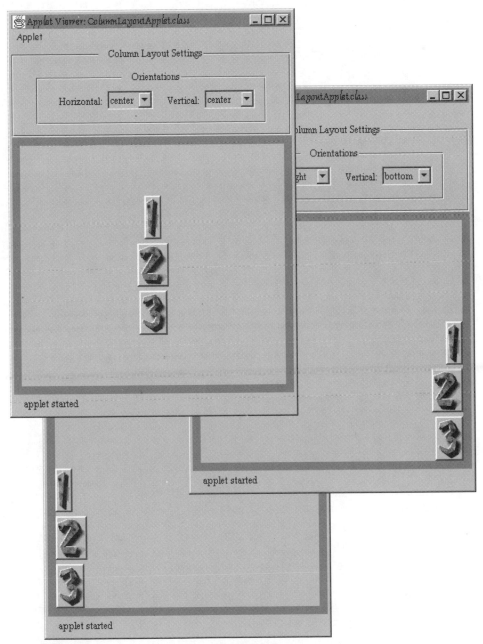

Figure 7-17 ColumnLayout at Work
This sequence of pictures shows a sample of ColumnLayout positioning buttons in their container.

Example 7-14 shows the `ColumnLayoutApplet` code, so you can see how it employs the `ColumnLayout` layout manager.

Example 7-14 `ColumnLayoutApplet` **Class Source Code**

```java
import java.applet.Applet;
import java.net.URL;
import java.awt.*;
import gjt.*;

public class ColumnLayoutApplet extends Applet {
  private ColumnButtonPanel buttonPanel;

  public void init() {
      setLayout(new BorderLayout());
      add("Center", buttonPanel = new ColumnButtonPanel(this));
      add("North", new Box(new ColumnPicker(buttonPanel),
                           "Column Layout Settings"));
  }
}

class ColumnButtonPanel extends Panel implements DialogClient {
  private ImageButton     one, two, three;
  private Panel           panel  = new Panel();
  private TenPixelBorder border = new TenPixelBorder(panel);

  public ColumnButtonPanel(Applet applet) {
      URL cb = applet.getCodeBase();

      one   = new ImageButton(applet.getImage(cb,
                                      "gifs/one.gif"));
      two   = new ImageButton(applet.getImage(cb,
                                      "gifs/two.gif"));
      three = new ImageButton(applet.getImage(cb,
                                      "gifs/three.gif"));

      panel.setLayout(new ColumnLayout(0));
      panel.add(one);
      panel.add(two);
      panel.add(three);

      setLayout(new BorderLayout());
      add       ("Center", border);
  }
  public void updateOrientations(Orientation horient,
                                 Orientation vorient,
                                 int gap) {
      panel.setLayout(new ColumnLayout(horient, vorient, gap));
```

```
        border.validate();
  }
  public void dialogDismissed(Dialog d) { }
}

class ColumnPicker extends Panel {
  private Label  horientLabel = new Label("Horizontal:");
  private Label  vorientLabel = new Label("Vertical:");
  private Label  gapLabel     = new Label("Gap:");

  private Choice hchoice   = new Choice();
  private Choice vchoice   = new Choice();
  private Choice gapChoice = new Choice();

  private ColumnButtonPanel buttonPanel;

  public ColumnPicker(ColumnButtonPanel buttonPanel) {
      Panel orientations = new Panel();
      Panel gap          = new Panel();

      this.buttonPanel = buttonPanel;
      hchoice.addItem("left");
      hchoice.addItem("center");
      hchoice.addItem("right");
      hchoice.select(1);

      vchoice.addItem("top");
      vchoice.addItem("center");
      vchoice.addItem("bottom");
      vchoice.select(1);

      gapChoice.addItem("0");
      gapChoice.addItem("5");
      gapChoice.addItem("10");
      gapChoice.addItem("15");
      gapChoice.addItem("20");

      orientations.add(horientLabel);
      orientations.add(hchoice);
      orientations.add(vorientLabel);
      orientations.add(vchoice);

      gap.add(gapLabel);
      gap.add(gapChoice);

      add(new Box(orientations, "Orientations"));
      add(new Box(gap,         "Gap"));
  }
```

```
public boolean action(Event event, Object what) {
    String horient, vorient;
    int     gap;

    horient = hchoice.getSelectedItem();
    vorient = vchoice.getSelectedItem();
    gap     =
    (new Integer(gapChoice.getSelectedItem())).intValue();

    buttonPanel.updateOrientations(
        Orientation.fromString(horient),
        Orientation.fromString(vorient), gap);

    return true;
    }
}
```

Summary

The AWT includes a comprehensive set of standard layout managers that can do most of the work necessary for automatically positioning and resizing components in a container. All classes that extend `Container` have default layout managers assigned to them, so for simple applets, you need never specify a layout manager. However, if you want to choose a layout manager to achieve a particular look in your applet, you can simply use the `setLayout()` method and specify which layout manager you want to use, like this:

```
setLayout(new FlowLayout());
```

The `GridBagLayout` layout manager is an exception to this simplicity. It is the most complex and powerful of the AWT layout managers. It implicitly lays out components in a grid (that is, at construction time you don't explicitly specify the number of rows and columns that you want it to use). `GridBagLayout` relies on instance variables set in a `GridBagConstraints` object to create a grid layout *on the-fly*. These `GridBagConstraints` instance variables, generically referred to as *constraints*, provide the raw material for `GridBagLayout` to determine how many rows and columns are necessary to position and size the container's components. For every component you want laid out by `GridBagLayout`, you set `GridBagConstraints` variables and then call `setConstraints()` to access those instance variables.

The tricky part about using the standard AWT layout managers is knowing when to use which one, but there are a few tips (see *Decisions, Decisions—Which Layout Manager to Use?* on page 169) that can help you until you've gained enough practice and experience that the decision is second nature.

The standard layout managers are fairly comprehensive in terms of the number of ways they can arrange components in a display. However, for those occasions when they just don't provide the desired behavior, you can devise your own implementation of the `LayoutManager` interface and create your own custom layout manager. This is as simple as defining the five methods in the `LayoutManager` interface, as we've shown in the Graphic Java Toolkit's `BulletinLayout`, `RowLayout`, and `ColumnLayout` custom layout managers.

The Graphic Java Toolkit—Extending the AWT

PART TWO

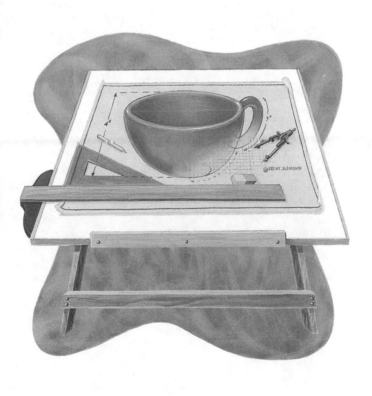

CHAPTER

8

- **Overview of the Graphic Java Toolkit on page 238**

    - **The GJT Packages on page 238**

    - **The GJT Classes on page 239**

    - **Custom Components in the Graphic Java Toolkit on page 242**

    - **Packaging Custom Components on page 242**

    - **The GJT Utility Classes on page 242**

    - **Assertions on page 242**

    - **Type-Checked Constants on page 244**

    - **The gjt.Util Class on page 246**

    - **The GJT test Package on page 246**

- **Summary on page 249**

Introducing the Graphic Java Toolkit

Graphic Java comes with a toolkit of high-level custom components built on top of the AWT. While the AWT provides low-level components such as buttons, scrollbars, and checkboxes, the Graphic Java Toolkit (GJT) provides high-level custom components such as image buttons, component and image scrollers, bargauges, convenience dialogs, and more. The GJT also provides packages for double buffered sprite animation, rubberbanding, and image filters.

The intent of the Graphic Java Toolkit is threefold:

- To provide a comprehensive set of high-level custom components built on top of the AWT that you may incorporate into your Java applets and applications

- To provide a vehicle for exploring the AWT in depth

- To illustrate techniques and good practices for developing your own custom components

Each of the chapters that follow examines a custom component from the GJT. In these chapters, we will burrow deeper into the AWT than we have thus far. We'll subclass `Canvas` and `Panel`, use the Java layout managers (we'll uncover the mysteries of the often confusing `GridBagLayout` layout manager), further explore `Font` and `FontMetrics`, show techniques for double buffered sprite animation, and perhaps most importantly, illustrate how to develop custom components.

The GJT is fully documented, and each custom component in the GJT comes with its own unit test applet. We suggest that you use your favorite Java-enabled browser to peruse the documentation on each custom component and use `appletviewer` to run each unit test as we work our way through the GJT and the AWT in the chapters to come.

Overview of the Graphic Java Toolkit

The Graphic Java Toolkit (GJT) is a set of Java packages that extend the capabilities of the AWT. The packages include a suite of custom components, double buffered sprite animation, rubberbanding, image filters and a comprehensive set of test applets for all of the above.

The GJT Packages

Table 8-1 shows the packages that compose the GJT.

Table 8-1 Graphic Java Toolkit Packages

Package Name	Contents
gjt	High-level custom components for developing user interfaces, including separators, borders, dialogs, image buttons, toolbars, scrollers, and more. The gjt package also includes utility classes and a set of custom layout managers.
gjt.animation	A set of classes for double buffered sprite animation. Animation takes place on a Playfield, where Sprites are animated by cycling through a sequence of images. Collision detectors detect collisions between sprites, and between sprites and the edges of the playfield.
gjt.image	A set of classes that support image manipulation, such as the bleaching, fading in, and fading out of images.
gjt.rubberband	A collection of classes that provide the infrastructure for rubberbanding. Included are classes for rubberbanding lines, rectangles, and ellipses, along with a RubberbandPanel, which is a Panel that can be fitted with any rubberband; user interaction for rubberbanding is automatically handled.
gjt.test	A comprehensive set of unit tests for all of the custom components in the other GJT packages. In addition to unit tests, all classes in the GJT are fully documented. HTML files for the entire GJT are provided on the CD that accompanies this book.

The GJT Classes

The next set of tables lists the classes available in each of the GJT packages. Table 8-2 shows the classes that compose the gjt package.

Table 8-2 gjt **Package Classes**

Classes	Use
Utility Classes	
Assert	Assertion checking.
Etching	Defines styles of etching – either etched-in or etched-out.
Orientation	Defines orientations and alignments.
Stopwatch	A thread masquerading as a stopwatch.
ThreeDBorderStyle	Defines styles of 3-D borders – either raised or inset.
Util	A collection of static utility methods.
Custom Components	
Bargauge	A 3-D rectangle filled with a specified color.
Border	A border drawn around a Component.
EtchedBorder	A Border that draws either etched-in or etched-out.
ThreeDBorder	A Border that draws either raised or inset.
Box	An etched border and title around a Component.
ButtonPanel	A separator above a row of buttons that can be placed in a container.
ChoiceCardPanel	A Choice controls display of any number of Panels.
IconCardPanel	A set of image buttons controls display of any number of panels.
DrawingPanel	The basis for a paint program.
ComponentScroller	A scroller that automatically scrolls any Component.
ImageScroller	A scroller that enables smooth scrolling of an Image.
ImageCanvas	A canvas for painting images.
DrawnRectangle	A rectangle drawn with varying degrees of thickness and shades of color.

Table 8-2 gjt **Package Classes (Continued)**

Classes	Use
EtchedRectangle	A DrawnRectangle that draws either etched-in or etched-out.
ThreeDRectangle	A DrawnRectangle that draws either raised or inset.
ImageButton	A button that displays an image.
ImageButtonEvent	Events associated with an image button.
StateButton	An ImageButton that cycles images.
ImageButtonPanel	A Panel containing image buttons.
ExclusiveImageButtonPanel	Only one ImageButton selected at a time.
Toolbar	A panel with a horizontal ImageButtonPanel plus a HorizontalSeparator.
LabelCanvas	A Canvas simulating a selectable label.
ImageCanvas	A Canvas that displays an Image.
QuestionDialog	A Dialog that asks for user input.
FontDialog	A Dialog for selecting a font.
MessageDialog	A Dialog that displays a String.
ProgressDialog	A Dialog with a Bargauge that monitors activity.
QuestionDialog	A Dialog that asks a Yes/No question.
Separator	Etched lines used to separate logical compartments of user interface widgets.
SelectionEvent	A select or deselect event.
Toolbar	A row of image buttons.
YesNoDialog	A Dialog that asks a question and provides Yes/No buttons for a response.

Custom Layout Managers

ColumnLayout	Positions components in a column.
RowLayout	Positions components in a row.
BulletinLayout	Positions components in a bulletin-board style.
ScrollerLayout	Lays out two scrollbars and a viewport for a scroller.

Table 8-3 shows the classes that compose the gjt.animation package.

Table 8-3 gjt.animation **Package Classes**

Class Name	Use
EdgeCollisionDetector	Detects collisions between sprites and playfield boundaries.
Playfield	Canvas on which sprites are animated.
Sprite	Animated objects on a Playfield.
SpriteCollisionDetector	Detects collisions between sprites.

Table 8-4 shows the classes that compose the gjt.rubberband package.

Table 8-4 gjt.rubberband **Package Classes**

Class Name	Use
RubberbandLine	Rubberband that does lines.
RubberbandRectangle	Rubberband that does rectangles.
RubberbandEllipses	Rubberband that does ellipses.
RubberbandPanel	Panel that can be fitted with a rubberband.

Table 8-5 shows the classes that compose the gjt.test package.

Table 8-5 gjt.test **Package Classes**

Class Name	Use
TiledPanel	Panel with a title and horizontal separator.
UnitTest	Applet extension for unit testing components.

Table 8-6 shows the classes that compose the gjt.image package.

Table 8-6 gjt.image **Package Classes**

Class Name	Use
BleachImageFilter	Filter that creates a bleached version of an image.
DissolveFilter	Filter that creates an image of varying degrees of opacity/transparency.
ImageDissolver	Fades images in or out of a component.

Custom Components in the Graphic Java Toolkit

Each custom component in the GJT is composed of a set of classes that are designed to work together to provide a useful tool for developing user interfaces.

All of the classes in each custom component have been documented and run through the `javadoc` program; you can find the HTML files for all of the classes in the GJT in the `graphicJava` directory on the CD.

AWT Tip

Packaging Custom Components

All of the custom components in this book come with a unit test—an applet that exercises the components. Unit tests serve three very important purposes: They exercise the custom component, they guard against bugs that might be introduced when the component is extended or reworked in the future, and they provide example code for potential clients. The best unit tests offer a balance between putting their custom components through every imaginable scenario and being simple enough to be understood by the curious developer. Additionally, all custom components in this book come with Booch class diagrams. These show the static relationships between classes, such as which classes extend or implement other classes and how classes are associated with one another. Such diagrams do wonders for quickly providing an overview of how collaborating classes are associated and enhance understanding of your custom components.

The GJT Utility Classes

The Graphic Java Toolkit comes with a number of utility classes that are used by many of the other classes in the GJT. The utility classes fall into three categories: assertions, type-safe constants, and utility. We will discuss each briefly.

Assertions

In his excellent book *Object-Oriented Software Construction*, Bertand Meyer discusses the concept of programming by contract [1]. Essentially, the relationship between a class and its clients is viewed as a formal agreement—a contract of sorts. The methods of a class should guarantee that they will hold up their end of the contract by reliably performing their intended function. However, the caller of such methods has to hold up its end of the contract by invoking the method with arguments that are correct. As a result, methods of a class should ensure that arguments they are passed are correct—only then can they fulfill their end of the contract.

---

1. See Meyer, Bertrand. *Object-Oriented Software Construction*, chapter 7. Prentice Hall.

For instance, consider the gjt.Bargauge class, which provides a method for setting the fill percent of the bargauge: setFillPercent(double). Obviously, the Bargauge class should *assert* that the value passed into its setFillPercent() method lies between 0 and 100. If this check is not made, and a Bargauge is passed a bogus percentage, it will not fulfill its end of the contract and will work unreliably. Java provides an exception for use in asserting the validity of arguments, the aptly named IllegalArgumentException. Such an exception would be used like this:

```
public setFillPercent(double percent) {
   if(percent < 0 || percent > 100)
      throw new IllegalArgumentException("Bargauge: bad percent");
   .
   .
   .
}
```

If Bargauge.setFillPercent() is passed a value that does not lie between 0 and 100, it will throw an IllegalArgumentException. However, littering one's code with conditional checks followed by a throw statement is often more overhead than many developers are willing to bear. As a result, the GJT provides an assertion class that provides a shorthand notation for asserting arguments. The same method written with the gjt.Assert class looks like this:

```
public setFillPercent(double percent) {
   Assert.notFalse(percent > 0 && percent < 100);
   .
   .
   .
}
```

The gjt.Assert class provides a number of convenience methods for asserting arguments, as listed in Table 8-7.The last two methods are passed a string, which is forwarded to the IllegalArgumentException constructor.

Table 8-7 gjt.Assert **Methods**

Methods
notFalse(boolean)
notNull(Object)
notFalse(boolean, String)
notNull(Object, String)

Type-Checked Constants

It is common practice in the AWT to designate constants by declaring `public static final` members of the class to which the constants pertain. For instance, `java.awt.Label` defines a set of integers used to specify its justification:

```
public static final int LEFT = 0;
public static final int CENTER = 1;
public static final int RIGHT= 2;
```

The `Label` class provides a constructor that allows you to specify the string the `Label` displays and its orientation:

```
public Label(String label, int alignment)
```

After our discussion concerning programming by contract, you would expect the `Label` constructor to assert that the `alignment` passed in is a valid value, either 0, 1 or 2. And sure enough, the `Label` constructor will throw an `IllegalArgumentException` if you attempt to slip it something other than 0, 1, or 2 [2].

Such a strategy for coding constants, however, puts the responsibility for checking arguments such as `alignment` squarely on the shoulders of the class that has declared the constants—in this case the `Label` class. In addition, other classes that need to specify LEFT, RIGHT, and CENTER must declare their own constants and perform the same checking when they are passed integer values for representing the constants.

The Graphic Java Toolkit approach is to provide classes that act as *type-checked* constants. For instance, the `gjt.ThreeDBorderStyle` class defines constants representing raised and inset borders:

```
public class ThreeDBorderStyle {
  public static final ThreeDBorderStyle RAISED =
                                    new ThreeDBorderStyle();
  public static final ThreeDBorderStyle INSET   =
                                    new ThreeDBorderStyle();
  public String toString() {
     if(this == ThreeDBorderStyle.RAISED)
         return getClass().getName() + "=RAISED";
     else
         return getClass().getName() + "=INSET";
  }
  private ThreeDBorderStyle() { }  // defeat instantiation
}
```

2.   Other AWT classes are not so disciplined at checking arguments representing constants and will simply misbehave when passed a invalid value.

The `gjt.ThreeDRectangle` class takes an instance of `ThreeDBorderStyle` as an argument to one of its constructors:

```
public ThreeDRectangle(Component drawInto,
                       ThreeDBorderStyle state,
                       int thickness, int x, int y,
                       int w, int h)
```

Clients constructing a `ThreeDRectangle` pass the constructor one of the two `public static final ThreeDBorderStyle` *objects*:

```
rect = new ThreeDRectangle(c, ThreeDBorderStyle.RAISED, ...);
```

Since an object is being passed to the `ThreeDRectangle` constructor for specifying the border style, it is the compiler that does the checking for us, thus the name type-checked constants. Any method that takes a `ThreeDBorderStyle` object as an argument is guaranteed that the object will be either `ThreeDBorderStyle.RAISED` or `ThreeDBorderStyle.INSET`, for these are the only two instances of `ThreeDBorderStyle` in existence [3].

The type-checked constant approach has other benefits as well. For instance, since the constants are defined within the confines of their own class, we can provide a `toString()` method for printing out the values of the constants, as we have done for `gjt.ThreeDBorderStyle`. To print a `ThreeDBorderStyle` object, you can simply do the following:

```
void someFictitiousMethod(ThreeDBorderStyle style) {
  System.out.println(style);
}
```

The `System.out.println()` call results in the invocation of `ThreeDBorderStyle.toString()`, which prints one of the following:

- `ThreeDBorderStyle=RAISED`

- `ThreeDBorderStyle=INSET`

Conversely, printing an integer representing a constant requires the method doing the printing to match up the string representation with the integer value, like this:

```
void anotherFictitiousMethod(int leftCenterOrRight) {
  if(leftCenterOrRight == LEFT)
     System:out.println("LEFT");
  else if(leftCenterOrRight == CENTER)
```

---

3. The private default constructor in `ThreeDBorderStyle` ensures that no other objects of type `ThreeDBorderStyle` can ever be instantiated.

```
        System.out.println("CENTER");
    else if(leftCenterOrRight == RIGHT)
        System.out.println("RIGHT");
}
```

The gjt.Util Class

The Graphic Java Toolkit provides a Util class which, as its name suggests provides a number of utility methods. All of the methods are static and may therefore be invoked by Util.*name*(), where *name* is the name of the method. The utility methods provided by gjt.Util are summarized in Table 8-8.

Table 8-8 gjt.Util **Methods**

Methods	Action
Frame getFrame(Component)	Returns frame in which component resides.
Applet getApplet(Component)	Returns applet in which component resides.
void waitForImage(Component, Image)	Waits for an image to load.
void wallPaper(Component, Graphics, Image)	Wallpapers component with image.
void setCursor(int, Component)	Sets cursor for component.

The GJT test Package

Each custom component comes with an applet that serves as a unit test for the component. All of the unit test applets reside in the gjt.test package and consist of .java, .class, and .html files. The HTML files are meant to be run with appletviewer or, alternatively, in a Java-enabled browser.

The gjt.test package includes two simple classes that provide some infrastructure for the unit tests: TitledPanel and UnitTest.

TitledPanel is simply a Panel that is fitted with a BorderLayout, with a Label in the north and a HorizontalSeparator in the south:

```
class TitledPanel extends Panel {
  public TitledPanel(String title) {
     setLayout(new BorderLayout());
     add("North", new Label(title, Label.CENTER));
     add("South", new HorizontalSeparator());
```

UnitTest is an abstract class that extends Applet and that is fitted with a BorderLayout. UnitTest places a TitledPanel in the north and a Panel created by derived classes in the center:

```
abstract public class UnitTest extends Applet {
  abstract public String title();
  abstract public Panel centerPanel();

  public void init() {
     Util.getFrame(this).setCursor(Frame.WAIT_CURSOR);
     Panel titledPanel = new TitledPanel(title());
     setLayout(new BorderLayout());
     add("North", titledPanel);
     add("Center", centerPanel());
  }
  public void start() {
     Util.getFrame(this).setCursor(Frame.DEFAULT_CURSOR);
  }
}
```

Note that classes derived from UnitTest must provide a title for the unit test and they must supply a Panel that is placed below the TitledPanel. Figure 8-1 shows the layout of UnitTest.

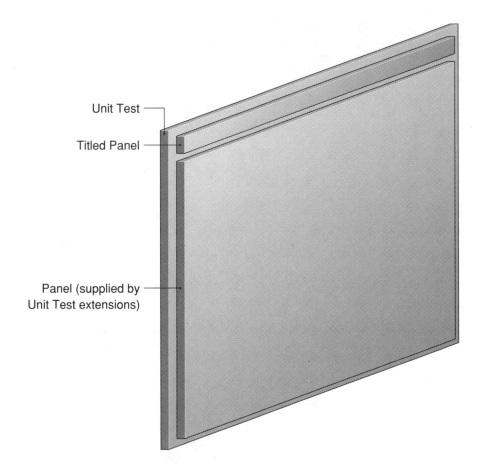

Figure 8-1 Unit Test Layout Diagram

Another feature of `UnitTest` is that it sets the cursor to `WAIT_CURSOR` in `init()` and subsequently changes the cursor back to `DEFAULT_CURSOR` in `start()`. Since some applets take awhile to load, it's nice to provide some feedback to the user that the applet is truly being loaded and not just stuck in limbo.

Summary

Each custom component in the GJT consists of the following:

- A set of collaborating classes

- A set of class diagrams

- A unit test that exercises the custom component

As a general rule, we suggest that custom components you develop on your own also include these items.

All custom components obviously must consist of the first item: a set of collaborating classes, although sometimes the number of classes is simply one (for example, refer to the Box component).

Class diagrams are excellent for portraying the static relationships between classes; they also communicate a great deal of information that is not easily gleaned from verbiage alone. If you have access to a tool that produces class diagrams, we highly recommend that you include class diagrams as part of your own custom components.

The third item serves three essential purposes: it exercises the custom component, it guards against bugs that might be introduced when the component is extended or reworked in the future, and it provides example code for potential clients interested in using the custom component.

CHAPTER

9

- gjt.Separator on page 251

- Separator Associations and Responsibilities on page 252

- Exercising the Separator on page 258

- gjt.Bargauge on page 262

- Bargauge Associations and Responsibilities on page 262

- Exercising the Bargauge on page 267

- Summary on page 275

Separators and Bargauges

This chapter covers two GJT custom components: Separator and Bargauge. These custom components will shed some light on developing custom components that extend java.awt.Canvas. Also, in our quest to demystify GridBagLayout, the separator unit test provides yet another example of GridBaglayout in action.

gjt.Separator

Nearly every modern-day user-interface toolkit comes with something akin to a separator: etched lines used to separate logical compartments of user interface widgets. We've seen the GJT version of separator (gjt.Separator) in action in a number of applets from Part 1 of the book, along with our previous discussion concerning the gjt.UnitTest class.

gjt.Separator is one of the simplest custom components the GJT provides. Its simplicity merits it the distinction of being the one of the first custom component we present.

Separator Associations and Responsibilities

Like the rest of the first group of GJT custom components presented in this book, gjt.Separator is an extension of Canvas. Since a separator contains no other components and simply draws an etched line, Canvas is the logical superclass to use. Figure 9-1 shows the class diagram for gjt.Separator.

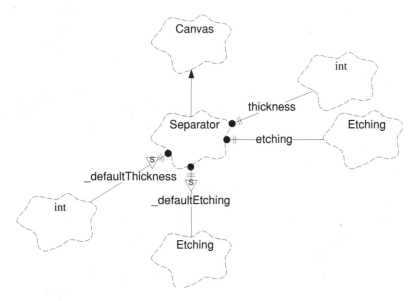

Figure 9-1 gjt.Separator Class Diagram

As you can see, gjt.Separator is a simple custom component that keeps track of the state of its etching and its thickness. The Etching object associated with the Separator is either Etching.IN or Etching.OUT.

To highlight the responsibilities of gjt.Separator, Table 9-1 lists its public methods.

Table 9-1 gjt.Separator **Responsibilities**

Methods	Description
void paint(Graphics g)	Overrides Component paint(). Paints either a horizontal or vertical separator.
Dimension minimumSize()	Overrides Component minimumSize(). Returns the preferredSize().
Dimension preferredSize()	Overrides Component preferredSize(). Sets preferredSize to something other than 0,0.

Table 9-2 lists the associations maintained by a Separator.

Table 9-2 gjt.Separator **Associations**

Variables	Description
Etching etching	Defines the etching style used by the separator.
int thickness	Defines the thickness of the separator.

A Separator also has two static private variables that define the default etching style and etching thickness:

```
static private Etching _defaultEtching   = Etching.IN;
static private int     _defaultThickness = 2;
```

These define the default etching and thickness for all instances of Separator.

Before looking through the code in Example 9-1 on page 256, we'll point out several items of particular interest. First, you'll notice when you look through the source that Separator overrides preferredSize() in order to return thickness for both width and height:

```
public Dimension preferredSize() {
   return new Dimension(thickness, thickness);
}
```

Using the default Separator constructor results in a separator two pixels wide and two pixels tall—a separator that's barely visible. Setting them both to thickness essentially gives the layout manager something to work with. For example, if a separator were positioned and sized with BorderLayout and the separator were positioned in the north or south, BorderLayout would respect the preferred height of the separator, but would ignore its preferred width. The height would be the default thickness, two pixels, and the width would be the width of the container in which the separator resides.

The Separator class counts on a layout manager to size the separator in one dimension. The unaffected dimension ends up being the default thickness.

AWT Tip

Avoid Hardcoding Orientation

Notice that the Graphic Java Toolkit does not have separate classes for horizontal and vertical separators. In some cases, changing the size of a container may change the orientation of a custom component from horizontal to vertical, or vice versa. Because of this, it is best if your custom components can cope with either orientation, as does gjt.Separator. Note that if a gjt.Separator starts out as a horizontal separator and is laid out such that its orientation changes to vertical, it is able to cope and repaints itself correctly.

The `Separator. paint()` method sets `brighter` to two shades brighter than the canvas background color and `darker` to two shades darker than the canvas background color:

```
public void paint(Graphics g) {
    Dimension size = size();
    Color brighter = getBackground().brighter().brighter();
    Color darker   = getBackground().darker().darker();

    if(etching == Etching.IN) {
        if(size.width > size.height)
            paintHorizontal(g, size, darker, brighter);
        else
            paintVertical(g, size, darker, brighter);
    }
    else {
        if(size.width > size.height)
            paintHorizontal(g, size, brighter, darker);
        else
            paintVertical(g, size, brighter, darker);
    }
}
```

AWT Tip

Avoid Hardcoding Colors Used for Shading

Notice that Separator uses its background color to derive the bright and dark shades that it uses to create an etched effect. We could have taken a different approach and specified Color.white and Color.darkGray (or some other explicit combination) for our etching color shades. However, if a client had set the background color of the Separator to something other than the default (light gray), we would get undesirable effects.

The paint() method also calls either paintHorizontal() or
paintVertical(). Each of these methods takes the Graphics object passed to
the paint() method, and each fills two rectangles to represent the etched-in or
etched-out lines of the separator:

```
private void paintHorizontal(Graphics g, Dimension size,
                             Color top, Color bottom) {
    g.setColor(top);
    g.fillRect(0, (size.height/2) - (thickness/2),
               size.width, thickness/2);
    g.setColor(bottom);
    g.fillRect(0, size.height/2, size.width, thickness/2);
}
private void paintVertical(Graphics g, Dimension size,
                           Color left, Color right) {
    g.setColor(left);
    g.fillRect((size.width/2) - (thickness/2),
               0, thickness/2, size.height);
    g.setColor(right);
    g.fillRect(size.width/2, 0, thickness/2, size.height);
}
}
```

Notice that to achieve the etched appearance, these methods fill two offset
rectangles, one with a color two shades darker than the background and one with
a color two shades brighter than the background. Also notice that a Separator
may have its thickness set to any desired value; however, values greater than 4
pixels tend to loose the etching effect.

With these relationships and responsibilities as a backdrop, let's take a look at the
code for the Separator class in Example 9-1. You'll notice that, as is the custom
in GJT components, there are a number of constructors, all of which call the final
constructor. A Separator may be constructed with either thickness or etching
specified, with both specified, or with neither specified, in which case the default
values are used. Separators are most often constructed with the default
constructor, which relies on the default values for etching and thickness, but it is a
nice touch to provide clients with a wide range of choices when constructing
custom components.

Example 9-1 gjt.Separator **Class Source Code**

```java
package gjt;

import java.awt.*;

public class Separator extends Canvas {
    static private Etching _defaultEtching   = Etching.IN;
    static private int     _defaultThickness = 2;

    private Etching etching;
    private int     thickness;

    public Separator() {
        this(_defaultThickness, _defaultEtching);
    }
    public Separator(int thickness) {
        this(thickness, _defaultEtching);
    }
    public Separator(Etching etching) {
        this(_defaultThickness, etching);
    }
    public Separator(int thickness, Etching etching) {
        this.etching   = etching;
        this.thickness = thickness;
        resize(thickness, thickness);
    }
    public Dimension minimumSize() {
        return preferredSize();
    }
    public Dimension preferredSize() {
        return new Dimension(thickness, thickness);
    }
    public void paint(Graphics g) {
        Dimension size     = size();
        Color brighter = getBackground().brighter().brighter();
        Color darker   = getBackground().darker().darker();
```

```
        if(etching == Etching.IN) {
            if(size.width > size.height)
                paintHorizontal(g, size, darker, brighter);
            else
                paintVertical(g, size, darker, brighter);
        }
        else {
            if(size.width > size.height)
                paintHorizontal(g, size, brighter, darker);
            else
                paintVertical(g, size, brighter, darker);
        }
    }
    public String paramString() {
        Dimension   size = size();
        Orientation orient = size.width > size.height ?
                        Orientation.HORIZONTAL :
                        Orientation.VERTICAL;
        return super.paramString() + "thickness=" +
            thickness + "," + etching + "," + orient;
    }
    private void paintHorizontal(Graphics g, Dimension size,
                                Color top, Color bottom) {
        g.setColor(top);
        g.fillRect(0, (size.height/2) - (thickness/2),
                    size.width, thickness/2);
        g.setColor(bottom);
        g.fillRect(0, size.height/2, size.width, thickness/2);
    }
    private void paintVertical(Graphics g, Dimension size,
                                Color left, Color right) {
        g.setColor(left);
        g.fillRect((size.width/2) - (thickness/2),
                    0, thickness/2, size.height);
        g.setColor(right);
        g.fillRect(size.width/2, 0, thickness/2, size.height);
    }
}
```

Exercising the Separator

When putting `gjt.Separator` to use in our unit test, `SeparatorTest` draws two separators, as shown in Figure 9-2.

```
Applet Viewer: gjt.test.SeparatorTest.class
Applet

                           Separator Test
North Of Etched—In Separator








West Of Etched—Out Separator








applet started
```

Figure 9-2 `gjt.Separator` Unit Test

As you can see from Figure 9-2, the unit test draws one horizontal and one vertical separator. The horizontal separator is etched-in, the vertical separator is etched-out, and each separator has an accompanying label. To see exactly how this set of components and containers is laid out in three dimensions, look at Figure 9-3.

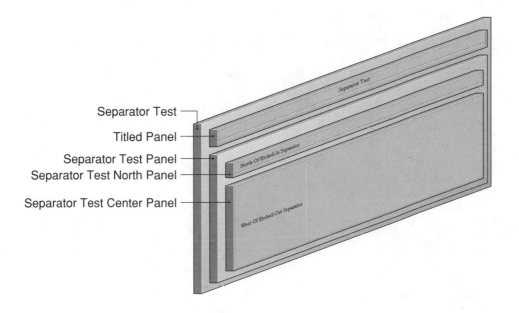

Separator Test
Titled Panel
Separator Test Panel
Separator Test North Panel
Separator Test Center Panel

Figure 9-3 `SeparatorTest` Layout Diagram

You'll want to refer to Figure 9-3 as you look through the `Separator` unit test in
Example 9-2. Pay attention to the layering of components within containers. Also,
note the use of different layout managers in different containers and the way they
position components in the display. We'll spend some time describing exactly
how `GridBagLayout` is being used after you've read through the code.

Example 9-2 `gjt.test.SeparatorTest` **Class Source Code**

```
package gjt;

import java.awt.*;
import gjt.Etching;
import gjt.Separator;

public class SeparatorTest extends UnitTest {
  public String title     () { return "Separator Test"; }
  public Panel  centerPanel() {
      return new SeparatorTestPanel();
  }
}

class SeparatorTestPanel extends Panel {
  public SeparatorTestPanel() {
```

```
        setLayout(new BorderLayout());
        add("North",  new SeparatorTestNorthPanel ());
        add("Center", new SeparatorTestCenterPanel());
    }
}

class SeparatorTestNorthPanel extends Panel {
  Separator separator = new Separator();

  public SeparatorTestNorthPanel() {
      setLayout(new BorderLayout());
      add("North", new Label("North Of Etched-In Separator"));
      add("South", separator);
  }
}

class SeparatorTestCenterPanel extends Panel {
  Separator separator = new Separator(Etching.OUT);

  public SeparatorTestCenterPanel() {
      GridBagConstraints gbc = new GridBagConstraints();
      GridBagLayout      gbl = new GridBagLayout();
      Label label = new Label("West Of Etched-Out Separator");

      setLayout(gbl);
      gbc.anchor  = GridBagConstraints.WEST;
      gbc.insets  = new Insets(0,0,0,10);
      gbl.setConstraints(label, gbc);
      add(label);

      gbc.insets  = new Insets(0,0,0,0);
      gbc.weightx = 1.0;
      gbc.weighty = 1.0;
      gbc.fill    = GridBagConstraints.VERTICAL;
      gbl.setConstraints(separator, gbc);
      add(separator);

  }
}
```

First, note that the horizontal separator and its associated label are laid out by a BorderLayout, with the label in the north and the separator in the south. The vertical separator and its associated label are laid out by a GridBagLayout, in the SeparatorTestCenterPanel:

```
   class SeparatorTestCenterPanel extends Panel {
❶    Separator separator = new Separator(Etching.OUT);

     public SeparatorTestCenterPanel() {
         GridBagConstraints gbc = new GridBagConstraints();
         GridBagLayout       gbl = new GridBagLayout();
         Label label = new Label("West Of Etched-Out Separator");

         setLayout(gbl);
❷        gbc.anchor  = GridBagConstraints.WEST;
❸        gbc.insets  = new Insets(0,0,0,10);
         gbl.setConstraints(label, gbc);
         add(label);

         gbc.insets  = new Insets(0,0,0,0);
         gbc.weightx = 1.0;
         gbc.weighty = 1.0;
❹        gbc.fill    = GridBagConstraints.VERTICAL;
         gbl.setConstraints(separator, gbc);
         add(separator);


     }
   }
```

The separator is constructed in line ❶, with its etching specified as Etching.OUT.
After the Label is constructed, the GridBagConstraints anchor and insets
are set (lines ❷ and ❸) for the label. Note that the insets are set so as to provide
some space between the label and the vertical separator. Otherwise, the separator
would butt up against the right edge of the label.

The same GridBagConstraints instance is used for both the label and the
separator, so the anchor constraint is still WEST for the Separator. However,
we override the previous insets and set the weightx, weighty, and fill
constraints. The weighty constraint is set to 1 to ensure that the grid cell in
which the Separator resides stretches in the vertical direction (refer to
page 189). The weightx value of 1 causes the cell in which the vertical separator
resides to take up the remaining space to the right of the vertical separator.
Specifying the fill constraint to GridBagConstraints.VERTICAL in line ❹
ensures that the separator itself fills the entire container in the vertical direction.

gjt.Bargauge

The Graphic Java Toolkit provides a `Bargauge` class that draws a 3-D border that can be filled with a color. Clients of `gjt.Bargauge` can specify both the fill color and the percentage of the bargauge that will be filled on the next call to `Bargauge.fill()`.

A bargauge's fill color is specified at construction time, but clients can specify both fill percentage and fill color after construction.

Bargauge Associations and Responsibilities

To see how `Bargauge` relates to the AWT and the GJT, look at Figure 9-4.

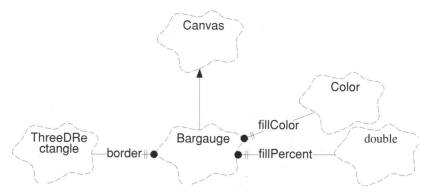

Figure 9-4 `gjt.Bargauge` Class Diagram

As you can see, `gjt.Bargauge` is another a simple custom component that extends `Canvas`. A bargauge maintains an association with a `ThreeDRectangle`, which it uses to paint a 3-D border around itself. `Bargauge` also maintains a fill color and a percentage of the bargauge that will be filled upon the next call to `Bargauge.fill()`.

Table 9-3 shows the responsibilities of a `gjt.Bargauge`.

Table 9-3 `gjt.Bargauge` **Responsibilities**

Methods	Description
`void fill()`	Fills the bargauge rectangle.
`Dimension minimumSize()`	Overrides `Component minimumSize()`. Returns the `preferredSize()`.
`void paint(Graphics g)`	Overrides `Component paint()`. Redraws the border and fills a rectangle.
`Dimension preferredSize()`	Overrides `Component preferredSize()`. Sets `preferredSize` to something other than 0,0.
`void resize(int w, int h)`	Overrides `Component resize()`.
`void reshape(int x, int y, int w, int h)`	Overrides `Component reshape()`. Resizes the border by calling `ThreeDRectangle resize()`
`void setFillColor( Color fillColor)`	Sets the color for filling the bargauge.
`void setFillPercent( double percentage)`	Sets the percentage of the bargauge to be filled. Default is 0, so it must be explicitly set.

Table 9-4 shows the associations of a `gjt.Bargauge`.

Table 9-4 `gjt.Bargauge` **Associations**

Variables	Description
`ThreeDRectangle border`	Draws a 3-D border around the bargauge.
`Color fillColor`	The color to be used for filling the bargauge.
`double fillPercent`	The percent of the bargauge to be filled.

We'll focus our discussion less on how `Bargauge` works and more on those things we've done peculiar to developing a custom component. For instance, when you look through the implementation of `gjt.Bargauge` in Example 9-3 on page 265, you'll notice that it overrides `resize()` and `reshape()`:

```
      public void resize(int w, int h) {
❶         reshape(location().x, location().y, w, h);
      }
      public void reshape(int x, int y, int w, int h) {
❷         super.reshape(x,y,w,h);
          border.resize(w,h);
      }
```

Notice how resize() calls reshape() in line ❶, using the
Component.location() method to determine the upper left-hand corner of
the bargauge. reshape() passes those coordinates, along with the width and
height, to super.reshape() in line ❷. Then, we resize the border in line ❸,
ensuring that it sizes proportionately to the bargauge.

AWT Tip

Call super.reshape() When Overriding reshape()

It is often necessary when developing custom components to override
reshape(). For instance, gjt.Bargauge overrides reshape() so that it can reshape
its border. One thing that is easily forgotten and can lead to a frustrating debugging session is the fact that when overriding reshape(), you must remember to
call super.reshape() or the component will not reshape correctly.

Let's also take a closer look at how gjt.Bargauge overrides the
preferredSize() method:

```
      public Dimension preferredSize() {
          int w = border.getThickness() * 3;
          return new Dimension(w, w*4);
      }
```

gjt.Bargauge specifies its preferred width as three times the border thickness,
and its height as four times the width. The height calculation is somewhat
arbitrary. The width, however is important because we want to ensure that when
a bargauge is filled, we can see the color. If the width were less than three times
the border thickness, there would not be enough room inside the border to
display the color. As it is, we provide room for the border on the left, the border
on the right, and the width of the border in the middle for the color.

You'll notice that gjt.Bargauge overrides the paint() method in order to
raise and paint the border and to fill the bargauge by invoking the fill()
method. The fill() method clears the interior of the bargauge and, depending
on its orientation, fills it accordingly:

```
public void fill() {
    Graphics g = getGraphics();

    if((g != null) && (percentFill > 0)) {
        Rectangle b      = border.getInnerBounds();
        int       fillw  = b.width;
        int       fillh  = b.height;

        if(b.width > b.height) fillw *= percentFill/100;
        else                   fillh *= percentFill/100;

        g.setColor(fillColor);
        border.clearInterior();

        if(b.width > b.height)
            g.fillRect(b.x, b.y, fillw, b.height);
        else
            g.fillRect(b.x, b.y + b.height - fillh,
                       b.width, fillh);
    }
}
```

Now, with these relationships with `Canvas` and its public methods in mind, let's take a look at the code for the `gjt.Bargauge` class in Example 9-3.

Notice while you look through the code that the `gjt.Bargauge` constructor does not provide a default color. We assume that anyone using `Bargauge` wants to specify a color that has some relevance rather than an arbitrary color, so we require clients to specify a color at the time of construction.

Example 9-3 `gjt.Bargauge` **Class Source Code**

```
package gjt;

import java.awt.*;

public class Bargauge extends Canvas {
    private double         percentFill = 0;
    private ThreeDRectangle border = new ThreeDRectangle(this);
    private Color          fillColor;

    public Bargauge(Color fillColor) {
        setFillColor(fillColor);
    }
    public void setFillColor(Color fillColor) {
        this.fillColor = fillColor;
    }
```

```
public void setFillPercent(double percentage) {
    Assert.notFalse(percentage >= 0 && percentage <= 100);
    percentFill = percentage;
}
public void resize(int w, int h) {
    reshape(location().x, location().y, w, h);
}
public void reshape(int x, int y, int w, int h) {
    super.reshape(x,y,w,h);
    border.resize(w,h);
}
public Dimension minimumSize() { return preferredSize(); }

public Dimension preferredSize() {
    int w = border.getThickness() * 3;
    return new Dimension(w, w*4);
}
public void paint(Graphics g) {
    border.raise();
    border.paint();
    fill();
}
public void fill() {
    Graphics g = getGraphics();

    if((g != null) && (percentFill > 0)) {
        Rectangle b      = border.getInnerBounds();
        int       fillw  = b.width;
        int       fillh  = b.height;

        if(b.width > b.height) fillw *= percentFill/100;
        else                   fillh *= percentFill/100;

        g.setColor(fillColor);
        border.clearInterior();

        if(b.width > b.height)
            g.fillRect(b.x, b.y, fillw, b.height);
        else
            g.fillRect(b.x, b.y + b.height - fillh,
                       b.width, fillh);
    }
}
```

```
protected String paramString() {
    Dimension size = size();
    Orientation orient = size.width > size.height ?
                            Orientation.HORIZONTAL :
                            Orientation.VERTICAL;
    String    str = "fill percent=" + percentFill + "," +
                        "orientation=" + orient       + "," +
                        "color"        + fillColor;
    return str;
    }
}
```

You've probably noticed that we've used paramString() in several components already described, but it's worth noting here because it leads us to one of our AWT Tips.

AWT Tip

Implement paramString() For Custom Components

If you've done any significant AWT development without a debugger, you've come to appreciate the fact that you can invoke toString() on any of the standard AWT components and obtain some meaningful information about the component. Custom components should also provide the same service by implementing paramString(). Note that the Component class implements a toString(), whioh invokcs Component.paramStriny(). Overrldlng param-String() to supply a string representing the parameters of your custom component is a nice touch that clients of your custom components will be grateful for.

Exercising the Bargauge

We've provided a couple of test applets to show gjt.Bargauge in action. The first one, called SimpleBargaugeTest in Example 9-4 on page 269, illustrates how the applet can be resized to the point that it changes the bargauge's orientation from vertical to horizontal, and the bargauge continues to function normally. Figure 9-5 shows a picture of the simple bargauge test.

Figure 9-5 gjt.Bargauge Class Simple Test
The bargauge continues to operate properly, even when it is
resized and changes orientation from horizontal to vertical.

This simple test creates a single, animated Bargauge. (Run this test with the
appletviewer, so that the window can be resized such that the bargauge
changes its orientation.)

WARNING: An AWT bug causes this test to be a gluttonous consumer of resources, especially under Windows 95. A mouse down will halt the animation thread and its consumption of resources.

Example 9-4 `gjt.test.SimpleBargaugeTest` **Class Source Code**

CD-Rom

```java
package gjt.test;

import java.awt.*;
import gjt.Bargauge;

public class SimpleBargaugeTest extends UnitTest {
    public String title() {
        return "Simple Bargauge Test";
    }
    public Panel centerPanel() {
        return new SimpleBargaugeTestPanel();
    }
}

class SimpleBargaugeTestPanel extends Panel implements Runnable {
    private Bargauge gauge = new Bargauge(Color.blue);
    private boolean  running = true;
    private Thread   t;

    public SimpleBargaugeTestPanel() {
        setLayout(new BorderLayout());
        add("Center", gauge);

        t = new Thread(this);
        t.start();
    }
    public void run() {
        while(true) {
            try { Thread.currentThread().sleep(500,0); }
            catch(InterruptedException e) { }

            gauge.setFillPercent(Math.random() * 100);
            gauge.fill();
        }
    }
    public boolean mouseDown(Event event, int x, int y) {
        if(running)  { t.suspend(); running = false; }
        else         { t.resume (); running = true;  }
        return true;
    }
}
```

The full-blown unit test for gjt.Bargauge creates a set of vertical or horizontal gauges filled with random colors, as in Figure 9-6.

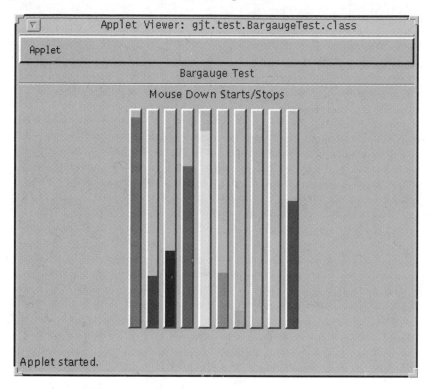

Figure 9-6 gjt.Bargauge Unit Test

As you can see, the gjt.Bargauge unit test creates an array of horizontal (or vertical) animated bargauges. The bargauges are horizontal or vertical, based on the orientation parameter passed to the applet. Figure 9-7 shows a layout diagram of the bargauge unit test.

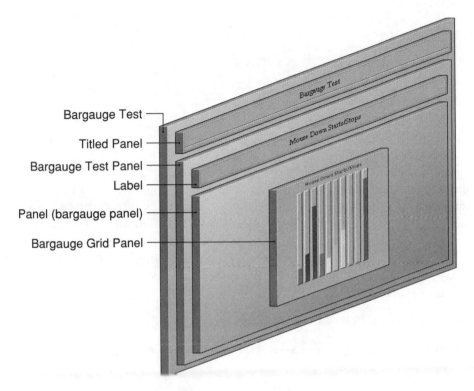

Bargauge Test

Titled Panel

Bargauge Test Panel

Label

Panel (bargauge panel)

Bargauge Grid Panel

Figure 9-7 BargaugeTest Layout Diagram

Example 9-5 shows how this unit test uses the Bargauge class. You'll want to reference Figure 9-7 as you look through the BargaugeTest unit test.

WARNING: An AWT bug causes this test to be a gluttonous consumer of resources, especially under Windows 95. A mouse down will halt the animation thread and its consumption of resources.

One specific topic of interest in this unit test is the use of layout managers, particularly, in the BargaugeTestPanel class:

```
    class BargaugeTestPanel extends Panel {
      public BargaugeTestPanel(Bargauge[] gauges, String orient) {
❶        Panel bargaugePanel = new Panel();

          setLayout(new BorderLayout());
          add("North",
              new Label("Mouse Down Starts/Stops",Label.CENTER));
          add("Center", bargaugePanel);

❷        bargaugePanel.add(new BargaugeGridPanel(gauges,orient));
      }
    }
```

Line ❶ creates a new panel that will be centered in `BargaugeTestPanel` (see Figure 9-7), which has a `BorderLayout` layout manager. Line ❷ then adds a `BargaugeGridPanel` to `bargaugePanel`, which by default uses a `FlowLayout` layout manager. This ensures that the `BargaugeGridPanel` is always centered in the `bargaugePanel`. (You can see this in the unit test output in Figure 9-6 on page 270. Whenever the applet is resized, `BargaugeGridPanel` remains centered in the horizontal direction.)

Here's the unit test in its entirety.

Example 9-5 `gjt.test.BargaugeTest` **Class Source Code**

```
package gjt;

import java.awt.*;
import java.applet.*;
import gjt.Bargauge;

public class BargaugeTest extends UnitTest {
    private Bargauge[] gauges = new Bargauge[10];
    private Thread      animatorThread;
    private boolean     running;

    public String title() {
        return "Bargauge Test";
    }
    public Panel   centerPanel() {
        return new BargaugeTestPanel(
                    gauges, getParameter("orientation"));
    }
    public boolean mouseDown(Event event, int x, int y) {
        if(running == true) {
            animatorThread.suspend();
            running = false;
        }
```

```
        else {
            animatorThread.resume ();
            running = true;
        }
        return true;
    }
  public void start() {
        super.start();
        animatorThread = new BargaugeAnimator(gauges);
        animatorThread.start();
        running = true;
    }
  public void stop() {
        super.stop();
        animatorThread.suspend();
        running = false;
    }
}


class BargaugeTestPanel extends Panel {
  public BargaugeTestPanel(Bargauge[] gauges, String orient) {
        Panel bargaugePanel = new Panel();

        setLayout(new BorderLayout());
        add("North",
            new Label("Mouse Down Starts/Stops",Label.CENTER));
        add("Center", bargaugePanel);

        bargaugePanel.add(new BargaugeGridPanel(gauges,orient));
    }
}

class BargaugeGridPanel extends Panel {
  private Dimension  preferredSize = new Dimension(200, 250);

  public BargaugeGridPanel(Bargauge[] gauges, String orient) {
        Bargauge nextGauge;
        Color    color = Color.gray;

        if("horizontal".equals(orient))
            setLayout(new GridLayout(gauges.length,0,5,5));
        else
            setLayout(new GridLayout(0,gauges.length,5,5));

        for(int i=0; i < gauges.length; ++i) {
            switch(i) {
                case 1:  color = Color.darkGray;    break;
                case 2:  color = Color.blue;        break;
```

```
                    case 3:   color = Color.magenta;      break;
                    case 4:   color = Color.yellow;       break;
                    case 5:   color = Color.green;        break;
                    case 6:   color = Color.cyan;         break;
                    case 7:   color = Color.orange;       break;
                    case 8:   color = Color.pink;         break;
                    case 9:   color = Color.red;          break;
                    case 10:  color = Color.yellow;       break;
                }
            nextGauge = new Bargauge(color);
            gauges[i] = nextGauge;
            add(nextGauge);
        }
    }
    public Dimension preferredSize() { return preferredSize; }
    public Dimension minimumSize  () { return preferredSize; }
}

class BargaugeAnimator extends Thread {
    private Bargauge[] gauges;
    private boolean     firstAnimation = true;

    public BargaugeAnimator(Bargauge[] gauges) {
        this.gauges = gauges;
    }
    public void run() {
        int count = gauges.length;

        while(true) {
            try { Thread.currentThread().sleep(500,0); }
            catch(InterruptedException e) { }
            for(int i=0; i < count; ++i) {
                gauges[i].setFillPercent(Math.random() * 100);
                gauges[i].fill();

                if(firstAnimation)
                    System.out.println(gauges[i].toString());
            }
            firstAnimation = false;
        }
    }
}
```

Summary

In this chapter, we've explored the `gjt.Separator` and `gjt.Bargauge` custom components from the Graphic Java Toolkit and described their implementations and unit tests. Presenting these custom components has prompted a few guidelines you can use in creating your own custom components. For example, when overriding `reshape()`, it's imperative to call `super.reshape()` or else the component will not reshape correctly. (The peer will never be given a chance to reshape.) Also, it's useful practice in custom components to override `paramString()`. By so doing, you supply clients of your component with a string representing parameters in the custom component.

CHAPTER 10

- gjt.Border on page 277

- gjt.ThreeDBorder on page 282

- gjt.EtchedBorder on page 283

- Exercising Border on page 284

- Summary on page 295

Borders

For a variety of reasons, it is sometimes useful to draw a border around a component. Perhaps you'd like to use a flat border around a component to signify focus, or maybe you'd like to jazz up your components by drawing a 3-D or etched border around them.

This chapter introduces three classes from the Graphic Java Toolkit: `Border`, `EtchedBorder`, and `ThreeDBorder`. Similar to `gjt.Box`, which we introduced in *Components, Containers, and Layout Managers*, `Border`, `EtchedBorder`, and `ThreeDBorder` all contain a single component. The job of the border classes is to contain the component and draw a border around it with a specified gap between the inside of the border and the outside of the component.

Discussing the border classes will afford us an opportunity to focus on overriding `Panel` and redefining insets.

gjt.Border

The `gjt.Border` class extends `Panel` and tracks the thickness of the border, along with the gap between the border and the component it contains. Additionally, `Border` employs a `DrawnRectangle` to draw a flat border around the component, as illustrated in Figure 10-1.

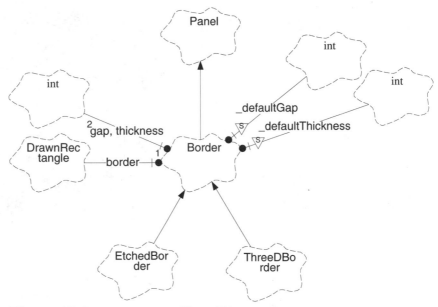

Figure 10-1 `gjt.Border` Class Diagram

AWT Tip

Canvas or Panel?

A Canvas, as its name implies, is a surface on which you can paint. What may be surprising is that you can also paint on a Panel.

The difference between a Canvas and a Panel is that a Panel is a Container, whereas a Canvas is a mere Component. Think of a Panel as a Canvas that can contain components.

The responsibilities of `gjt.Border` are listed in Table 10-2.

Table 10-1 gjt.Border **Responsibilities**

Methods	Description
void paint(Graphics g)	Overrides Component paint(). Paints the border.
Dimension minimumSize()	Overrides Component minimumSize(). Returns preferredSize().
void resize(int w, int h)	Overrides Component resize(). This is a precautionary measure.
void reshape(int x, int y, int w, int h)	Overrides Component reshape(). Reshapes the border.
Insets insets()	Overrides Component insets(). Returns insets equal to the border thickness plus the gap.
Rectangle getInnerBounds()	Returns the inner bounds of the border.
void setLineColor(Color c)	Sets the line color for the border.
Color getLineColor()	Returns current line color for the border.
String paramString()	Returns parameters particular to the border.

Table 10-1 lists the associations of a gjt.Border.

Table 10-2 gjt.Border **Associations**

Variables	Description
int gap	Sets the gap between inside of border and outside of component.
int thickness	Sets the thickness of the border.
DrawnRectangle border	Paints the border.

As we've established, a Border is a Panel containing a single Component, around which a border is drawn. Now that we've got a good idea about what a Border does and how it does it, let's look at the actual class code in Example 10-1.

Example 10-1 `gjt.Border` **Class Source Code**

```java
package gjt;

import java.awt.*;

public class Border extends Panel {
    protected int           thickness;
    protected int           gap;
    protected DrawnRectangle border;

    protected static int _defaultThickness = 2;
    protected static int _defaultGap       = 0;

    public Border(Component borderMe) {
        this(borderMe, _defaultThickness, _defaultGap);
    }
    public Border(Component borderMe, int thickness) {
        this(borderMe, thickness, _defaultGap);
    }
    public Border(Component borderMe, int thickness, int gap) {
        this.thickness = thickness;
        this.gap       = gap;

        setLayout(new BorderLayout());
        add("Center", borderMe);
    }
    public Insets insets() {
        return new Insets(thickness+gap, thickness+gap,
                          thickness+gap, thickness+gap);
    }
    public Rectangle getInnerBounds() {
        return border().getInnerBounds();
    }
    public void setLineColor(Color c) {
        border().setLineColor(c);
    }
    public Color getLineColor()            {
        return border().getLineColor();
    }
    public void paint(Graphics g) {
        border().paint();
    }
```

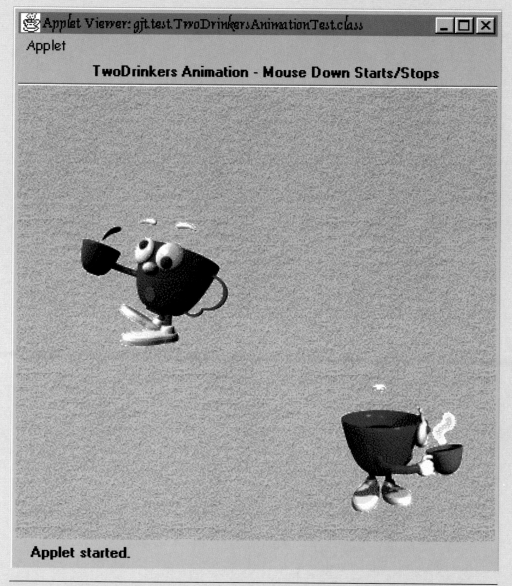

TwoDrinkers Animation

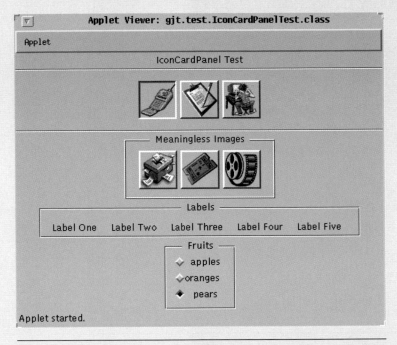

IconCardPanel Test

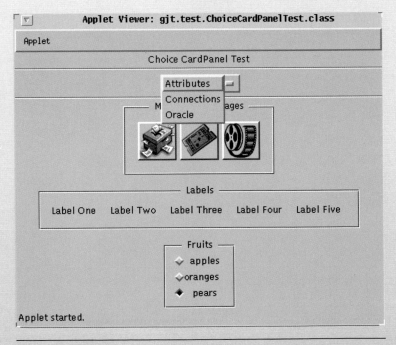

ChoiceCardPanel Test

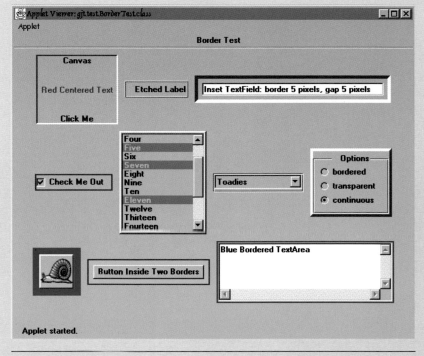

BorderTest

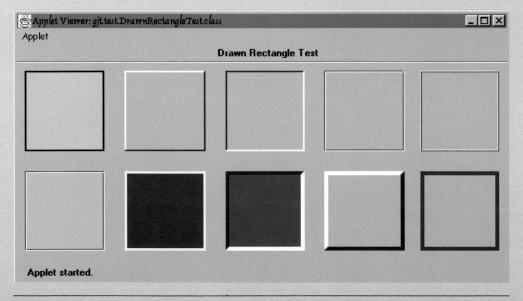

DrawRectangleTest

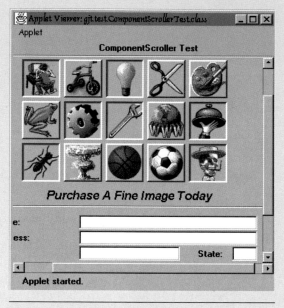

ComponentScroller Test

RowLayout Test

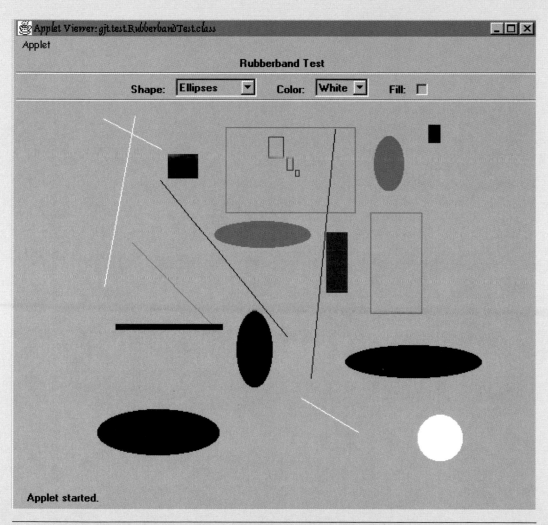

Rubberband Test

ImageDissolver Test

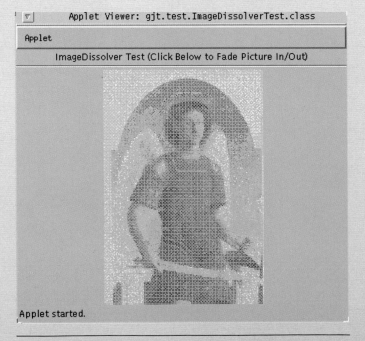

ImageDissolver Test

ImageDissolver Test

BleachImageFilter Test

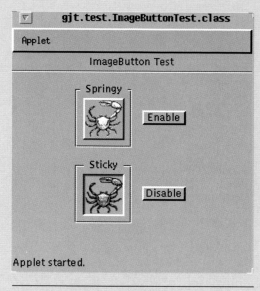

ImageButton Test

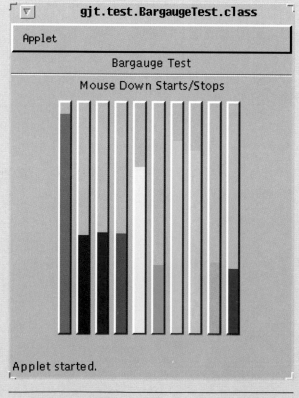

Bargauge Test

```
public void resize(int w, int h) {
    Point location = location();
    reshape(location.x, location.y, w, h);
}
public void reshape(int x, int y, int w, int h) {
    super.reshape(x, y, w, h);
    border().resize(w, h);
}
protected String paramString() {
    return super.paramString() + ",border=" +
            border().toString() + ",thickness=" + thickness
        + ",gap=" + gap;
}
protected DrawnRectangle border() {
    if(border == null)
        border = new DrawnRectangle(this, thickness);
    return border;
}
}
```

Notice that the thickness of the border and the gap between the `Component` and the border are specified at construction time:

```
public Border(Component borderMe, int thickness, int gap) {
    this.thickness = thickness;
    this.gap       = gap;

    setLayout(new BorderLayout());
    add("Center", borderMe);
}
```

`gjt.Border` employs a `gjt.DrawnRectangle` to actually paint the border:

```
protected DrawnRectangle border() {
    if(border == null)
        border = new DrawnRectangle(this, thickness);
    return border;
}
```

Derived classes are free to override `DrawnRectangle border()` in order to use an extension of `DrawnRectangle` for drawing their border.

gjt.ThreeDBorder

The `gjt.ThreeDBorder` class extends `Border` and, as its name indicates, draws a 3-D border. Notice as you look through Example 10-2 that the border can be drawn either raised, which is the default, or inset.

Example 10-2 `gjt.ThreeDBorder` **Class Source Code**

```
package gjt;

import java.awt.*;

public class ThreeDBorder extends Border {
  public ThreeDBorder(Component borderMe) {
      this(borderMe, _defaultThickness, _defaultGap);
  }
  public ThreeDBorder(Component borderMe,
                      int borderThickness) {
      this(borderMe, borderThickness, _defaultGap);
  }
  public ThreeDBorder(Component borderMe,
                      int borderThickness, int gap) {
      super(borderMe, borderThickness, gap);
  }
  public void inset() { ((ThreeDRectangle)border()).inset(); }
  public void raise() { ((ThreeDRectangle)border()).raise(); }

  public void paintRaised() {
      ((ThreeDRectangle)border()).paintRaised();
  }
  public void paintInset() {
      ((ThreeDRectangle)border()).paintInset ();
  }
  public boolean isRaised() {
      return ((ThreeDRectangle)border()).isRaised();
  }
  protected DrawnRectangle border() {
      if(border == null)
          border = new ThreeDRectangle(this, thickness);
      return border;
  }
 }
```

Notice that the drawing style used by `paint()` is controlled by `raise()` and `inset()`. Those methods do not cause any painting to be done; they just set the state for the next call to `paint()`. Using the `paintRaised()` and `paintInset()` methods provides the means to set the state and paint in one operation.

gjt.EtchedBorder

`gjt.EtchedBorder` is a `Border` that does just what it suggests; it draws an etched border. An `EtchedBorder` can be drawn either etched-in (the default) or etched-out. Example 10-3 shows the `EtchedBorder` class in its entirety. Notice as you look through the code that the drawing style used by `paint()` is controlled by the `etchedIn()` and `etchedOut()` methods. Those methods do not result in anything being painted but only set the state for the next call to `paint()`. Using the `paintEtchedIn()` and `paintEtchedOut()` methods provides the means to set the state and to paint in one operation.

Example 10-3 `gjt.EtchedBorder` **Class Source Code**

```java
package gjt;

import java.awt.*;

public class EtchedBorder extends Border {
  public EtchedBorder(Component borderMe) {
      this(borderMe, _defaultThickness, _defaultGap);
  }
  public EtchedBorder(Component borderMe,
                      int borderThickness) {
      this(borderMe, borderThickness, _defaultGap);
  }
  public EtchedBorder(Component borderMe,
                      int borderThickness, int gap) {
      super(borderMe, borderThickness, gap);
  }
  public void etchedIn() {
      ((EtchedRectangle)border()).etchedIn();
  }
  public void etchedOut() {
      ((EtchedRectangle)border()).etchedOut();
  }
  public void paintEtchedIn() {
      ((EtchedRectangle)border()).paintEtchedIn ();
  }
  public void paintEtchedOut() {
      ((EtchedRectangle)border()).paintEtchedOut();
  }
  public boolean isEtchedIn() {
      return ((EtchedRectangle)border()).isEtchedIn();
  }
  protected String paramString() {
      return super.paramString() + (EtchedRectangle)border();
  }
```

```
protected DrawnRectangle border() {
    if(border == null)
        border = new EtchedRectangle(this, thickness);
    return border;
}
}
```

Exercising Border

When we put the Border class to use in our very busy unit test, it looks like the applet in Figure 10-2.

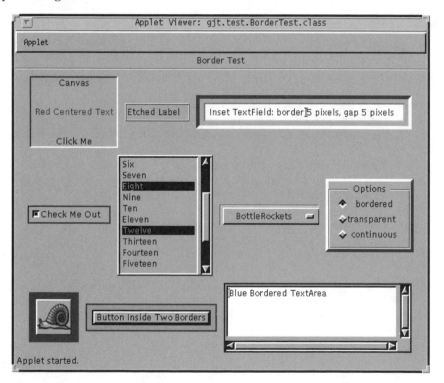

Figure 10-2 gjt.Border Unit Test

Figure 10-3 illustrates in three dimensions how this test is constructed.

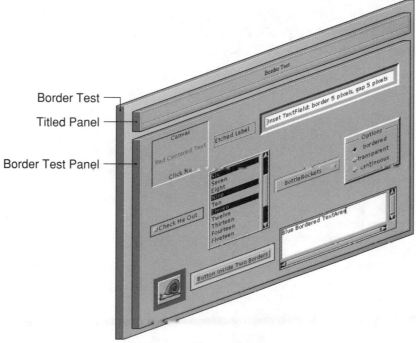

Figure 10-3 BorderTest Layout Diagram

You may want to refer to Figure 10-2 and Figure 10-3 as you look through the unit test in Example 10-4 on page 291. As you can see, the layout for the Border unit test is quite simple. As with all unit tests, the applet lays out a TitledPanel in the north for which we provide the title string, while we provide the Panel to be laid out in the center of the applet [1]:

```
public class BorderTest extends UnitTest {
  public String title() {
      return "Border Test";
  }
  public Panel  centerPanel() {
      return new BorderTestPanel(this);
  }
}
```

1. See *Introducing the Graphic Java Toolkit* on page 237 for a discussion of the UnitTest and TitledPanel classes.

Our `BorderTestPanel`, which is laid out in the center of the applet, uses a `FlowLayout` with a centered alignment and horizontal and vertical gaps between components of ten pixels. From there on out, we add ten borders, all of which are constructed by private `BorderTestPanel` methods:

```
public BorderTestPanel(Applet applet) {
    setLayout(new FlowLayout(FlowLayout.CENTER, 10, 10));

    add(new BorderedCanvas());
    add(etchedLabel =
            new EtchedBorder(new Label("Etched Label")));
    add(threeDBorder = new ThreeDBorder(tf, 5, 5));
    add(new Border(new Checkbox("Check Me Out")));
    add(makeThreeDBorderedList        ());
    add(makeEtchedBorderedChoice      ());
    add(makeThreeDBorderedCheckboxes());
    add(makeBorderedImageButton       (applet));
    add(makeBorderedAWTButton         ());
    add(makeBorderedTextArea          ());

    threeDBorder.inset();
    etchedLabel.etchedOut();
}
```

The important thing to note here is that each of the private methods returns a `Border`. Therefore, each `add()` call in the `BorderTestPanel` constructor is adding a `Border` to itself.

Each private method creates a component and a border. The component is passed to the `Border` constructor, and the border is returned to be added to the `BorderTestPanel`. For instance, the `makeBorderedTextArea()` method looks like this:

```
private Border makeBorderedTextArea() {
    Border border;

    border = new Border(
            new TextArea("Blue Bordered TextArea", 5, 30));
    border.setLineColor(Color.blue);

    return border;
}
}
```

We pass the `Border` constructor a newly constructed `TextArea`, set the border line color to blue, and return the `border`.

Remember that a `Border` can contain multiple components simply by passing its constructor a `Container` [2]. The `makeThreeDBorderedCheckboxes()` method creates a `Panel`, to which it adds three checkboxes. Then a `Box` is constructed, which is passed the `panel` and the string "Options." Finally, a `ThreeDBorder` is constructed by passing it the box. The result is that the bordered checkboxes you see in the unit test are actually a `ThreeDBorder` containing a `Box` [3] that contains the three checkboxes:

Through the magic of inheritance, we are able to return a `ThreeDBorder` from a method that returns a `Border`:

```
private Border makeThreeDBorderedCheckboxes() {
    Panel          panel = new Panel();
    Box            box   = new Box(panel, "Options");
    CheckboxGroup  group = new CheckboxGroup();

    panel.setLayout(new GridLayout(3,0));
    panel.add(new Checkbox("bordered",    group, false));
    panel.add(new Checkbox("transparent", group, false));
    panel.add(new Checkbox("continuous",  group, true));

    return new ThreeDBorder(box, 4);
}
```

---

2. Recall that a `Container` is an extension of `Component`.
3. Recall that a `Box` is similar to a `Border` in that it surrounds a component. See the *Components, Containers, and Layout Managers* chapter for details.

The CheckBoxGroup ensures that only one of the checkboxes in the group is checked at any given time. The checkboxes are added to the group by passing group to their constructor.

Since a Border is a Panel to which a component may be added, it is perfectly acceptable to add a border to another border, thus wrapping a component in multiple borders. This is done in the makeBorderedAWTButton() method:

```
private Border makeBorderedAWTButton() {
    Button button;
    Border cyanBorder, blackBorder;

    button = new Button("Button Inside Two Borders");
    cyanBorder = new Border(button, 7);
    cyanBorder.setLineColor(Color.cyan);

    blackBorder = new Border(cyanBorder);

    return blackBorder;
}
```

makeBorderedAWTButton() places a java.awt.Button in the cyanBorder. (Refer to the color inserts to see the cyan in the cyan border.) The thickness of the cyanBorder, specified at construction time is seven pixels, and the line color of the cyanBorder is set to cyan. The cyanBorder is subsequently placed inside the blackBorder, and it is the blackBorder that is returned and added to the BorderTestPanel. The result is a button bordered by a seven pixel thick cyan border, bordered by a black border. (The black border that surrounds the button itself is a focus indicator):

The last thing to note about the Border unit test is that we add a bordered Canvas, which is an extension of ThreeDBorder:

```
class BorderedCanvas extends ThreeDBorder {
  public BorderedCanvas() {
      super(new TestCanvas());
  }
  public boolean mouseDown(Event event, int x, int y) {
      if(isRaised()) paintInset ();
      else            paintRaised();
      return true;
  }
}
```

The rationale for extending `ThreeDBorder` is that we wish to react to mouse down events, which we accomplish by overriding `mouseDown()`. If the border is raised, a mouse down event results in painting the border inset. If the border is inset, a mouse down results in painting the border raised. The result of all this is that the border is toggled between raised and inset every time a mouse down occurs in the canvas.

Notice that the `BorderedCanvas` constructor passes an instance of `TestCanvas` to the `ThreeDBorder` constructor. `TestCanvas` displays two strings, one centered at the top of the canvas ("Canvas") and one centered at the bottom of the canvas ("Click Me"). Additionally, every time a mouse up event occurs in the `TestCanvas`, a string ("Red Centered Text") is drawn or erased from the center of the canvas. If the canvas is raised, the string is erased. If the canvas is inset, the string is drawn. All of the centering of the text strings is accomplished by using the canvas size and the border's `FontMetrics` [4]:

4.   See *Graphics, Colors, and Fonts* for more information on use of `FontMetrics`.

```
class TestCanvas extends Canvas {
  private boolean centeredShowing = false;
  private String  centered = new String ("Red Centered Text");

  public void paint(Graphics g) {
      String      canvas = "Canvas";
      String      click  = "Click Me";
      Dimension   size   = size();
      FontMetrics fm     = g.getFontMetrics();

      g.drawString(canvas, (size.width/2) -
                          (fm.stringWidth(canvas)/2),
                          fm.getHeight() - fm.getDescent());

      g.drawString(click, (size.width/2) -
                          (fm.stringWidth(click)/2),
                          size.height - fm.getHeight() +
                          fm.getAscent());

      if(centeredShowing == true) {
          g.setColor(Color.red);
          g.drawString(centered,
              size.width/2-(fm.stringWidth(centered)/2),
              size.height/2 - (fm.getHeight()/2) +
              fm.getAscent());
      }
  }
  public Dimension preferredSize() {
      FontMetrics fm = getGraphics().getFontMetrics();
      return new Dimension(fm.stringWidth(centered)+10, 100);
  }
  public boolean mouseUp(Event event, int x, int y) {
      if(centeredShowing == false) centeredShowing = true;
      else                         centeredShowing = false;
      repaint();
      return true;
  }
}
```

Before we present the Border unit test source code in its entirety in Example 10-4, we should point out that the etched border around the Choice has its left and bottom edges obliterated. This is because of an AWT bug under Motif that results in an incorrect size being calculated for Choice objects.

Example 10-4 gjt.test.BorderTest **Class Source Code**

```java
package gjt.test;

import java.applet.Applet;
import java.awt.*;
import gjt.Border;
import gjt.Box;
import gjt.EtchedBorder;
import gjt.ImageButton;
import gjt.ThreeDBorder;

public class BorderTest extends UnitTest {
  public String title() {
      return "Border Test";
  }
  public Panel  centerPanel() {
      return new BorderTestPanel(this);
  }
}

class BorderTestPanel extends Panel {
  TextField tf = new TextField(
          "Inset TextField: border 5 pixels, gap 5 pixels ");
  ThreeDBorder threeDBorder;
  EtchedBorder etchedLabel;
  Border        border;

  public BorderTestPanel(Applet applet) {
      setLayout(new FlowLayout(FlowLayout.CENTER, 10, 10));

      add(new BorderedCanvas());
      add(etchedLabel =
              new EtchedBorder(new Label("Etched Label")));
      add(threeDBorder = new ThreeDBorder(tf, 5, 5));
      add(new Border(new Checkbox("Check Me Out")));
      add(makeThreeDBorderedList        ());
      add(makeEtchedBorderedChoice      ());
      add(makeThreeDBorderedCheckboxes());
      add(makeBorderedImageButton       (applet));
      add(makeBorderedAWTButton         ());
      add(makeBorderedTextArea          ());

      threeDBorder.inset();
      etchedLabel.etchedOut();
  }
  private Border makeThreeDBorderedList() {
      List list = new List(10, true);
```

```
        list.addItem("One");
        list.addItem("Two");
        list.addItem("Three");
        list.addItem("Four");
        list.addItem("Five");
        list.addItem("Six");
        list.addItem("Seven");
        list.addItem("Eight");
        list.addItem("Nine");
        list.addItem("Ten");
        list.addItem("Eleven");
        list.addItem("Twelve");
        list.addItem("Thirteen");
        list.addItem("Fourteen");
        list.addItem("Fiveteen");
        list.addItem("Sixteen");
        list.addItem("Seventeen");
        list.addItem("Eightteen");
        list.addItem("Nineteen");
        list.addItem("Twenty");

        return new ThreeDBorder(list);
    }
    private Border makeEtchedBorderedChoice() {
        Choice choice = new Choice();

        choice.addItem("Toadies");
        choice.addItem("SilverChair");
        choice.addItem("Rug Burns");
        choice.addItem("Cracker");
        choice.addItem("Seven Mary Three");
        choice.addItem("Dishwalla");
        choice.addItem("Blues Traveler");
        choice.addItem("BottleRockets");
        choice.addItem("SpaceHog");

        return new EtchedBorder(choice);
    }
    private Border makeBorderedImageButton(Applet applet) {
        Image  snail;
        Border border;

        snail = applet.getImage(applet.getCodeBase(),
                                "gifs/snail.gif");
        border = new Border(new ImageButton(snail), 10);
        border.setLineColor(Color.red);

        return border;
```

```
    }
    private Border makeBorderedAWTButton() {
        Button button;
        Border cyanBorder, blackBorder;

        button = new Button("Button Inside Two Borders");
        cyanBorder = new Border(button, 7);
        cyanBorder.setLineColor(Color.cyan);

        blackBorder = new Border(cyanBorder);

        return blackBorder;
    }
    private Border makeThreeDBorderedCheckboxes() {
        Panel          panel = new Panel();
        Box            box   = new Box(panel, "Options");
        CheckboxGroup group = new CheckboxGroup();

        panel.setLayout(new GridLayout(3,0));
        panel.add(new Checkbox("bordered",    group, false));
        panel.add(new Checkbox("transparent", group, false));
        panel.add(new Checkbox("continuous",  group, true));

        return new ThreeDBorder(box, 4);
    }
    private Border makeBorderedTextArea() {
        Border border;

        border = new Border(
                 new TextArea("Blue Bordered TextArea", 5, 30));
        border.setLineColor(Color.blue);

        return border;
    }
}

class BorderedCanvas extends ThreeDBorder {
  public BorderedCanvas() {
        super(new TestCanvas());
  }
  public boolean mouseDown(Event event, int x, int y) {
        if(isRaised()) paintInset ();
        else           paintRaised();
        return true;
  }
}

class TestCanvas extends Canvas {
```

```
private boolean centeredShowing = false;
private String  centered = new String ("Red Centered Text");

public void paint(Graphics g) {
    String       canvas = "Canvas";
    String       click  = "Click Me";
    Dimension    size   = size();
    FontMetrics  fm     = g.getFontMetrics();

    g.drawString(canvas, (size.width/2) -
                      (fm.stringWidth(canvas)/2),
                      fm.getHeight() - fm.getDescent());

    g.drawString(click, (size.width/2) -
                      (fm.stringWidth(click)/2),
                      size.height - fm.getHeight() +
                      fm.getAscent());

    if(centeredShowing == true) {
        g.setColor(Color.red);
        g.drawString(centered,
            size.width/2-(fm.stringWidth(centered)/2),
            size.height/2 - (fm.getHeight()/2) +
            fm.getAscent());
    }
}
public Dimension preferredSize() {
    FontMetrics fm = getGraphics().getFontMetrics();
    return new Dimension(fm.stringWidth(centered)+10, 100);
}
public boolean mouseUp(Event event, int x, int y) {
    if(centeredShowing == false) centeredShowing = true;
    else                         centeredShowing = false;
    repaint();
    return true;
}
}
```

Summary

Borders are useful in a number of situations and can be used to spruce up components displayed in an applet. They can also be used in grouping components together [5]. The GJT provides three types of borders: Border, which draws a flat border, EtchedBorder, which draws a border either etched-in or etched-out, and ThreeDBorder, which draws a 3-D border either raised or inset.

Borders extend Pane, and must be supplied with a component at construction time. The component supplied at construction time is centered in the border with the assistance of a BorderLayout. A border may contain multiple components by passing it a Container at construction time. Finally, since a GJT border is a Panel and a Panel is a Container, we can pass a border to another border's constructor, thereby surrounding a component with multiple borders.

---

5.   If you simply want to group components together and give the group a title, Box is more suited to your needs.

CHAPTER
11

- gjt.Image Button on page 297

- gjt.ImageButton Associations and Responsibilities on page 298

- Image Button Controllers on page 306

- ImageButton Events on page 314

- Exercising the Image Button and Its Controllers on page 315

- gjt.StateButton on page 322

- Exercising the StateButton and Its Controllers on page 324

- Summary on page 327

ImageButton and StateButton

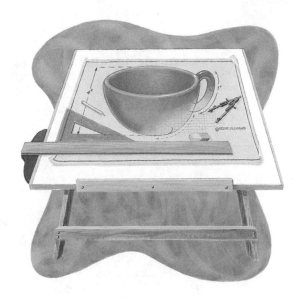

Of all the components missing from the AWT in the initial release of Java, probably the most asked-for is an image button. For this and a number of other reasons, we've included an image button in the Graphic Java Toolkit. In so doing, we'll demonstrate a few particulars about custom component development, including how to delegate event handling and more use of `GridBagLayout`.

gjt.Image Button

Image buttons are similar to an AWT `Button`, except that they display an image instead of text. The Graphic Java Toolkit's version of image button delegates handling of mouse events—much as a container delegates laying out components—to another object, an image button controller. This provides a great deal of flexibility as far as defining and reusing image button behavior. Although it does not pertain directly to developing custom components, delegating event handling greatly improves code maintainability and modularity, two of the major benefits of object-oriented design.[1]

To begin our discussion of the `gjt.ImageButton`, let's look at its associations and responsibilities.

---

1. See Budd, Timothy. *An Introduction To Object-Oriented Programming*. Addison-Wesley.

gjt.ImageButton Associations and Responsibilities

Figure 11-1 shows the manly class diagram for the gjt.ImageButton class.

Figure 11-1 gjt.ImageButton Class Diagram

As you can see in Figure 11-1, gjt.ImageButton extends Canvas. An image button needs to be a Component so that it can be laid out and displayed just like any other component, and it also needs to display an Image. Since an image button does not contain any components, it does not need to be a container, and therefore the logical choice for its superclass is Canvas[2]. ImageButton employs a ThreeDRectangle for drawing a 3-D border around the Image it displays.

---

2.   Refer to *Canvas or Panel?* on page 278 for factors in selecting an applet's super-
     class.

An `ImageButton` can be enabled and disabled. By default, every `ImageButton` is enabled; calling `disable()` causes the `ImageButton` image to be bleached. (Refer to *Filtering Images* on page 135 for a discussion of `gjt.BleachImageFilter`). Subsequent mouse events are ignored until `enable()` is called. Calling `enable()` on a disabled `ImageButton` restores the original image and causes the `ImageButton` to once again respond to mouse events.

One instance of `gjt.image.BleachImageFilter` is shared by all instances of `ImageButton`, the `_bleachFilter` member, which provides a bleached version of the original image the first time an image button is disabled.

Each `ImageButton` maintains an association with a single `ImageButtonController`; an instance of `ImageButton` forwards mouse events to its controller. By default, an `ImageButton` is fitted with a `SpringyImageButtonController`, which implements the same behavior with respect to reacting to mouse events as an `awt.Button` does. After constructing an image button, clients are free to change its controller by invoking `ImageButton.setController(ImageButtonController)`. This allows clients to fit an `ImageButton` with a different derivation of `ImageButtonController`.

The Graphic Java Toolkit comes with three derivations of `ImageButtonController`:

- `SpringyImageButtonController` – Causes its associated `ImageButton` to behave exactly as an `awt.Button` with respect to mouse events

- `StickyImageButtonController` – Causes the associated `ImageButton` to stick instead of springing back when activated

- `StateButtonController` – Is associated with a `StateButton` (an extension of `ImageButton`) that cycles through a set of images when activated

Let's look at Table 11-1, which lists the responsibilities of a `gjt.ImageButton`. Pay special attention to the `Component` methods `gjt.ImageButton` is overriding and the rationale for doing so

Table 11-1 gjt.ImageButton **Responsibilities**

Methods	Description
boolean isRaised(Graphics g)	Queries the current state—raised or inset.
boolean isDisabled(Graphics g)	Queries whether ImageButton is enabled or disabled.
boolean isInside(int x, int y)	Returns true if the point lies within the image button, false otherwise.
void enable()	Restores the original image and enables response to input.
void disable()	Disables response to input and repaints the image with a bleached version of the original image.
ImageButtonController getController()	Returns controller currently in use.
boolean mouseDown(Event event, int w, int y)	Overrides Component mouseDown(). Delegates to the controller.
boolean mouseDrag(Event event, int w, int y)	Overrides Component mouseDrag(). Delegates to the controller.
boolean mouseUp(Event event, int w, int y)	Overrides Component mouseUp(). Delegates to the controller.
void paint(Graphics g)	Overrides Component paint(). Paints the border and the image.
void paintInset()	Paints the border inset.
void paintRaised()	Paints the border raised.
Dimension minimumSize()	Overrides Component minimumSize(). Returns preferredSize().
Dimension preferredSize()	Overrides Component preferredSize(). Sets preferred size to the image size plus the border thickness.
void resize(int x, int y)	Overrides Component resize().
void reshape(int x, int y, int w, int h)	Overrides Component reshape(). Reshapes the border.
void setController(ImageButtonController controller)	Specifies a controller to use.
void setImage(Image image)	Sets the image to be displayed.

Table 11-2 lists the associations of a gjt.ImageButton.

Table 11-2 gjt.ImageButton **Associations**

Variables	Description
static BleachImageFilter _bleachFilter	Creates a bleached version of the image the first time the image button is disabled.
static int _bleachPercent	Specifies extent of bleaching for the disabled image.
static int _offset	Specifies the pixel amount image recesses when image button is painted inset.
static int _defaultThickness	Specifies the default border thickness.
ThreeDRectangle border	Paints a 3-D border around an image.
boolean isDisabled	Indicates whether button is currently enabled or disabled.
Dimension preferredSize	Specifies the preferred size of the button.
int thickness	Specifies the thickness of the button.
ImageButtonController controller	Implements the algorithm for reacting to mouse events.
Image image	The image displayed when enabled.
Image disabledImage	The image displayed when disabled.

gjt.ImageButton is a fairly complex class, so set's look at a few specific areas of interest before looking the entire class. First, notice that the gjt.ImageButton constructors assert that an image passed to the constructor is not null[3]. Also, as previously mentioned, a gjt.ImageButton is fitted by default with a gjt.SpringyImageButtonController:

```
public ImageButton(Image image, int thickness,
                   ImageButtonController controller) {
    Assert.notNull(image);
    Assert.notFalse(thickness > 0);

    if(controller == null)
        this.controller =
            new SpringyImageButtonController(this);
    else
        this.controller = controller;
        .
        .
        .
}
```

3. Refer to *Assertions* on page 242 for more information on assertions in the Graphic Java Toolkit.

ImageButton overrides `preferredSize()`; the preferred size is calculated in the `setImage()` method as the size of the image plus twice the thickness of the border, like this:

```
preferredSize.width  = image.getWidth (this) +
                          (2*thickness);
preferredSize.height = image.getHeight(this) +
                          (2*thickness);
```

You'll notice that the `gjt.ImageButton paint()` method determines whether the image button is raised or inset and calls the appropriate helper method to do the actual painting:

```
public void paint(Graphics g) {
    if(isRaised()) paintRaised();
    else           paintInset ();
}
```

You might also pay attention to the image button controllers used by the `ImageButton` and how they work. The overridden mouse handler methods delegate control to the controller, except when the `ImageButton` is disabled. In that case, the methods simply return `false`, like this:

```
public boolean mouseDown(Event event, int x, int y) {
    if(isDisabled()) return false;
    else             return controller.mouseDown(event,x,y);
}
public boolean mouseUp(Event event, int x, int y) {
    if(isDisabled()) return false;
    else             return controller.mouseUp(event,x,y);
}
public boolean mouseDrag(Event event, int x, int y) {
    if(isDisabled()) return false;
    else             return controller.mouseDrag(event,x,y);
}
```

Now that we've covered the highlights of the `ImageButton` implementation, let's look at the `gjt.ImageButton` code in Example 11-1. As you're looking through the code, pay attention to the `Component` methods it overrides. Also, notice how `createDisabledImage()` is called by `disable()` such that a bleached (i.e., *disabled*) image is created and used only when necessary. Most image buttons will likely live their entire lives without ever being disabled—as a result, it would be wasteful to create a bleached version of every image button's image when the image button is instantiated. This is another example of employing lazy instantiation, which we've seen previously in our *OO Tip* on page 106.

Example 11-1 gjt.ImageButton **Class Source Code**

```java
package gjt;

import java.awt.*;
import java.awt.image.FilteredImageSource;

import gjt.image.BleachImageFilter;

public class ImageButton extends Canvas {
  private static BleachImageFilter _bleachFilter;
  private static int              _bleachPercent   = 50;
  private static int              _offset          = 1;
  private static int              _defaultThickness = 2;

  private ThreeDRectangle border  = new ThreeDRectangle(this);
  private boolean         isDisabled    = false;
  private Dimension       preferredSize = new Dimension(0,0);
  private int             thickness;
  private Image           image, disabledImage;
  private ImageButtonController controller;

  public static int setBleachPercent() {
      return _bleachPercent;
  }
  public static void getBleachPercent(int p) {
      _bleachPercent = p;
  }
  public ImageButton(Image image) {
      this(image, _defaultThickness, null);
  }
  public ImageButton(Image image,
                    ImageButtonController controller) {
      this(image, _defaultThickness, controller);
  }
  public ImageButton(Image image, int thickness,
                    ImageButtonController controller) {
      Assert.notNull(image);
      Assert.notFalse(thickness > 0);

      if(controller == null)
          this.controller =
              new SpringyImageButtonController(this);
      else
          this.controller = controller;

      border.setThickness(this.thickness = thickness);
      setImage(image);
```

```
    }
    public void setImage(Image image) {
        Util.waitForImage(this, this.image = image);

        preferredSize.width  = image.getWidth (this) +
                               (2*thickness);
        preferredSize.height = image.getHeight(this) +
                               (2*thickness);
    }
    public Dimension minimumSize() {
        return preferredSize;
    }
    public Dimension preferredSize() {
        return preferredSize;
    }
    public boolean isRaised  () { return border.isRaised(); }
    public boolean isDisabled() { return isDisabled;        }

    public void enable() {
        isDisabled = false;
        repaint();
    }
    public void disable() {
        isDisabled = true;

        if(disabledImage == null)
            createDisabledImage();

        repaint();
    }
    public void resize(int w, int h) {
        reshape(location().x, location().y, w, h);
    }
    public void reshape(int x, int y, int w, int h) {
        super.reshape(x,y,w,h);
        border.resize(w,h);
    }
    public void paint(Graphics g) {
        if(isRaised()) paintRaised();
        else           paintInset ();
    }
    public void paintInset() {
        Point     upperLeft = findUpperLeft();
        Graphics  g         = getGraphics();
        Image     image     = isDisabled() ?
                              disabledImage : this.image;
        Dimension size      = size();
```

```
    if(g != null) {
        border.clearInterior();
        g.drawImage(image,
                    upperLeft.x + thickness + _offset,
                    upperLeft.y + thickness + _offset,this);

        g.setColor(getBackground().darker());
        for(int i=0; i < _offset; ++i) {
            g.drawLine(thickness+i,thickness+i,
                       size.width-thickness-i,thickness+i);
            g.drawLine(thickness+i,thickness+i,
                       thickness+i,size.height-thickness-i);
        }
        border.paintInset();
    }
}
public void paintRaised() {
    Point    upperLeft = findUpperLeft();
    Graphics g         = getGraphics();
    Image    image     = isDisabled() ?
                          disabledImage : this.image;

    if(g != null) {
        border.clearInterior();
        g.drawImage(image, upperLeft.x + thickness,
                           upperLeft.y + thickness, this);
        border.paintRaised();
    }
}
public boolean isInside(int x, int y) {
  Dimension size = size();
  return x >= 0 && x < size.width && y >= 0 &&
         y < size.height;
}
public void setController(ImageButtonController controller){
    this.controller = controller;
}
public ImageButtonController getController() {
    return controller;
}
public boolean mouseDown(Event event, int x, int y) {
    if(isDisabled()) return false;
    else             return controller.mouseDown(event,x,y);
}
public boolean mouseUp(Event event, int x, int y) {
    if(isDisabled()) return false;
    else             return controller.mouseUp(event,x,y);
}
```

```
public boolean mouseDrag(Event event, int x, int y) {
    if(isDisabled()) return false;
    else                 return controller.mouseDrag(event,x,y);
}

private void createDisabledImage() {
    if(_bleachFilter == null)
        _bleachFilter =
            new BleachImageFilter(_bleachPercent);

    if(_bleachPercent != _bleachFilter.percent())
        _bleachFilter.percent(_bleachPercent);

    FilteredImageSource fis =
        new FilteredImageSource(image.getSource(),
                                _bleachFilter);

    Util.waitForImage(this, disabledImage=createImage(fis));
}
private Point findUpperLeft() {
    Dimension size = size();
    return new Point((size.width/2) -
                    (preferredSize.width/2),
                    (size.height/2) -
                    (preferredSize.height/2));
}
}
```

Image Button Controllers

As we mentioned in our chapter on *Components, Containers, and Layout Managers*, the developers of the AWT were wise to introduce layout managers, which decouple containers from the algorithms for laying out their components. This allows for a great deal of flexibility when laying out a container; layout managers are independent of any single container and therefore can be used by any container that deems their services appropriate.

We have done much the same with image buttons by decoupling the handling of mouse events from the image buttons themselves. At first glance, this may seem to be an insignificant reshuffling of responsibilities, but let's consider over the next few pages the benefits to be gained by decoupling the handling of mouse events from image buttons.

Flexibility

Since the algorithm for reacting to mouse events is not hardcoded into the gjt.ImageButton class, image buttons are not required to always react to mouse events in the same manner. Image buttons may be fitted with an appropriate image button controller, or they may rely upon the default controller (gjt.SpringyImageButtonController), which implements the same behavior found in the awt.Button class.

For instance, on the one hand, a toolbar image button may be content to rely upon the default behavior provided by gjt.SpringyImageButtonController. On the other hand, a set of image buttons used to select a graphical operation in a drawing program should not spring back when selected but should remain painted inset after activation to indicate the current graphical operation. Such an effect is easily achieved by fitting such an image button with a gjt.StickyImageButtonController.

Hierarchies of Image Button Controllers

Hierarchies of image button controllers can be developed. In fact, the Graphic Java Toolkit provides a small hierarchy of such controllers. Hierarchies of image button controllers take advantage of existing controllers to provide specialized behavior, as illustrated in Figure 11-2.

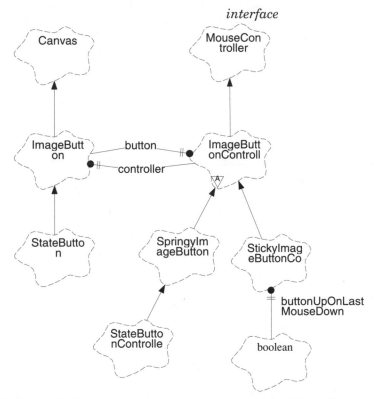

Figure 11-2 `gjt.ImageButtonController` Class Diagram

We have already mentioned the `SpringyImageButtonController` and `StickyImageButtonController` classes. The `StateButtonController` is used by `StateButton` objects, an extension of `gjt.ImageButton` that cycles through a series of images every time the button is activated.

Dynamically Setting Controllers

Image buttons can be fitted with different image button controllers at runtime. During the course of an image button's lifetime, an image button may be fitted with different types of controllers, depending upon the needs of the moment. While such situations are admittedly rare, this capability is enabled by decoupling the image buttons from the algorithms for reacting to mouse events. Note that it would be difficult to obtain this capability if reacting to mouse events were hardcoded into the `ImageButton` class itself.

Reduced Complexity in ImageButton

By moving mouse event handling out of the `ImageButton` class, we have reduced the complexity of image buttons, making them easier to understand, maintain, and extend. Of course, by decoupling mouse event handling, we are increasing the number of overall classes, but the classes have simple, clearly defined sets of responsibilities—the hallmark of good object-oriented design[4].

OO Tip

Design Classes With a Clearly Defined Set of Responsibilities

Each class in an object-oriented system should have a small, well-defined set of responsibilities. These responsibilities are often measured by the number of public methods the class implements. A small number of well-defined public methods per class ensures a fine granularity of functionality. ImageButton already has a basic set of public methods that provide core functionality. As a result, we have given the responsibility for reacting to mouse events to another class, which keeps ImageButton from having too many responsibilities and thus becoming difficult to understand and extend.

The MouseController Interface

Image button controllers implement a very simple interface: `MouseController`:

```
public interface MouseController {
   public boolean mouseEnter(Event event, int x, int y);
   public boolean mouseExit (Event event, int x, int y);

   public boolean mouseMove (Event event, int x, int y);
   public boolean mouseDown (Event event, int x, int y);
   public boolean mouseUp   (Event event, int x, int y);
   public boolean mouseDrag (Event event, int x, int y);
}
```

`MouseController` defines the methods through which an image button communicates with its controller. (Note that `MouseController` is usable in contexts other than image buttons.) `ImageButtonController` implements `MouseController`, but notice that it does not actually implement the methods defined in `MouseController` and, therefore, is an abstract class.

```
public abstract class ImageButtonController
      implements MouseController {
   private ImageButton button;
```

---

4. See Wirfs-Brock, Wilkerson, and Wiener. *Designing Object-Oriented Software,* chapter 4. Prentice Hall.

```
ImageButtonController(ImageButton button) {
    Assert.notNull(button);
    this.button = button;
    button.setController(this);
}
public ImageButton getButton() {
    return button;
}
public boolean mouseEnter(Event event, int x, int y) {
    return false;
}
public boolean mouseExit (Event event, int x, int y) {
    return false;
}
public boolean mouseMove (Event event, int x, int y) {
    return false;
}

protected void armButton(Event event) {
    button.deliverEvent(
        new ImageButtonEvent(button,
                             event,
                             ImageButtonEvent.ARM));
}
protected void disarmButton(Event event) {
    button.deliverEvent(
        new ImageButtonEvent(button,
                             event,
                             ImageButtonEvent.DISARM));
}
protected void activateButton(Event event) {
    button.deliverEvent(
        new ImageButtonEvent(button,
                             event,
                             ImageButtonEvent.ACTIVATE));
}
}
```

Note that the ImageButtonController constructor sets the image button's controller.

The ImageButtonController class is responsible for establishing the relationship with its associated image button—it leaves the methods from MouseController for extensions to implement. ImageButtonController also provides protected methods for arming, disarming, and activating the image button that deliver an ImageButtonEvent to the image button's container. These methods are invoked by subclasses of ImageButtonController. (We will shortly introduce the ImageButtonEvent class.)

As we've previously indicated, each image button is fitted by default with a `SpringyImageButtonController` at construction time. Example 11-2 shows the implementation of `SpringyImageButtonController`.

Example 11-2 `gjt.SpringyImageButtonController` **Class Source Code**

```
package gjt;

import java.awt.Event;
import java.awt.Graphics;

   extends ImageButtonController {
   public SpringyImageButtonController(ImageButton ib) {
       super(ib);
   }
   public boolean mouseDown(Event event, int x, int y) {
       if(event.modifiers == 0) {
           getButton().paintInset();
           armButton(event);
       }
       return false;
   }
   public boolean mouseUp(Event event, int x, int y) {
       if(event.modifiers == 0) {
           if(getButton().isRaised() == false) {
               getButton().paintRaised();
               activateButton(event);
           }
       }
       return false;
   }
   public boolean mouseDrag(Event event, int x, int y) {
       if(event.modifiers == 0) {
           if(getButton().isInside(x,y)) {
               if(getButton().isRaised()) {
                   getButton().paintInset();
                   armButton(event);
               }
           }
           else {
               if(getButton().isRaised() == false) {
                   getButton().paintRaised();
                   disarmButton(event);
               }
           }
       }
       return false;
   }
}
```

Notice that by using the `Event modifiers` field, which we introduced in our chapter on *Event Handling*, only mouse button one is honored [5]. This is the same algorithm used by `awt.Button`.

Although image buttons are perfectly content to rely on their default controllers perhaps 90 percent of the time, there are times when a different controller is a necessity. The Graphic Java Toolkit also comes with a `StickyImageButtonController`, which causes the image button to stick to its current orientation (raised or inset) when activated. The `StickyImageButtonController` is a little more complicated than its springy sibling, so let's take a look at it in Example 11-3.

Example 11-3 `gjt.StickyImageButtonController` **Class Source Code**

```
package gjt;

import java.awt.Event;
import java.awt.Graphics;

public class StickyImageButtonController
                  extends ImageButtonController {
  private boolean buttonUpOnLastMouseDown = true;

  public StickyImageButtonController(ImageButton ib) {
      super(ib);
  }
  public boolean mouseDown(Event event, int x, int y) {
      ImageButton button = getButton();

      if(event.modifiers == 0) {
          if(button.isRaised()) button.paintInset();
          else                  button.paintRaised();

          buttonUpOnLastMouseDown = getButton().isRaised();
          armButton(event);
      }
      return false;
  }
  public boolean mouseUp(Event event, int x, int y) {
      activateButton(event);
      return false;
  }
}
```

5.   There is currently a bug under Windows 95 where a mouse button 2 up is detected as a mouse button 1 up; therefore, image buttons can be activated with mouse button 2 under Windows 95.

```
public boolean mouseDrag(Event event, int x, int y) {
    ImageButton button = getButton();

    if(event.modifiers == 0) {
        if(button.isInside(x,y)) {
            if(buttonUpOnLastMouseDown) {
                if(button.isRaised() == false) {
                    button.paintRaised();
                    armButton(event);
                }
            }
            else {
                if(button.isRaised()) {
                    button.paintInset();
                    armButton(event);
                }
            }
        }
        else {
            if(buttonUpOnLastMouseDown) {
                if(button.isRaised()) {
                    button.paintInset();
                    disarmButton(event);
                }
            }
            else {
                if(button.isRaised() == false) {
                    button.paintRaised();
                    disarmButton(event);
                }
            }
        }
    }
    return false;
}
```

A mouse down event results in the image button being toggled between raised and inset. Additionally, mouseDown() calls armButton() to generate an ImageButtonEvent and propagate it to the image button's container.

A mouse up event simply results in the creation and propagation of an ImageButtonEvent for activating the image button by calling activateButton().

Most of the complexity resides in the mouseDrag() method. (While we will describe the algorithm implemented in mouseDrag(), it is much easier to see the behavior by running the ImageButton unit test and experimenting with the sticky image button). After a mouse drag is initiated inside the image button, dragging the mouse outside of the image button restores it to the state it was in before the mouse down occurred. Subsequently, dragging the mouse back into the image button toggles its state between inset and raised. Dragging the mouse out of the image button results in a call to `disarmButton()`. Dragging the mouse back into the image button results in a call to `armButton()`.

ImageButton Events

As we noted in *Custom Component Events* on page 87, events for custom components are best defined by extending `java.awt.Event`. The Graphic Java Toolkit provides such a class for image button events: `gjt.ImageButtonEvent`. The `ImageButtonEvent` is very similar to the `gjt.SelectionEvent` class, which we covered in detail in *Extending java.awt.Event* on page 89. Image button events are used in exactly the same manner as selection events, except that it is the image button's controller that delivers the events to the image button's container. Example 11-4 shows the source for the `gjt.ImageButtonEvent` class:

Example 11-4 `gjt.ImageButtonEvent` **Class Source Code**

```
package gjt;

import java.awt.Event;

public class ImageButtonEvent extends Event {
    public static final int ARM      = 1;
    public static final int DISARM   = 2;
    public static final int ACTIVATE = 3;

    private int eventType;

    public ImageButtonEvent(ImageButton button,
                            Event       event,
                            int         type) {
        super(button, event.when, event.id, event.x, event.y,
                      event.key,  event.modifiers, event.arg);

        Assert.notFalse(type == ARM    ||
                        type == DISARM ||
                        type == ACTIVATE);

        eventType = type;
        id = -1;
    }
    public boolean isArmed() {
        return eventType == ARM;
```

```
    }
    public boolean isDisarmed() {
        return eventType == DISARM;
    }
    public boolean isActivated() {
        return eventType == ACTIVATE;
    }
    protected String paramString() {
        String str = new String();

        if(eventType == ImageButtonEvent.ARM)
            str = "ARM";
        else if(eventType == ImageButtonEvent.DISARM)
            str = "DISARM";
        else if(eventType == ImageButtonEvent.ACTIVATE)
            str = "ACTIVATE";

        return super.paramString() + str;
    }
}
```

Notice that an image button has three valid states for an image button event: ARM, DISARM, and ACTIVATE. An image button has been armed when a mouse down occurs inside of the image button; a subsequent mouse up inside the image button activates the image button, while a subsequent mouse up *outside* the image button disarms the image button.

Note that ImageButtonController provides convenience methods for extensions that create and deliver an ImageButtonEvent to the image button (and consequently to the image button's container).

Mouse enter and exit events are detected by an image button's container in exactly the same manner as mouse enter and exit events are detected normally in the AWT, by using the java.awt.Event id and target fields.

Exercising the Image Button and Its Controllers

Now that we've seen all the gjt.ImageButton code and the controllers that manage its mouse events—everything that's under the hood, so to speak—let's put this vehicle in motion and test drive it. To begin with, look at the ImageButton unit test in Figure 11-5.

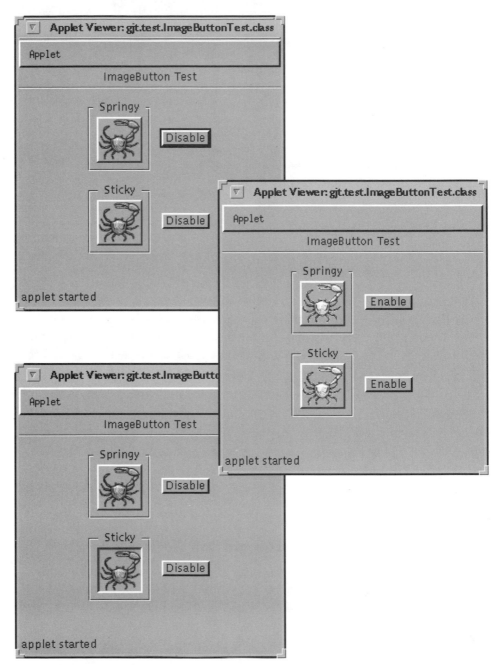

Figure 11-3 gjt.ImageButton Unit Test
This series of pictures shows, from top to bottom, image buttons
enabled, disabled, and in use.

Also, to see how components and containers are nested in this unit test, refer to Figure 11-4, which shows the layout in three dimensions.

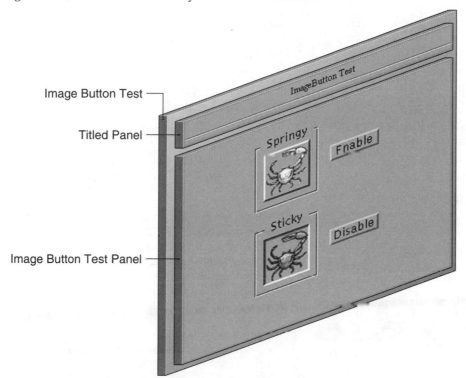

Figure 11-4 `ImageButtonTest` Layout Diagram

Before diving into the unit test code, let's take a brief look at how `ImageButtonTest` employs `GridBagLayout`, now that we've seen the unit test and the 3-D diagram of its layout:

```
❶      gbc.anchor    = GridBagConstraints.NORTH;
       springyBox    = new Box(springyButton, "Springy");
❷      gbc.insets    = new Insets(10,0,0,0);
       gbl.setConstraints(springyBox, gbc); add(springyBox);


❸      gbc.gridwidth = GridBagConstraints.REMAINDER;
❹      gbc.insets    = new Insets(45,10,0,0);
       gbl.setConstraints(springyButtonEnabler, gbc);
       add(springyButtonEnabler);


❺      gbc.anchor    = GridBagConstraints.NORTH;
❻      gbc.gridwidth = 1;
       stickyBox     = new Box(stickyButton, "Sticky");
       gbc.insets    = new Insets(10,0,0,0);
```

❼   ```
         gbc.weighty   = 1.0;
         gbl.setConstraints(stickyBox, gbc); add(stickyBox);
         ```

❽        ```
         gbc.gridwidth = GridBagConstraints.REMAINDER;
         gbc.insets    = new Insets(45,10,0,0);
         gbl.setConstraints(stickyButtonEnabler, gbc);
         add(stickyButtonEnabler);
         ```

In this unit test, `GridBagLayout` has four components to lay out: a `springyButton` and its enable/disable button, and a `stickyButton` and its enable/disable button. We set up the `GridBagConstraints` such that each pair of buttons resides in its own grid cell, like this:

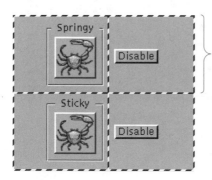

The springy and sticky buttons and their corresponding enable/disable buttons each reside in one grid cell. This is achieved by setting the anchor constraints to North for the sticky and springy buttons (lines ❶ and ❺) and setting the gridwidth constraints to REMAINDER for the enable/disable buttons (lines ❸ and ❽). Using REMAINDER for gridwidth ensures that the next component will be positioned underneath the previous component. Note that the anchor set in line ❺ is really unnecessary, since the anchor has already been set in line ❶ for this instance of GridBagConstraints. However, we've left it in to draw attention to the sticky button positioning.

Notice that the insets are set for the top of the `springyButton` in lines ❷ and the top and left for the enable/disable button in line ❹. (The `stickyButton` and its enable/disable button are set up the same way.) We've hardcoded the top insets for the enable/disable buttons to 45 pixels in order to center them next to the springy and sticky buttons. We could have calculated this location, but we've hardcoded these insets to keep the code simple.

You might wonder why `gridwidth` in line ❻ and `weighty` in line ❼ are set for the `stickyButton`. The `gridwidth` is set to override the previous `gridwidth` setting (line ❸), ensuring that the `stickyButton` consumes one grid cell. The `weighty` constraint is somewhat conspicuous by its presence. We set `weighty` because when the window is resized, we want the sticky button and its enable/disable button to retain their relative position below the springy button and its enable/disable button. The `weighty` setting ensures the bottom button grid cells consume any extra space in the vertical direction, as in the next illustration:

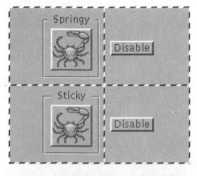

The `weighty` constraints are set to 1 for the bottom buttons. This ensures that these grid cells consume any extra space in the vertical direction when the window is stretched taller. The result is that the bottom row buttons maintain their relative position below the top row of buttons.

Note that the buttons themselves do not resize to fit the space; only the grid cells change size.

AWT Tip

Expanding the Component vs. Expanding the Grid Cell

The GridBagConstraints weightx and weighty members control how much extra space is consumed by a component's *grid cell*. The GridBagConstraints fill member controls how much extra space is consumed by the *component*. In order for the component to consume extra space in both directions, all three constraints must be set. If only the fill constraint is set, the component will fill its grid cell in the specified direction, but the grid cell itself will not consume any extra space.

You might want to refer to Figure 11-4 on page 317 as you look through the unit test code. Also, notice as you look through the code that `ImageButtonTest` class creates an instance of `StickyImageButtonController` rather than using the default controller. The `stickyButton` is associated with a new instance of `StickyImageButtonController`:[6]

```
stickyButton.setController(
        new StickyImageButtonController(stickyButton));
```

Example 11-5 `gjt.test.ImageButtonTest` **Class Source Code**

```
package gjt.test;

import java.applet.Applet;
import java.awt.*;
import gjt.Box;
import gjt.ImageButton;
import gjt.ImageButtonEvent;
import gjt.SpringyImageButtonController;
import gjt.StickyImageButtonController;

public class ImageButtonTest extends UnitTest {
  public String title() {
      return "ImageButton Test";
  }
  public Panel centerPanel() {
      return new ImageButtonTestPanel(this);
  }
}

class ImageButtonTestPanel extends Panel {
  private ImageButton springyButton;
  private Button      springyButtonEnabler;
  private ImageButton stickyButton;
  private Button      stickyButtonEnabler;

  public ImageButtonTestPanel(Applet applet) {
      Image               image;
      Box                 springyBox, stickyBox;
      GridBagLayout       gbl = new GridBagLayout();
      GridBagConstraints  gbc = new GridBagConstraints();

      image =
      applet.getImage(applet.getCodeBase(), "gifs/crab.gif");
```

6. Note that we do not *have* to call `setController()` for the `stickyButton`—merely creating the controller will associate it with the image button.

```
springyButton        = new ImageButton(image);
springyButtonEnabler = new Button      ("Disable");
stickyButton         = new ImageButton(image);
stickyButtonEnabler  = new Button      ("Disable");

new StickyImageButtonController(stickyButton);

setLayout(gbl);

gbc.anchor    = GridBagConstraints.NORTH;
springyBox    = new Box(springyButton, "Springy");
gbc.insets    = new Insets(10,0,0,0);
gbl.setConstraints(springyBox, gbc); add(springyBox);


gbc.gridwidth = GridBagConstraints.REMAINDER;
gbc.insets    = new Insets(45,10,0,0);
gbl.setConstraints(springyButtonEnabler, gbc);
add(springyButtonEnabler);

gbc.anchor    = GridBagConstraints.NORTH;
gbc.gridwidth = 1;
stickyBox     = new Box(stickyButton, "Sticky");
gbc.insets    = new Insets(10,0,0,0);
gbc.weighty   = 1.0;
gbl.setConstraints(stickyBox, gbc); add(stickyBox);

gbc.gridwidth = GridBagConstraints.REMAINDER;
gbc.insets    = new Insets(45,10,0,0);
gbl.setConstraints(stickyButtonEnabler, gbc);
add(stickyButtonEnabler);
}
public boolean action(Event event, Object what) {
    Button button = (Button)event.target;
    String label  = (String)what;

    if(button == stickyButtonEnabler) {
        if(label.equals("Disable")) stickyButton.disable();
        else                        stickyButton.enable();
    }
    else {
        if(label.equals("Disable")) springyButton.disable();
        else                        springyButton.enable();
    }
    if(label.equals("Disable")) button.setLabel("Enable");
    else                        button.setLabel("Disable");
```

```
            return true;
    }
    public boolean handleEvent(Event event) {
        boolean eventHandled = false;

        if(event instanceof ImageButtonEvent) {
            System.out.println("ImageButton " + event);
            eventHandled = true;
        }
        if(event.id == Event.MOUSE_ENTER) {
            if(event.target == stickyButton)
                System.out.println("Sticky Button Entered");

            else if(event.target == springyButton)
                System.out.println("Springy Button Entered");

            eventHandled = true;
        }
        if(event.id == Event.MOUSE_EXIT) {
            if(event.target == stickyButton)
                System.out.println("Sticky Button Exited");

            else if(event.target == springyButton)
                System.out.println("Springy Button Exited");

            eventHandled = true;
        }
        if(eventHandled) return true;
        else             return super.handleEvent(event);
    }
}
```

gjt.StateButton

Next we'll take a look at an `ImageButton` extension: `gjt.StateButton`.
`StateButton`, in conjunction with its controller (`StateButtonController`),
cycles through a series of images; the next image in the series is displayed after
the state button has been activated. As you can see in Example 11-6, a
`gjt.StateButton` has a very modest implementation, mostly because its event
handling has been encapsulated in a different class.

Example 11-6 gjt.StateButton **Class Source Code**

```java
package gjt;

import java.awt.Image;

public class StateButton extends ImageButton {
  private Image[] images;
  private int     state = 0;
  private int     numStates;

  public StateButton(Image[] images) {
      super(images[0]);

      this.images = images;
      numStates   = images.length;
      setController(new StateButtonController(this));
      waitForImages();
  }
  public Image nextImage() {
      if(state + 1 < numStates) state++;
      else                      state = 0;

      return images[state];
  }
  public int state() {
      return state;
  }
  private void waitForImages() {
      for(int i=0; i < images.length; ++i)
          Util.waitForImage(this, images[i]);
  }
}
```

gjt.StateButton explicitly sets its controller to StateButtonController. (Note that ImageButton.setController(ImageButtonController) is still available to clients if they need to fit a StateButton with some other extension of ImageButtonController.)

Notice also that by virtue of the gjt.Util.waitForImage() method, which encapsulates a standard implementation of MediaTracker, a StateButton waits for all of its images to load before displaying any of them.

All instances of `StateButton`, of course, are fitted by default with a `StateButtonController`. It is the controller that actually cycles the state button through the next image when the state button is activated. `StateButtonController` also has a simple implementation, as illustrated in Example 11-7.

Example 11-7 `gjt.StateButtonController` **Class Source Code**

```java
package gjt;

import java.awt.Event;

class StateButtonController extends SpringyImageButtonController{
   public StateButtonController(StateButton button) {
      super(button);
   }
   public boolean mouseUp(Event event, int x, int y) {
      StateButton button = (StateButton)getButton();
      button.setImage(button.nextImage());
      return super.mouseUp(event, x, y);
   }
}
```

Notice particularly the simplicity and readability of `StateButtonController`. It's only 8 lines of code, yet it serves its associated `StateButton` by cycling through a series of images; each time a mouse up is detected in the `StateButton`, the button's image is set to the next image in the array. In addition, `SpringyImageButtonController`, which is the superclass of `StateButtonController`, takes care of creating and delivering ARM, DISARM, and ACTIVATE events to the image button.

Exercising the StateButton and Its Controllers

Figure 11-5 shows sample output from the unit test implementation of the `gjt.StateButton` class.

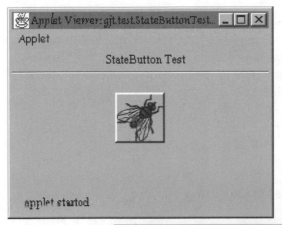

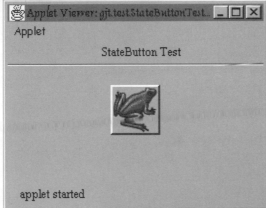

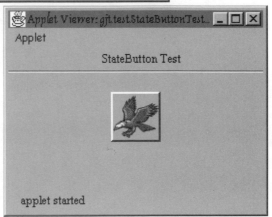

Figure 11-5 `gjt.StateButton` Unit Test
The series of three pictures results from three consecutive mouse clicks.

Now let's look at the `StateButtonTest` class in Example 11-8. As you look through the code, notice how `gjt.test.StateButtonTest` obtains three images and passes in an array to the `StateButton` constructor in line ❶. `StateButton` waits for all the images to be loaded, so the unit test does not concern itself with this. Also pay attention to the use of `FlowLayout`, which centers the state button with a horizontal gap of 20 and a vertical gap of 20.

Example 11-8 `gjt.test.StateButtonTest` **Class Source Code**

```
package gjt;

import java.applet.Applet;
import java.awt.*;
import java.net.URL;
import gjt.StateButton;

public class StateButtonTest extends UnitTest {
  public String title     () { return "StateButton Test";  }
  public Panel   centerPanel() {
      return new StateButtonTestPanel(this);
  }
}

class StateButtonTestPanel extends Panel {
    private URL          codeBase;
    private Image[]      images;
    private StateButton button;

    public StateButtonTestPanel(Applet applet) {
        codeBase  = applet.getCodeBase();
        images    = new Image[3];
        images[0] = applet.getImage(codeBase, "gifs/fly.gif");
        images[1] = applet.getImage(codeBase, "gifs/frog.gif");
        images[2] = applet.getImage(codeBase, "gifs/eagle.gif");
        button    = new StateButton(images);

        setLayout(new FlowLayout(FlowLayout.CENTER, 20, 20));
        add        (button);
    }
}
```
❶ (line marker at `button = new StateButton(images);`)

Summary

In the course of developing the GJT `ImageButton` and `StateButton` classes, we've tried to highlight the benefits of separating event handling from the custom component itself. This leads to more modular and maintainable code that can be easily extended and utilized for a range of purposes.

We've also once again looked `GridBagLayout` in use, showing yet another example of it in action.

CHAPTER 12

- Overview of Toolbar on page 329

- gjt.ImageButtonPanel on page 331

- gjt.Toolbar Associations and Responsibilities on page 336

- ImageButtonPanel Mouse Event Controllers on page 338

- ExclusiveImageButtonPanel on page 341

- Exercising the Toolbar on page 342

- Summary on page 348

Toolbars

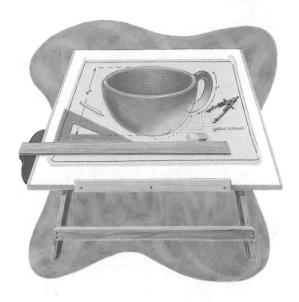

Most graphical user interfaces today include a toolbar—a row of icons at the top of a window. The icons contained in a toolbar are typically used as shortcuts to the most common tasks the software in question provides. The Graphic Java Toolkit provides a `Toolbar` class, which we explore in this chapter.

Overview of Toolbar

It is important to realize that there is an underlying abstraction present in the concept of a toolbar: a row of icons (image buttons). The GJT also provides a class that encapsulates that abstraction: an `ImageButtonPanel`, which is a `Panel` containing image buttons that can be oriented either horizontally or vertically. Our discussion of `gjt.Toolbar` encompasses the `ImageButtonPanel`, its mouse event controllers, as well as the `Toolbar` class itself.

We'll start by looking at Figure 12-1, which shows the relationships maintained by `gjt.Toolbar`.

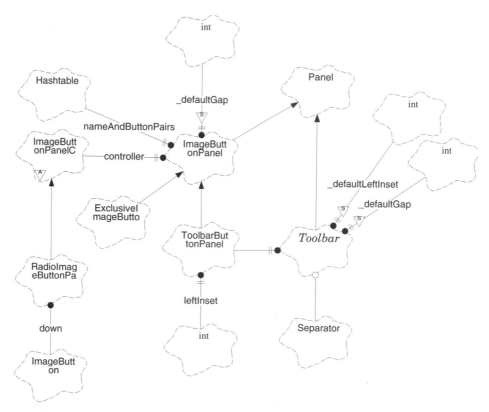

Figure 12-1 gjt.Toolbar Class Diagram

gjt.Toolbar is an extension of Panel, which employs by default a
BorderLayout to lay out a ToolbarButtonPanel (an extension of
ImageButtonPanel) as its north component and a separator as its south
component, as illustrated in Figure 12-2. Note that Toolbar does not maintain a
reference to the Separator, so the class diagram depicts the relationship between
a toolbar and separator as a *uses* relationship, and not a *has* relationship. Toolbar
does, however, maintain a reference to an instance of ToolbarButtonPanel, and
therefore that relationship is depicted as a *has* relationship.

Figure 12-2 A Toolbar
The Toolbar has an ToolbarButtonPanel as its north
component and a separator as its south component.

gjt.Toolbar itself is a very simple custom component that delegates most of its work to the ToolBarButtonPanel it contains. In fact, if you look at Figure 12-1, it is really the ImageButtonPanel (superclass of ToolbarButtonPanel) that we need to investigate. ToolbarButtonPanel extends ImageButtonPanel but adds very little to it. Therefore, before we look at the Toolbar class implementation, we're going to cover ImageButtonPanel in some detail.

gjt.ImageButtonPanel

As is evident from its name, ImageButtonPanel is an extension of Panel that contains image buttons. An ImageButtonPanel may be oriented either horizontally or vertically; as a result, an ImageButtonPanel sets its layout manager to an instance of gjt.RowLayout or gjt.ColumnLayout, depending upon its orientation[1].

ImageButtonPanel Associations and Responsibilities

Table 12-1 lists the responsibilities of an ImageButtonPanel.

Table 12-1 gjt.ImageButtonPanel **Responsibilities**

Methods	Description

void setController(
  ImageButtonPanelController
  controller)
	Sets the controller type.

Insets insets()	Sets insets.
ImageButton add(Image image, String name)	Creates an image button, adds it to a panel, and returns a reference to the newly created image button.
ImageButton add(Image image)	Creates an image button with a default name, adds it to a panel, and returns a reference to the newly created image button.
void add(ImageButton button)	Adds an existing image button.
void add(ImageButton button, String name)	Adds an existing image button with a specific name.
ImageButton getButtonByName(String name)	Returns an ImageButton by name.
void addSpacer(int sizeInPixels)	Adds space between buttons.

1. See *Custom Layout Managers* on page 207 for a discussion of gjt.RowLayout and gjt.ColumnLayout.

Table 12-1 `gjt.ImageButtonPanel` **Responsibilities (Continued)**

Methods	Description
`boolean mouseDown(Event event, int x, int y)`	Overrides `Component mouseDown()`.
`boolean mouseDrag(Event event, int x, int y)`	Overrides `Component mouseDrag()`.
`boolean mouseUp(Event event, int x, int y)`	Overrides `Component mouseUp()`.

Also look at Table 12-2, which shows the associations of an `ImageButtonPanel`.

Table 12-2 `gjt.ImageButtonPanel` **Associations**

Variables	Description
`static int _defaultGap`	Specifies the default gap between image buttons as 5 pixels.
`Hashtable nameAndButtonPairs`	Keeps track of image buttons by name.
`ImageButtonPanelController controller`	Reacts to mouse events.

A gap of five pixels is used by default between image buttons in an `ImageButtonPanel`. If a different gap is desired, clients may specify a gap at construction time. An `ImageButtonPanel` also keeps track of its buttons by name; when clients add an image button to an `ImageButtonPanel`, they can optionally specify a name for the image button. An `ImageButtonPanel` is equipped to return the appropriate image button, given its name, or to return a name, given an image button.

As is the case with image buttons themselves, each `ImageButtonPanel` has a controller (`RadioImageButtonPanelController`), which encapsulates the algorithm for reacting to mouse events. As we saw in our *ImageButton and StateButton* chapter, this affords a great deal of flexibility for mixing and matching image button panels and their controllers.

You'll notice that `ImageButtonPanel` provides three constructors, offering a range of settings at construction time. The last of the constructors sets the appropriate layout manager, as determined by the orientation of the `ImageButtonPanel`:

```
public ImageButtonPanel(Orientation orient, Orientation horient,
                        Orientation vorient, int gap) {
    Assert.notFalse      (orient == Orientation.HORIZONTAL ||
                          orient == Orientation.VERTICAL);
```

```
    if(orient == Orientation.VERTICAL)
        setLayout(new ColumnLayout(horient, vorient, gap));
    else
        setLayout(new RowLayout(horient, vorient, gap));

    setController(new RadioImageButtonPanelController(this));
}
```

The three orientations specified in this constructor are:

- `Orientation orient` – orientation of `ImageButtonPanel`

- `Orientation horient` – horizontal orientation of image buttons within panel

- `Orientation vorient` – vertical orientation of image buttons within panel

Mouse events in an `ImageButtonPanel` are delegated to a controller. It is permissible for an `ImageButtonPanel` to have a null controller. If an image button panel's controller is null, then the mouse event handler methods simply return `false` and the event is propagated up to the `ImageButtonPanel` container. Notice that the default controller is an instance of `RadioImageButtonPanelController`, which implements mutually exclusive selection behavior. (We'll discuss the mouse controllers in more detail shortly.) Just as with the `gjt.ImageButton` class, clients of `gjt.ImageButtonPanel` can set the controller explicitly by calling:

```
    setController(ImageButtonPanelController)
```

`ImageButtonPanel` arbitrarily sets its insets to (10, 10, 10, 10). If different insets are desired, `ImageButtonPanel` must be subclassed.[2]

The `add()` methods enable clients to add an image button to an `ImageButtonPanel`:

```
public ImageButton add(Image image, String name) {
    ImageButton button = new ImageButton(image);
    add(button);
    nameAndButtonPairs.put(name, button);
    return button;
}
```

---

2. For more information about insets, see the discussion of *Peers and Insets* on page 162.

In this case, the image button panel creates an image button using the image, adds the image button to itself, and then returns the image button to the caller. Clients can add image buttons with or without a name. If they do provide a name, getButtonByName(String) and getButtonName(ImageButton) can be called to return the appropriate name or button.

Space can be added between the image buttons of an ImageButtonPanel by specifying a pixel size for the space.

```
public void addSpacer(int sizeInPixels) {
  Assert.notFalse(sizeInPixels > 0);
  Canvas spacer = new Canvas();
  spacer.resize(sizeInPixels, sizeInPixels);
  add(spacer);
}
```

addSpacer() creates a Canvas, sizes it to the size passed in, and adds the Canvas to itself in order to provide spacing.

Now that we have a high-level understanding of ImageButtonPanel, let's take a look at its implementation in Example 12-1.

Example 12-1 gjt.ImageButtonPanel **Class Source Code**

```
package gjt;

import java.awt.*;
import java.util.Enumeration;
import java.util.Hashtable;

public class ImageButtonPanel extends Panel {
  static private int _defaultGap = 5;

  private Hashtable nameAndButtonPairs = new Hashtable();
  private ImageButtonPanelController controller;

  public ImageButtonPanel(Orientation orient) {
      this(orient, Orientation.CENTER,
                  Orientation.CENTER, _defaultGap);
  }
  public ImageButtonPanel(Orientation orient, int gap) {
      this(orient, Orientation.CENTER,
                  Orientation.CENTER, gap);
  }
  public ImageButtonPanel(Orientation orient,
                          Orientation horient,
                          Orientation vorient, int gap) {
      Assert.notFalse(orient == Orientation.HORIZONTAL ||
                  orient == Orientation.VERTICAL);
```

```
        if(orient == Orientation.VERTICAL)
            setLayout(new ColumnLayout(horient, vorient, gap));
        else
            setLayout(new RowLayout(horient, vorient, gap));

        setController(
            new RadioImageButtonPanelController(this));
    }
    public void setController(ImageButtonPanelController c) {
        this.controller = c;
    }
    public Insets insets() { return new Insets(10,10,10,10); }

    public ImageButton add(Image image, String name) {
        ImageButton button = new ImageButton(image);
        add(button);
        nameAndButtonPairs.put(name, button);
        return button;
    }
    public ImageButton add(Image image) {
        return add(image, "noname");
    }
    public void add(ImageButton button) {
        add(button, "noname");
    }
    public void add(ImageButton button, String name) {
        nameAndButtonPairs.put(name, button);
        super.add(button);
    }
    public ImageButton getButtonByName(String name) {
        return (ImageButton)nameAndButtonPairs.get(name);
    }
    public String getButtonName(ImageButton button) {
        Enumeration e = nameAndButtonPairs.keys();
        ImageButton nbutt;
        String nstr;

        while(e.hasMoreElements()) {
            nstr = (String)e.nextElement();
            nbutt = (ImageButton)nameAndButtonPairs.get(nstr);

            if(nbutt.equals(button))
              return nstr;
        }
        return null;
    }
    public void addSpacer(int sizeInPixels) {
        Assert.notFalse(sizeInPixels > 0);
```

```
        Canvas spacer = new Canvas();
        spacer.resize(sizeInPixels, sizeInPixels);
        add(spacer);
    }
    public boolean mouseDown(Event event, int x, int y) {
        return controller != null ?
            controller.mouseDown(event,x,y) : false;
    }
    public boolean mouseDrag(Event event, int x, int y) {
        return controller != null ?
            controller.mouseDrag(event,x,y) : false;
    }
    public boolean mouseUp(Event event, int x, int y) {
        return controller != null ?
            controller.mouseUp(event,x,y) : false;
    }
}
```

At this point, you may be scratching your head wondering, where's the toolbar? In fact, there isn't a toolbar without the ImageButtonPanel (the superclass of ToolbarButtonPanel). Now that we've covered ImageButtonPanel, we're ready to take a look at the implementation of gjt.Toolbar.

gjt.Toolbar Associations and Responsibilities

As shown in the previous sections, gjt.Toolbar is a simple class that delegates a good deal of its functionality to an enclosed ToolbarButtonPanel. Table 12-3 lists the responsibilities of the Toolbar class.

Table 12-3 gjt.Toolbar **Responsibilities**

Methods	Description
ImageButton add(Image image)	Creates and adds an image button.
void add(ImageButton button)	Adds a new image button.
void addSpacer(int sizeInPixels)	Adds space between image buttons.

Table 12-4 lists the associations of a gjt.Toolbar.

Table 12-4 gjt.Toolbar **Associations**

Variables	Description
static int _defaultGap	Sets the default gap to 5 pixels if not explicitly set.
static int _defaultLeftInset	Sets the default left inset to 0 pixels if not explicitly set.
ToolbarButtonPanel buttonpanel	Is the panel in which the buttons reside.
Hashtable nameAndButtonPairs	Keeps track of image buttons by name.
ImageButtonPanelController controller	Reacts to mouse events.

Now, let's take a look at the gjt.Toolbar source code in Example 12-2. Notice that Toolbar uses a BorderLayout and specifies a ToolbarButtonPanel as the north component and a separator as the south component.

Example 12-2 gjt.Toolbar **Class Source Code**

```
package gjt;

import java.awt.';

public class Toolbar extends Panel {
    static private int _defaultGap       = 0;
    static private int _defaultLeftInset = 0;

    private ToolbarButtonPanel buttonPanel;

    public Toolbar() {
        this(_defaultLeftInset, _defaultGap);
    }
    public Toolbar(int leftInset, int gap) {
        buttonPanel = new ToolbarButtonPanel(leftInset, gap);

        setLayout(new BorderLayout());
        add       ("North", buttonPanel);
        add       ("South", new Separator());
    }
    public ImageButton add(Image image) {
        return buttonPanel.add(image);
    }
    public void add(ImageButton button) {
        buttonPanel.add(button);
    }
    public void addSpacer(int sizeInPixels) {
        Assert.notFalse(sizeInPixels > 0);
```

```
        buttonPanel.addSpacer(sizeInPixels);
    }
  }
```

Note that both add() methods simply delegate responsibility to the associated image button panel.

Toolbar delegates its responsibilities to a ToolbarButtonPanel, which extends ImageButtonPanel, hardcodes its orientation to horizontal, and hardcodes the orientation of the buttons that it contains to left in the horizontal direction and centered in the vertical direction. ToolbarButtonPanel also sets its controller to null (otherwise it would use the default controller for an ImageButtonPanel). ToolbarButtonPanel also overrides insets to (5, leftInset, 5, 5), where leftInset is specified by the Toolbar or perhaps by the client. Here is the implementation of ToolbarButtonPanel:

```
class ToolbarButtonPanel extends ImageButtonPanel {
  private int leftInset;

  public ToolbarButtonPanel(int leftInset, int gap) {
     super(Orientation.HORIZONTAL,
           Orientation.LEFT,
           Orientation.CENTER,
           gap);

     this.leftInset = leftInset;
     setController(null);
  }
  public Insets insets() {
     return new Insets(5,leftInset,5,5);
  }
}
```

ImageButtonPanel Mouse Event Controllers

Before we launch into a discussion of the Toolbar unit test, we need to take a slight detour to describe the mouse event controllers available to an ImageButtonPanel. Specifically, that means we need to look at:

- ImageButtonPanelController – An abstract class that simply establishes a relationship with an ImageButtonPanel

- RadioImageButtonPanelController – A class that ensures that only one ImageButton in its ImageButtonPanel is painted inset at one time

ImageButtonPanelController

The `ImageButtonPanelController` class is functionally identical to an `ImageButtonController`. Both implement the `MouseController` interface (refer to *The MouseController Interface* on page 309) but decline to actually implement the methods that `MouseController` defines; therefore, they are both abstract classes. An `ImageButtonPanelController` simply establishes the relationship between itself and its `ImageButtonPanel`. It accomplishes this by invoking the `ImageButtonPanel setController(ImageButtonPanelController)` method. Example 12-3 shows how `ImageButtonPanelController` is implemented.

Example 12-3 `gjt.ImageButtonPanelController` **Class Source Code**

```
package gjt;

import java.awt.Event;

abstract class ImageButtonPanelController implements
                                    MouseController {
  private ImageButtonPanel panel;

  ImageButtonPanelController(ImageButtonPanel panel) {
      Assert.notNull(panel);
      this.panel = panel;
      panel.setController(this);
  }
  public ImageButtonPanel panel() {
      return panel;
  }
  public boolean mouseEnter(Event event, int x, int y) {
      return false;
  }
  public boolean mouseExit (Event event, int x, int y) {
      return false;
  }
  public boolean mouseMove (Event event, int x, int y) {
      return false;
  }
}
```

RadioImageButtonPanelController

The GJT comes with only one concrete `ImageButtonPanelController`, and that is `RadioImageButtonPanelController`. This class ensures that only one `ImageButton` at a time in its `ImageButtonPanel` is painted inset. Example 12-4 shows the `RadioImageButtonPanelController` implementation.

Example 12-4 `gjt.RadioImageButtonPanelController` **Class Source Code**

```java
package gjt;

import java.awt.Event;

class RadioImageButtonPanelController
              extends ImageButtonPanelController {
    ImageButton down;

    public RadioImageButtonPanelController(
              ImageButtonPanel panel) {
        super(panel);
    }
    public boolean mouseDown(Event event, int x, int y) {
        ImageButton button;

        if(event.target instanceof ImageButton) {
            button = (ImageButton)event.target;
            if(down == button) return false;

            if(down != null)
                down.paintRaised();

            down = button;
        }
        return false;
    }
    public boolean mouseUp(Event event, int x, int y) {
        return false;
    }
    public boolean mouseDrag(Event event, int x, int y) {
        return false;
    }
}
```

This class monitors which mouse button was last down. Upon a mouse down event, if the target of the event was an image button and an image button was activated previously, then the button activated previously is painted raised and a reference to the current button is kept.

The mouseUp() and mouseDrag() events are ignored and simply return false. The RadioImageButtonPanelController class must implement these methods in order for it to be a concrete (that is, not an abstract) class.

ExclusiveImageButtonPanel

ExclusiveImageButtonPanel is an extension of ImageButtonPanel that relies on RadioImageButtonPanelController, which is the default controller from its superclass. ExclusiveImageButtonPanel redefines methods for adding an image button with the express purpose of fitting the image button with a StickyImageButtonController, as illustrated in Example 12-5.

Example 12-5 gjt.ExclusiveImageButtonPanel **Class Source Code**

```
package gjt;

import java.awt.Image;

public class ExclusiveImageButtonPanel extends
                                    ImageButtonPanel {
  public ExclusiveImageButtonPanel(Orientation orient) {
      this(orient, 5);
  }
  public ExclusiveImageButtonPanel(Orientation orient,
                                   int gap) {
      super(orient, gap);
  }
  public ExclusiveImageButtonPanel(Orientation orient,
                                   Orientation horient,
                                   Orientation vorient,
                                   int gap) {
      super(orient, horient, vorient, gap);
  }
  public void add(ImageButton button) {
      super.add(button);
      new StickyImageButtonController(button);
  }
```

```
public ImageButton add(Image image) {
    ImageButton button = super.add(image);
    new StickyImageButtonController(button);
    return button;
}
public ImageButton add(Image image, String name) {
    ImageButton button = super.add(image, name);
    new StickyImageButtonController(button);
    return button;
}
}
```

Notice in this class that associating an `ImageButton` with a
`StickyImageButtonController` is achieved simply by virtue of creating a
new `StickyImageButtonController` and passing it an `ImageButton`. The
`StickyImageButtonController` constructor calls
`ImageButton.setController(ImageButtonController)` for the image
button passed to it.

Exercising the Toolbar

Now that we have a fairly detailed understanding of `Toolbar` and
`ExclusiveImageButtonPanel`, let's take a look at the unit test that exercises
them. Figure 12-3 shows the unit test for the `Toolbar` class.

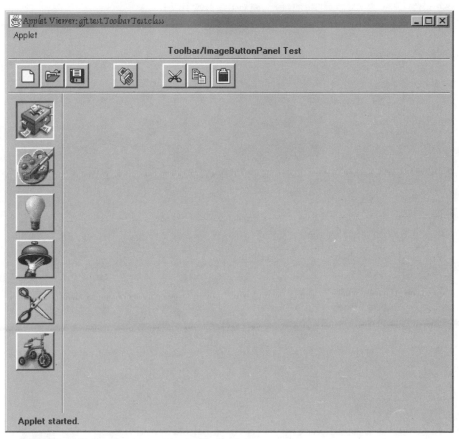

Figure 12-3 gjt.Toolbar Unit Test
Notice the sticky button (painted inset) at the top of the horizontal column.

To see how the `ToolbarTest` is laid out, refer to Figure 12-4.

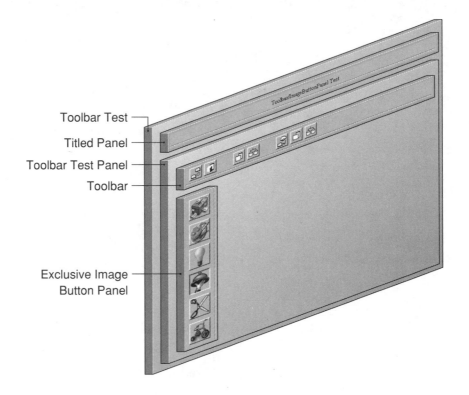

Toolbar Test

Titled Panel

Toolbar Test Panel

Toolbar

Exclusive Image
Button Panel

Figure 12-4 `ToolbarTest` Layout Diagram

Now that we've seen the layout characteristics of the unit test, let's take a look at its implementation. As usual, to make the most out of this discussion, you will want to run `appletviewer` on `ToolbarTest.html` in order to see the unit test in action. You may also want to refer back to Figure 12-3 and Figure 12-4 as you read through the code.

As you look through the unit test in Example 12-6 on page 346, notice that the `ToolbarTest` class sets its layout manager to a `BorderLayout` and specifies a `Toolbar` as the north component and an `ExclusiveImageButtonPanel` as its west component. Remember from our earlier discussion (see *ExclusiveImageButtonPanel* on page 341) that an `ExclusiveImageButtonPanel` fits all of its image buttons with a `StickyImageButtonController`, so when an image button is activated, it stays painted inset until another image button is activated.

There are a couple methods worth pointing out before we look at the code in its entirety. To begin with, the makeToolbar() method is used to create a Toolbar, and add image buttons to it:

```
private Toolbar makeToolbar(Applet app, URL cb) {
     Toolbar tb  = new Toolbar(10, 0);

     newButton   = tb.add(app.getImage(cb, "gifs/new.gif"));
     openButton  = tb.add(app.getImage(cb, "gifs/open.gif"));
     diskButton  = tb.add(app.getImage(cb, "gifs/disk.gif"));

     tb.addSpacer(newButton.preferredSize().width);

     printButton = tb.add(app.getImage(cb, "gifs/print.gif"));

     tb.addSpacer(newButton.preferredSize().width);

     cutButton   = tb.add(app.getImage(cb, "gifs/cut.gif"));
     copyButton  = tb.add(app.getImage(cb, "gifs/copy.gif"));
     pasteButton = tb.add(app.getImage(cb, "gifs/paste.gif"));

     return tb;
}
```

The Applet is passed in order to use its getImage() and getCodeBase() methods. As a convenience, we don't have to create the image buttons that will reside in the toolbar; we just pass Toolbar the images we want associated with the image buttons, and the toolbar creates and returns the image buttons.

The makePalette() method creates a new ExclusiveImageButtonPanel—the west component—which is constructed with vertical, center, and top orientations. The vertical orientation specifies the orientation of the panel itself. The center and top orientations specify the horizontal and vertical orientations of the image buttons within the ExclusiveImageButtonPanel:

```
iconPalette = new ExclusiveImageButtonPanel(
                    Orientation.VERTICAL,
                    Orientation.CENTER,
                    Orientation.TOP, 10);
```

You might notice that we've contradicted ourselves. Earlier, we cautioned you not to hardcode orientations. However, that was for components that extend Canvas. Canvas is just used for drawing graphics. Here, we're hardcoding the orientations for a Panel in which a layout manager is going to control the ultimate layout of components within the container.

Example 12-6 shows the entire unit test code.

Example 12-6 `gjt.test.ToolbarTest` **Class Source Code**

```
package gjt;

import java.net.URL;
import java.awt.*;
import java.applet.Applet;
import gjt.ExclusiveImageButtonPanel;
import gjt.ImageButton;
import gjt.ImageButtonEvent;
import gjt.Orientation;
import gjt.Toolbar;
import gjt.Separator;

 public String title() {
     return "Toolbar/ImageButtonPanel Test";
 }
 public Panel centerPanel() {
     return new ToolbarTestPanel(this);
 }
}

class ToolbarTestPanel extends Panel {
    ImageButton     newButton,   openButton, diskButton,
                    printButton, cutButton,  copyButton,
                    pasteButton;

 public ToolbarTestPanel(Applet app) {
     setLayout(new BorderLayout());
     add("North", makeToolbar(app, app.getCodeBase()));
     add("West",  makePalette(app, app.getCodeBase()));
 }
 public boolean handleEvent(Event event) {
     if(event instanceof ImageButtonEvent &&
        event.id == ImageButtonEvent.ACTIVATE) {

         if(event.target == newButton)
             System.out.println("New Button Activated");
         if(event.target == openButton)
             System.out.println("Open Button Activated");
         if(event.target == diskButton)
             System.out.println("Disk Button Activated");
         if(event.target == printButton)
             System.out.println("Print Button Activated");
         if(event.target == cutButton)
             System.out.println("Cut Button Activated");
         if(event.target == copyButton)
             System.out.println("Copy Button Activated");
```

```
            if(event.target == pasteButton)
                System.out.println("Paste Button Activated");

            return true;
        }
        else
            return super.handleEvent(event);
}
private Toolbar makeToolbar(Applet app, URL cb) {
    Toolbar tb  = new Toolbar(10, 0);

    newButton   = tb.add(app.getImage(cb, "gifs/new.gif"));
    openButton  = tb.add(app.getImage(cb, "gifs/open.gif"));
    diskButton  = tb.add(app.getImage(cb, "gifs/disk.gif"));

    tb.addSpacer(newButton.preferredSize().width);

    printButton = tb.add(app.getImage(cb, "gifs/print.gif"));

    tb.addSpacer(newButton.preferredSize().width);

    cutButton   = tb.add(app.getImage(cb, "gifs/cut.gif"));
    copyButton  = tb.add(app.getImage(cb, "gifs/copy.gif"));
    pasteButton = tb.add(app.getImage(cb, "gifs/paste.gif"));

    return tb;
}
private Panel makePalette(Applet app, URL cb) {
    ExclusiveImageButtonPanel iconPalette;
    Panel                     iconPalettePanel = new Panel();

    iconPalette = new ExclusiveImageButtonPanel(
                        Orientation.VERTICAL,
                        Orientation.CENTER,
                        Orientation.TOP, 10);

    iconPalette.add(app.getImage(cb,"gifs/ballot_box.gif"));
    iconPalette.add(app.getImage(cb,"gifs/palette.gif"));
    iconPalette.add(app.getImage(cb,"gifs/light_bulb1.gif"));
    iconPalette.add(app.getImage(cb,"gifs/Dining.gif"));
    iconPalette.add(app.getImage(cb,"gifs/scissors.gif"));
    iconPalette.add(app.getImage(cb,"gifs/tricycle.gif"));
```

```
        iconPalettePanel = new Panel();
        iconPalettePanel.setLayout(new BorderLayout());
        iconPalettePanel.add        ("Center", iconPalette);
        iconPalettePanel.add        ("East",   new Separator());
        return iconPalettePanel;
    }
}
```

Summary

We've looked at the implementation of the `Toolbar` and ExclusiveImageButtonPanel classes, along with the implementations of their supporting cast: `ImageButtonPanel` and its controller classes. We've squeezed extensive mileage out of `BorderLayout` in a number of classes covered in this chapter. As we alluded to in *Components, Containers, and Layout Managers*, `BorderLayout` is one of the most generally useful layout managers provided by the AWT. Additionally, we've once again demonstrated the technique of encapsulating algorithms for reacting to mouse events from a component.

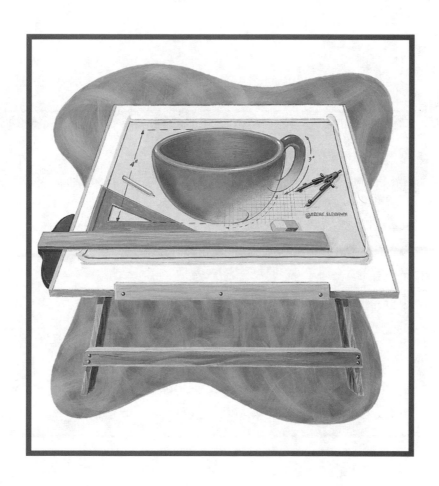

CHAPTER 13

- **The Graphic Java Toolkit Rubberband Package** on page 352

- **The Rubberband Base Class** on page 352

- **Rubberband Associations and Responsibilities** on page 353

- **Painting in XOR Mode** on page 357

- **Drawing Rubberband Lines** on page 358

- **Drawing Rubberband Rectangles and Ellipses** on page 359

- **A Rubberband Panel** on page 360

- **Exercising the Rubberband Package** on page 361

- **Refactoring the Unit Test** on page 366

- **The GJT DrawingPanel Class** on page 367

- **Summary** on page 371

Rubberbanding

Rubberbanding is an essential tool in the applet developer's toolkit. Rubberbands are useful in a number of different contexts; for instance, one method for selecting multiple items is to stretch a *rubberband* rectangle around the items to be selected. Drawing programs typically employ rubberbands that enable users to *rubberband* the shape they wish to draw before it is actually drawn on-screen.

Rubberbanding involves dynamically updating a geometric shape whose boundary changes as the cursor moves on-screen. A rubberband must be careful not to disturb any existing graphics beneath it, which is accomplished by painting in XOR mode, as we shall see shortly.

This chapter presents a handful of classes for rubberbanding, including a RubberbandPanel, an extension of Panel that can be fitted with a rubberband. A RubberbandPanel takes care of reacting to mouse events in a rubberband-savvy manner. The chapter culminates with a simple drawing program that illustrates the use of rubberbands and RubberbandPanel.

The Graphic Java Toolkit Rubberband Package

The Graphic Java Toolkit includes a separate package for rubberbanding:
gjt.rubberband. Figure 13-1 shows the class diagram for the rubberband
package.

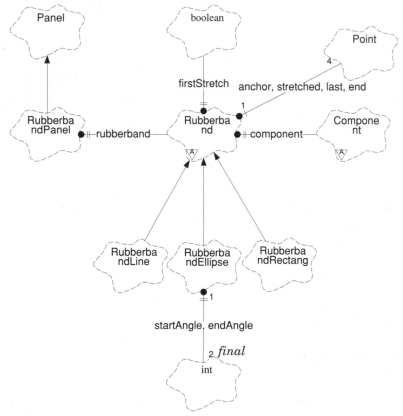

Figure 13-1 gjt.rubberband Package Diagram

The Rubberband Base Class

Before looking at the code for the Rubberband base class, let's briefly outline the
steps involved in rubberbanding a shape on-screen:

1. A mouse down event occurs in a Component equipped with a
   Rubberband.
2. The mouse is dragged inside the Component where the mouse down event
   occurred.
3. A mouse up event occurs in the same Component.

Step one defines the *anchor* point for the rubberband. The anchor point remains constant throughout the remaining steps. Step two involves dynamically updating the *stretch* point for the rubberband; the stretch point is kept in synch with the last mouse drag location. Step three defines the *endpoint* for the rubberband. After a rubberbanding operation is complete, a rubberband should be able to report the anchor point and the endpoint of the last rubberbanding operation that occurred, so that the rubberband client can determine the boundary of the rubberbanding operation and take whatever action is appropriate.

The Rubberband base class encapsulates the steps outlined above. Extensions of Rubberband, namely, RubberbandLine, RubberbandRectangle, and RubberbandEllipse, simply implement the actual drawing of the rubberband.

Rubberband Associations and Responsibilities

Table 13-1 and Table 13-2 summarize the responsibilities and associations of the Rubberband class. Note the two abstract methods in Table 13-1. Subclasses of Rubberband must implement drawLast() and drawNext() if they are to be concrete classes.

Table 13-1 gjt.rubberband.Rubberband **Responsibilities**

Methods	Description
void drawLast(Graphics g)	**Abstract** method that must be implemented by extensions of Rubberband. Draws the appropriate geometric shape at the last rubberband location.
void drawNext(Graphics g)	**Abstract** method that must be implemented by extensions of Rubberband. Draws the appropriate geometric shape at the next rubberband location.
Point getAnchor()	Returns the point of origin of a rubberband operation.
Point getStretched()	Returns the current stretched location for a rubberband operation.
Point getLast()	Returns the last point in a rubberband operation.
Point getEnd()	Returns the final point in a rubberband operation.
void anchor(Point p)	Sets the anchor point for a rubberband operation.

Table 13-1 gjt.rubberband.Rubberband **Responsibilities (Continued)**

Methods	Description
void stretch(Point p)	Sets the stretched location for a rubberband operation.
void end(Point p)	Sets the final point in a rubberband operation.
Rectangle bounds()	Returns the current boundary of the rubberband.
Rectangle lastBounds()	Returns the last boundary of the rubberband.

Table 13-2 gjt.rubberband.Rubberband **Associations**

Variables	Description
Point anchor	The point of origin for a rubberband operation. Initialized to 0,0.
Point stretched	The current point in a rubberband operation. Initialized to 0,0.
Point last	The last point in a rubberband operation. Initialized to 0,0.
Point end	The final point in a rubberband operation. Initialized to 0,0.
boolean firstStretch	drawLast() not invoked if firstStretch is true.
Component component	The component where rubberbanding will take place.

Now let's look at the Rubberband base class in Example 13-1. Recall that it encapsulates the steps outlined on page 352 for providing rubberbanding functionality.

Example 13-1 gjt.rubberband.Rubberband **Class Source Code**

```
package gjt.rubberband;

import java.awt.*;

abstract public class Rubberband {
   protected Point anchor    = new Point(0,0);
   protected Point stretched = new Point(0,0);
   protected Point last      = new Point(0,0);
   protected Point end       = new Point(0,0);
```

```java
private Component component;
private boolean   firstStretch = true;

abstract public void drawLast(Graphics g);
abstract public void drawNext(Graphics g);

public Rubberband(Component component) {
    this.component = component;
}
public Point getAnchor   () { return anchor;    }
public Point getStretched() { return stretched; }
public Point getLast      () { return last;      }
public Point getEnd       () { return end;       }

public void anchor(Point p) {
    firstStretch = true;
    anchor.x = p.x;
    anchor.y = p.y;

    stretched.x = last.x = anchor.x;
    stretched.y = last.y = anchor.y;
}
public void stretch(Point p) {
    last.x       = stretched.x;
    last.y       = stretched.y;
    stretched.x = p.x;
    stretched.y = p.y;

    Graphics g = component.getGraphics();
    if(g != null) {
        g.setXORMode(component.getBackground());

        if(firstStretch == true) firstStretch = false;
        else                      drawLast(g);

        drawNext(g);
    }
}
public void end(Point p) {
    last.x = end.x = p.x;
    last.y = end.y = p.y;

    Graphics g = component.getGraphics();
    if(g != null) {
        g.setXORMode(component.getBackground());
        drawLast(g);
    }
}
```

```
public Rectangle bounds() {
   return new Rectangle(stretched.x < anchor.x ?
                        stretched.x : anchor.x,
                        stretched.y < anchor.y ?
                        stretched.y : anchor.y,
                        Math.abs(stretched.x - anchor.x),
                        Math.abs(stretched.y - anchor.y));
}

public Rectangle lastBounds() {
   return new Rectangle(
               last.x < anchor.x ? last.x : anchor.x,
               last.y < anchor.y ? last.y : anchor.y,
               Math.abs(last.x - anchor.x),
               Math.abs(last.y - anchor.y));
   }
}
```

Rubberbanding, like all other graphical activities in the AWT, takes place in a component. Therefore, a rubberband must be supplied with a component at the time of construction:

```
public Rubberband(Component component) {
    this.component = component;
}
```

When a mouse down occurs in a component equipped with a rubberband, the component invokes the rubberband's anchor() method:

```
public void anchor(Point p) {
    firstStretch = true;
    anchor.x = p.x;
    anchor.y = p.y;

    stretched.x = last.x = anchor.x;
    stretched.y = last.y = anchor.y;
}
```

Rubberband.anchor() is passed the point where the mouse down event occurred. The rubberband sets the anchor, stretched, and last points to the point passed in, and firstStretch is set to true.

Subsequent mouse move events in a component equipped with a rubberband require the component to invoke the rubberband's stretch() method. Finally, when a mouse up occurs in the component, the rubberband's end() method must be invoked [1].

1.   RubberbandPanel, as we shall see, makes the appropriate rubberband calls when
     mouse events occur.

Painting in XOR Mode

As we've pointed out, Rubberband is an abstract class that leaves two methods for extensions to implement:

```
abstract public void drawLast(Graphics g);
abstract public void drawNext(Graphics g);
```

Both of these methods are invoked from within Rubberband stretch() and end() methods:

```
    public void stretch(Point p) {
❶       last.x = stretched.x;
        last.y      = stretched.y;
❷       stretched.x = p.x;
        stretched.x = p.x;
        stretched.y = p.y;

        Graphics g = component.getGraphics();
        if(g != null) {
❸          g.setXORMode(component.getBackground());

           it(firstStretch == true) firstStretch = false;
           else                      drawLast(g);

           drawNext(g);
        }
    }
    public void end(Point p) {
        last.x = end.x = p.x;
        last.y = end.y = p.y;

        Graphics g = component.getGraphics();
        if(g != null) {
            g.setXORMode(component.getBackground());
            drawLast(g);
        }
    }
```

The stretch() method is called when a mouse drag occurs. The first order of business for stretch() is to update both the stretch point and the last point in lines ❶ and ❷. Next, the Graphics object associated with the component upon which rubberbanding is taking place is set to XOR mode in line ❸. Setting XOR mode with the background color results in the following for all subsequent graphical operations using the Graphics object:

- Existing pixels with the current Graphics color are changed to the background color, and vice versa.

- Existing pixels that are not in the current color are changed unpredictably but reversibly—drawing the same color over the same pixel twice returns the pixel to its original color.

In essence, this difficult-to-explain operation effectively lets us paint on top of existing pixels without disturbing them.

Drawing Rubberband Lines

As the astute reader will probably figure out, the RubberbandLine class *rubberbands* lines. Example 13-2 shows the RubberbandLine class source code.

Example 13-2 gjt.rubberband.RubberbandLine **Class Source Code**

```
package gjt.rubberband;

import java.awt.Component;
import java.awt.Graphics;

public class RubberbandLine extends Rubberband {
   public RubberbandLine(Component component) {
❶      super(component);
   }
   public void drawLast(Graphics graphics) {
❷      graphics.drawLine(anchor.x, anchor.y, last.x, last.y);
   }
   public void drawNext(Graphics graphics) {
❸      graphics.drawLine(anchor.x, anchor.y, stretched.x,
                         stretched.x, stretched.y);
   }
}
```

Like all extensions of Rubberband, RubberbandLine must be constructed with a component, which it passes along to its superclass constructor in line ❶.

In line ❷, drawLast() draws a line from the anchor point to the last point. In line ❸, drawNext() draws a line from the anchor point to the current stretched point. drawNext() and drawLast() both use the anchor, stretched, and last points from the Rubberband class.

Note that RubberbandLine does not concern itself with drawing in XOR mode or tracking the anchor, stretch, or endpoints of the rubberbanding operation; all of that infrastructure is provided by Rubberband, its superclass.

Drawing Rubberband Rectangles and Ellipses

RubberbandRectangle and RubberbandEllipse work exactly the same as
RubberbandLine except that they draw rectangles and ellipses, as shown in
Example 13-3 and Example 13-4, respectively.

Example 13-3 gjt.rubberband.RubberbandRectangle **Class Source Code**

```java
package gjt.rubberband;

import java.awt.Component;
import java.awt.Graphics;
import java.awt.Rectangle;

public class RubberbandRectangle extends Rubberband {
  public RubberbandRectangle(Component component) {
      super(component);
  }
  public void drawLast(Graphics graphics) {
      Rectangle rect = lastBounds();
      graphics.drawRect(rect.x, rect.y,
                         rect.width, rect.height);
  }
  public void drawNext(Graphics graphics) {
      Rectangle rect = bounds();
      graphics.drawRect(rect.x, rect.y,
                         rect.width, rect.height);
  }
}
```

Example 13-4 gjt.rubberband.RubberbandEllipse **Class Source Code**

```java
package gjt.rubberband;

import java.awt.Component;
import java.awt.Graphics;
import java.awt.Rectangle;

public class RubberbandEllipse extends Rubberband {
  private final int startAngle = 0;
  private final int endAngle   = 360;

  public RubberbandEllipse(Component component) {
      super(component);
  }
  public void drawLast(Graphics graphics) {
      Rectangle r = lastBounds();
      graphics.drawArc(r.x, r.y,
```

```
            r.width, r.height, startAngle, endAngle);
    }
    public void drawNext(Graphics graphics) {
        Rectangle r = bounds();
        graphics.drawArc(r.x, r.y,
            r.width, r.height, startAngle, endAngle);
    }
}
```

Note that both RubberbandRectangle and RubberbandEllipse invoke the Rubberband.lastBounds() and Rubberband.bounds() methods to access the last and next boundaries that the rubberband enclosed, respectively.

RubberbandRectangle invokes the graphics.drawRect() method to draw its rectangles; RubberbandEllipse invokes the graphics.drawEllipse() method to draw its ellipses.

A Rubberband Panel

Example 13-5 shows the RubberbandPanel class, a simple extension of Panel that maintains an association with an instance of Rubberband and overrides its mouse event handling methods to manipulate the rubberband. The mouse event handlers all return false, so that the events are propagated to the panel's container.

Example 13-5 gjt.rubberband.RubberbandPanel **Class Source Code**

```
package gjt.rubberband;

import java.awt.*;

public class RubberbandPanel extends Panel {
  private Rubberband rubberband;

  public void setRubberband(Rubberband rubberband) {
      this.rubberband = rubberband;
  }
  public Rubberband getRubberband() {
      return rubberband;
  }
  public boolean mouseDown(Event event, int x, int y) {
      rubberband.anchor(new Point(x,y));
      return false;
  }
  public boolean mouseDrag(Event event, int x, int y) {
      rubberband.stretch(new Point(x,y));
      return false;
```

```
    }
    public boolean mouseUp(Event event, int x, int y) {
        rubberband.end(new Point(x,y));
        return false;
    }
}
```

Exercising the Rubberband Package

Figure 13-2 shows the gjt.rubberband package in action. As usual, feel free to run the unit test applet by invoking appletviewer on RubberbandTest.html. Running the unit test should help you to better understand the discussion of the unit test.

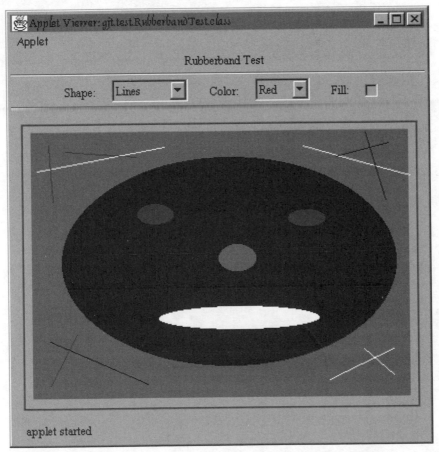

Figure 13-2 gjt.rubberband.Rubberband Unit Test

To see exactly how RubberbandTest is laid out in three dimensions, look at Figure 13-3.

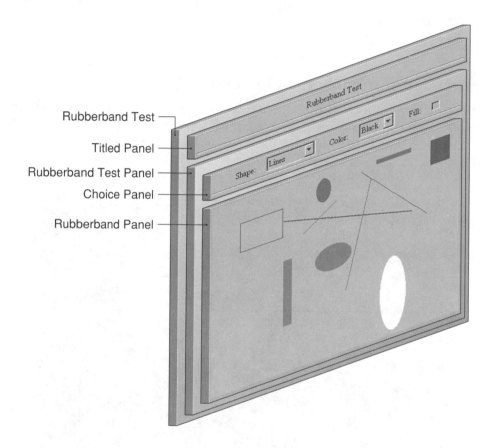

Rubberband Test

Titled Panel

Rubberband Test Panel

Choice Panel

Rubberband Panel

Figure 13-3 RubberbandTest Layout Diagram

As you may have gathered from looking at the unit test, RubberbandTest is a small drawing program for drawing basic lines, rectangles, and ellipses. Users can specify color and can choose to fill or not fill shapes.

As you look through the `RubberbandTest` class in Example 13-8, note that the
`RubberbandTestPanel` maintains references to three different rubberbands,
each fitted to the `rubberbandPanel` when an appropriate choice is made in the
`shapeChoice` component. Also notice that the `mouseUp()` method uses the
current rubberband to obtain either the bounds of the last rubberbanding operation
(when drawing rectangles or ellipses) or the anchor and endpoints (when drawing
lines). The `mouseUp()` method then draws the appropriate shape and fills it if the
shape is a rectangle or ellipse and the fill checkbox has been checked.

Example 13-6 `gjt.test.RubberbandTest` **Class Source Code, Take I**

```
public class RubberbandTest extends UnitTest {
    public String title()        { return "Rubberband Test";            }
    public Panel  centerPanel() { return new RubberbandTestPanel(); }
}

class RubberbandTestPanel extends Panel {
    private ChoicePanel     choicePanel     = new ChoicePanel(this);
    private RubberbandPanel rubberbandPanel = new RubberbandPanel();
    private Rubberband      rbLine, rbRect, rbEllipse,

    public RubberbandTestPanel() {
        rbLine     = new RubberbandLine      (rubberbandPanel);
        rbRect     = new RubberbandRectangle(rubberbandPanel);
        rbEllipse  = new RubberbandEllipse   (rubberbandPanel);

        rubberbandPanel.setRubberband(rbLine);

        setLayout(new BorderLayout());
        add("North",  choicePanel);
        add("Center", rubberbandPanel);
    }
    public void lines() {
        rubberbandPanel.setRubberband(rbLine);
    }
    public void rectangles() {
        rubberbandPanel.setRubberband(rbRect);
    }
    public void ellipses() {
        rubberbandPanel.setRubberband(rbEllipse);
    }
```

```java
    public boolean mouseUp(Event event, int x, int y) {
        Rubberband rb = rubberbandPanel.getRubberband();
        Graphics   g  = rubberbandPanel.getGraphics();
        Color      c  = choicePanel.getColor();

        g.setColor(c);

        if(rb == rbLine) {
            Point anchor = rb.getAnchor(), end = rb.getEnd();
            g.drawLine(anchor.x, anchor.y, end.x, end.y);
        }
        else if(rb == rbRect || rb == rbEllipse) {
            Rectangle r    = rb.bounds();
            boolean   fill = choicePanel.fill();

            if(rb == rbRect) {
                if(fill) g.fillRect(r.x, r.y, r.width, r.height);
                else     g.drawRect(r.x, r.y, r.width, r.height);
            }
            if(rb == rbEllipse) {
                if(fill) g.fillArc(r.x, r.y, r.width, r.height, 0, 360);
                else     g.drawArc(r.x, r.y, r.width, r.height, 0, 360);
            }
        }
        return true;
    }
}

class ChoicePanel extends Panel {
    private RubberbandTestPanel panel;
    private Color               color;
    private Checkbox            fillCheckbox = new Checkbox();

    public ChoicePanel(RubberbandTestPanel panel) {
        Panel    choicePanel    = new Panel();
        Choice   geometricChoice = new Choice();
        Choice   colorChoice    = new Choice();

        this.panel = panel;

        geometricChoice.addItem("Lines");
        geometricChoice.addItem("Rectangles");
        geometricChoice.addItem("Ellipses");
```

```java
        colorChoice.addItem("Black");
        colorChoice.addItem("Red");
        colorChoice.addItem("Blue");
        colorChoice.addItem("Gray");
        colorChoice.addItem("White");

        choicePanel.setLayout(new RowLayout(10));
        choicePanel.add(new Label("Shape:  "));
        choicePanel.add(geometricChoice);
        choicePanel.add(new Label("Color:  "));
        choicePanel.add(colorChoice);
        choicePanel.add(new Label("Fill:  "));
        choicePanel.add(fillCheckbox);

        setLayout(new BorderLayout());
        add("Center", choicePanel);
        add("South",  new Separator());
    }
    public boolean action(Event event, Object what) {
        if(event.target instanceof Choice) {
            if(((String)what).equals("Lines")) {
                fillCheckbox.setState(false);
                panel.lines();
            }
            else if(((String)what).equals("Rectangles"))
                panel.rectangles();
            else if(((String)what).equals("Ellipses"))
                panel.ellipses  ();

            else if(((String)what).equals("Black"))
                color = Color.black;
            else if(((String)what).equals("Red"))
                color = Color.red;
            else if(((String)what).equals("Blue"))
                color = Color.blue;
            else if(((String)what).equals("Gray"))
                color = Color.gray;
            else if(((String)what).equals("White"))
                color = Color.white;
        }
        return true;
    }
    public Insets   insets () { return new Insets(5,0,5,0);      }
    public Color   getColor() { return color;                    }
    public boolean fill    () { return fillCheckbox.getState(); }
}
```

Realize that `RubberbandTestPanel.mouseUp()` detects mouse up events in the `ChoicePanel` that do not occur in one of the `Choice` objects or the `Checkbox`. (This happens because by default, a panel's `mouseUp()` returns `false` and the event is propagated to the container, which in this case is the `RubberbandTestPanel`). Therefore, you can draw a shape in a specific color, change the color in the color choice, and then simply click anywhere outside a component in the `ChoicePanel`, and the shape will be redrawn in the new color [2].

One last thing to note about the unit test is that it does not keep track of which shapes have been drawn; therefore, when the window is covered and then brought to front, the shapes previously drawn vanish.

Refactoring the Unit Test

The object-oriented design process is an iterative one[3]. Classes are written, and as other classes are added to a system, insights are gained which often result in existing classes being *refactored*, meaning their implementations are modified to some degree according to a number of criterion. One of the mainstays of refactoring is to identify basic abstractions that may be shared among a number of different classes in the midst of specialized pieces of functionality. When such code is identified, it is separated from the specialized code and packaged into its own class or classes. The specialized code is then refactored to use the newly created class or classes.

For instance, the unit test above is a specialized piece of functionality, namely, a unit test for the `rubberband` package, that contains an abstraction which is much better placed in a class that is available for all to take advantage of. That abstraction is a drawing panel—a panel equipped with a set of rubberbands that can used to draw geometric shapes.

---

2. Is this a bug or a feature? We'll let you make the call.
3. See Booch, Grady. *Object-Oriented Analysis And Design*, section 6.1. Benjamin/Cummings.

The GJT DrawingPanel Class

Let's take a look at the gjt.DrawingPanel class, which, coincidentally, grew out of the original rubberband unit test in the manner described above. You will note that much of the functionality of the original unit test has been placed into the gjt.DrawingPanel class.

Example 13-7 gjt.DrawingPanel **Class Source Code**

```
package gjt;

import java.awt.*;
import gjt.rubberband.*;

public class DrawingPanel extends RubberbandPanel {
  private Rubberband rbLine, rbRect, rbEllipse;
  private Color    color;
  private boolean fill;

  public DrawingPanel() {
      rbLine    = new RubberbandLine     (this);
      rbRect    = new RubberbandRectangle(this);
      rbEllipse = new RubberbandEllipse  (this);

      setRubberband(rbLine);
  }
  public void drawLines      () { setRubberband(rbLine);    }
  public void drawRectangles() { setRubberband(rbRect);    }
  public void drawEllipses   () { setRubberband(rbEllipse); }

  public void  setColor(Color color) { this.color = color; }
  public Color getColor()            { return color;       }

  public void    setFill(boolean b) { fill = b;   }
  public boolean getFill()          { return fill; }
```

```
public boolean mouseUp(Event event, int x, int y) {
    Rubberband rb = getRubberband();
    Graphics   g  = getGraphics();

    super.mouseUp(event, x, y);
    g.setColor(color);

    if(rb == rbLine)         drawLine      (rb, g);
    else if(rb == rbRect)    drawRectangle(rb, g);
    else if(rb == rbEllipse) drawEllipse   (rb, g);

    return true;
}
protected void drawLine(Rubberband rb, Graphics g) {
    Point anchor = rb.getAnchor(), end = rb.getEnd();
    g.drawLine(anchor.x, anchor.y, end.x, end.y);
}
protected void drawRectangle(Rubberband rb, Graphics g) {
    Rectangle r = rb.bounds();

    if(fill) g.fillRect(r.x, r.y, r.width, r.height);
    else     g.drawRect(r.x, r.y, r.width, r.height);
}
protected void drawEllipse(Rubberband rb, Graphics g) {
    Rectangle r = rb.bounds();

    if(fill) g.fillArc(r.x, r.y, r.width, r.height, 0, 360);
    else     g.drawArc(r.x, r.y, r.width, r.height, 0, 360);
}
}
```

Now we present the refactored gjt.test.RubberbandTest class implementation [4] in Example 13-8.

---

4. Note that the CD contains only the refactored version of the unit test.

Example 13-8 gjt.test.RubberbandTest **Class Source Code**

```
package gjt.test;

import java.awt.*;
import gjt.DrawingPanel;
import gjt.Separator;
import gjt.RowLayout;
import gjt.rubberband.*;

public class RubberbandTest extends UnitTest {
  public String title() {
      return "Rubberband Test";
  }
  public Panel centerPanel() {
      return new RubberbandTestPanel();
  }
}

class RubberbandTestPanel extends Panel {
  private DrawingPanel drawingPanel;
  private ChoicePanel  choicePanel;

  public RubberbandTestPanel() {
      drawingPanel = new DrawingPanel();
      choicePanel  = new ChoicePanel(drawingPanel);

      setLayout(new BorderLayout());
      add("North",  choicePanel);
      add("Center", drawingPanel);
  }
}

class ChoicePanel extends Panel {
  private DrawingPanel drawingPanel;
  private Color        color;
  private Checkbox     fillCheckbox = new Checkbox();
```

```java
    public ChoicePanel(DrawingPanel drawingPanel) {
        Panel    choicePanel     = new Panel();
        Choice   geometricChoice = new Choice();
        Choice   colorChoice     = new Choice();

        this.drawingPanel = drawingPanel;

        geometricChoice.addItem("Lines");
        geometricChoice.addItem("Rectangles");
        geometricChoice.addItem("Ellipses");

        colorChoice.addItem("Black");
        colorChoice.addItem("Red");
        colorChoice.addItem("Blue");
        colorChoice.addItem("Gray");
        colorChoice.addItem("White");

        choicePanel.setLayout(new RowLayout(10));
        choicePanel.add(new Label("Shape:"));
        choicePanel.add(geometricChoice);
        choicePanel.add(new Label("Color:"));
        choicePanel.add(colorChoice);
        choicePanel.add(new Label("Fill:"));
        choicePanel.add(fillCheckbox);

        setLayout(new BorderLayout());
        add("Center", choicePanel);
        add("South",  new Separator());
    }
    public boolean action(Event event, Object what) {
        if(event.target instanceof Checkbox) {
            drawingPanel.setFill(fillCheckbox.getState());
        }
        else if(event.target instanceof Choice) {
            if(((String)what).equals("Lines")) {
                fillCheckbox.setState(false);
                drawingPanel.drawLines();
            }
            else if(((String)what).equals("Rectangles")) {
                System.out.println("Rectangles");
                drawingPanel.drawRectangles();
            }
            else if(((String)what).equals("Ellipses"))
                drawingPanel.drawEllipses  ();
            else if(((String)what).equals("Black"))
                drawingPanel.setColor(Color.black);
            else if(((String)what).equals("Red"))
                drawingPanel.setColor(Color.red);
```

```
        else if(((String)what).equals("Blue"))
            drawingPanel.setColor(Color.blue);
        else if(((String)what).equals("Gray"))
            drawingPanel.setColor(Color.gray);
        else if(((String)what).equals("White"))
            drawingPanel.setColor(Color.white);
    }
    return true;
}

public Insets insets() { return new Insets(5,0,5,0); }
}
```

Summary

The `gjt.rubberband` package serves as a good reminder that all graphical activities in the AWT occur in a `Component`. All the work is accomplished by the use of a component's `Graphics` object.

We have discussed one of the cornerstones of object-oriented software development—refactoring existing code. One of the principal activities of refactoring is to identify basic abstractions that have been implemented in specialized code. Once the basic abstractions have been identified, they are extracted from the specialized code and placed in a class (or classes) of their own, and the original specialized code is refactored to use the newly created classes.

CHAPTER

14

- The AWT Dialog on page 373

- Dismissing a Dialog on page 375

- gjt.DialogClient on page 376

- GJT Dialog Classes on page 379

- GJTDialog Base Class on page 381

- gjt.ButtonPanel on page 382

- gjt.MessageDialog on page 383

- gjt.YesNoDialog on page 388

- gjt.QuestionDialog on page 390

- gjt.ProgressDialog on page 395

- Exercising the GJT Dialogs on page 397

- Summary on page 402

Dialogs

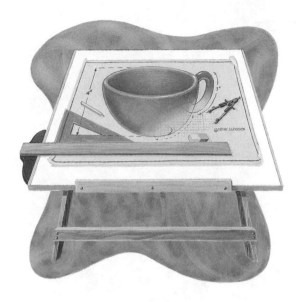

You may have noticed that we we've been conspicuously silent about dialog boxes in Part 1 of *Graphic Java*. We decided to cover dialog boxes in Part 2 mainly because AWT dialogs are largely uninteresting and the Graphic Java Toolkit's suite of dialogs provides more food for thought and discussion. This chapter, therefore, both introduces AWT dialogs and describes the four GJT convenience dialogs: MessageDialog, QuestionDialog, YesNoDialog, and ProgressDialog.

The AWT Dialog

Before we embark on our discussion of the GJT dialog classes, we'll briefly introduce the AWT Dialog class. To begin with, look at Figure 14-1.

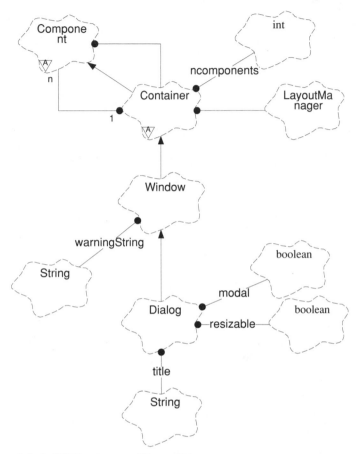

Figure 14-1 AWT `Dialog` Class Diagram

As you can see, `awt.Dialog` extends `awt.Window`, and, as such, can be shown, packed, disposed of, and sent to the front or back. Most of these `Window` methods are straightforward to use. For instance, `show()` does as you might expect—it shows the window. `pack()` is the most interesting `Window` method. It packs the contents of the window and resizes the window so that its size is just large enough to accommodate the contents of the window. Note that the 1.0.2 version of the AWT has introduced a bug that causes the `pack()` method to work incorrectly under Windows 95. As a result, under Windows 95, you will need to manually resize the GJT dialogs when they are shown for the first time.

Dialog adds a handful of methods to those it inherits from Window, the most interesting of which are the setTitle(String) method and the isModal() method.

setTitle(String) allows setting of the dialog's title, and the isModal() method returns a boolean indicating whether the dialog is modal. A modal dialog does not allow access to any other window until it has been addressed and dismissed.

Dismissing a Dialog

One thing you must decide when working with dialogs in the AWT is how you will react to a dialog being dismissed. When a dialog is shown by invoking its show() method, it does not block program execution; execution continues after the dialog is shown. For instance, if we have a method that shows a dialog, like this—

```
public void someMethod() {
    Dialog dialog = new Dialog(Util.getFrame(this), false);
    dialog.show();
    // do something interesting
}
```

—the "do something interesting" part of someMethod() is executed immediately after the dialog is shown.

As an aside, note that an AWT Dialog must be constructed with a Frame as an argument to its constructor. Luckily for us, the GJT Util class provides a method that will return the Frame associated with any Component. Also note that we assume that someMethod() resides in some extension of Component and therefore the this argument will suffice as the Component reference that Util.getFrame(Component) expects.

In any event, the point here is that showing a dialog does not block program execution. Of course, this begs the question: If showing a dialog does not block program execution, then how can the client that showed the dialog be notified that the dialog has been dismissed? There are a number of ways to handle such notification. Three possibilities are:

- Creating a thread that shows the dialog and constantly polls to see if the dialog has been dismissed

- Defining a dialog base class with a dismiss() method that must be overridden by subclasses

- Defining an interface for clients to implement

Of the three techniques, our preference is for the last one because it is the simplest and most direct approach and does not require a proliferation of dialog extensions for every dialog in existence.

gjt.DialogClient

A class in the GJT that needs to be notified that a dialog has been dismissed must implement the gjt.DialogClient interface:

```
public interface DialogClient {
    abstract public void dialogDismissed(Dialog d);
}
```

As you can certainly deduce, implementing the gjt.DialogClient interface involves implementing one lone method: dialogDismissed(). Implementors of gjt.DialogClient are passed a reference to the dialog that was dismissed, in case the implementor is intimately involved with more than one dialog. We will see an example of this in action when we look at the unit test for all of the GJT dialogs.

For now, let's take look at a simple example that shows a gjt.MessageDialog and illustrates implementing the dialogDismissed() method. First, look at Figure 14-2, which shows the MessageDialog in action.

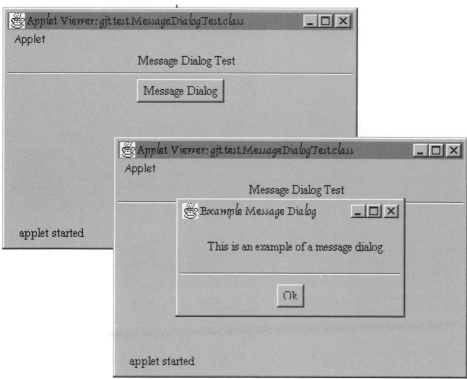

Figure 14-2 MessageDialog Output
The first picture shows the MessageDialog button, and the
second includes the dialog itself.

(Remember that all GJT unit tests are available on the CD accompanying this
book. We encourage you to run the unit test by invoking appletviewer. In this
case, run appletviewer on MessageDialogTest.html.)

Now that you've seen the unit test output, let's take a look at the code in
Example 14-1.

Example 14-1 `gjt.test.MessageDialotTest` **Class Source Code**

```
package gjt.test;

import java.awt.*;
import java.applet.Applet;

import gjt.MessageDialog;
import gjt.DialogClient;
import gjt.Util;

public class MessageDialogTest extends UnitTest {
  public String title() {
      return "Message Dialog Test";
  }
  public Panel centerPanel() {
      return new MessageDialogLauncher();
  }
}

class MessageDialogLauncher extends Panel
                          implements DialogClient {
  private MessageDialog  messageDialog;

  public MessageDialogLauncher() {
      add(new Button("Show Message Dialog"));
  }
  public boolean action(Event event, Object what) {
      messageDialog = MessageDialog.getMessageDialog(
                  Util.getFrame(this), this,
                  "Example Message Dialog",
                  "This is an example of a message dialog.");
      messageDialog.show();
      return true;
  }
  public void dialogDismissed(Dialog d) {
      System.out.println("MessageDialog Down");
  }
}
```

❶
❷

Like all of the other GJT unit tests, we're extending the `gjt.test.UnitTest`
class. `MessageDialogTest` returns an instance of `MessageDialogLauncher`
from the `centerPanel()` method. The `MessageDialogLauncher` contains a
single button that, when activated, shows the `gjt.MessageDialog`. For now,
we'll ignore the particulars of the `gjt.MessageDialog` itself and just focus on
`DialogClient`.

MessageDialogLauncher implements the dialogDismissed() method in line ❷. Note that in line ❶, the second argument to MessageDialog.getMessageDialog() is this, which is a reference to a DialogClient. The MessageDialogLauncher implementation of dialogDismissed() simply prints a message that indicates it has indeed been notified of the message dialog's dismissal.

From a client's perspective, that's all there is to reacting to a dialog's dismissal. Now let's take a look at the dialogs the Graphic Java Toolkit provides.

GJT Dialog Classes

As previously mentioned, the Graphic Java Toolkit provides four dialog classes: MessageDialog, QuestionDialog, YesNoDialog, and ProgressDialog. Figure 14-3 shows a class diagram that is an overview of the GJT dialog classes.

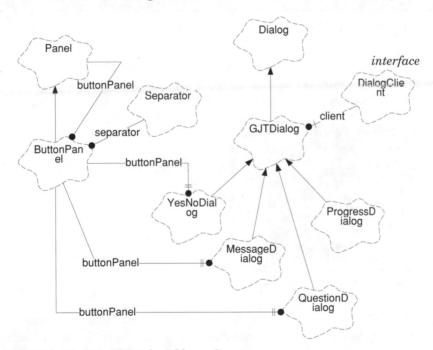

Figure 14-3 GJT Dialog Class Overview

MessageDialog displays a message; viewers of a MessageDialog have only one option upon seeing the message, and that is to activate the Ok button, which signifies that they are tired of looking at the message. We've already seen the MessageDialog in action in Figure 14-2 on page 377.

`QuestionDialog` poses a question and expects a response. `QuestionDialog` includes a prompt and a `TextField` into which a response can be typed. Additionally, `QuestionDialog` contains two buttons: an Ok button, which indicates that the question has been answered, and a Cancel button, which indicates that the entire operation be cancelled. Figure 14-4 shows a sample `QuestionDialog`.

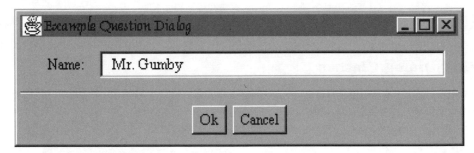

Figure 14-4 `QuestionDialog` Applet

`YesNoDialog`, like `QuestionDialog`, asks a question but accepts only a yes or no response. Therefore, `YesNoDialog` does not provide a `TextField`. Instead, it provides two buttons: a Yes button and a No button, as illustrated in Figure 14-5.

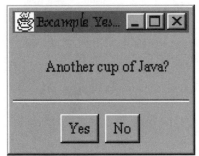

Figure 14-5 `YesNoDialog` Applet

Finally, the GJT provides a `ProgressDialog`, which contains a bargauge that shows the progress of some task that takes long enough to cause one to wonder if the software is in limbo or just extremely busy. In such a case, it is often a nice touch to provide a dialog that shows progress, and that is exactly the role of the `ProgressDialog`. Note that `ProgressDialog` is somewhat of a black sheep of the GJT dialog family, as it has no buttons and does not notify clients of its impending dismissal. In fact, it is the client who causes the `ProgressDialog` dismissal by telling it that the task is 100 percent complete. Figure 14-6 shows a `ProgressDialog` in use.

Figure 14-6 ProgressDialog Applet

GJTDialog Base Class

All of the dialogs provided with the Graphic Java Toolkit extend the same base class: GJTDialog. The role of GJTDialog is twofold:

- To establish the relationship between a dialog and its DialogClient
- To ensure that the dialog is centered in the frame specified as its parent

Example 14-2 shows GJTDialog class implementation.

Example 14-2 GJTDialog **Class Source Code**

```
package gjt;

import java.awt.*;

public class GJTDialog extends Dialog {
❶   protected DialogClient client;

    public GJTDialog(Frame      frame,
                     String     title,
                     DialogClient client,
                     boolean    modal) {
        super(frame, title, modal);
        setClient(client);
    }
    public void setClient(DialogClient client) {
        this.client = client;
    }
❷   public void show() {  // Fixes bug under Win95
        Dimension frameSize = getParent().size();
        Point     frameLoc  = getParent().location();
        Dimension mySize    = size();
        int       x,y;

        x = frameLoc.x + (frameSize.width/2) -(mySize.width/2);
        y = frameLoc.y + (frameSize.height/2)-(mySize.height/2);
        reshape(x,y,size().width,size().height);
```

```
        super.show();
    }
}
```

The one constructor in GJTDialog must be provided with a reference to a
DialogClient, which is set to the protected member client in line ❶. Note
also that the client can be changed after construction by means of the
setClient(DialogClient) method.

GJTDialog also overrides show() in line ❷ to ensure that the dialog is always
centered in the frame that is specified as its parent in the constructor. Although all
dialogs are supposed to be centered automatically in their parent frame, a bug
under the Windows 95 implementation of the AWT forces us to take matters into
our own hands to ensure proper positioning of the dialog.

gjt.ButtonPanel

Three of the four GJT dialogs are equipped with at least one button. As a result, it
is worthwhile to encapsulate that functionality inside an extension of Panel so
that dialogs can easily add a panel that contains buttons. This, of course, is the
role of gjt.ButtonPanel, as illustrated in Example 14-3. Note that
ButtonPanel is a general-purpose class that is useful outside of the realm of
dialogs.

Example 14-3 gjt.ButtonPanel **Class Source Code**

CD-Rom

```
package gjt;

import java.awt.*;

public class ButtonPanel extends Panel {
    Panel      buttonPanel = new Panel();
    Separator separator   = new Separator();

    public ButtonPanel() {
❶      setLayout(new BorderLayout(0,5));
        add("North",  separator);
        add("Center", buttonPanel);
    }
```

```
    public void add(Button button) {
        buttonPanel.add(button);
    }
    public Button add(String buttonLabel) {
        Button addMe = new Button(buttonLabel);
        buttonPanel.add(addMe);
        return addMe;
    }
    protected String paramString() {
        return super.paramString() + "buttons=" +
        countComponents();
    }
}
```

ButtonPanel is a simple extension of Panel that houses buttons.
ButtonPanel allows adding of buttons by two methods, one that takes an
awt.Button and, as a convenience, one that simply takes a String. The latter
method creates an awt.Button given the string that will be used as the button's
label, adds the newly created button to itself, and returns a reference to the button
in case the caller needs to make reference to the button at a later time.

Note that in line ❶, ButtonPanel employs a BorderLayout to lay out a
separator as its north component and a panel containing the buttons as its center
component. The ButtonPanel BorderLayout is constructed with a horizontal
gap of 0 and a vertical gap of 5 between components. This provides a small
amount of breathing room between the separator and the panel that houses the
buttons.

gjt.MessageDialog

Now we are finally in a position to take a look at the implementation of the four
GJT dialog classes. We start with MessageDialog, which displays a message
and comes equipped with a lone button used to dismiss the dialog. Figure 14-7
shows the class diagram for the GJT MessageDialog.

Figure 14-7 GJT `MessageDialog` Class

The `MessageDialog` maintains a string that is used as the message in the dialog and also maintains a reference to the Ok button.

Example 14-4 shows the `MessageDialog` source code. Notice that `MessageDialog` overrides `show()` in order to allow the Ok button to request focus, which lets a user dismiss the dialog by pressing the space bar to activate the button instead of having to go through the pain and agony of wheeling the cursor over to the button and clicking on it. After the Ok button requests focus, the `GJTDialog show()` method is invoked, which ensures that the dialog is centered in its parent's frame.

`MessageDialog` also overrides `action(Event,Object)` in order to dismiss the dialog. As we saw in our chapter on *Event Handling*, only four types of objects are capable of generating action events: `Button`, `CheckBox`, `TextField`, and `Choice`. Of those four objects, the GJT dialog classes use only one: a `Button`. Since there is only one button in the dialog, we need not bother to check and see

where the action event originated—we know the Ok button triggered the action—
and we proceed to hide() the dialog, which removes it from the screen; after
that, we notify the DialogClient that the dialog has indeed been dismissed.

Example 14-4 gjt.MessageDialog **Class Source Code**

```java
package gjt;

import java.awt.*;

public class MessageDialog extends GJTDialog {
   static private MessageDialog _theMessageDialog;

   private Button      okButton;
   private String      message;
   private ButtonPanel buttonPanel = new ButtonPanel();

   static public MessageDialog getMessageDialog(Frame frame,
                              DialogClient client,
                              String       title,
                              String       message) {
      if(_theMessageDialog == null)
         _theMessageDialog = new MessageDialog(frame,
                                      client,
                                      title,
                                      message);
      else {
         _theMessageDialog.setClient (client);
         _theMessageDialog.setTitle  (title);
         _theMessageDialog.setMessage(message);
      }
      return _theMessageDialog;
   }
   private MessageDialog(Frame  frame, DialogClient client,
                        String title, String       message) {
      super(frame, title, client, true);
      okButton = buttonPanel.add("Ok");

      setLayout(new BorderLayout());
      add("Center", new MessagePanel(message));
      add("South", buttonPanel);
      pack();
   }
   public void show() {
      okButton.requestFocus();
      super.show();
   }
   public boolean action(Event event, Object what) {
```

```
        hide();
        client.dialogDismissed(this);
        return true;
    }
    private void setMessage(String message) {
        this.message = message;
    }
}

class MessagePanel extends Panel {
    public MessagePanel(String message) {
        add("Center", new Label(message, Label.CENTER));
    }
    public Insets insets() {
        return new Insets(10,10,10,10);
    }
}
```

For the moment, let's ignore both the static member _theMessageDialog and the static method getMessageDialog() and go straight to the MessageDialog constructor:

```
private MessageDialog(Frame  frame, DialogClient client,
                        String title, String        message) {
    super(frame, title, client, true);
    okButton = buttonPanel.add("Ok");

    setLayout(new BorderLayout());
    add("Center", new MessagePanel(message));
    add("South", buttonPanel);
    pack();
}
```

The MessageDialog constructor takes four arguments:

- A Frame, which is the parent of the dialog

- A DialogClient, which is notified when the dialog is dismissed

- A String, which serves as a title for the dialog

- A String, which serves as the message to be displayed when the dialog is shown.

The constructor first calls its superclass (GJTDialog) constructor and then commences to add an Ok button to its ButtonPanel instance. It then creates a MessagePanel, which is laid out by a BorderLayout as the center component, while the ButtonPanel is laid out as the south component.

Finally, MessageDialog implements a private setMessage(String) method whose purpose will become apparent after we've uncovered the mystery of the static method and variable, which we have up until now ignored.

The Singleton Pattern and the MessageDialog

Now it's time to take a look at the static members that we told you to ignore:

```
static private MessageDialog _theMessageDialog;
    .
    .
    .
 static public MessageDialog getMessageDialog(Frame frame,
                          DialogClient client,
                          String      title,
                          String      message) {
        if(_theMessageDialog == null)
            _theMessageDialog = new MessageDialog(frame,
                                          client,
                                          title,
                                          message);
        else {
            _theMessageDialog.setClient (client);
            _theMessageDialog.setTitle  (title);
            _theMessageDialog.setMessage(message);
        }
        return _theMessageDialog;
    }
```

As long as we can vary the message displayed in a MessageDialog, we really have need of only one instance of MessageDialog. (In fact, in this day and age of recycling, we cannot, with good conscience, go about creating a brand-new MessageDialog whenever we want to display a message.) As a result, we provide a means to reuse the same MessageDialog over and over again.

The private _theMessageDialog is simply that. It is *the* MessageDialog. Clients of MessageDialog can request to use it by invoking the static MessageDialog.getMessageDialog() method. Note that getMessageDialog() first checks to see if the MessageDialog exists. If not, it creates it. From there on, getMessageDialog() simply sets up the MessageDialog client, title, and message and returns the same old MessageDialog for reuse.

You may have also noticed that the MessageDialog constructor is private, which prohibits clients from directly instantiating a MessageDialog. Since MessageDialog.getMessageDialog() is a method of the MessageDialog class, it has the right to invoke the private constructor, whereas methods outside of the `MessageDialog` class do not. Therefore, the only access that clients have to the `MessageDialog` is through the static `getMessageDialog()` method.

This implementation is known in object-oriented circles as the *singleton pattern* [1]. We will use the singleton pattern with two other GJT dialogs: the `YesNoDialog` and the `ProgressDialog`.

gjt.YesNoDialog

The `YesNoDialog` is very similar to the `MessageDialog`, except that its message is a question and it contains two buttons: a Yes button and a No button. The class diagram for `YesNoDialog` is shown in Figure 14-8.

Figure 14-8 GJT `YesNoDialog` Class

---

1.   For more information on the singleton pattern, see Gamma, Helm, Johnson, Vlissides. *Design Patterns, page 127.* Addison-Wesley.

Since `MessageDialog` and `YesNoDialog` are nearly identical in their
implementations, we will show you its implementation in Example 14-5 and be
on with our business.

Example 14-5 `gjt.YesNoDialog` **Class Source Code**

```java
package gjt;

import java.awt.*;

public class YesNoDialog extends GJTDialog {
  static private YesNoDialog _theYesNoDialog;
  private Button       yesButton;
  private Button       noButton;
  private String       message;
  private boolean      answer       = false;
  private ButtonPanel buttonPanel = new ButtonPanel();

  static public YesNoDialog getYesNoDialog( Frame frame,
                             DialogClient client,
                             String       title,
                             String       message) {
      if(_theYesNoDialog == null)
          _theYesNoDialog = new YesNoDialog(frame,client,
                                            title,message);
      else {
          _theYesNoDialog.setClient (client);
          _theYesNoDialog.setTitle  (title);
          _theYesNoDialog.setMessage(message);
      }
      return _theYesNoDialog;
  }
  private YesNoDialog(Frame  frame, DialogClient client,
                     String title, String       message) {
      super(frame, title, client, true);
      yesButton = buttonPanel.add("Yes");
      noButton  = buttonPanel.add("No");

      setLayout(new BorderLayout());
      add("Center", new YesNoPanel(message));
      add("South", buttonPanel);
      pack();
  }
  public void show() {
      yesButton.requestFocus();
      super.show();
  }
  public boolean answeredYes() {
```

```
            return answer;
    }
    public boolean action(Event event, Object what) {
        if(event.target == yesButton) answer = true;
        else                          answer = false;

        hide();
        client.dialogDismissed(this);
        return true;
    }
    private void setMessage(String message) {
        this.message = message;
    }
}

class YesNoPanel extends Panel {
    public YesNoPanel(String question) {
        add("Center", new Label(question, Label.CENTER));
    }
    public Insets insets() {
        return new Insets(10,10,10,10);
    }
}
```

gjt.QuestionDialog

The gjt.QuestionDialog presents a prompt and a TextField into which a response may be entered. It also comes with an Ok button and a Cancel button, as you can see from Figure 14-9.

Figure 14-9 GJT `QuestionDialog` Class

The first thing that may strike you about `QuestionDialog` is that we do not employ the singleton pattern for the `QuestionDialog`. Because it is impossible to resize the number of columns in a java.awt.`TextField` after its construction and because we want clients to be able to explicitly state the desired size of the `TextField`, we eschew the singleton pattern for the `QuestionDialog`. (Since we do not employ the singleton pattern, we are careful to `dispose()` of the dialog directly after it is hidden. This ensures that the resources associated with the dialog are cleaned up.)

We once again override `show()` in `QuestionDialog` in order to allow the `TextField` to request focus. By the way, realize that a request for focus in the AWT never seems to be denied. Of course, we request the focus as a convenience to the user so that the `TextField` has a blinking cursor from the beginning and the user can type into it without having to position the mouse in the `TextField`. Also, note that when an action occurs in the `QuestionPanel`, we are assured that the action was generated by a return in the `TextField` (again, refer to our chapter on *Event Handling* for details) and that the `QuestionDialog` `returnInTextField()` method is invoked in order to give focus to the Ok button. All of this requesting of focus business results in the user being able to type in a response and dismiss the dialog without ever having to use the mouse.

Example 14-6 shows the `QuestionDialog` implementation.

Example 14-6 gjt.`QuestionDialog` **Class Source Code**

CD-Rom

```
package gjt;

import java.awt.*;

public class QuestionDialog extends GJTDialog {
    static private int  _defaultTextFieldSize = 20;
    private Button       okButton;
    private Button       cancelButton;
    private String       question;
    private TextField    textField;
    private boolean      wasCancelled;
    private ButtonPanel buttonPanel = new ButtonPanel();

    public QuestionDialog(Frame   frame, DialogClient client,
                          String title, String       question,
                          String initialResponse) {
        this(frame, client, title, question, initialResponse,
            _defaultTextFieldSize);
    }
    public QuestionDialog(Frame   frame, DialogClient client,
                          String title, String       question) {
        this(frame, client, title,
            question, null, _defaultTextFieldSize);
    }
    public QuestionDialog(Frame   frame, DialogClient client,
                          String title, String       question,
                          int    textFieldSize) {
        this(frame, client, title,
            question, null, textFieldSize);
    }
```

```
public QuestionDialog(Frame  frame, DialogClient client,
                      String title, String        question,
                      String initialResponse,
                      int textFieldSize) {
    super(frame, title, client, true);

    QuestionPanel questionPanel;

    okButton    = buttonPanel.add("Ok");
    cancelButton = buttonPanel.add("Cancel");

    setLayout(new BorderLayout());
    add("North", questionPanel =
        new QuestionPanel(this, question,
                          initialResponse, textFieldSize));
    add("South", buttonPanel);
    textField = questionPanel.getTextField();
    pack();
}
public boolean action(Event event, Object what) {
    if(event.target == cancelButton) wasCancelled = true;
    else                             wasCancelled = false;

    hide();
    dispose();
    client.dialogDismissed(this);
    return true;
}
public void show() {
    textField.requestFocus();
    super.show();
}
public void returnInTextField() {
    okButton.requestFocus();
}
public TextField getTextField() {
    return textField;
}
public String getAnswer() {
    return textField.getText();
}
public boolean wasCancelled() {
    return wasCancelled;
}
private void setQuestion(String question) {
    this.question = question;
}
}
```

```java
class QuestionPanel extends Panel {
  private TextField      field;
  private QuestionDialog dialog;

  public QuestionPanel(QuestionDialog dialog,
                       String question) {
     this(dialog, question, null, 0);
  }
  public QuestionPanel(QuestionDialog dialog, String question,
                       int columns) {
     this(dialog, question, null, columns);
  }
  public QuestionPanel(QuestionDialog dialog, String question,
                       String initialResponse, int cols) {
     this.dialog = dialog;
     setLayout(new RowLayout());
     add(new Label(question));

     if(initialResponse != null) {
        if(cols != 0)
           add(field=new TextField(initialResponse, cols));
        else
           add(field=new TextField(initialResponse));
     }
     else {
        if(cols != 0) add(field = new TextField(cols));
        else          add(field = new TextField());
     }
  }
  public TextField getTextField() {
     return field;
  }
  public boolean action(Event event, Object what) {
     dialog.returnInTextField();
     return false;
  }
  public Insets insets() {
     return new Insets(10,10,10,10);
  }
}
```

gjt.ProgressDialog

Finally, we come to the gjt.ProgressDialog, which, unlike its GJT dialog siblings, does not contain any buttons nor does it notify a DialogClient when it is dismissed. As we previously mentioned, a ProgressDialog indicates to the user the percentage of a time-consuming task that has completed. Figure 14-10 shows the class diagram for the ProgressDialog.

Figure 14-10 GJT ProgressDialog Class

Since there normally is only one time-consuming task at a time that is holding matters up, we once again employ the singleton pattern to reuse the one and only instance of ProgressDialog.

Note that the `gjt.ProgressDialog` constructor creates a `gjt.Bargauge` and sets its color. The `setPercentComplete()` method updates the bargauge's fill percentage (see our chapter on *Separators and Bargauges* for a discussion of the Bargauge class). If the task is 100 percent complete, this method calls `done()`, which hides and disposes of the dialog.

Also, notice that `ProgressDialog` overrides `preferredSize()` to return a `Dimension` of 400,75, which is arbitrary but visually appealing.

Example 14-6 shows the `ProgressDialog` source code.

Example 14-7 `gjt.ProgressDialog` **Class Source Code**

```java
package gjt;

import java.awt.*;

public class ProgressDialog extends GJTDialog {
    static private ProgressDialog _theProgressDialog;
    static private int       _preferredWidth  = 400;
    static private int       _preferredHeight = 75;
    static private Color     _color;
    static private boolean _dialogUp;

    private Bargauge bargauge;

    static public ProgressDialog getProgressDialog(
                                      Frame   frame,
                                      String title,
                                      Color   color){
        if(_theProgressDialog == null)
            _theProgressDialog = new ProgressDialog(frame,
                                                    title,
                                                    color);
        else {
            _theProgressDialog.setTitle (title);
            _theProgressDialog.reset    ();
        }
        return _theProgressDialog;
    }
    private ProgressDialog(Frame frame,
                           String title,
                           Color color) {
        super(frame, title, null, true);
        setLayout(new BorderLayout());
        add("Center", bargauge = new Bargauge(color));
        pack();
    }
```

```
public void setPercentComplete(double percent) {
    bargauge.setFillPercent(percent);
    bargauge.fill();

    if(percent == 100)
      hide();
}
public void reset() {
    bargauge.setFillPercent(0);
}
public Dimension preferredSize() {
    return new Dimension(_preferredWidth, _preferredHeight);
}
}
```

Exercising the GJT Dialogs

At long last, we have come to the gjt.DialogTest, which exercises each of the dialogs we've discussed. We'll show you the customary picture of the unit test in Figure 14-11 and its corresponding 3-D layout diagram, followed by the code in its entirety. Once again, to get the full effect, you should run appletviewer on DialogTest.html.

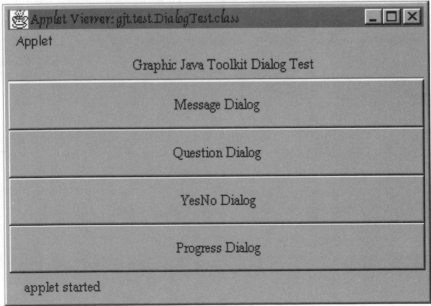

Figure 14-11 DialogTest Unit Test

Figure 14-12 shows the `DialogTest` layout in three dimensions.

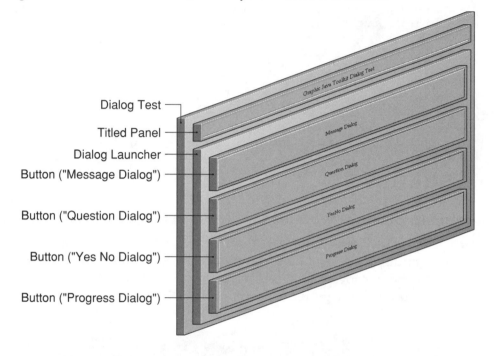

Dialog Test
Titled Panel
Dialog Launcher
Button ("Message Dialog")
Button ("Question Dialog")
Button ("Yes No Dialog")
Button ("Progress Dialog")

Figure 14-12 `DialogTest` Layout Diagram

One of the things to note in `DialogTest` in Example 14-8 is that the `DialogLauncher.dialogDismissed(Dialog)` method uses the `Dialog` reference passed in to determine what to print out. This is required because `DialogLauncher` must deal with three different dialogs. Remember that the progress dialog does not alert clients of its impending dismissal.

```
public void dialogDismissed(Dialog d) {
    if(d == messageDialog)  {
        System.out.println("MessageDialog Down");
    }
    if(d == questionDialog) {
        if(questionDialog.wasCancelled())
            System.out.println("CANCELLED");
        else
        System.out.println(
            "Name:   " +
            questionDialog.getTextField().getText());
    }
    if(d == yesNoDialog) {
```

```
        if(yesNoDialog.answeredYes())
            System.out.println("YES");
        else
            System.out.println("NO");
    }
}
```

Also note the role of `ProgressThread`. Given a `ProgressDialog`, the `ProgressThread` `run()` method bumps up the percent complete for the dialog by 10 percent every half second:

```
public void run() {
    while(percentComplete <= 100) {
        try { Thread.currentThread().sleep(500); }
        catch(InterruptedException e) { }

        dialog.setPercentComplete(percentComplete);
        percentComplete += 10;
    }
}
```

We must warn you that the 1.0.2 version of the AWT has introduced a bug that causes the thread that updates the progress dialog to work incorrectly, therefore the progress dialog in the unit test will not work properly under Motif. It is interesting to note that the dialog worked properly under version 1.0.1 of the AWT, and still functions correctly under Windows 95.

Example 14-8 shows the `gjt.test.DialogTest` source code.

Example 14-8 `gjt.test.DialogTest` **Class Source Code**

```
package gjt.test;

import java.awt.*;
import java.applet.Applet;

import gjt.Util;
import gjt.DialogClient;
import gjt.MessageDialog;
import gjt.ProgressDialog;
import gjt.QuestionDialog;
import gjt.YesNoDialog;

public class DialogTest extends UnitTest {
  public String title() {
      return "Graphic Java Toolkit Dialog Test";
  }
  public Panel centerPanel() {
```

```
         return new DialogLauncher();
   }
}

class DialogLauncher extends Panel implements DialogClient {
  private MessageDialog  messageDialog;
  private QuestionDialog questionDialog;
  private YesNoDialog    yesNoDialog;
  private ProgressDialog progressDialog;

  private Button messageDialogButton, questionDialogButton,
                 yesNoDialogButton,   progressDialogButton;

  public DialogLauncher() {
      setLayout(new GridLayout(0,1));

      add(messageDialogButton  =
          new Button("Message Dialog"));

      add(questionDialogButton =
          new Button("Question Dialog"));

      add(yesNoDialogButton    =
          new Button("YesNo Dialog"));

      add(progressDialogButton =
             new Button("Progress Dialog"));
  }
  public boolean action(Event event, Object what) {
      if(event.target == messageDialogButton) {
          messageDialog = MessageDialog.getMessageDialog(
              Util.getFrame(this), this,
              "Example Message Dialog",
              "This is an example of a message dialog.");

          messageDialog.show();
      }
      else if(event.target == questionDialogButton) {
          questionDialog =
              new QuestionDialog(Util.getFrame(this), this,
                                 "Example Question Dialog",
                                 "Name:  ", "Gumby", 45);
          questionDialog.show();
      }
      else if(event.target == yesNoDialogButton) {
          yesNoDialog =
              YesNoDialog.getYesNoDialog(Util.getFrame(this),
                                    this,
```

```
                                        "Example YesNo Dialog",
                                        "Another cup of Java?");

            yesNoDialog.show();
        }
        else if(event.target == progressDialogButton) {
            progressDialog =
                ProgressDialog.getProgressDialog(
                    Util.getFrame(this),
                    "Example Progress Dialog",
                    Color.blue);

            progressDialog.show();

            ProgressThread thread =
                new ProgressThread(progressDialog);
            thread.start();
        }

        return true;
    }
    public void dialogDismissed(Dialog d) {
        if(d == messageDialog)   {
            System.out.println("MessageDialog Down");
        }
        if(d == questionDialog) {
            if(questionDialog.wasCancelled())
                System.out.println("CANCELLED");
            else
            System.out.println(
                "Name:   " +
                questionDialog.getTextField().getText());
        }
        if(d == yesNoDialog) {
            if(yesNoDialog.answeredYes())
                System.out.println("YES");
            else
                System.out.println("NO");
        }
    }
}

class ProgressThread extends Thread {
    private ProgressDialog dialog;
    private double         percentComplete = 0;

    public ProgressThread(ProgressDialog dialog) {
        this.dialog = dialog;
    }
```

```
public void run() {
    while(percentComplete <= 100) {
        try { Thread.currentThread().sleep(500); }
        catch(InterruptedException e) { }

        dialog.setPercentComplete(percentComplete);
        percentComplete += 10;
    }
}
}
```

Summary

In this chapter, we've introduced the AWT `Dialog` class and explored four GJT extensions of it. In the process, we've suggested when it is appropriate to reuse an instance of an object rather than to always create new instances of it. (This is a technique referred to as the *singleton pattern*.)

We've also illustrated a technique for handling the dismissal of a dialog. Although dialog dismissal can be handled in a number of ways, the GJT dialog extensions introduce the `DialogClient` interface for this purpose. Clients of the GJT dialog classes can simply implement the interface and define its `dialogDismissed()` method to manage the dismissal of a dialog.

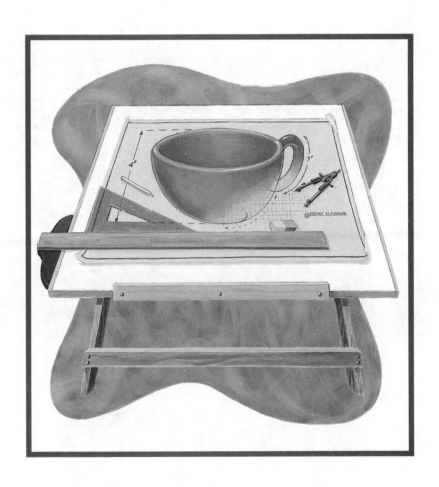

CHAPTER 15

- gjt.FontDialog on page 406

- A Font Panel on page 413

- Forcing a Container to Lay Out Its Components on page 415

- The Font Selection Panel on page 418

- The Font Picker Panel on page 419

- The Font Buttons Panel on page 422

- Exercising the gjt.FontDialog on page 424

- Summary on page 428

FontDialog

This chapter discusses the implementation of the Graphic Java Toolkit
FontDialog—a dialog that is used to select a font. While the font dialog is not as
generally useful as a general-purpose custom component such as an image
button, it is nonetheless handy for applets and applications that manipulate fonts.
Furthermore, the gjt.FontDialog implementation illustrates a number of
useful techniques for developing custom components, such as overriding the
addNotify() method, forcing a container to lay out its components in response
to some event, and obtaining a list of system fonts available. Finally, we provide
yet another example that illustrates GridBagLayout in use.

gjt.FontDialog

To begin with, look at Figure 15-1, which shows the `gjt.FontDialog` class diagram.

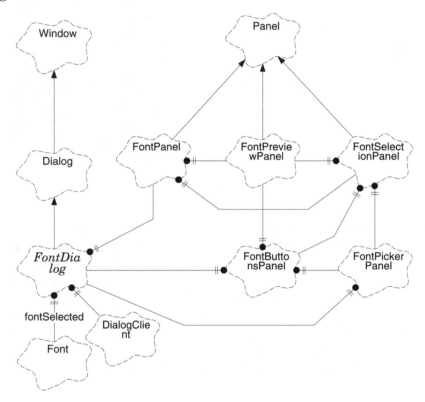

Figure 15-1 `gjt.FontDialog` Class Diagram

`gjt.FontDialog` extends `awt.Dialog` and maintains associations with a `FontPanel`, a `DialogClient`, and a `Font`. Note that `FontDialog` does not inherit from `GJTDialog` because we are not interested in inheriting the positioning of the dialog as implemented in `GJTDialog.show()`. (Refer to our chapter on *Dialogs* for a discussion of `GJTDialog`). The responsibilities of `gjt.FontDialog` are listed in Table 15-1.

Table 15-1 gjt.FontDialog **Responsibilities**

Methods	Description
boolean handleEvent(Event event)	Checks for WINDOW_DESTROY events.
String[] getFontNames()	Returns a list of font names.
String[] getFontSizes()	Returns a list of font sizes.
String getPreviewButtonLabel()	Returns the text displayed in the preview button.
String getOkButtonLabel()	Returns the text displayed in the ok button.
String getCancelButtonLabel()	Returns the text displayed in the cancel button.
void show()	Explicitly shapes dialog and calls super.show().
void done(Font font)	Invokes client's dialogDismissed() and disposes and hides dialog.
Font getFontSelected()	Returns the font selected. If dialog was cancelled, returns null.
void listSelectedPicker()	Invoked when a list in the FontPicker panel is selected. Requests focus for preview button.

Table 15-2 lists the associations of a gjt.FontDialog.

Table 15-2 gjt.FontDialog **Associations**

Variables	Description
private FontPanel fontpanel	Panel housing FontPreview panel and FontSelectionPanel.
private Font fontSelected	The font selected. Is null if dialog is cancelled.
private DialogClient client	Client that gets notified when font dialog is dismissed.

Before we dive into the code for gjt.FontDialog and its associates, let's look at a picture of a gjt.FontDialog in use in Figure 15-2 and a corresponding layout diagram in Figure 15-3.

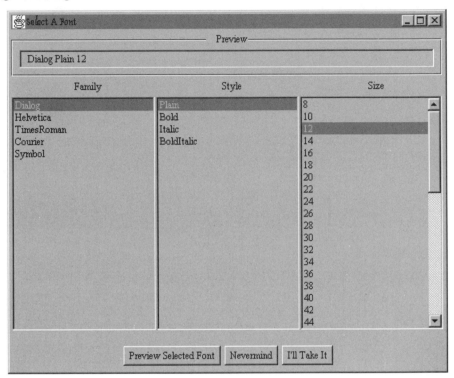

Figure 15-2 FontDialog In Action

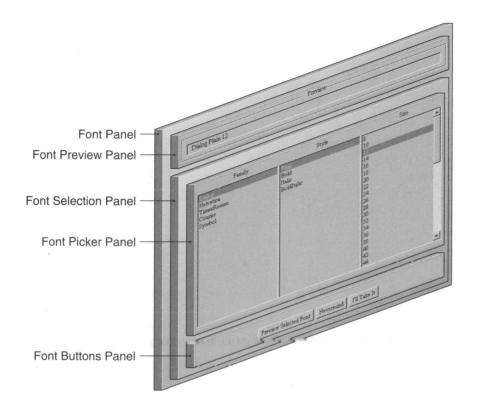

Figure 15-3 FontPanel Layout Diagram

FontDialog uses a BorderLayout layout manager, which centers an instance of FontPanel. FontPanel likewise employs a BorderLayout and lays out an instance of FontPreviewPanel in the north and an instance of FontSelectionPanel in the center.

`FontSelectionPanel` also uses a `BorderLayout` and lays out a
`FontPickerPanel` instance in the center and a `FontButtonsPanel` in the
south.

As an aside, this layout, along with others in the GJT, attests to the versatility of
`BorderLayout`. It is the layout manager of choice for many layout situations, as
mentioned in our chapter on *Components, Containers, and Layout Managers*.

Now that you have a good grasp of the anatomy of `FontDialog`, we are ready to
take a look at its implementation. Specifically, we'll be looking at:

- `FontDialog`

- `FontPanel`

- `FontPreviewPanel`

- `FontSelectionPanel`

- `FontPickerPanel`

- `FontButtonsPanel`

`gjt.FontDialog`, like many of the classes in the Graphic Java Toolkit, has a
fairly simple implementation, as illustrated in Example 15-1. Take a look through
the code, and then we'll make a few points about how it works.

Example 15-1 `gjt.FontDialog` **Class Source Code**

```
package gjt;

import java.awt.*;

public class FontDialog extends Dialog {
  private static String _defaultSizes[] =
      { "8",  "12", "14", "16", "18", "24", "48", "64" };

  private FontPanel     fontPanel;
  private Font          fontSelected;
  private DialogClient  client;

  public FontDialog(Frame         frame,
                    DialogClient client,

                    Font          font,    // initial font
                    boolean       modal) {
      super(frame, "Select A Font", modal);
      this.client = client;

      setLayout(new BorderLayout());
```

```
        add("Center", fontPanel = new FontPanel(this, font));
    }
    public boolean handleEvent(Event event) {
        if(event.id == Event.WINDOW_DESTROY)
            done(null);

        return super.handleEvent(event);
    }
    public String[] getFontNames() {
        return getToolkit().getFontList();
    }
    public String[] getFontSizes() {
        return _defaultSizes;
    }

    public String getPreviewButtonLabel() { return "Preview"; }
    public String getOkButtonLabel      () { return "Ok";      }
    public String getCancelButtonLabel () { return "Cancel";  }

    public void show() {
        Point frameLoc = getParent().location();
        reshape(frameLoc.x + 50, frameLoc.x + 50, 550, 450);
        super.show();
    }
    public void done(Font font) {
        fontSelected = font;
        client.dialogDismissed(this);
        hide    ();
        dispose();
    }
    public Font getFontSelected() {
        return fontSelected;
    }
    public void listSelectedInPicker() {
        fontPanel.getPreviewButton().requestFocus();
    }
}
```

❶ (marker at `client.dialogDismissed(this);` line)

Although gjt.FontDialog does not extend GJTDialog, as described in
GJTDialog Base Class on page 381, it uses the same technique for notifying clients
that it has been dismissed (see *Dismissing a Dialog* on page 375). FontDialog
maintains a reference to a DialogClient and invokes the client's
dialogDismissed() method from FontDialog.done() in line ❶.

The `FontDialog` does not employ the singleton pattern as do some of the other dialogs in the GJT. We decided not to implement `FontDialog` as a singleton because we expect `FontDialog` to be subclassed fairly often, which makes implementing the singleton pattern somewhat problematic.

`FontDialog` implements five methods that subclasses may wish to override in order to customize the look of the `FontDialog`:

```
public String[] getFontNames() {
  return getToolkit().getFontList();
}

public String[] getFontSizes() { return _defaultSizes; }

public String getPreviewButtonLabel() { return "Preview"; }

public String getOkButtonLabel () { return "Ok"; }

public String getCancelButtonLabel () { return "Cancel"; }
```

By invoking the `static Toolkit.getFontList()`, the `getFontNames()` method returns a list of system fonts available. Should subclasses wish to expand or restrict this list, they can do so by overriding `getFontNames()`.

The `getFontSizes()` method returns the `FontDialog` list of default sizes, which includes only a handful of sizes: 8, 12, 14, 16, 18, 24, 48, and 64. Subclasses can substitute a different list of sizes by overriding the `getFontSizes()` method. As we shall see, our unit test for `FontDialog` does exactly this and provides an expanded list of font sizes.

`FontDialog` also implements three methods that define the labels on the buttons that reside in the `FontButtonsPanel`; subclasses can override these methods to customize the labels of the buttons.

The `show()` method of `FontDialog` positions the dialog 50 pixels to the left and 50 pixels below the upper left-hand corner of the frame designated as its parent. Additionally, `show()` hardcodes the initial size of the dialog as 550 pixels wide and 450 pixels high:

```
public void show() {
  Point frameLoc = getParent().location();
  reshape(frameLoc.x + 50, frameLoc.x + 50, 550, 450);
  super.show();
}
```

In general, it is not a good idea to hardcode sizes of anything in the AWT. For windows and dialogs, it is much better to use `Window.pack()` to pack the contents of the window or dialog instead of hardcoding the size. However, using `pack()` for the font dialog results in a tiny dialog that we thought looked ridiculous and would probably be resized immediately anyway. Therefore, we've elected to indulge in a small bit of bad practice and hardcode the size to something that we find aesthetically appealing.

Note the `listSelectedInPicker()` method, which is called in response to a selection that is made in the `FontPickerPanel`:

```
public void listSelectedInPicker() {
   fontPanel.getPreviewButton().requestFocus();
}
```

`FontPickerPanel`, as you can see from the layout diagram in Figure 15-3 on page 409, contains three lists: one for font names, one for font styles, and one for font sizes. Whenever a selection is made from one of the lists, `FontPickerPanel` calls `FontDialog.listSelectedInPicker()`, which requests focus for the font panel's preview button. Essentially, we are trying to implement a cornerstone of good user interface design—anticipation of the user's next move. Most likely, when a selection is made from one of the three lists, the user will want to preview the selection. As a result, we give the focus to the preview button so that the user does not have to mouse around to preview the new selection. (You may remember that we employed the same technique with the Graphic Java Toolkit's `QuestionDialog`, described in Example 14-6 on page 392.)

Lastly, `FontDialog` implements the simple, but crucial `getFontSelected()` method, which clients can invoke to obtain the font selected in the dialog.

```
public Font getFontSelected() {
   return fontSelected;
}
```

A Font Panel

Of course, `gjt.FontDialog` is a mere shell of a dialog that contains an instance of `FontPanel`:

```
   class FontPanel extends Panel {
❶  private static Font defaultFont =
       new Font("TimesRoman", Font.PLAIN, 12);

❷  private FontPreviewPanel preview;
❸  private FontSelectionPanel fsp;
```

```
public FontPanel(FontDialog dialog, Font f) {
    Font font = f == null ? defaultFont : f;

    setLayout(new BorderLayout());
    add("North",  preview = new FontPreviewPanel  ());
    add("Center", fsp     =
        new FontSelectionPanel(dialog, preview, font));
}
public Button getPreviewButton() {
    return fsp.getPreviewButton();
}
}
```

FontPanel is a panel extension that lays out the preview panel and the selection panel. FontPanel is constructed with an initial font to be displayed in the font selection panel. If the font passed to the FontPanel constructor is null, FontPanel defaults the initial font to TimesRoman PLAIN 12 in line ❶.

The FontSelectionPanel declared in line ❸, as its name implies, enables selection of a font, and the FontPreviewPanel in line ❷ previews the font before it is selected. Note that the functionality of both panels is easily gleaned from their names. Coming up with good names for classes is one of the most overlooked activities of solid object-oriented design and can sometimes be one of the more difficult part of designing a set of classes.

In any event, we digress, so let's take a look at the implementation of FontPreviewPanel:

```
class FontPreviewPanel extends Panel {
TextField textField = new TextField();
Box        box        = new Box(textField, "Preview");

public FontPreviewPanel() {
    textField.setEditable(false);

    setLayout(new BorderLayout());
    add("Center", box);
}
public void setPreviewFont(Font font) {
    String name  = font.getName();
    String size  = String.valueOf(font.getSize());
    String style = new String();

    if(font.isPlain () == true) style = "Plain";
    else {
        if(font.isBold () == true) style += "Bold";
        if(font.isItalic() == true) style += "Italic";
    }
```

```
          textField.setFont(font);
          textField.setText(name + " " + style + " " + size);
          retrofitPreviewPanel();
      }
    private void retrofitPreviewPanel() {
          Dimension tfps, tfs;
          FontPanel fontPanel = (FontPanel)getParent();

          tfps = textField.preferredSize();
          tfs  = textField.size();

          if(tfps.width != tfs.width ||
             tfps.height != tfs.height) {
            fontPanel.invalidate();
            fontPanel.getParent().validate();
            box.repaint();              // Only necessary on Win95
          }
      }
    }
  }
```

FontPreviewPanel uses a BorderLayout to lay out an instance of the versatile gjt.Box, which contains a TextField that will display the currently selected font.

In setPreviewFont(), we determine the style of the font passed in by invoking the Font class isPlain(), isBold(), and isItalic() methods in lines **❶**, **❷**, and **❸**, respectively.

After determining the style of the font, we set the TextField font by invoking the Component method setFont(), and then we set the text to a string that displays the name, style, and size of the font selected. After we are done with the TextField, we then invoke retrofitPreviewPanel(), which we shall discuss next.

Forcing a Container to Lay Out Its Components

We're going to discuss the retrofitPreviewPanel() method separately from the others in FontPreviewPanel because, in general, we consider the mechanics of forcing a layout to be worthy of its own discussion.

We briefly introduced this topic in our chapter on *Components, Containers, and Layout Managers*, but it is worth our time here to revisit and expand somewhat on that discussion.

Realize that setting the font of the text field in setPreviewFont() may cause the text field to resize when its text is set. In response to this change in size, we must force a layout of the contents of the dialog; otherwise we may only see a fraction of the text in the text field or the text field may be too big for the text. Either way, when the font of the preview panel is set, we want to cause the dialog to lay out its components. In practice, forcing containers to lay out their components is common in the world of the AWT.

Forcing a layout is accomplished by invoking validate() on a container. However, calling validate() will result in a no-op if the components contained in the container are all valid. In reality, forcing a layout is accomplished by a two-step process:

1. Invalidating components, either explicitly with the invalidate() method or implicitly with the Container methods that invalidate a component (see Table 7-8 on page 203)

2. Calling validate() on the container that contains those components

This is exactly what we do in the retrofitPreviewPanel() method:

```
       private void retrofitPreviewPanel() {
           Dimension tfps, tfs;
           FontPanel fontPanel = (FontPanel)getParent();

           tfps = textField.preferredSize();
           tfs  = textField.size();

❶          if(tfps.width != tfs.width ||
              tfps.height != tfs.height) {
❷             fontPanel.invalidate();
❸             fontPanel.getParent().validate();
              box.repaint();              // Only necessary on Win95
           }
       }
```

Notice that we get the text field's preferred size and its actual size. If the preferred size is different from the actual size, as determined in line ❶, then we know that we need to force a layout. We accomplish this by invalidating the font panel in line ❷ and then invoking validate on the font panel's parent in line ❸. (A component's parent is its container.) Also, notice that repainting of the gjt.Box instance is necessary under Windows 95 or the box will contain remnants of the previous rendering of the text field. This is a bug with the AWT implementation under Windows 95 and is unnecessary (and in fact is harmless) with the Solaris versions of the AWT.

Although you will want to run the unit test applet for FontDialog, you can see the forced layout in action in Figure 15-4.

Figure showing two "Select A Font" dialog windows.

Top window:
- Title bar: Select A Font
- Preview: Dialog Plain 12
- Family: Dialog (selected), Helvetica, TimesRoman, Courier, Symbol
- Style: Plain (selected), Bold, Italic, BoldItalic
- Size: 8, 10, 12 (selected), 14, 16, 18, 20, 22, 24, 26, 28, 30, 32, 34, 36, 38, 40, 42, 44
- Buttons: Preview Selected Font, Nevermind, I'll Take It

Bottom window:
- Title bar: Select A Font
- Preview: *TimesRoman Italic 42*
- Family: Dialog, Helvetica, TimesRoman (selected), Courier, Symbol
- Style: Plain, Bold, Italic (selected), BoldItalic
- Size: 28, 30, 32, 34, 36, 38, 40, 42 (selected), 44, 46, 48, 50, 52, 54, 56, 58, 60
- Buttons: Preview Selected Font, Nevermind, I'll Take It

Figure 15-4 FontDialog With Preview Panel Resized

The Font Selection Panel

Next, let's take a look at the FontSelectionPanel implementation:

```
class FontSelectionPanel extends Panel {
  private FontPickerPanel  picker;
  private FontButtonsPanel buttons;
  private FontPreviewPanel preview;
  private Font             initialFont;

  public FontSelectionPanel(FontDialog     dialog,
                            FontPreviewPanel preview,
                            Font initialFont) {
      this.preview     = preview;
      this.initialFont = initialFont;

      picker  = new FontPickerPanel (dialog, initialFont);
      buttons = new FontButtonsPanel(dialog, picker, preview);

      setLayout(new BorderLayout());
      add("Center", picker);
      add("South",  buttons);
  }
  public void addNotify() {
      super.addNotify();
      preview.setPreviewFont(initialFont);
  }
  public Button getPreviewButton() {
      return buttons.getPreviewButton();
  }
}
```

FontSelectionPanel lays out a FontPickerPanel in the center and a FontButtonsPanel in the south. The FontSelectionPanel is passed the initial font, which it uses in setting the preview panel's initial font. Note that we override addNotify(), which ensures that all of the underlying peers have been created and that the setting of the font will work correctly.

> **AWT Tip**
>
> ***Overriding addNotify()***
>
> The grossly misnamed Component.addNotify() method creates the component's peer (createPeer() would have been a much better choice for a name). Therefore, if you need to ensure that the peer is created before performing some function, you may override addNotify() and take care of business. However, you must *always* call super.addNotify() when overriding addNotify() or else the platform-specific peers will not be created. Only after invoking super.addNotify() can you be assured that the component's peer has been created.

The Font Picker Panel

Now we've come to the most complicated panel contained in our FontDialog — the FontPickerPanel. The FontPickerPanel has a fairly long-winded implementation—in general, something we like to avoid. However, the FontPickerPanel has a good deal of work to do and a number of components to contain, so it merits being the heavyweight among its associates. Let's look at some of the particulars of its implementation before dropping you into the entire source code.

As mentioned before, and as you can see from the Figure 15-2 on page 408 and Figure 15-3 on page 409, FontPickerPanel contains lists for:

- Font names
- Font styles
- Font sizes

FontPickerPanel also has more complicated layout needs, so we turn to the powerful GridBagLayout to lend a hand. Here is how GridBagLayout is used:

```
❶       gbc.anchor    = GridBagConstraints.NORTH;
❷       gbc.gridwidth = 1;
        gbl.setConstraints(family, gbc); add(family);
        gbl.setConstraints(style,  gbc); add(style);
❸       gbc.gridwidth = GridBagConstraints.REMAINDER;
        gbl.setConstraints(size,    gbc); add(size);
```

```
        gbc.gridwidth = 1;
❹       gbc.weighty   = 1.0;
❺       gbc.weightx   = 1.0;
❻       gbc.fill      = GridBagConstraints.BOTH;
        gbl.setConstraints(fonts,  gbc); add(fonts);
        gbl.setConstraints(styles, gbc); add(styles);
        gbl.setConstraints(sizes,  gbc); add(sizes);
```

First, we set the constraints for each of the labels (family, style, and size) to NORTH in line ❶. In line ❷, we set the gridwidth for the first two labels to 1. By default, gridwidth is set to 1, but we like being explicit as to our intentions here. We set the constraints for the size label in line ❸ to REMAINDER so that it will be the last component in its row.

We once again set the gridwidth to 1, and then in lines ❹, ❺ and ❻, we set weightx and weighty to 1.0, and fill to BOTH. Setting weightx and weighty to 1.0, along with setting fill to BOTH, ensures that each list will fill all available extra space equally when a resize occurs, which is just the effect that we desire.

Now, with this background on how FontPickerPanel employs GridBagLayout, let's look at the class in its entirety:

```
class FontPickerPanel extends Panel {
  private FontDialog dialog;
  private Button       previewButton;
  private List         fonts  = new List();
  private List         styles = new List();
  private List         sizes  = new List();
  private Font         initialFont;

  public FontPickerPanel(FontDialog dialog,
                         Font         initialFont) {
    GridBagLayout       gbl    = new GridBagLayout();
    GridBagConstraints  gbc    = new GridBagConstraints();
    Label               family = new Label("Family");
    Label               style  = new Label("Style");
    Label               size   = new Label("Size");

    this.initialFont = initialFont;
    this.dialog      = dialog;

    populateFonts  ();
    populateStyles ();
    populateSizes  ();

    setLayout(gbl);

    gbc.anchor     = GridBagConstraints.NORTH;
```

```
        gbc.gridwidth = 1;
        gbl.setConstraints(family, gbc); add(family);
        gbl.setConstraints(style,  gbc); add(style);
        gbc.gridwidth = GridBagConstraints.REMAINDER;
        gbl.setConstraints(size,   gbc); add(size);

        gbc.gridwidth = 1;
        gbc.weighty   = 1.0;
        gbc.weightx   = 1.0;
        gbc.fill      = GridBagConstraints.BOTH;
        gbl.setConstraints(fonts,  gbc); add(fonts);
        gbl.setConstraints(styles, gbc); add(styles);
        gbl.setConstraints(sizes,  gbc); add(sizes);
    }
    public boolean handleEvent(Event event) {
        if(event.id  == Event.LIST_SELECT) {
            dialog.listSelectedInPicker();
            return true;
        }
        return false;
    }
    public void addNotify() {
        super.addNotify();
        String initialFamily = initialFont.getName();
        int    initialSize   = initialFont.getSize();
        int    initialStyle  = initialFont.getStyle();

        styles.select(initialStyle);

        for(int i=0; i < fonts.countItems(); ++i) {
            String nextFamily = fonts.getItem(i);
            if(nextFamily.equals(initialFamily))
                fonts.select(i);
        }
        for(int i=0; i < sizes.countItems(); ++i) {
            String nextSize = sizes.getItem(i);
            if(nextSize.equals(String.valueOf(initialSize)))
                sizes.select(i);
        }
    }
    public String fontSelected() {
        return fonts.getSelectedItem ();
    }
    public String styleSelected() {
        return styles.getSelectedItem();
    }
    public int sizeSelected() {
        String szstring = sizes.getSelectedItem();
```

```
        if(szstring != null) {
            Integer integer = new Integer(szstring);
            return integer.intValue();
        }
        else
            return 0;
    }
    private void populateFonts() {
        String names[] = dialog.getFontNames();

        for(int i=0; i < names.length; ++i) {
            fonts.addItem(names[i]);
        }
    }
    private void populateSizes() {
        String sizeArray[] = dialog.getFontSizes();

        for(int i=0; i < sizeArray.length; ++i) {
            sizes.addItem(sizeArray[i]);
        }
    }
    private void populateStyles() {
        styles.addItem("Plain");
        styles.addItem("Bold");
        styles.addItem("Italic");
        styles.addItem("BoldItalic");
    }
}
```

Note that FontPicker overrides addNotify() for the express purpose of selecting the appropriate items in each list corresponding to the initial font. FontPicker needs to ensure that the lists are created before selecting items in them; overriding addNotify() and invoking super.addNotify() guarantees that the lists and their associated peers are accessible and that we can select items in the lists.

The Font Buttons Panel

Now let's take a look at the last panel of which the gjt.FontDialog is composed—the FontButtonsPanel:

```
class FontButtonsPanel extends Panel {
    private FontDialog       dialog;
    private FontPickerPanel  picker;
    private FontPreviewPanel preview;
    private Button           previewButton,
```

```
                         okButton,
                         cancelButton;

   public FontButtonsPanel(FontDialog       dialog,
                           FontPickerPanel  picker,
                           FontPreviewPanel preview) {
      this.picker  = picker;
      this.preview = preview;
      this.dialog  = dialog;

      add(previewButton =
          new Button(dialog.getPreviewButtonLabel()));
      add(cancelButton  =
          new Button(dialog.getCancelButtonLabel()));
      add(okButton      =
          new Button(dialog.getOkButtonLabel()));
   }
❶  public void addNotify() {
      super.addNotify();
      cancelButton.requestFocus();
   }
❷  public boolean action(Event event, Object object) {
      Button  button = (Button)event.target;
      boolean handledEvent = true;

      if(event.target == previewButton) {
         Font selectedFont = fontSelected();

         if(selectedFont != null) {
            preview.setPreviewFont(selectedFont);
            okButton.requestFocus();
         }
      }
      else if(event.target == okButton)
         dialog.done(fontSelected());
      else if(event.target == cancelButton)
         dialog.done(null);
      else
         handledEvent = false;

      return handledEvent;
   }
   public Button getPreviewButton() {
      return previewButton;
   }
   private Font fontSelected() {
      String font  = picker.fontSelected ();
      String style = picker.styleSelected();
```

```
int    size  = picker.sizeSelected ();
int    istyle = Font.PLAIN;

if(font != null && style != null && size > 0) {
    if(style.equals("Bold"))   istyle = Font.BOLD;
    if(style.equals("Plain"))  istyle = Font.PLAIN;
    if(style.equals("Italic")) istyle = Font.ITALIC;

    if(style.equals("BoldItalic"))
        istyle = Font.BOLD + Font.ITALIC;

    return new Font(font, istyle, size);
}
else
    return null;
    }
}
```

There are a few points we should make about FontButtonsPanel. First, notice that we override addNotify() in line ❶ with the express purpose of giving the Cancel button focus. When the FontDialog first comes up, since a font has not yet been selected, the user has no need for either the preview button or the Ok button, so we give the Cancel button focus to start. As we indicated in our previous discussion, the preview button is given focus when a list selection is made from the font picker panel.

Second, we override the action() method in line ❷ to give the Ok button focus after the font has been set in the preview panel. Presumably, the next logical task after previewing a font is to choose it, which is done by activating the Ok button. Therefore, after a preview is complete, we give focus to the Ok button in anticipation of the user selecting the font previewed. If the user decides that the previewed font is not desirable, no harm has been done in giving the Ok button focus—the user is still free to choose a different font or select the Cancel button. Once again, we are just trying to make the font dialog user's life a little easier.

Exercising the gjt.FontDialog

Figure 15-5 shows sample output from the unit test implementation of the FontDialog class.

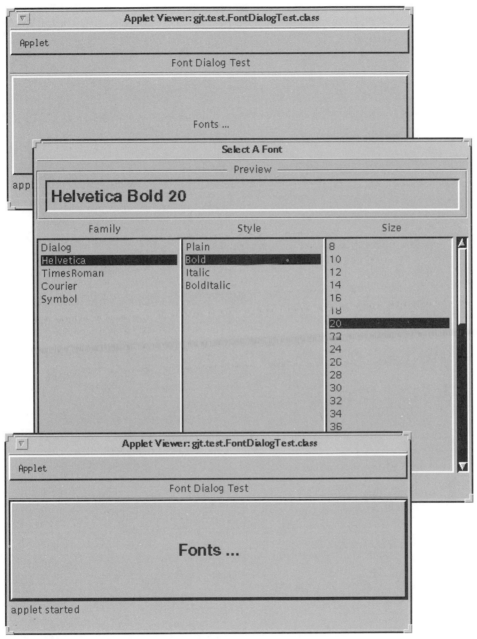

Figure 15-5 gjt.FontDialog Unit Test
This series of pictures shows the unit test in its initial state and
then final state after a Helvetica 20 point bold font is selected
from the font dialog.

Now, given Figure 15-5, look through the `FontDialog` unit test in Example 15-2. As you do, notice that it creates a font button. Activating the button causes the `FontDialog` to be displayed. Selecting a font from the `FontDialog` causes the button to use the selected font.

Example 15-2 `gjt.test.FontDialogTest` **Class Source Code**

```java
package gjt.test;

import java.awt.*;

import gjt.FontDialog;
import gjt.DialogClient;
import gjt.Util;

class LotsOfSizesFontDialog extends FontDialog {
  private static String _defaultSizes[] =
      { "8", "10", "12", "14", "16",
        "18", "20", "22", "24",
        "26", "28", "30", "32", "34",
        "36", "38", "40", "42", "44",
        "46", "48", "50", "52", "54",
        "56", "58", "60", "62", "64",
        "66", "68", "70", "72", "74",
        "76", "78", "80", "82", "84",
        "86", "88", "90", "92", "94",
        "96", "98", "100" };

    public LotsOfSizesFontDialog(Frame          frame,
                                 DialogClient client,
                                 Font           font) {
        super(frame, client, font, true);
    }
    public String getPreviewButtonLabel() {
        return "Preview Selected Font";
    }
    public String getOkButtonLabel      () {
        return "I'll Take It";
    }
    public String getCancelButtonLabel () {
        return "Nevermind";
    }
    public String[] getFontSizes          () {
        return _defaultSizes;
    }
}
  public class FontDialogTest extends UnitTest {
```

```
    public String title() { return "Font Dialog Test"; }
    public Panel centerPanel() {
        return new FontDialogTestPanel();
    }
}


class FontDialogTestPanel extends     Panel
                        implements DialogClient {
    private Button fontButton;

    public FontDialogTestPanel() {
        setLayout(new BorderLayout());
        add("Center", fontButton = new Button("Fonts ..."));
    }
    public boolean handleEvent(Event event) {
        if(event.id == Event.ACTION_EVENT) {
            LotsOfSizesFontDialog d;
            d = new LotsOfSizesFontDialog(Util.getFrame(this),
                                          this,
                                          fontButton.getFont());

            d.show();
        }
        return true;
    }
    public void dialogDismissed(Dialog d) {
        FontDialog fontDialog   = (FontDialog)d;
        Font        fontSelected = fontDialog.getFontSelected();

        if(fontSelected != null)
            fontButton.setFont(fontSelected);

        fontButton.requestFocus();
    }
}
```

Notice that LotsOfSizesFontDialog extends FontDialog and overrides a
number of methods to customize the dialog, namely:

- getPreviewButtonLabel()

- getOkButtonLabel()

- getCancelButtonLabel()

- getFontSizes()

The FontDialogTestPanel adds a centered Button, whose activation causes
the LotsOfSizesFontDialog to be displayed in the action() method. The
dialogDismissed() method casts the Dialog reference passed in to a

FontDialog and calls `FontDialog.getFontSelected()` to obtain the font selected in the `LotsOfSizesFontDialog`. Lastly, the `fontButton` has its font set to the font selected in the `LotsOfSizesFontDialog`, and requests focus.

Summary

In this chapter, we've introduced the Graphic Java Toolkit `FontDialog` class and a number of supporting classes. Besides discussing the general utility of the `FontDialog`, we've spent some time highlighting exactly how to force a container to lay out its components—a commonly required task in response to an event within an applet. We've also taken yet another pass at showing the powerful `GridBagLayout` layout manager in use. Finally, we have discussed overriding `addNotify()` in order to perform functions that require a component's peer to exist.

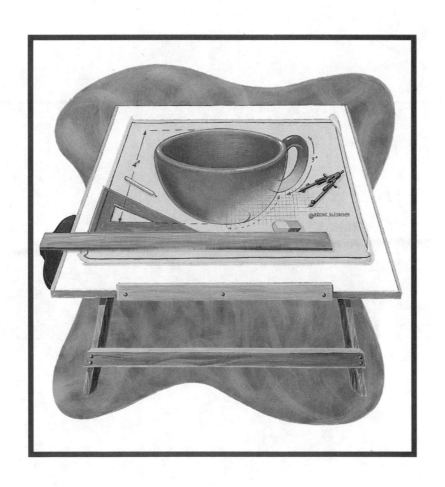

CHAPTER
16

- Scrollbars on page 432

- Scrolling With the Graphic Java Toolkit on page 435

- gjt.Scroller on page 445

- gjt.ComponentScroller on page 454

- gjt.ImageCanvas and gjt.ImageScroller on page 457

- Exercising the gjt.ImageScroller on page 459

- Exercising the gjt.ComponentScroller on page 463

- Summary on page 471

Scrollers

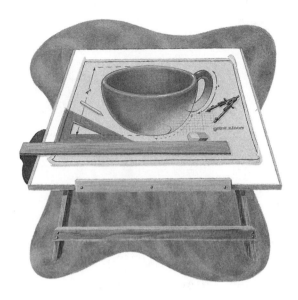

When developing applets, or any graphical user interface, for that matter, it usually doesn't take long before the need arises to scroll something. In the world of the AWT, that *something* is nearly always a component—usually a container—or an image.

Creating a scrollbar and attaching it to a container is a simple matter when using the AWT; however, actually scrolling a component or an image requires you to handle a myriad of details concerning the monitoring of and reacting to scrollbar events.

The Graphic Java Toolkit comes with a set of classes that encapsulate all the details of scrolling a component or image, freeing you to work on the higher-level aspects of your applet instead of spending time manually scrolling components and images.

Scrollbars

We will discuss the GJT classes and their unit tests, but let's start out by looking at a simple applet that creates a couple of scrollbars, attaches them to a container, and monitors scrollbar events:

```
import java.applet.Applet;
import java.awt.*;
public class ScrollbarTest extends Applet {
  private Scrollbar hbar, vbar;
  public void init() {
     setLayout(new BorderLayout());
     add("South", hbar = new Scrollbar(Scrollbar.HORIZONTAL));
     add("East", vbar = new Scrollbar(Scrollbar.VERTICAL));
     hbar.setValues(0, 100, 0, 1000);
     hbar.setLineIncrement(50);
     hbar.setPageIncrement(100);
     vbar.setValues(100, 500, 0, 1000);
     hbar.setLineIncrement(100);
     hbar.setPageIncrement(500);
  }
  public boolean handleEvent(Event event) {
     if(event.target instanceof Scrollbar)
         System.out.println(event);
     return false;
  }
}
```

This applet employs a `BorderLayout` to lay out a horizontal scrollbar to the south and a vertical scrollbar to the east. Subsequently, whenever a scrollbar event occurs, the applet's `handleEvent(Event)` method simply prints out the event.

Lines ❶ and ❹ set the *values* for the horizontal and vertical scrollbars, respectively. The four values passed to the `Scrollbar.setValues()` method are:

- `value` — Sets the scrollbar's slider position
- `visible` — Indicates the amount of the object being scrolled that is visible
- `minimum` — Indicates the minimum value the scrollbar can have
- `maximum` — Indicates the maximum size of the object being scrolled

For the horizontal scrollbar, we have set the initial value to 0, which means the slider will start out on the far-left side of the scrollbar. We have set the amount visible to 100, indicating that the visible portion of the object being scrolled is one tenth of its overall width. Finally, we have set the minimum value for the scrollbar to 0 and the maximum to 1000.

Realize that "setValues" is somewhat of a misnomer for this method. You might reasonably expect such a method to set all the values with which a scrollbar is concerned. However, if you look at lines ❷ and ❸, you will see that we have invoked two additional `Scrollbar` methods that also set values for the scrollbar: `setLineIncrement()` and `setPageIncrement()`. The line increment is the amount that the scrollbar's slider moves when the line gadgets of the scrollbar (the arrows) are activated. The page increment represents the amount that the scrollbar's slider moves when a mouse click occurs either above or below the slider.

It is worthwhile to take a look at the `ScrollBarTest` applet under both Windows 95 and Motif, as illustrated in Figure 16-1.

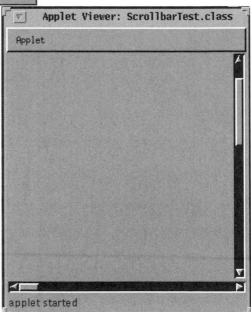

Figure 16-1 Scrollbar in Windows 95 and Motif
The top picture shows a Windows 95 scrollbar and the bottom a
Motif scrollbar.

Scrolling With the Graphic Java Toolkit

As our `ScrollBarTest` applet illustrates and as we mentioned previously, it is a simple matter to create scrollbars, attach them to a container, and monitor the events associated with the scrollbar. However, when trying to scroll a component or image, the developer must handle many details; this is where the AWT leaves off and the scrolling classes of the Graphic Java Toolkit begin. Figure 16-2 shows the relationships between the GJT scroller classes.

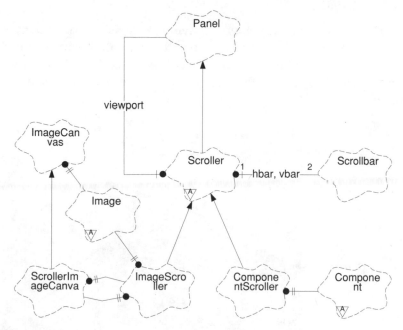

Figure 16-2 `gjt.Scroller` Class Diagram

When using the Graphic Java Toolkit, most of the time you will simply create an `ImageScroller` or a `ComponentScroller` and fit each with an image or component, respectively. `ImageScroller` and `ComponentScroller` automatically handle all of the grunt work associated with scrolling an image or component.

`ImageScroller` and `ComponentScroller` both extend `Scroller`. `Scroller` is a very general class that handles most aspects of scrolling, without regard for the object being scrolled. Notice that `Scroller` extends `Panel`. Since `ImageScroller` and `ComponentScroller` are both components, they can be added to containers and laid out just like any other component.

Each `Scroller` contains three components:

- Horizontal scrollbar
- Vertical scrollbar
- A panel

From here on, we will generically refer to the panel contained in a scroller as its *viewport*. The viewport displays the visible portion of whatever is being scrolled.

gjt.Scroller Layout

Each `Scroller` has a `ScrollerLayout` layout manager. `ScrollerLayout` is a good place to begin our discussion because it illustrates the components contained in a `Scroller` and, of course, how they are laid out. In order to better visualize a scroller, take a look at the diagram in Figure 16-3 showing its components.

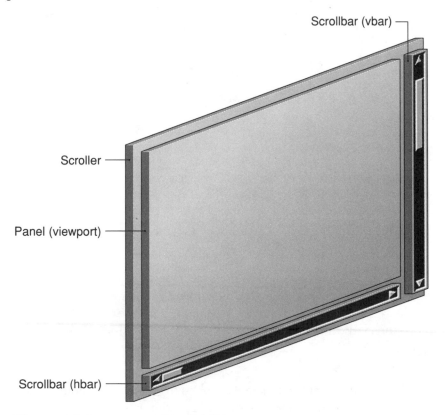

Figure 16-3 `ScrollerLayout` Diagram

A gjt.ScrollerLayout is responsible for placing and sizing the scrollbars and viewport associated with its Scroller. We'll dissect ScrollerLayout in the next few pages and then show the entire implementation in Example 16-1 on page 442.

A ScrollerLayout maintains references to its scroller, along with the scroller's scrollbars and viewport:

```
public class ScrollerLayout implements LayoutManager {
    private Scroller   scroller;
    private Scrollbar hbar, vbar;
    private String     hbarPosition, vbarPosition;
    private Component viewport;
    private int        top, bottom, right, left;

    public ScrollerLayout(Scroller scroller) {
        this.scroller = scroller;
    }
```

ScrollerLayout must be handed a scroller at construction time. Let's look at how components are added to and removed from a scroller layout:

```
    public void addLayoutComponent(String name,
                                   Component comp) {
        Assert.notFalse(comp != null);

❶      if(comp instanceof Scrollbar) {
            Scrollbar sbar = (Scrollbar)comp;

            if(sbar.getOrientation() == Scrollbar.VERTICAL) {
                Assert.notFalse("East".equals(name) == true ||
                                "West".equals(name) == true);
                vbar          = sbar;
                vbarPosition = name;
            }
            else {
                Assert.notFalse("North".equals(name) == true ||
                                "South".equals(name) == true);
                hbar          = sbar;
                hbarPosition = name;
            }
        }
        else {
❷          Assert.notFalse("Scroll".equals(name) == true);
            Assert.notFalse("Scroll".equals(name) == true);
            viewport = comp;
        }
    }
```

If the component to be added is an instance of Scrollbar (line ❶), then we proceed to check the scrollbar's orientation. If it is vertical, then we assert that the name passed in is either East or West. If it is horizontal, we assert that the name is either North or South.

If the component is not a Scrollbar, an assertion is made in line ❷ to ensure that the name passed in is equal to "Scroll."[1]

As an aside, notice that ScrollerLayout will not allow you to incorrectly specify an orientation or give it an unexpected type of object. This may seem like we're indulging in paranoia, but consider the following code:

```
       .
       .
       .
setLayout(new BorderLayout());
add("center", new TextField());
       .
       .
       .
```

After you've spent some time staring at code like this and trying to figure out why your text field is not showing up, you will come to appreciate correct code and aggressive use of assertions[2]. Note that the code above will compile correctly but will silently ignore your request to place the text field in the center. BorderLayout does not enforce correct usage; the "center" argument should actually be "Center"; however BorderLayout simply ignores requests to add components if the string supplied with the component is invalid. Therefore, the above code will compile and run without a hitch, but you'll never see the text field until you spell Center with a capital C.

Let's quickly cover the ScrollerLayout implementations of preferredLayoutSize() and minimumLayoutSize():

```
   public Dimension preferredLayoutSize(Container parent) {
       Dimension dim = new Dimension(0,0);

❶      if(vbar != null && vbar.isVisible()) {
           Dimension d = vbar.preferredSize();
           dim.width += d.width;
           dim.height = d.height;
       }
❷      if(hbar != null && hbar.isVisible()) {
           Dimension d = hbar.preferredSize();
```

1. In retrospect, "Viewport" would have been a better choice.
2. Refer to *Assertions* on page 242 for more on assertions.

```
            dim.width += d.width;
            dim.height = Math.max(d.height, dim.height);
        }
❸       if(viewport != null && viewport.isVisible()) {
            Dimension d = viewport.preferredSize();
            dim.width += d.width;
            dim.height = Math.max(d.height, dim.height);
        }
        return dim;
    }
    public Dimension minimumLayoutSize(Container parent) {
        Dimension dim = new Dimension(0,0);

❹       if(vbar != null && vbar.isVisible()) {
            Dimension d = vbar.minimumSize();
            dim.width += d.width;
            dim.height = d.height;
        }
❺       if(hbar != null && hbar.isVisible()) {
            Dimension d = hbar.minimumSize();
            dim.width += d.width;
            dim.height = Math.max(d.height, dim.height);
        }
❻       if(viewport != null && viewport.isVisible()) {
            Dimension d = viewport.minimumSize();
            dim.width += d.width;
            dim.height = Math.max(d.height, dim.height);
        }
        return dim;
    }
```

The most important thing worth noting about these two methods is that they must be careful to check that each component is not null and is visible before applying the component's size to the total size of the container. These checks occur in lines ❶ through ❻, respectively.

The most interesting part of the ScrollerLayout is the layoutContainer() method:

```
public void layoutContainer(Container target) {
    Insets insets      = target.insets();
    Dimension targetSize = target.size();

    top    = insets.top;
    bottom = targetSize.height - insets.bottom;
    left   = insets.left;
    right  = targetSize.width - insets.right;
```

❶
```
        scroller.manageScrollbars();

        reshapeHorizontalScrollbar();
        reshapeVerticalScrollbar  ();
        reshapeViewport           ();

        scroller.setScrollbarValues();
    }
```
❷
```
    private void reshapeHorizontalScrollbar() {
        if(hbar != null && hbar.isVisible()) {
            if("North".equals(hbarPosition)) {
                Dimension d = hbar.preferredSize();
                hbar.reshape(left, top, right - left, d.height);
                top += d.height;
            }
            else {   // South
                Dimension d = hbar.preferredSize();
                hbar.reshape(left, bottom - d.height,
                            right - left,d.height);
                bottom -= d.height;
            }
        }
    }
```
❸
```
    private void reshapeVerticalScrollbar() {
        if(hbar != null && vbar.isVisible()) {
            if("East".equals(vbarPosition)) {
                Dimension d = vbar.preferredSize();
                vbar.reshape(right - d.width, top,
                                d.width, bottom - top);
                right -= d.width;
            }
            else { // West
                Dimension d = vbar.preferredSize();
                vbar.reshape(left, top,
                                d.width, bottom - top);
                left += d.width;
            }
        }
    }
```
❹
```
    private void reshapeViewport() {
        if(viewport != null && viewport.isVisible()) {
            viewport.reshape(left, top,
                                right - left, bottom - top);
        }
    }
```

After we calculate the top, left, bottom, and right sides of the container, given the container's size and insets, we have the scroller manage its scrollbars. `Scroller.manageScrollbars()` called in line ❶ determines whether each of its two scrollbars should be visible and ensures that their visibility is set appropriately.

Once the two scrollbars have been either hidden or shown, as appropriate, `ScrollerLayout` commences to reshape each component it is responsible for laying out.

After each of the three components has been laid out, the scroller sets the values for each of its scrollbars.

The only mystery left to uncover is how each component is laid out. First, notice that each reshape method in lines ❷, ❸, and ❹ uses the top, left, bottom, and right class members that were set in `layoutContainer()`. Furthermore, the scrollbar reshape methods (`reshapeHorizontalScrollbar()` and `reshapeVerticalScrollbar()`) potentially modify all of the four variables, so the order of invocation in `layoutContainer()` is important.

First, `reshapeHorizontalScrollbar()` in line ❷ checks to see if there's a horizontal scrollbar and if it is visible. If so, `reshapeHorizontalScrollbar()` reshapes the scrollbar and updates either the top or bottom dimension, depending upon whether the scrollbar is in the North or the South.

Second, `reshapeVerticalScrollbar()` in line ❸, which is almost a mirror image of `reshapeHorizontalScrollbar()`, reshapes the vertical scrollbar and adjusts either the right or left dimensions.

By the time we get to `reshapeViewport()` in line ❹, left, top, bottom, and right have all been adjusted to account for the horizontal and vertical scrollbars. (Notice that `reshapeViewport()` is invoked after the scrollbar reshape methods in `layoutContainer()`). All that is left, then, is to reshape the viewport, assuming that it is non-null and visible.

Now that we've thoroughly discussed the manner in which `ScrollerLayout` performs its duties, we're ready to take a look at its complete implementation in Example 16-1.

Example 16-1 `gjt.ScrollerLayout` **Class Source Code**

CD-Rom

```java
package gjt;

import java.awt.*;

public class ScrollerLayout implements LayoutManager {
   private Scroller   scroller;
   private Scrollbar hbar, vbar;
   private String    hbarPosition, vbarPosition;
   private Component viewport;
   private int       top, bottom, right, left;

   public ScrollerLayout(Scroller scroller) {
       this.scroller = scroller;
   }

   public void addLayoutComponent(String name,
                                  Component comp) {
       Assert.notFalse(comp != null);

       if(comp instanceof Scrollbar) {
           Scrollbar sbar = (Scrollbar)comp;

           if(sbar.getOrientation() == Scrollbar.VERTICAL) {
               Assert.notFalse("East".equals(name) == true ||
                               "West".equals(name) == true);
               vbar          = sbar;
               vbarPosition = name;
           }
           else {
               Assert.notFalse("North".equals(name) == true ||
                               "South".equals(name) == true);
               hbar          = sbar;
               hbarPosition = name;
           }
       }
       else {
           Assert.notFalse("Scroll".equals(name) == true);
           viewport = comp;
       }
   }
   public void removeLayoutComponent(Component comp) {
       if(comp == vbar)     vbar     = null;
       if(comp == hbar)     hbar     = null;
       if(comp == viewport) viewport = null;
   }
   public Dimension preferredLayoutSize(Container parent) {
```

```java
        Dimension dim = new Dimension(0,0);

        if(vbar != null && vbar.isVisible()) {
            Dimension d = vbar.preferredSize();
            dim.width += d.width;
            dim.height = d.height;
        }
        if(hbar != null && hbar.isVisible()) {
            Dimension d = hbar.preferredSize();
            dim.width += d.width;
            dim.height = Math.max(d.height, dim.height);
        }
        if(viewport != null && viewport.isVisible()) {
            Dimension d = viewport.preferredSize();
            dim.width += d.width;
            dim.height = Math.max(d.height, dim.height);
        }
        return dim;
    }
    public Dimension minimumLayoutSize(Container parent) {
        Dimension dim = new Dimension(0,0);

        if(vbar != null && vbar.isVisible()) {
            Dimension d = vbar.minimumSize();
            dim.width += d.width;
            dim.height = d.height;
        }
        if(hbar != null && hbar.isVisible()) {
            Dimension d = hbar.minimumSize();
            dim.width += d.width;
            dim.height = Math.max(d.height, dim.height);
        }
        if(viewport != null && viewport.isVisible()) {
            Dimension d = viewport.minimumSize();
            dim.width += d.width;
            dim.height = Math.max(d.height, dim.height);
        }
        return dim;
    }
    public void layoutContainer(Container target) {
        Insets insets       = target.insets();
        Dimension targetSize = target.size();

        top    = insets.top;
        bottom = targetSize.height - insets.bottom;
        left   = insets.left;
        right  = targetSize.width - insets.right;
```

```
                scroller.manageScrollbars();

                reshapeHorizontalScrollbar();
                reshapeVerticalScrollbar  ();
                reshapeViewport           ();

                scroller.setScrollbarValues();
        }
        private void reshapeHorizontalScrollbar() {
            if(hbar != null && hbar.isVisible()) {
                if("North".equals(hbarPosition)) {
                    Dimension d = hbar.preferredSize();
                    hbar.reshape(left, top, right - left, d.height);
                    top += d.height;
                }
                else {  // South
                    Dimension d = hbar.preferredSize();
                    hbar.reshape(left, bottom - d.height,
                                right - left,d.height);
                    bottom -= d.height;
                }
            }
        }
        private void reshapeVerticalScrollbar() {
            if(hbar != null && vbar.isVisible()) {
                if("East".equals(vbarPosition)) {
                    Dimension d = vbar.preferredSize();
                    vbar.reshape(right - d.width, top,
                                d.width, bottom - top);
                    right -= d.width;
                }
                else { // West
                    Dimension d = vbar.preferredSize();
                    vbar.reshape(left, top,
                                d.width, bottom - top);
                    left += d.width;
                }
            }
        }
        private void reshapeViewport() {
            if(viewport != null && viewport.isVisible()) {
                viewport.reshape(left, top,
                                right - left, bottom - top);
            }
        }
    }
```

gjt.Scroller

Table 16-1 lists the gjt.Scroller class responsibilities and Example 16-2 on page 451 shows its implementation.

Table 16-1 gjt.Scroller **Responsibilities**

Methods	Description
void scrollTo(int x, int y)	Abstract method. Passed current values for horizontal scrollbar's value and vertical scrollbar's value.
Dimension getScrollAreaSize()	Abstract method. Returns size of object being scrolled.
Scrollbar getHorizontalScrollbar()	Returns the horizontal scrollbar.
Scrollbar getVerticalScrollbar()	Returns the vertical scrollbar.
Panel getViewport()	Returns the viewport.
boolean handleEvent(Event event)	Reacts to scrolling events, otherwise calls super.handleEvent()
void paint(Graphics g)	Calls scroll().
void update(Graphics g)	Calls update().
void manageScrollbars()	Sets visibility of scrollbars.
void setScrollbarValues()	Sets values of scrollbars.

Table 16-2 lists the associations of a gjt.Scroller.

Table 16-2 gjt.Scroller **Associations**

Variables	Description
protected Panel viewport	Panel in which object being scrolled is displayed.
protected Scrollbar hbar	Horizontal scrollbar
protected Scrollbar vbar	Vertical scrollbar

However, there are a number of details about it worth pointing out before showing you the complete source code.

gjt.Scroller is an abstract class that encapsulates all aspects of scrolling that are independent of the object being scrolled. As it turns out, that includes just about all of the scrolling functionality. Extensions of gjt.Scroller are left to implement but two methods:

```
abstract public void        scrollTo(int x, int y);
abstract public Dimension getScrollAreaSize();
```

Each extension of `Scroller` must be able to scroll to a given location. The x and y values passed to `scrollTo()` represent the current values for the horizontal and vertical scrollbars, respectively. It is up to extensions of `gjt.Scroller` to do the actual work of scrolling to those coordinates.

Each extension of `gjt.Scroller` must also be able to report the size of whatever it is that is being scrolled. Note that this is very much dependent upon what is being scrolled. The size of an `Image`, for instance, is obtained by invoking the `Image` methods:

- `Image.getWidth(ImageObserver)`

- `Image.getHeight(ImageObserver)`

The size of a `Container` is obtained by invoking `Container.size()`.

Now that we understand the responsibilities of extensions of `gjt.Scroller`, let's take a look at how `gjt.Scroller` works.

In its constructor, `gjt.Scroller` creates the viewport and two scrollbars. `gjt.Scroller` also provides accessors for each component:

```
public Scroller() {
    setLayout(new ScrollerLayout(this));
    add("Scroll", viewport = new Panel());
    add("East", vbar = new Scrollbar(Scrollbar.VERTICAL));
    add("South",hbar = new Scrollbar(Scrollbar.HORIZONTAL));
}
public Scrollbar getHorizontalScrollbar() {return hbar;    }
public Scrollbar getVerticalScrollbar  () {return vbar;    }
public Panel     getViewport            () {return viewport;}
```

You may think it somewhat wasteful to always create both horizontal and vertical scrollbars, when one or both may be unnecessary, and you would be correct—we are wasting the space of an object or two once in a while. However, the clarity of the code would suffer if we were always checking to see if a scrollbar existed before we did anything with it, so we've taken the liberty to waste an object or two.

By the way, `gjt.ScrollerLayout` is very careful to check that a component is not null before it goes about laying it out. As `gjt.Scroller` is currently implemented, of course, `ScrollerLayout` need not be so cautious about invoking a method on a null scrollbar or viewport, because they are always there.

However, ScrollerLayout is careful *not* to rely upon the implementation of Scroller (even though the author of Scroller and ScrollerLayout are one and the same) so as to achieve the object-oriented "Quality Without A Name"[3].

Now, let's look at the handleEvent() method:

```
public boolean handleEvent(Event event) {
    boolean handledEvent;

    switch(event.id) {
        case Event.SCROLL_LINE_UP:    scrollLineUp(event);
        break;
        case Event.SCROLL_LINE_DOWN:  scrollLineDown(event);
        break;
        case Event.SCROLL_PAGE_UP:    scrollPageUp  (event);
        break;
        case Event.SCROLL_PAGE_DOWN:  scrollPageDown(event);
        break;
        case Event.SCROLL_ABSOLUTE:   scrollAbsolute(event);
        break;
    }
    handledEvent = event.id == Event.SCROLL_LINE_UP    ||
                   event.id == Event.SCROLL_LINE_DOWN  ||
                   event.id == Event.SCROLL_PAGE_UP    ||
                   event.id == Event.SCROLL_PAGE_DOWN  ||
                   event.id == Event.SCROLL_ABSOLUTE;

    if(handledEvent) return true;
    else             return super.handleEvent(event);
}
```

Similar to the implementation of Component.handleEvent(Event), as described in our chapter on *Event Handling*, this implementation of handleEvent() is an event sifter, resulting in calls to other Scroller methods if the event is a scrollbar event and resulting in a no-op if the event has nothing to do with scrolling. If the event has nothing to do with scrolling, we return super.handleEvent(event) which gives the superclass a crack at the event, as we've discussed previously in the *Event Handling* chapter.

Now let's take a look at the Scroller implementation of paint() and update():

```
public void paint (Graphics g) {
  scroll();
}
```

---

3.   See Alexander, Christopher. *The Timeless Way of Building*. Oxford University Press.

```
public void update(Graphics g) {
   paint(g);
}
```

We've overridden `update()` so that it just calls `paint()`. Normally, `update()` paints the entire component with the background color and then invokes `paint()`. Overriding `update()` to call `paint()` directly dispenses with erasing the scroller before painting, thus eliminating some distracting flashing.

The `paint()` method is overridden to simply call `scroll()`, which looks like this:

```
protected void scroll() {
   scrollTo(hbar.getValue(), vbar.getValue());
}
```

Note that the `scrollTo()` method is an abstract method in `Scroller` and therefore must be implemented by `Scroller` extensions.

The result of all this maneuvering is that a call to either `paint()` or `update()` results in a call to the `scrollTo()` method, which is implemented by `Scroller` extensions. `scrollTo()` is passed the current values for each scrollbar.

This brings us to the management (that is, the hiding and showing) of the scroller's scrollbars. Remember that `Scroller.manageScrollbars()` is invoked from `ScrollerLayout.layoutContainer(Container)`:

```
public void manageScrollbars() {
    manageHorizontalScrollbar();
    manageVerticalScrollbar   ();
}
 protected void manageHorizontalScrollbar() {
    Dimension size          = size();
    Dimension scrollAreaSize = getScrollAreaSize();

    if(vbar.isVisible())
        size.width -= vbar.size().width;

❶      if(scrollAreaSize.width > size.width) {
❷          if( ! hbar.isVisible()) hbar.show();
    }
    else if(hbar.isVisible()) {
❸        hbar.hide();
        hbar.setValue(0);
        repaint();
    }
}
 protected void manageVerticalScrollbar() {
```

```
        Dimension size           = size();
        Dimension scrollAreaSize = getScrollAreaSize();

        if(hbar.isVisible())
            size.height -= hbar.size().height;

        if(scrollAreaSize.height > size.height) {
            if( ! vbar.isVisible())
                vbar.show();
        }
        else if(vbar.isVisible()) {
            vbar.hide();
            vbar.setValue(0);
            repaint();
        }
    }
```

Each of the scrollbar management methods determines whether its particular
scrollbar is necessary at the moment by comparing the scroll area size to the size
of the scroller. (Remember that getScrollAreaSize() is to be implemented by
extensions of Scroller). Notice also that each of the scrollbar management
methods must be careful to check whether the other scrollbar is visible and factor
that into its calculation.

If the width of the scroll area in line ❶ is greater than the width of the scroller
(adjusted for the presence of the other scrollbar), then the scrollbar should be
visible. In such a case, we check to see if the scrollbar is currently not visible; if
that is the case, we call its show() method in line ❷.

If the width of the scroll area is less than the width of the scroller (adjusted for the
presence of the other scrollbar), then the scrollbar should not be visible. In such a
case, we check to see if the scrollbar is currently visible; if so, we call its hide()
method in line ❸, set its value to 0, and then invoke repaint() for the scroller.

Now let's take a look at the other Scroller methods invoked from
ScrollerLayout.layoutContainer(Container):

```
    public void setScrollbarValues() {
        if(hbar.isVisible()) setHorizontalScrollbarValues();
        if(vbar.isVisible()) setVerticalScrollbarValues();
    }
❶   protected void setHorizontalScrollbarValues() {
        Dimension vsize          = viewport.size();
        Dimension scrollAreaSize = getScrollAreaSize();
        int max = scrollAreaSize.width - vsize.width;

        hbar.setValues(hbar.getValue(), // value
```

```
                                 vsize.width,      // amt visible/page
                                 0,                // minimum
                                 max);             // maximum

          setHorizontalLineAndPageIncrements();
    }
❷   protected void setVerticalScrollbarValues() {
          Dimension vsize          = viewport.size();
          Dimension scrollAreaSize = getScrollAreaSize();
          int max = scrollAreaSize.height - vsize.height;

          vbar.setValues(vbar.getValue(), // value
                         vsize.height,    // amt visible/page
                         0,               // minimum
                         max);            // maximum

          setVerticalLineAndPageIncrements();
    }
```

Notice that setHorizontalScrollbarValues() and
setVerticalScrollbarValues() in lines ❶ and ❷, respectively, have nearly
identical implementations. Each sets its scrollbars value to the current value and
sets the amount visible to the size of the viewport. The minimum value is set to 0,
and the maximum value is set to the size of the scroll area minus the size of the
viewport.

Following are the implementations of the various methods invoked from
Scroller.handleEvent():

```
    protected void scrollLineUp   (Event event) { scroll(); }
    protected void scrollLineDown (Event event) { scroll(); }
    protected void scrollPageUp   (Event event) { scroll(); }
    protected void scrollPageDown (Event event) { scroll(); }
    protected void scrollAbsolute (Event event) { scroll(); }
```

As is evident, these methods simply call scroll(), resulting in a call to
scrollTo(). Therefore, by default, every scrolling event results in a call to
scrollTo(), which should scroll as appropriate, depending upon the current
values of the scrollbars.

Finally, we have two methods that set the line and page increments for the
scrollbars:

```
    protected void setHorizontalLineAndPageIncrements() {
         Dimension size = getScrollAreaSize();
         hbar.setLineIncrement(size.width/10);
         hbar.setPageIncrement(size.width/5);
    }
```

```
protected void setVerticalLineAndPageIncrements() {
    Dimension size = getScrollAreaSize();
    vbar.setLineIncrement(size.height/10);
    vbar.setPageIncrement(size.height/5);
}
```

Notice that all of the methods that react to scrolling events are protected, meaning you are free to override them in extensions of Scroller. For instance, if you are unhappy with a line increment that is one tenth of the scroll area size, you can override setHorizontalLineAndPageIncrements() in an extension of Scroller. On the other hand, if you need to customize the reaction to a scroll line up event, you are free to override scrollLineUp() in a Scroller extension. This technique is nearly identical to that employed by Component.handleEvent(Event), which delegates responsibility to no-op methods such as mouseDown() and mouseDrag(), which may be overridden by subclasses when the no-op implementation is not sufficient.

Now that we've seen the significant parts of the gjt.Scroller, let's look at the entire implementation in Example 16-2.

Example 16-2 gjt.Scroller **Class Source Code**

CD-Rom

```
package gjt;

import java.awt.*;

public abstract class Scroller extends Panel {
    protected Panel      viewport;
    protected Scrollbar hbar, vbar;

    abstract public void      scrollTo(int x, int y);
    abstract public Dimension getScrollAreaSize();

    public Scroller() {
        setLayout(new ScrollerLayout(this));
        add("Scroll", viewport = new Panel());
        add("East", vbar = new Scrollbar(Scrollbar.VERTICAL));
        add("South",hbar = new Scrollbar(Scrollbar.HORIZONTAL));
    }
    public Scrollbar getHorizontalScrollbar() {return hbar;    }
    public Scrollbar getVerticalScrollbar  () {return vbar;    }
    public Panel     getViewport           () {return viewport;}

    public boolean handleEvent(Event event) {
        boolean handledEvent;

        switch(event.id) {
```

```
                case Event.SCROLL_LINE_UP:   scrollLineUp(event);
                break;
                case Event.SCROLL_LINE_DOWN: scrollLineDown(event);
                break;
                case Event.SCROLL_PAGE_UP:   scrollPageUp  (event);
                break;
                case Event.SCROLL_PAGE_DOWN: scrollPageDown(event);
                break;
                case Event.SCROLL_ABSOLUTE:  scrollAbsolute(event);
                break;
        }
        handledEvent = event.id == Event.SCROLL_LINE_UP    ||
                       event.id == Event.SCROLL_LINE_DOWN  ||
                       event.id == Event.SCROLL_PAGE_UP    ||
                       event.id == Event.SCROLL_PAGE_DOWN  ||
                       event.id == Event.SCROLL_ABSOLUTE;

        if(handledEvent) return true;
        else             return super.handleEvent(event);
    }
    public void paint (Graphics g) { scroll(); }
    public void update(Graphics g) { paint(g); }

    public void manageScrollbars() {
        manageHorizontalScrollbar();
        manageVerticalScrollbar  ();
    }
    protected void manageHorizontalScrollbar() {
        Dimension size          = size();
        Dimension scrollAreaSize = getScrollAreaSize();

        if(vbar.isVisible())
            size.width -= vbar.size().width;

        if(scrollAreaSize.width > size.width) {
            if( ! hbar.isVisible())
                hbar.show();
        }
        else if(hbar.isVisible()) {
            hbar.hide();
            hbar.setValue(0);
            repaint();
        }
    }
    protected void manageVerticalScrollbar() {
        Dimension size          = size();
        Dimension scrollAreaSize = getScrollAreaSize();
```

```
        if(hbar.isVisible())
            size.height -= hbar.size().height;

        if(scrollAreaSize.height > size.height) {
            if( ! vbar.isVisible())
                vbar.show();
        }
        else if(vbar.isVisible()) {
            vbar.hide();
            vbar.setValue(0);
            repaint();
        }
    }
    public void setScrollbarValues() {
        if(hbar.isVisible()) setHorizontalScrollbarValues();
        if(vbar.isVisible()) setVerticalScrollbarValues();
    }
    protected void setHorizontalScrollbarValues() {
        Dimension vsize          = viewport.size();
        Dimension scrollAreaSize = getScrollAreaSize();
        int max = scrollAreaSize.width - vsize.width;

        hbar.setValues(hbar.getValue(), // value
                     vsize.width,      // amt visible/page
                     0,                // minimum
                     max);             // maximum

        setHorizontalLineAndPageIncrements();
    }

    protected void setVerticalScrollbarValues() {
        Dimension vsize          = viewport.size();
        Dimension scrollAreaSize = getScrollAreaSize();
        int max = scrollAreaSize.height - vsize.height;

        vbar.setValues(vbar.getValue(), // value
                     vsize.height,     // amt visible/page
                     0,                // minimum
                     max);             // maximum

        setVerticalLineAndPageIncrements();
    }
    protected void scrollLineUp  (Event event) { scroll(); }
    protected void scrollLineDown(Event event) { scroll(); }
    protected void scrollPageUp  (Event event) { scroll(); }
    protected void scrollPageDown(Event event) { scroll(); }
    protected void scrollAbsolute(Event event) { scroll(); }
```

```
    protected void setHorizontalLineAndPageIncrements() {
        Dimension size = getScrollAreaSize();
        hbar.setLineIncrement(size.width/10);
        hbar.setPageIncrement(size.width/5);
    }
    protected void setVerticalLineAndPageIncrements() {
        Dimension size = getScrollAreaSize();
        vbar.setLineIncrement(size.height/10);
        vbar.setPageIncrement(size.height/5);
    }
    protected void scroll() {
        scrollTo(hbar.getValue(), vbar.getValue());
    }
}
```

gjt.ComponentScroller

gjt.Scroller has encapsulated all of the event handling, management of the visibility of its scrollbars, and the setting of scrollbar values. It leaves the specifics of actually scrolling an object to its extensions: gjt.ComponentScroller and gjt.ImageScroller.

gjt.ComponentScroller, as a result of encapsulating the lower-level details in the gjt.Scroller class, has a modest implementation, as illustrated in Example 16-3.

Example 16-3 gjt.ComponentScroller **Class Source Code**

```
package gjt;

import java.awt.*;

public class ComponentScroller extends Scroller {
  private Component scrollMe;

  public ComponentScroller() {
  }
  public ComponentScroller(Component component) {
      setComponent(component);
  }
  public void setComponent(Component component) {
      scrollMe = component;
      viewport.setLayout(new BulletinLayout());
      viewport.add        (scrollMe);
      viewport.move        (0,0);
  }
  public void scrollTo(int x, int y) {
```

```
        scrollMe.move(-x,-y);
    }
    public Dimension getScrollAreaSize() {
        return scrollMe.preferredSize();
    }
}
```

A gjt.ComponentScroller may be constructed with or without a component. It is assumed that a ComponentScroller constructed without a component will call setComponent() before the component scroller is displayed. If not, a null pointer exception will occur in either scrollTo() or getScrollAreaSize().

By the way, you may find the implementation of the default constructor somewhat curious. Java will automatically supply a default constructor *only* when no constructor has been implemented for the class. If we do not implement a default constructor, then none will be available for clients to use, so we must have a default constructor implementation. That begs the question—what is the default constructor to do? The answer is nothing. You might think that scrollMe should be set to null in the default constructor, but that is taken care of automatically; in Java, objects that are members of a class are set to null if they are not initialized. Therefore, there is nothing for the default constructor to do, but we must implement it in order for it to be available to clients. Thus, the peculiar (but bug-free) implementation.

Let's take a look at the two methods that were defined as abstract in Scroller and that are implemented in ComponentScroller:

```
    public void scrollTo(int x, int y) {
        scrollMe.move(-x,-y);
    }
    public Dimension getScrollAreaSize() {
        return scrollMe.preferredSize();
    }
```

scrollTo() simply moves the component such that it is placed at -x,-y, which causes the appropriate visible area of the component to be displayed in the viewport, as in Figure 16-4.

Figure 16-4 gjt.ComponentScroller Unit Test

getScrollAreaSize() simply returns the preferred size of the component being scrolled.

Finally, we have setComponent(Component), which is called to set the component being scrolled:

```
public void setComponent(Component component) {
    scrollMe = component;
    viewport.setLayout(new BulletinLayout());
    viewport.add       (scrollMe);
    viewport.move      (0,0);
}
```

`ComponentScroller` sets the viewport's layout to a `BulletinLayout` (described in our chapter on *Components, Containers, and Layout Managers*), and adds the component to be scrolled (`scrollMe`), which is initially placed at 0,0.

gjt.ImageCanvas and gjt.ImageScroller

Before we look at `ImageScroller`, we must take a slight detour and introduce another GJT component: `ImageCanvas`. `gjt.ImageCanvas` is a canvas onto which an image is painted. It exists solely because `Image` is not a component, which leaves us hanging, for instance, when we want to add an image to a container. Example 16-4 shows how it is implemented.

Example 16-4 `gjt.ImageCanvas` **Class Source Code**

```
package gjt;

import java.awt.*;

class ImageCanvas extends Canvas {
    private Image image;

    public ImageCanvas(Image image) {
        this.image = image;
        Util.waitForImage(this, image);
        resize(image.getWidth(this), image.getHeight(this));
    }
    public void paint(Graphics g) {
        g.drawImage(image, 0, 0, this);
    }
    public void update(Graphics g) {
        paint(g);
    }
}
```

`gjt.ImageCanvas` is constructed with an image. After waiting for the image to load, `ImageCanvas` adjusts its size to accommodate the image. When told to paint, the `ImageCanvas` draws the image at 0,0. Notice that `ImageCanvas` overrides `update()` for the same reason we override it in `Scroller`—to eliminate erasing of the background when an update occurs.

Now we are ready to take a look at `gjt.ImageScroller` in Example 16-5.

Example 16-5 `gjt.ImageScroller` **Class Source Code**

CD-Rom

```java
package gjt;

import java.awt.*;

public class ImageScroller extends Scroller {
  private Image   image;
  private ScrollerImageCanvas canvas;

  public ImageScroller(Image image) {
      viewport.setLayout(new BorderLayout());
      setImage(image);
  }
  public void resetImage(Image image) {
      viewport.remove(canvas);
      setImage(image);
      invalidate();
      validate();
  }
  public void scrollTo(int x, int y) {
      Graphics g = canvas.getGraphics();
      if(g != null) {
          g.translate(-x,-y);
          g.drawImage(image, 0, 0, this);
      }
  }
  public Dimension getScrollAreaSize() {
      return new Dimension(image.getWidth(this),
                           image.getHeight(this));
  }
  private void setImage(Image image) {
      this.image = image;
      hbar.setValue(0);
      vbar.setValue(0);
      viewport.add("Center",
          canvas = new ScrollerImageCanvas(this, image));
  }
}

class ScrollerImageCanvas extends ImageCanvas {
  private ImageScroller scroller;

  public ScrollerImageCanvas(ImageScroller scroller,
                             Image         image) {
      super(image);
      this.scroller = scroller;
  }
```

```
    public void paint(Graphics g) {
        scroller.repaint();
    }
}
```

Notice that `ScrollerImageCanvas` is an extension of `ImageCanvas` that keeps track of its scroller. `ScrollerImageCanvas` overrides `paint()` and forces its scroller to `repaint()`. This is necessary because of an AWT bug that results in components not being repainted correctly when a resize event occurs.

An `ImageScroller` is constructed with an image. After the constructor sets the viewport's layout manager to an instance of `BorderLayout`, the image is sent to the private `setImage()` method.

The `setImage()` method creates an instance of `ScrollerImageCanvas` and centers it in the viewport. `setImage()` also sets the initial values of the scrollbars to 0,0.

The `scrollTo()` is overridden as follows:

```
    public void scrollTo(int x, int y) {
        Graphics g = canvas.getGraphics();
        if(g != null) {
❶           g.translate(-x,-y);
            g.drawImage(image, 0, 0, this);
        }
    }
```

The `scrollTo()` method obtains the `Graphics` object for the `ImageScrollerCanvas` and translates the `Graphics` object before drawing the image at 0,0. The `g.translate()` method in line ❶ translates the origin of the Graphics object, which results in all subsequent graphics operations being relative to the translated origin. `getScrollAreaSize()` simply returns the size of the image being scrolled.

Image scrolling is very smooth, with no flashing whatsoever. This is accomplished by overriding the `Scroller update()` method to eliminate erasure of the scroller when updating and by translating and drawing the image in the `ImageScroller.scrollTo()` method.

Exercising the gjt.ImageScroller

`ImageScrollerTest` creates images and cycles through them on each mouse up event, as illustrated in Figure 16-5.

Figure 16-5 gjt.ImageScroller Unit Test
Each mouse up event causes a new image to be displayed.
Scrollbars only appear when an image is larger than the display
area.

ImageScrollerTest extends UnitTest and supplies an instance of an
ImageScrollerTestPanel. Figure 16-6 shows the unit test layout.

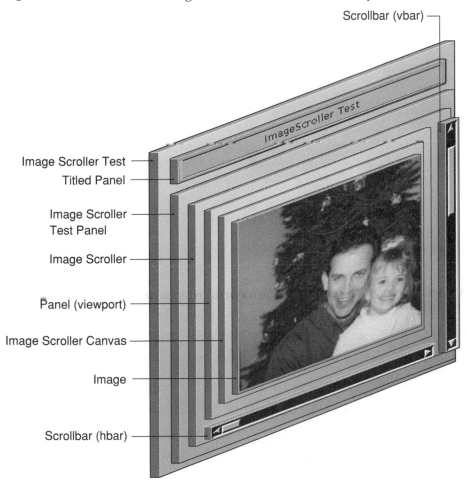

Scrollbar (vbar)

Image Scroller Test
Titled Panel

Image Scroller
Test Panel

Image Scroller

Panel (viewport)

Image Scroller Canvas

Image

Scrollbar (hbar)

Example 16-6 shows the source code for the ImageScrollerTest class.

Example 16-6 gjt.test.ImageScrollerTest **Class Source Code**

```
package gjt.test;

import java.awt.*;
import java.applet.Applet;
import java.net.URL;

import gjt.ImageScroller;
import gjt.Util;
```

```
public class ImageScrollerTest extends UnitTest {
  public String title() {
      return "ImageScroller Test";
  }
  public Panel centerPanel() {
      return new ImageScrollerTestPanel(this);
  }
}

class ImageScrollerTestPanel extends Panel {
  private Image[]        images    = new Image[4];
  private int            imageIndex = 0;
  private ImageScroller scroller;

  public ImageScrollerTestPanel(Applet applet) {
      URL cb = applet.getCodeBase();

      images[0]=applet.getImage(cb,"gifs/ashleyAndRoy.gif");
      images[1]=applet.getImage(cb,"gifs/ashleyAndSabre.gif");
      images[2]=applet.getImage(cb,"gifs/anjinAndMariko.gif");
      images[3]=applet.getImage(cb,"gifs/ashleyAndAnjin.gif");

      setLayout(new BorderLayout());
      add("Center", scroller = new ImageScroller(images[0]));
  }
  public boolean mouseUp(Event event, int x, int y) {
      if(imageIndex == images.length-1) imageIndex = 0;
      else                              imageIndex++;

      Util.setCursor(Frame.WAIT_CURSOR, this);
      scroller.resetImage(images[imageIndex]);
      Util.setCursor(Frame.DEFAULT_CURSOR, this);

      return true;
  }
}
```

The ImageScrollerTestPanel constructor uses a BorderLayout and places an ImageScroller in the center of the panel.

This applet illustrates the ease with which an image can be scrolled with the Graphic Java Toolkit. As clients of ImageScroller, our only responsibilities are to ensure that ImageScroller is passed a valid image at construction time and that a valid image is also passed to the ImageScroller.resetImage(Image) method.

Exercising the gjt.ComponentScroller

In our quest to demysify `GridBagLayout`, we have gone to some lengths in the `ComponentScroller` unit test to put together a modest, yet practical, layout. The unit test is a contrived applet for purchasing a number of images, which are displayed above the purchase form, as illustrated in Figure 16-7.

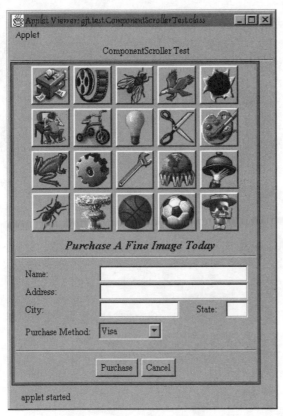

Figure 16-7 `gjt.ComponentScroller` Unit Test

`ComponentScrollerTest` has an insanely complicated layout, as illustrated in Figure 16-8.

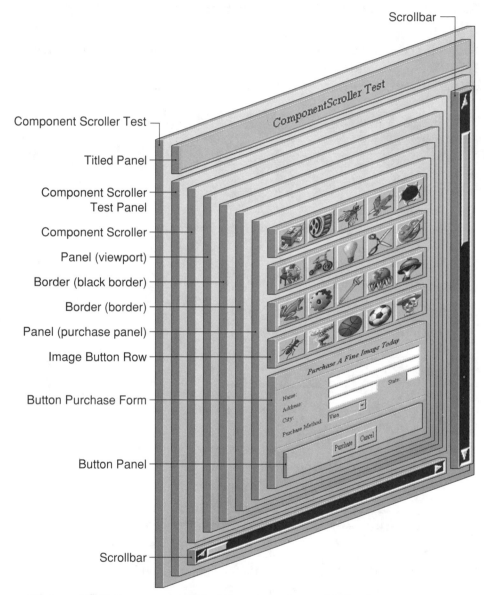

Scrollbar

Component Scroller Test

Titled Panel

Component Scroller
Test Panel

Component Scroller

Panel (viewport)

Border (black border)

Border (border)

Panel (purchase panel)

Image Button Row

Button Purchase Form

Button Panel

Scrollbar

Figure 16-8 `ComponentScrollerTest` Layout Diagram

As you might guess by the complexity of the layout, this unit test is similarly complex. Before biting off the whole class, let's nibble on some interesting pieces of it.

First, this unit test uses two instances of the `gjt.Border` class to put two borders around the component to be scrolled: a thick gray border and a thin black border:

```
scroller    = new ComponentScroller();
border      = new Border(purchasePanel, 3, 2);
blackBorder = new Border(border, 1, 0);

border.setLineColor(Color.gray);
blackBorder.setLineColor(Color.black);
scroller.setComponent(blackBorder);
```

The `border` instance is constructed with a reference to the `purchasePanel` (`purchasePanel` is the panel that contains all of the image buttons and the `ButtonPurchaseForm`). As a result, the `purchasePanel` is centered in the border. Remember that a `Border` is a `Panel` that centers the component passed to its constructor.

The `blackBorder` instance is constructed with a reference to the `border` object; therefore, the `blackBorder` contains the `border`, which contains the `purchasePanel`. Got that? Again, refer to Figure 16-8, which clearly shows these relationships.

Also, notice that the `ButtonPurchaseForm` uses a `GridBagLayout` to lay out the text fields, choice, and buttons. If you look at the row of components beginning with "City:," you can see that there are four components in the row: the "City:" label, a text field, the "State:" label, and the state text field.

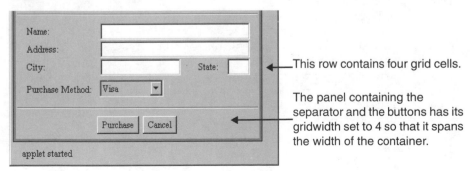

This row contains four grid cells.

The panel containing the separator and the buttons has its gridwidth set to 4 so that it spans the width of the container.

To accomplish this layout with `GridBagLayout`, we specify a `gridwidth` constraint of 4 for the `ButtonPanel`, so that it stretches across the entire width of the `ButtonPurchaseForm`.

There's one last item we want to mention before showing you the unit test. In this applet, we have an `ImageButtonRow`, which extends `Panel`, for the express purpose of fitting every image button in an `ImageButtonRow` with a `StickyImageButtonController`. When an image button in an `ImageButtonRow` is activated, it will stay depressed until it is activated again. This is just the behavior we desire, so that a potential customer can see at a glance which images have been selected for purchase.

Finally, let's look at the code for `ComponentScrollerTest` in Example 16-7.

Example 16-7 `gjt.test.ComponentScrollerTest` **Class Source Code**

```
package gjt;

import java.awt.*;
import java.util.Vector;
import java.applet.Applet;
import java.net.URL;

import gjt.Border;
import gjt.ButtonPanel;
import gjt.ColumnLayout;
import gjt.ComponentScroller;
import gjt.EtchedBorder;
import gjt.ImageButton;
import gjt.RowLayout;
import gjt.Separator;
import gjt.StickyImageButtonController;

public class ComponentScrollerTest extends UnitTest {
  public String title() {
      return "ComponentScroller Test";
  }
  public Panel  centerPanel() {
      return new ComponentScrollerTestPanel(this);
  }
}

class ComponentScrollerTestPanel extends Panel {
  private ComponentScroller  scroller;
  private Panel              purchasePanel;
  private ImageButtonRow     nextRow;
  private String[][]         imageNames = {
```

```
       { "gifs/ballot_box.gif",   "gifs/filmstrip.gif",
         "gifs/fly.gif",          "gifs/eagle.gif",
         "gifs/bullet_hole.gif" },
       { "gifs/mad_hacker.gif",   "gifs/tricycle.gif",
         "gifs/light_bulb1.gif",  "gifs/scissors.gif",
         "gifs/palette.gif" },
       { "gifs/frog.gif",         "gifs/gear.gif",
         "gifs/wrench.gif",       "gifs/www.gif",
         "gifs/Dining.gif" },
       { "gifs/ant.gif",          "gifs/abomb.gif",
         "gifs/basketball.gif",   "gifs/soccer.gif",
         "gifs/skelly.gif" },
   };
   public ComponentScrollerTestPanel(Applet applet) {
       URL    base = applet.getCodeBase();
       Image  nextImage;
       Border border, blackBorder;

       purchasePanel = new Panel();
       purchasePanel.setLayout(new ColumnLayout());

       for(int r=0; r < imageNames.length; ++r) {
           nextRow = new ImageButtonRow(),
           nextRow.setLayout(new RowLayout());

           for(int c=0; c < imageNames[r].length; ++c) {
               nextImage = applet.getImage(base,
                                          imageNames[r][c]);
               nextRow.add(nextImage);
           }
           purchasePanel.add(nextRow);
       }
       purchasePanel.add(new ButtonPurchaseForm());

       scroller    = new ComponentScroller();
       border      = new Border(purchasePanel, 3, 2);
       blackBorder = new Border(border, 1, 0);

       border.setLineColor(Color.gray);
       blackBorder.setLineColor(Color.black);
       scroller.setComponent(blackBorder);

       setLayout(new BorderLayout());
       add("Center", scroller);
   }
}

class ButtonPurchaseForm extends Panel {
```

```
TextField nameField    = new TextField(25);
TextField addressField = new TextField(25);
TextField cityField    = new TextField(15);
TextField stateField   = new TextField(2);

Choice    paymentChoice = new Choice();

Button    paymentButton = new Button("Purchase");
Button    cancelButton  = new Button("Cancel");

public ButtonPurchaseForm() {
    GridBagLayout       gbl = new GridBagLayout();
    GridBagConstraints gbc = new GridBagConstraints();

    Separator sep = new Separator();
    Label title   =
        new Label("Purchase A Fine Image Today");
    Label name    = new Label("Name:");
    Label address = new Label("Address:");
    Label payment = new Label("Purchase Method:");
    Label phone   = new Label("Phone:");
    Label city    = new Label("City:");
    Label state   = new Label("State:");

    setLayout(gbl);

    paymentChoice.addItem("Visa");
    paymentChoice.addItem("MasterCard");
    paymentChoice.addItem("COD");

    title.setFont(new Font("Times-Roman",
                           Font.BOLD + Font.ITALIC,
                           16));
    gbc.anchor    = GridBagConstraints.NORTH;
    gbc.gridwidth = GridBagConstraints.REMAINDER;
    gbl.setConstraints(title, gbc);
    add(title);

    gbc.anchor    = GridBagConstraints.NORTH;
    gbc.gridwidth = GridBagConstraints.REMAINDER;
    gbc.fill      = GridBagConstraints.HORIZONTAL;
    gbc.insets    = new Insets(0,0,10,0);
    gbl.setConstraints(sep, gbc);
    add(sep);

    gbc.anchor    = GridBagConstraints.WEST;
    gbc.gridwidth = 1;
    gbc.insets    = new Insets(0,0,0,10);
```

```
gbl.setConstraints(name, gbc);
add(name);

gbc.gridwidth = GridBagConstraints.REMAINDER;
gbl.setConstraints(nameField, gbc);
add(nameField);

gbc.gridwidth = 1;
gbl.setConstraints(address, gbc);
add(address);

gbc.gridwidth = GridBagConstraints.REMAINDER;
gbc.fill = GridBagConstraints.HORIZONTAL;
gbl.setConstraints(addressField, gbc);
add(addressField);

gbc.gridwidth = 1;
gbl.setConstraints(city, gbc);
add(city);

gbl.setConstraints(cityField, gbc);
add(cityField);

gbl.setConstraints(state, gbc);
add(state);

gbl.setConstraints(stateField, gbc);
gbc.gridwidth = GridBagConstraints.REMAINDER;
gbl.setConstraints(stateField, gbc);
add(stateField);

gbc.gridwidth = 1;
gbl.setConstraints(payment, gbc);
gbc.insets = new Insets(5,0,5,0);
add(payment);

gbc.gridwidth = GridBagConstraints.REMAINDER;
gbc.fill      = GridBagConstraints.NONE;
gbl.setConstraints(paymentChoice, gbc);
add(paymentChoice);

ButtonPanel buttonPanel = new ButtonPanel();

buttonPanel.add(paymentButton);
buttonPanel.add(cancelButton);

gbc.anchor    = GridBagConstraints.SOUTH;
gbc.insets    = new Insets(5,0,0,0);
```

```
        gbc.fill       = GridBagConstraints.HORIZONTAL;
        gbc.gridwidth = 4;
        gbl.setConstraints(buttonPanel, gbc);
        add(buttonPanel);
    }
}
class ImageButtonRow extends Panel {
  public ImageButtonRow() {
      setLayout(new RowLayout());
  }
  public void add(Image image) {
      ImageButton button = new ImageButton(image);
      add(button);
      button.setController(
              new StickyImageButtonController(button));
  }
}
```

When you run the component scroller unit test, you will notice that the components flash horribly. This is because of the fact that when a component is moved, it is invalidated, which causes it to be updated. Component.update() erases the background of the component and then redraws it. As a result the components flash as they are being scrolled. While we can redefine update() for components such as panels and canvases, there is no way to redefine update() for all of the components in the AWT without subclassing everything in sight. We understand that this problem will be addressed in a future version of the AWT, but for now you are better off paging the scrollbar to reduce the flashing, rather than sliding the slider. Also, note that the flashing is evident regardless of the platform on which you are running.

Additionally, the Windows 95 version of scrollbars has had a myriad of problems since the first version of the AWT. For instance, up until version 1.0.2, the sliders in the scrollbars were a fixed size and the scrollbars bounced around like a ping-pong ball after they were moved. There is still some bouncing of the scrollbars in version 1.0.2, although it has been greatly reduced.

Summary

Creating scrollbars and fitting them to a container is a simple matter in the AWT. However, scrolling components or images is not nearly as simple, because many details of scrolling must be handled by the developer.

In this chapter we have discussed AWT scrollbars and scrolling in depth. We have pointed out some bugs and platform-specific discrepancies with the current AWT implementation of scrollbars and have presented a set of GJT classes that greatly simplify scrolling of components and images. As with all of the Graphic Java Toolkit custom components, we have presented unit tests for scrolling both components and images.

CHAPTER 17

- The Participants on page 473

- Sequences and Sprites on page 475

    - gjt.animation.Sequence on page 475

    - gjt.animation.Sprite on page 480

- Playfields and Double Buffering on page 488

    - gjt.animation.Playfield on page 488

    - Double Buffering on page 493

- Collision Detection on page 499

- Exercising the gjt.animation Package on page 502

    - Simple Animation on page 503

    - Bump Animation on page 507

    - Two-Sprite Collision on page 511

- Summary on page 515

Sprite
Animation

The Graphic Java Toolkit provides an animation package that encapsulates many of the low-level details of implementing animation. This chapter explores the gjt.animation package and discusses a number of animation-related topics, such as double buffering, animation sequences, sprites, and collision detection.

The Participants

Let's take a look at a class diagram in Figure 17-1, which shows the major classes in the gjt.animation package and their relationships.

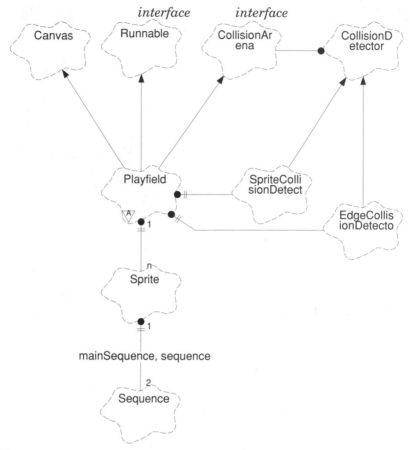

Figure 17-1 Animation Package Diagram

There are four major participants in the GJT `animation` package:

- `Playfield` — Is a `Canvas` on which sprite animation takes place

- `Sprite` — Is a sequence of images animated on a `Playfield`

- `Sequence` — Controls the animation of a sequence of images

- `CollisionDetector` — Detects collisions between two sprites and collisions between sprites and the `Playfield` boundaries

The premise behind the `gjt.animation` package is simple: Sprites are animated on a playfield and can collide with other sprites and with the boundaries of their playfield. The rate at which sprites cycle through their images and the speed at which they move can both be set.

We'll begin our discussion with sprites and sequences and then describe playfields and collision detection.

Sequences and Sprites

Sprites must be able to perform two major functions:

- Cycle through a sequence of images
- Move about on a playfield

As previously mentioned, the rate at which each of these functions occurs can be set. Sprite objects are responsible for moving themselves about and timing their movement; however, they delegate the responsibility for cycling through a sequence of images to another object: a Sequence.

gjt.animation.Sequence

Figure 17-2 shows the Sequence class diagram.

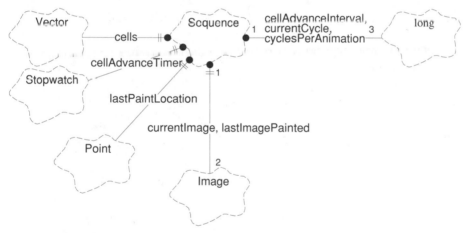

Figure 17-2 Sequence Class Diagram

As you can see, a Sequence maintains a vector of images that it cycles through. It also uses a stopwatch to control the rate at which it cycles through its images. The cellAdvanceInterval member of the Sequence class defines the elapsed time (in milliseconds) between the display of one image and the next.

If all Sequence objects simply cycled through their images only once, they wouldn't be of much use. Therefore, the number of cycles (defined as one complete pass through all the images) that a Sequence runs through can be set and is maintained in the cyclesPerAnimation member of the Sequence class.

Additionally, an instance of Sequence keeps track of its current cycle and is able to report whether its animation is over. The responsibilities of gjt.animation.Sequence are listed in Table 17-1.

Table 17-1 gjt.animation.Sequence **Responsibilities**

Methods	Description
void start()	Starts the sequence.
Image getLastImage()	Returns last image painted.
Point getLastLocation()	Returns location of last image painted.
int getNumImages()	Returns the number of images in the sequence.
long getCurrentCycle()	Returns the number of the current cycle.
void setCurrentCycle(long c)	Sets the current cycle.
long getCyclesPerAnimation()	Returns the number of cycles for one complete animation.
void setCyclesPerAnimation(long cyclesPerAnimation)	Sets the number of cycles per animation.
Image getFirstImage()	Returns the first image in the sequence.
Image getCurrentImage()	Returns the current image.
int getCurrentImagePosition()	Returns the position of the current image.
Image getnextImage()	Returns the next image in the sequence.
void setAdvanceInterval(long interval)	Sets the interval between image updates in milliseconds.
void addImage(Component component, Image image)	Adds an image to the sequence.
void removeImage(Image image)	Removes an image from the sequence.
boolean needsRepainting(Point point)	Whether the sequence needs to repaint at a particular location.
void paint(Graphics g, int x, int y, ImageObserver observer)	Draws the current image.
boolean isAtLastImage()	Whether the sequence is on the last image.
boolean timeToAdvanceCell()	Whether it is time to advance to the next image.
boolean animationOver()	Whether the animation is over.
void advance()	Advances to the next image.

Table 17-2 lists the associations of a gjt.animation.Sequence.

Table 17-2 gjt.animation.Sequence **Associations**

Variables	Description
private static long infiniteCycle	Defines an infinite cycle.
private Vector cells	Images used in sequence
private Point lastPaintLocation	Location last image was painted at.
private Stopwatch cellAdvanceTimer	Timer for timing interval between image advances.
private Image currentImage	The current image.
private Image lastImagePainted	The last image painted.
private long cellAdvanceInterval	The delay between image updates, in milliseconds.
private long currentCycle	The current cycle.
private long cyclesPerAnimation	The number of cycles per animation.

Now that we have a basic understanding of the inner workings of a Sequence, let's take a look at the implementation of the Sequence class in Example 17-1.

Example 17-1 gjt.animation.Sequence **Class Source Code**

```
package gjt.animation;

import java.util.Vector;
import java.awt.*;
import java.awt.image.ImageObserver;
import gjt.Util;
import gjt.Stopwatch;

public class Sequence {
  private static long infiniteCycle = -1;

  private Vector     cells                = new Vector();
  private Point      lastPaintLocation    = new Point(0,0);
  private Stopwatch  cellAdvanceTimer     = new Stopwatch();
  private Image      currentImage, lastImagePainted;
  private long       cellAdvanceInterval  = 0,
                     currentCycle         = 0,
                     cyclesPerAnimation   = 0;
```

```java
public Sequence() { }

public Sequence(Component component, Image[] images) {
    for(int i=0; i < images.length; ++i) {
        addImage(component, images[i]);
    }
    cyclesPerAnimation = infiniteCycle;
}
public void  start           () { cellAdvanceTimer.start(); }
public Image getLastImage    () { return lastImagePainted;  }
public Point getLastLocation() { return lastPaintLocation; }
public int   getNumImages    () { return cells.size();      }

public long getCurrentCycle()        { return currentCycle; }
public void setCurrentCycle(long c) { currentCycle = c;     }

public long getCyclesPerAnimation() {
    return currentCycle;
}
public void setCyclesPerAnimation(long cyclesPerAnimation) {
    this.cyclesPerAnimation = cyclesPerAnimation;
}
public Image getFirstImage() {
    return (Image)cells.firstElement();
}
public Image getCurrentImage() {
    return currentImage;
}
public int getCurrentImagePosition() {
    return cells.indexOf(currentImage);
}
public Image getNextImage() {
    int   index = cells.indexOf(currentImage);
    Image image;

    if(index == cells.size() - 1)
        image = (Image)cells.elementAt(0);
    else
        image = (Image)cells.elementAt(index + 1);
```

```
        return image;
    }
    public void setAdvanceInterval(long interval) {
        cellAdvanceInterval = interval;
    }
    public void addImage(Component component, Image image) {
        if(currentImage == null)
            currentImage = image;

        Util.waitForImage(component, image);
        cells.addElement(image);
    }
    public void removeImage(Image image) {
        cells.removeElement(image);
    }
    public boolean needsRepainting(Point point) {
        return (lastPaintLocation.x != point.x ||
                lastPaintLocation.y != point.y ||
                lastImagePainted    != currentImage);
    }
    public void paint(Graphics g, int x, int y,
                      ImageObserver observer) {
        g.drawImage(currentImage, x, y,  observer);
        lastPaintLocation.x = x;
        lastPaintLocation.y = y;
        lastImagePainted    = currentImage;
    }
    public boolean isAtLastImage() {
        return getCurrentImagePosition() == (cells.size() - 1);
    }
    public boolean timeToAdvanceCell() {
        return
          cellAdvanceTimer.elapsedTime() > cellAdvanceInterval;
    }
    public boolean animationOver() {
        return (cyclesPerAnimation != infiniteCycle) &&
               (currentCycle >= cyclesPerAnimation);
    }
    public void advance() {
        if(isAtLastImage())
            ++currentCycle;

        currentImage = getNextImage();
        cellAdvanceTimer.reset();
    }
}
}
```

A `Sequence` can be constructed with a component and an array of images. The sequence waits for all the images in the array to be loaded before returning from its constructor. The component's only role is as an accomplice to this loading of images, for it is passed to `gjt.Util.waitForImage(Component,Image)`.

Additionally, a `Sequence` can be constructed with no arguments. Presumably, images will be added to such a sequence through its `addImage()` method before sequencing through its images.

A `Sequence` is also able to report whether it needs repainting at a given location. If the last paint location is different from the given location or if the last image painted is not equal to the current image, then the sequence needs to be repainted.

A `Sequence` has a `paint(Graphics g, int x, int y, ImageObserver)` method that paints the current image at the location specified. Note that this method is not the familiar `Component paint(Graphics g)`, which we've overridden numerous times, because a `Sequence` is not a `Component`.

A `Sequence` also has methods that return information about the sequence:

- `isAtLastImage()`

- `timeToAdvanceCell()`

- `animationOver()`

gjt.animation.Sprite

It is important to realize that a `Sequence` is something of a simpleton that will continuously cycle through its sequence of images, no matter what its `cyclesPerAnimation` has been set to. It is up to another object to monitor the sequence's progress and determine if it is time to end the sequence. That object is a `Sprite`, as diagrammed in Figure 17-3.

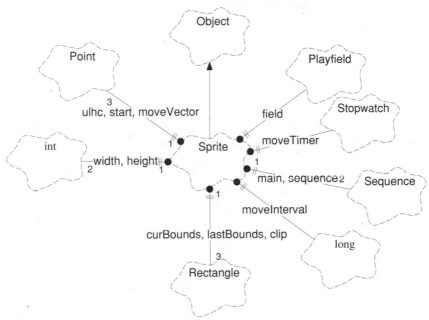

Figure 17-3 Sprite Class Diagram

The first thing that may strike you about the Sprite class is that it actually maintains two sequences: one main sprite sequence and one temporary one. Our sprites would be pretty boring if they endlessly cycled through only one sequence; thus, it is imperative that we give sprites the ability to change their sequence for a period of time. As a result, each sprite has a main sequence that it cycles through endlessly and a temporary sequence that upstages the main sequence for a specific number of cycles. Upstaging the main sequence is accomplished by the play(Sequence sequence, long cycles) method.

As we previously mentioned, a sprite is responsible for moving itself, so it is not surprising to see that a sprite has both a stopwatch, which is used to time its movement, and an interval, specified in milliseconds, which times its movement from one location to the next.

Of course, in addition to timing its movements, a sprite must know the direction in which to move. The direction in which a sprite moves is stored in its moveVector, a point that defines how many pixels the sprite moves in the x and y directions each time it is told to move.

A sprite also keeps track of its width, height, and current location.

Finally, a sprite keeps track of its current bounds, its last bounds, and something called its clip bounds. For reasons that will become apparent when we discuss the `Playfield` class, the clip bounds is the union of a `Sprite` object's last and current bounds. The responsibilities of `gjt.animation.Sprite` are listed in Table 17-3.

Table 17-3 `gjt.animation.Sprite` **Responsibilities**

Methods	Description
`Playfield getPlayfield()`	Returns the sprite's playfield.
`Rectangle clipRect()`	Returns the sprite's clip rectangle.
`Rectangle curBounds()`	Returns the sprite's current bounds.
`int width()`	Returns the width of the sprite.
`int height()`	Returns the height of the sprite.
`void reverseX()`	Reverses the sprite's horizontal direction.
`void reverseY`	Reverses the sprite's vertical direction.
`void reverse()`	Reverses both the horizontal and vertical directions of the sprite.
`void setMoveVector(Point p)`	Sets the direction the sprite moves.
`Point getMoveVector()`	Returns the move vector.
`void play(Sequence sequence, long cycles)`	Plays a sequence other than the main sequence for a specified number of cycles
`void animate()`	Animates the sprite.
`void setMainSequence(Sequence sequence)`	Sets the sprite's main sequence.
`Sequence getMainSequence()`	Returns the sprite's main sequence.
`void setSequence(Sequence sequence)`	Sets a temporary sequence.
`Sequence getSequence()`	Gets the current sequence.
`boolean intersects(Sprite otherSprite)`	Determines if the sprite intersects with another sprite.
`boolean willIntersect(Sprite otherSprite)`	Determines if the sprite will intersect with another sprite the next time they are moved.
`boolean timeToMove()`	Returns whether it is time for the sprite to move.
`boolean timeToChangeImage()`	Returns whether it is time for the sprite to advance to the next image.
`void moveTo(Point p)`	Moves the sprite to a specific location.

Table 17-3 `gjt.animation.Sprite` **Responsibilities (Continued)**

Methods	Description
`void needsRepainting()`	Returns whether the sprite needs to be repainted.
`void setMoveInterval(long interval)`	Sets the interval between movements.
`void setImageChangeInterval(long interval)`	Sets the interval between image advancement.
`void move()`	Move the sprite.
`Point location()`	Returns the sprite's current location.
`Point nextLocation()`	Returns the sprite's location after it is moved next.
`Rectangle nextBounds()`	Returns the sprite's next bounds.
`void paint(Graphics g)`	Paints the sprite.

Table 17-4 lists the associations of a `gjt.animation.Sprite`.

Table 17-4 `gjt.animation.Sprite` **Associations**

Variables	Description
`private Playfield playfield`	The sprite's playfield.
`private Sequence currentSequence`	The sprite's current sequence.
`private Sequence mainSequence`	The sprite's main sequence.
`private Stopwatch moveTimer`	Timer used to time movements.
`private Point ulhc`	Upper left hand corner of the sprite.
`private Point moveVector`	Defines the direction in which the sprite moves.
`private Rectangle clip`	Union of the sprite's current and last bounds.
`private Rectangle curBounds`	The sprite's current bounds.
`private int width`	Width of the sprite.
`private int height`	Height of the sprite.
`private long moveInterval`	Interval, in milliseconds, between movements.

Example 17-2 shows the implementation of the `Sprite` class.

Example 17-2 `gjt.animation.Sprite` **Class Source Code**

```java
package gjt.animation;

import java.awt.*;
import java.util.Vector;
import gjt.Assert;
import gjt.Stopwatch;
import gjt.Util;

public class Sprite {
  private Playfield field;
  private Sequence currentSequence, mainSequence;
  private Stopwatch moveTimer = new Stopwatch();

  private Point ulhc       = new Point(0,0);
  private Point start      = new Point(0,0);
  private Point moveVector = new Point(1,1);

  private Rectangle clip = new Rectangle(0,0);
  private Rectangle curBounds, lastBounds;

  private int  width, height;
  private long moveInterval = 0;

  public Sprite(Playfield field,
                Sequence  sequence,
                Point     ulhc) {
    Assert.notNull(field);
    Assert.notNull(sequence);
    Assert.notNull(ulhc);

    this.field = field;
    this.ulhc  = ulhc;
    start.x     = ulhc.x;
    start.y     = ulhc.y;

    setSequence(sequence);
    setMainSequence(sequence);

    initializeBounds();
    moveTimer.start();
    currentSequence.start();
  }
  public Playfield getPlayfield() { return field;          }
  public Rectangle clipRect    () { return clip;           }
  public Rectangle curBounds   () { return curBounds;      }
```

```java
public int    width    () { return width;                    }
public int    height   () { return height;                   }
public void   reverseX () { moveVector.x = 0-moveVector.x;    }
public void   reverseY () { moveVector.y = 0-moveVector.y;    }
public void   reverse  () { reverseX(); reverseY();           }
public Point  start    () { return start;                    }

public void  setMoveVector (Point p) { moveVector = p;        }
public Point getMoveVector()         { return moveVector;     }

public void play(Sequence sequence, long cycles) {
    setSequence(sequence);
    sequence.setCyclesPerAnimation(cycles);
    sequence.setCurrentCycle(0);
}
public void animate() {
    if(currentSequence.animationOver())
        currentSequence = mainSequence;

    if(timeToChangeImage()) currentSequence.advance();
    if(timeToMove())        move();
    if(needsRepainting())   field.paintSprite(this);
}
public void setMainSequence(Sequence sequence) {
    mainSequence = sequence;
}
public Sequence getMainSequence() {
    return mainSequence;
}
public void setSequence(Sequence sequence) {
    currentSequence = sequence;

    if(curBounds != null)
        updateBounds();
}
public Sequence getSequence() {
    return currentSequence;
}
public boolean intersects(Sprite otherSprite) {
    return curBounds().intersects(otherSprite.curBounds());
}
public boolean willIntersect(Sprite otherSprite) {
    return
      nextBounds().intersects(otherSprite.nextBounds());
}
public boolean timeToMove() {
    return moveTimer.elapsedTime() > moveInterval;
}
```

```
public boolean timeToChangeImage() {
    return currentSequence.timeToAdvanceCell();
}
public void moveTo(Point p) {
    ulhc = p;
    moveTimer.reset();
}
public boolean needsRepainting() {
    return currentSequence.needsRepainting(ulhc);
}
public void setMoveInterval(long interval) {
    moveInterval = interval;
}
public void setImageChangeInterval(long interval) {
    currentSequence.setAdvanceInterval(interval);
}
public void move() {
    ulhc.x += moveVector.x;
    ulhc.y += moveVector.y;
    updateBounds();
    moveTimer.reset();
}
public Point location() {
    return ulhc;
}
public Point nextLocation() {
    return new Point(ulhc.x + moveVector.x,
                     ulhc.y + moveVector.y);
}
public Rectangle nextBounds() {
    Image nextImage = currentSequence.getNextImage();
    Point nextLoc   = nextLocation();

    return new Rectangle(
                    nextLoc.x, nextLoc.y, width, height);
}
public void paint(Graphics g) {
    currentSequence.paint(g, ulhc.x, ulhc.y, field);
}
private void initializeBounds() {
    Image curImage = currentSequence.getCurrentImage();

    width  = curImage.getWidth (field);
    height = curImage.getHeight(field);

    curBounds =
      new Rectangle(ulhc.x, ulhc.y, width, height);
```

```
        lastBounds = new Rectangle(curBounds.x,
                                   curBounds.y,
                                   curBounds.width,
                                   curBounds.height);

        clip = lastBounds.union(curBounds);
    }
    private void updateBounds() {
        Image curImage = currentSequence.getCurrentImage();

        lastBounds.width  = curBounds.width;
        lastBounds.height = curBounds.height;

        curBounds.width  = width  = curImage.getWidth(field);
        curBounds.height = height = curImage.getHeight(field);

        lastBounds.move(curBounds.x, curBounds.y);
        curBounds.move (ulhc.x, ulhc.y);

        clip = lastBounds.union(curBounds);
    }
}
```

A sprite must be constructed with a Playfield, a main Sequence, and a starting location:

```
public Sprite(Playfield field, Sequence sequence, Point ulhc) {
```

An instance of a Sprite, of course, keeps track of its Playfield, main Sequence, and location; we leave nothing to chance by requiring that each of these is supplied at construction time.

Notice that a sprite also implements a number of convenient methods. It is able to reverse either its x direction, y direction, or both, and it may have its move vector and sequence set anytime after construction. Additionally, a sprite can tell whether it currently intersects with another Sprite or whether it *will* intersect with another sprite the next time it is moved.

One last thing to note about our implementation of the Sprite class is that it requires that each image in its current sequence be the same size. While this may seem restrictive, in practice it is usually not a problem; if a sprite wishes to grow or shrink, it can always be fitted with a new sequence with images that are larger or smaller. The only requirement is that each image in the sequence has the same size.

Playfields and Double Buffering

Of course, a sprite is useless without a `Playfield` upon which to frolic, so let's turn our attention to the `Playfield` class and then look at the mechanics of double buffering.

gjt.animation.Playfield

A `Playfield` is where all the action takes place, as is evident from the class diagram in Figure 17-4.

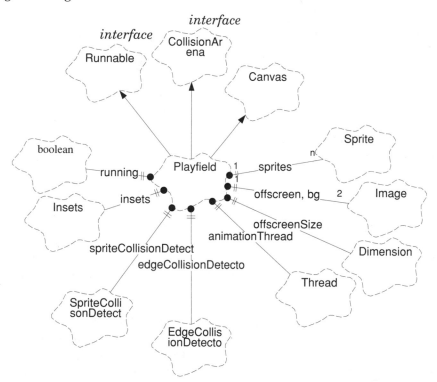

Figure 17-4 `Playfield` Class Diagram

`Playfield` is an extension of `Canvas`, and it also implements two interfaces:

- `Runnable`
- `CollisionArena`

A `Playfield` creates and maintains a thread that calls the `Playfield` run() method, as we shall see shortly. We will discuss the responsibilities of a collision arena when we discuss collision detection.

Each `Playfield` employs two collision detectors: a sprite collision detector and an edge collision detector. As their names suggest, these detect collisions either between two `Sprite` objects or between a `Sprite` and the boundary of the `Playfield`. These collision detectors call back to the `Playfield` to handle the collision. We will also expound on this relationship more when we cover collision detection.

Each instance of `Playfield` keeps track of `Sprite` objects that are currently animating on it. Each `Playfield` also keeps track of some off-screen images that are used for double buffering. Table 17-5 lists the responsibilities of the `gjt.animation.Playfield`.

Table 17-5 `gjt.animation.Playfield` **Responsibilities**

Methods	Description
void paintBackground(Graphics g)	Abstract method. Paints background.
void stop()	Stops the animation
boolean running()	Returns whether the animation is currently running.
Dimension getSize()	Returns the size of the playfield.
Insets getInsets()	Returns the insets of the playfield.
Vector getSprites()	Returns the sprites in the playfield.
void addSprite(Sprite sprite)	Adds a sprite to the playfield.
void setInsets(Insets insets)	Sets the insets of the playfield.
void start()	Starts the animation.
void reshape(int x, int y, int w, int h)	Overridden from Component.
void run()	Animation loop.

Table 17-6 lists the associations of a `gjt.animation.Playfield`.

Table 17-6 `gjt.animation.Playfield` **Associations**

Variables	Description
protected Vector sprites	Sprites on the playfield.
private boolean running	Whether the animation is running.
private Insets insets	Insets of the playfield.
private Thread animationThread	Thread controlling the animation.
private Image bgoffscreen	Background off-screen buffer.
private Image workplaceBuffer	Workplace off-screen buffer.

Table 17-6 `gjt.animation.Playfield` **Associations (Continued)**

Variables	Description
private Dimension offscreenSize	Size of off-screen buffer.
private EdgeCollisionDetector edgeCollisionDetector	Detects collisions between sprites and boundaries of the playfield.
private SpriteCollisionDetector spriteCollisionDetector	Detects collisions between sprites.

Let's take a look at the implementation of `Playfield` in Example 17-3.

Example 17-3 `gjt.animation.Playfield` **Class Source Code**

```
package gjt.animation;

import java.awt.*;
import java.util.Enumeration;
import java.util.Vector;
import gjt.Util;

public abstract class Playfield extends      Canvas
                             implements Runnable,
                                        CollisionArena {
    protected Vector      sprites = new Vector();
    private   boolean     running = false;
    private   Insets      insets  = new Insets(0,0,0,0);

    private   Thread                      animationThread;
    private   Image                       bgoffscreen,
                                          workplaceBuffer;
    private   Dimension                   offscreenSize;
    private   EdgeCollisionDetector       edgeCollisionDetector;
    private   SpriteCollisionDetector     spriteCollisionDetector;

    abstract public void paintBackground(Graphics g);

    public Playfield() {
        edgeCollisionDetector   =
            new EdgeCollisionDetector(this);
        spriteCollisionDetector =
            new SpriteCollisionDetector(this);
    }
    public void      stop      () { running = false;  }
    public boolean   running   () { return running;   }
    public Dimension getSize   () { return size();    }
    public Insets    getInsets () { return insets;    }
```

```java
    public Vector    getSprites() { return sprites;    }

    public void addSprite(Sprite sprite) {
        sprites.addElement(sprite);
    }
    public void setInsets(Insets insets) {
        this.insets = insets;
    }
    public void start() {
        animationThread = new Thread(this);
        running = true;
        animationThread.start();
    }
    public void paint(Graphics g) {
        if(needNewOffscreenBuffer()) {
            workplaceBuffer  = createOffscreenImage(size());
            bgoffscreen = createOffscreenImage(size());
            paintBackground(bgoffscreen.getGraphics());
        }
        g.drawImage(bgoffscreen, 0, 0, this);
        paintSprites();
    }
    public void reshape(int x, int y, int w  int h) {
        super.reshape(x,y,w,h);
        repaint();
    }
    public void run() {
        while(running) {
            edgeCollisionDetector.detectCollisions  ();
            spriteCollisionDetector.detectCollisions();

            animateSprites();
            Thread.currentThread().yield();
        }
        animationThread = null;
    }
    private boolean needNewOffscreenBuffer() {
        return (workplaceBuffer == null              ||
                bgoffscreen      == null              ||
                size().width  != offscreenSize.width ||
                size().height != offscreenSize.height);
    }
    private Image createOffscreenImage(Dimension size) {
        Image image = createImage(size.width, size.height);
        Util.waitForImage(this, image);
        offscreenSize = size;
        return image;
    }
```

```
protected void animateSprites() {
    Sprite        nextSprite;
    Enumeration e = sprites.elements();

    while(e.hasMoreElements()) {
        nextSprite = (Sprite)e.nextElement();
        nextSprite.animate();
    }
}
protected void paintSprites() {
    Sprite        nextSprite;
    Enumeration e = sprites.elements();

    while(e.hasMoreElements()) {
        nextSprite = (Sprite)e.nextElement();
        paintSprite(nextSprite);
    }
}
protected void paintSprite(Sprite sprite) {
    Graphics  g    = getGraphics();
    Graphics  wpg  = workplaceBuffer.getGraphics();
    Rectangle clip = sprite.clipRect();

    wpg.clipRect(clip.x, clip.y, clip.width, clip.height);
    wpg.drawImage(bgoffscreen, 0, 0, this);
    sprite.paint(wpg);

    g.clipRect (clip.x, clip.y, clip.width, clip.height);
    g.drawImage(workplaceBuffer, 0, 0, this);

    g.dispose();
    wpg.dispose();
}
}
```

The first thing to note is that Playfield is an abstract class that defines a lone abstract method: paintBackground(Graphics). The second point of interest is that a Playfield has both a start() and a stop() method, which start and stop the animation, respectively. The start() method creates a thread that is passed as a reference to the Playfield, and therefore the Playfield run() method is invoked when the thread is started. [1]

The implementation of the stop() method may seem odd, since it merely sets a boolean variable (running) to false and does nothing else. In reality, it does not stop anything. However, the run() method runs as long as the running

---

1. A number of Java language books from SunSoft Press/Prentice Hall discuss threads in more detail.

member is true; this is checked at the top of the run() method's while loop. If running has been set to false, run() returns after setting animationThread to null. The reason for this seemingly roundabout way of stopping the animation thread is to ensure that the thread is not stopped in the middle of painting one of the Playfield sprites.

Let's take a closer look at the run() method to see exactly what it is that a Playfield does over and over until someone calls the stop() method:

```
public void run() {
  while(running) {
❶         edgeCollisionDetector.detectCollisions  ();
❷         spriteCollisionDetector.detectCollisions();

          animateSprites();
          Thread.currentThread().yield();
     }
     animationThread = null;
  }
```

First, each of the Playfield collision detectors is told to detect collisions in lines ❶ and ❷, which they do. Next, the Playfield animates the Sprite objects, and last, it calls yield() on the current thread to give other processes some breathing room. (After all, when the boss walks by while you're playing the hottest new Internet game, a Playfield must be able to quickly allow someone else to take over the display.)

If the stop() method caused you to do a double take, surely the implementation of the reshape() method will do the same:

```
public void reshape(int x, int y, int w, int h) {
     super.reshape(x,y,w,h);
     repaint();
  }
```

There's a bug in the 1.0.2 release of the AWT that causes reshaping to sometimes trip over itself, forcing us to introduce an extra repaint when the Playfield is reshaped.

Double Buffering

Now that we've got the superficial stuff out of the way, it's time to explore how a Playfield implements its bread and butter, *double buffering*. Each Playfield maintains two buffers for off-screen images—one image contains nothing but the background and the other image is used as a scratch, or workplace, buffer, as illustrated in Figure 17-5.

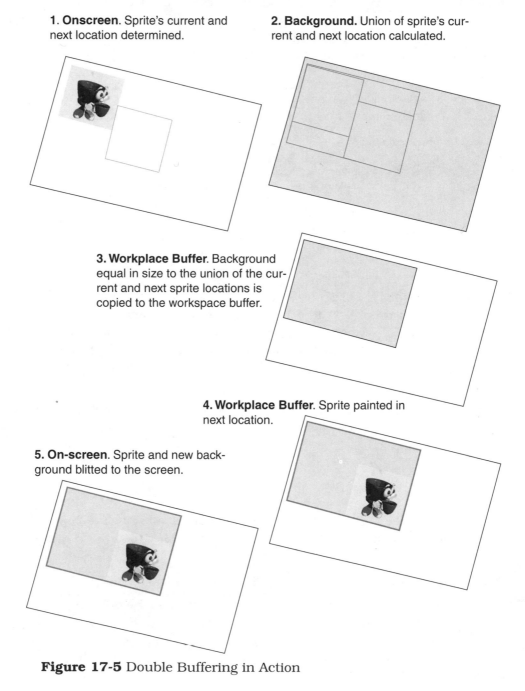

1. Onscreen. Sprite's current and next location determined.

2. Background. Union of sprite's current and next location calculated.

3. Workplace Buffer. Background equal in size to the union of the current and next sprite locations is copied to the workspace buffer.

4. Workplace Buffer. Sprite painted in next location.

5. On-screen. Sprite and new background blitted to the screen.

Figure 17-5 Double Buffering in Action

To illustrate how the off-screen buffers are used to provide smooth, flicker-free animation (the whole point of going to all this trouble), we need to take a look at the paint() and run() methods.

```
public void paint(Graphics g) {
    if(needNewOffscreenBuffer()) {
        workplaceBuffer = createOffscreenImage(size());
        bgoffscreen   = createOffscreenImage(size());
        paintBackground(bgoffscreen.getGraphics());
    }
    g.drawImage(bgoffscreen, 0, 0, this);
    paintSprites();
}
```

The paint() method's role in this double buffering business is to ensure that the off-screen buffers exist and are the correct size. It begins by inquiring whether a new off-screen buffer is needed:

```
private boolean needNewOffscreenBuffer() {
    return (workplaceBuffer == null            ||
            bgoffscreen      == null            ||
            size().width  != offscreenSize.width ||
            size().height != offscreenSize.height);
}
```

Notice that new off-screen buffers are needed if either of the two off-screen buffers is null or if the off-screen size is not the same as the current size of the Playfield.

If new off-screen buffers are needed, the paint() method goes ahead and creates them with the createOffscreenImage() method:

```
private Image createOffscreenImage(Dimension size) {
    Image image = createImage(size.width, size.height);
    Util.waitForImage(this, image);
    offscreenSize = size;
    return image;
}
```

createOffscreen() ensures that the image is loaded before it returns, by using the handy gjt.Util.waitForImage() method. It then updates the offscreenSize member and returns the off-screen image.

After paint() has created both off-screen images, it calls paintBackground(), which, as you recall, is the lone abstract method declared in Playfield. More interesting to note, however, is that the paintBackground() method is passed the bgoffscreen image, meaning that extensions of Playfield are inadvertently drawing the background into the background off-screen buffer and not directly into the Playfield itself.

After the background has been painted into the background off-screen buffer, the entire contents of the background buffer are copied (actually, *blitted*, in the parlance of the animation world) to the Playfield in one fell swoop. The reason for painting into the background off-screen buffer and then blitting to the screen is twofold:

- First, we need the background off-screen buffer to actually contain the background.

- Second, blitting [2] from the background off-screen buffer to the Playfield results in a nearly instantaneous painting of the background, instead of the background being painted in blotches.

After the background is blitted to the Playfield, it is time for the Playfield to paint the sprites, which leads us to the paintSprites() method:

```
protected void paintSprites() {
    Sprite        nextSprite;
    Enumeration e = sprites.elements();

    while(e.hasMoreElements()) {
        nextSprite = (Sprite)e.nextElement();
        paintSprite(nextSprite);
    }
}
```

paintSprites() simply cycles through each Sprite and passes it to the paintSprite() method. paintSprite() is where all of the double buffering action takes place:

```
     protected void paintSprite(Sprite sprite) {
❶        Graphics   g    = getGraphics();
         // wpg stands for workplace graphics
❷        Graphics   wpg  = workplaceBuffer.getGraphics();
         Rectangle clip = sprite.clipRect();

         wpg.clipRect(clip.x, clip.y, clip.width, clip.height);
         wpg.drawImage(bgoffscreen, 0, 0, this);
         sprite.paint(wpg);

         g.clipRect (clip.x, clip.y, clip.width, clip.height);
❸        g.drawImage(workplaceBuffer, 0, 0, this);

         g.dispose();
         wpg.dispose();
     }
```

2.   Refer to the *Images* chapter for some background on blitting.

The first thing `paintSprite()` does is obtain the `Graphics` object for the `Playfield` itself and the `Graphics` object for the `workplaceBuffer` in lines ❶ and ❷. The next thing it goes looking for is the return value of the sprite's `clipRect()` method. The rectangle returned from `Sprite.clipRect()` is the union of the `Sprite` object's previous position with the `Sprite` object's current position, like this:

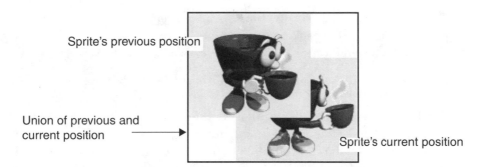

Sprite's previous position

Union of previous and current position ⟶

Sprite's current position

The next order of business is to call `wpg.clipRect()`, passing it the bounds of the `Sprite` object's clip rectangle. Invoking `Graphics.clipRect()` results in any subsequent graphics operations being restricted to the bounds passed in. [3] Any graphics operation outside the specified bounds will be ignored.

Next, `paintSprites()` blits the entire background off-screen image into the workplace buffer. Note, however, that since we set the workplace graphic's clip rectangle to the union of the sprite's previous and current bounds, only that region of the workplace buffer is affected by the `drawImage()` call in line ❸.

Let's summarize what we've done so far: We have clipped all subsequent graphics operations for the workplace buffer to the region occupied by the union of the `Sprite` object's previous and current boundaries and then blitted the background into that region alone in the workplace buffer. This erases the previous image of the `Sprite`. Note that we have also erased the `Sprite` object's current bounds, effectively clearing the way for the `Sprite` to be drawn in its current location.

All that's left now is to paint the `Sprite` into the workplace buffer:

```
sprite.paint(wpg);
```

3. This is not entirely true; it is actually the intersection of the current graphic's clip rectangle with the bounds passed in. However, for our purposes, our white lie will do no damage.

A `Sprite` is an unwitting accomplice to the double buffering the `Playfield` provides, for unbeknown to it, the `Sprite` is drawing into the workplace buffer, not into the `Playfield` itself.

It is important to note that all the action so far has taken place in the workplace buffer; we have not yet modified the `Playfield` itself, although that will change shortly.

At this point, we have painted over the `Sprite` object's previous location and its current location with the background into the workplace buffer and painted the `Sprite` at its current location. Now we are ready to blit to the screen:

```
g.clipRect (clip.x, clip.y, clip.width, clip.height);
g.drawImage(workplaceBuffer, 0, 0, this);
```

Notice that we also set the clip rectangle for the on-screen graphics to the `Sprite` object's clip rectangle; thus, we restrict graphic operations to the union of the `Sprite` object's previous and current boundaries for the on-screen `Playfield`. Next, we blit the entire workplace buffer into the on-screen buffer, but of course, only the region specified by the bounds passed to `g.clipRect()` is affected.

Nearly all of the painting that goes on takes place off-screen. Only when everything is prepared and ready to go do we blit a tiny (relative to the size of the `Playfield`) portion of the workplace buffer to the screen. All of this results in smooth, flicker-free animation that looks like it belongs on an Atari arcade game at your local bowling alley.

Now we must confess to a small white lie which, if you are a studious reader of footnotes, you are already aware of. Setting a graphic's clip rectangle actually restricts graphic operations to the intersection of the current clip rectangle and the boundary passed to `Graphics.clipRect()`—not simply the boundary passed in, as we've led you to believe. Consider what will happen the next time we come through `paintSprite()`: The *intersection* of the previous clip rectangle and the current clip rectangle will result in only a portion of the `Sprite` being updated, which results in some undesirable effects. Additionally, if you cover the `Playfield` with another window and bring the `Playfield` to the front, it will not repaint correctly because we have scrambled the graphic's clip rectangle. (In fact, some Java books on the market that cover animation suffer from this malady). As a result, we are forced to dispose of both the on-screen graphics and the workplace buffer's graphics to ensure that the clip rectangle is reset, and once again, all is well.

Collision Detection

Now that we've covered the Sequence, Sprite, and Playfield classes, and double buffering, the only topic left to discuss is collision detection. Collision detection is defined by an interface and an abstract class: CollisionArena and CollisionDetector, respectively. As we discuss collision detection, don't forget that Playfield implements CollisionArena, so everything we say concerning CollisionArena goes for Playfield.

gjt.animation.CollisionArena

The CollisionArena interface defines the behavior of an arena in which collisions take place, as you can see in Example 17-4.

Example 17-4 gjt.animation.CollisionArena **Class Source Code**

```
package gjt.animation;

import java.awt.Dimension;
import java.awt.Insets;
import java.util.Vector;
import gjt.Orientation;

public interface CollisionArena {
  abstract public Vector    getSprites();
  abstract public Dimension getSize   ();
  abstract public Insets    getInsets ();

  abstract public void spriteCollision(Sprite sprite,
                                       Sprite other);

  abstract public void edgeCollision(Sprite        sprite,
                                     Orientation orient);
}
```

A CollisionArena is responsible for producing a Vector of the Sprite objects it contains, reporting its size and insets and handling collisions between two Sprite objects and between a Sprite and a boundary. Notice that the CollisionArena is not responsible for actually *detecting* collisions, but is only responsible for handling the aftermath of a collision by implementing spriteCollision() and edgeCollision().

gjt.animation.CollisionDetector

The abstract class CollisionDetector also supports collision detection, as illustrated in Example 17-5.

Example 17-5 `gjt.animation.CollisionDetector` **Class Source Code**

```
package gjt.animation;

abstract public class CollisionDetector {
  protected CollisionArena arena;

  abstract public void detectCollisions();

  public CollisionDetector(CollisionArena arena) {
      this.arena = arena;
  }
}
```

A `CollisionDetector` must be constructed with a reference to a `CollisionArena`. Remember that a `CollisionArena` is responsible for handling the aftermath of a collision, whereas a `CollisionDetector` is only responsible for detecting collisions.

gjt.animation.SpriteCollisionDetector

`CollisionDetector` has two subclasses that do the grunt work of actually detecting collisions: `SpriteCollisionDetector` and `EdgeCollisionDetector`. Let's first look at `SpriteCollisionDetector` in Example 17-4, which detects collisions between `Sprite` objects.

Example 17-6 `gjt.animation.SpriteCollisionDetector` **Class Source Code**

```
package gjt.animation;

import java.awt.*;
import java.util.Enumeration;
import java.util.Vector;
import gjt.Orientation;

public class SpriteCollisionDetector extends CollisionDetector {
  public SpriteCollisionDetector(CollisionArena arena) {
      super(arena);
  }
  public void detectCollisions() {
      Enumeration sprites = arena.getSprites().elements();
      Sprite        sprite;

      while(sprites.hasMoreElements()) {
          sprite = (Sprite)sprites.nextElement();

          Enumeration otherSprites =
                          arena.getSprites().elements();
```

```
        Sprite otherSprite;

        while(otherSprites.hasMoreElements()) {
            otherSprite=(Sprite)otherSprites.nextElement();

            if(otherSprite != sprite)
                if(sprite.willIntersect(otherSprite))
                    arena.spriteCollision(sprite,otherSprite);
        }
    }
  }
}
```

Simply put, SpriteCollisionDetector gets all of the Sprite objects from its associated CollisionArena and cycles through each to see if it will intersect with other Sprite objects the next time they are moved. If so, SpriteCollisionDetector invokes its collision arena's spriteCollision() method, passing along the Sprite objects involved in the collision.

gjt.animation.EdgeCollision

EdgeCollisionDetector in Example 17-7 detects collisions between a Sprite object and the boundaries of its collision arena.

Example 17-7 gjt.animation.EdgeCollisionDetector **Class Source Code**

```
package gjt.animation;

import java.awt.*;
import java.util.Enumeration;
import java.util.Vector;
import gjt.Orientation;

public class EdgeCollisionDetector extends CollisionDetector {
  public EdgeCollisionDetector(CollisionArena arena) {
      super(arena);
  }
  public void detectCollisions() {
      Enumeration sprites    = arena.getSprites().elements();
      Dimension   arenaSize   = arena.getSize();
      Insets      arenaInsets = arena.getInsets();
      Sprite      sprite;

      while(sprites.hasMoreElements()) {
          sprite = (Sprite)sprites.nextElement();

          Point nl = sprite.nextLocation ();
```

```
            Point mv = sprite.getMoveVector();
            int   nextRightEdge   = nl.x + sprite.width();
            int   nextBottomEdge  = nl.y + sprite.height();
            int   arenaBottomEdge = arenaSize.height -
                                    arenaInsets.bottom;
            int   arenaRightEdge  = arenaSize.width -
                                    arenaInsets.right;

            if(nextRightEdge > arenaRightEdge)
                arena.edgeCollision(sprite, Orientation.LEFT);
            else if(nl.x < arenaInsets.left)
                arena.edgeCollision(sprite, Orientation.RIGHT);

            if(nextBottomEdge > arenaBottomEdge)
                arena.edgeCollision(sprite, Orientation.BOTTOM);
            else if(nl.y < arenaInsets.top)
                arena.edgeCollision(sprite, Orientation.TOP);
        }
    }
}
```

Note that when a Sprite collides with the boundary of the collision arena, it is not enough to simply state that a particular sprite ran into a boundary. We must also inform the collision arena which edge of the Sprite bumped into the boundary. This is the reason for the orientation argument in the arena's edgeCollision() method.

We've now plowed through all of the details of the Sprite, Playfield, and Sequence classes and collision detection and double buffering, so it's time to have a little fun and take a look at the unit test for the gjt.animation package.

Exercising the gjt.animation Package

Before we look at the animation unit test, we'll outline the steps necessary to create your own animations, using the gjt.animation package.

1. Since Playfield is an abstract class, the first order of business is to write an extension of Playfield. Remember that Playfield defines one abstract method:

    ```
    void paintBackground(Graphics)
    ```

    The Playfield class also does *not* implement two methods from the CollisionArena interface it professes to implement:

    ```
    void edgeCollision (Sprite, Orientation)
    ```

```
void spriteCollision(Sprite, Sprite)
```

Therefore, extensions of `Playfield` must implement the three methods listed above in order to paint their background and handle sprite/sprite and sprite/boundary collisions.

2. The only other requirement to get an animation up and running is to create the `Sprite` objects that will take part in the animation, define their move vectors and the rates at which they move, and their images.

Simple Animation

To start off, we'll look at a simple animation applet that you can use as a starting point for your own animations. Our simple animation will have one instance of `Sprite` that will bounce off the walls of the `Playfield`. Figure 17-6 shows some output from the test, but, of course, you can see the full animation by running the unit test yourself. Simply run `appletviewer` on the `SimpleAnimationTest.html` file.

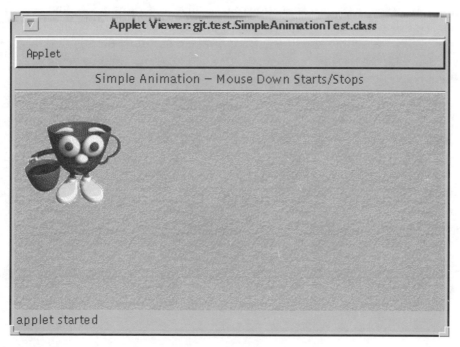

Figure 17-6 Simple Animation Unit Test
This sprite simply moves on the playfield and bumps off the walls.

As you look through the animation unit test in Example 17-8, notice that `SimpleAnimationTestPanel` centers a `SimplePlayfield` instance; once that is done, all that is left is to implement `SimplePlayfield`, Notice that `SimplePlayfield.paintBackground()` obtains an image from the `gifs` directory, which it passes, along with the `Graphics` object it was passed, to the `Util.wallPaper()` method. The `Util.wallPaper()` method wallpapers the image over the entire background of the image represented by the `Graphics` object.

We override `mouseDown()` (remember, a `Playfield` is a component—a `Canvas`, to be exact) to start and stop the animation, depending upon whether the animation is currently running.

We must also implement `spriteCollision()` if we want `SimplePlayfield` to be a concrete class. Notice, however, that since we have only one `Sprite` in our `Playfield`, there can never be any sprite/sprite collisions, so we implement the method as a no-op.

`edgeCollisions()` is implemented such that our `Sprite` bounces off the walls of the `Playfield`. If the orientation of the collision is right or left, then we know our `Sprite` has bumped into a vertical wall, and we reverse its x direction. If the orientation is anything else (top or bottom), then we know the `Sprite` has collided with the floor or ceiling of the `Playfield`, and we reverse its y direction.

`makeSequencesAndSprites()` first loads the 19 images used in the `Sprite` object's main sequence and then creates a sequence from the images loaded. Next, it creates the `Sprite` itself (`javaDrinker`), passing a reference to the `Playfield`, the main sequence, and the starting location for `javaDrinker`. We set the move vector to (2,2), meaning the `Sprite` will move 2 pixels in the x direction and 2 pixels in the y direction every time it moves. Lastly, we add the `Sprite` to the `Playfield`. Figure 17-7 depicts the layout for all three of the sprite animation unit tests.

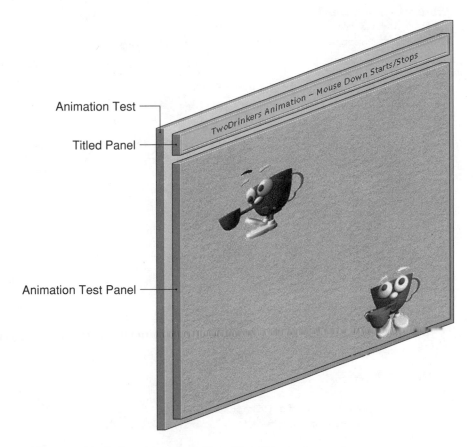

Animation Test

Titled Panel

Animation Test Panel

Figure 17-7 Sprite Animation Unit Tests Layout.

Now let's look at the unit test in Example 17-8.

Example 17-8 gjt.test.SimpleAnimationTest **Class Source Code**

```
package gjt.test;

import java.net.URL;
import java.applet.Applet;
import java.awt.*;

import gjt.Util;
import gjt.Orientation;
import gjt.animation.*;
```

```java
public class SimpleAnimationTest extends UnitTest {
  public String title() {
      return "Simple Animation - Mouse Down Starts/Stops";
  }
  public Panel centerPanel() {
      return new SimpleAnimationTestPanel(this);
  }
}

class SimpleAnimationTestPanel extends Panel {
  public SimpleAnimationTestPanel(Applet applet) {
      setLayout(new BorderLayout());
      add("Center", new SimplePlayfield(applet));
  }
}

class SimplePlayfield extends Playfield {
  private Applet    applet;
  private URL       cb;
  private Sprite    javaDrinker;
  private Sequence  spinSequence;

  public SimplePlayfield(Applet applet) {
      this.applet = applet;
      cb          = applet.getCodeBase();
      makeSequencesAndSprites();
  }
  public void paintBackground(Graphics g) {
      Image bg = applet.getImage(cb, "gifs/background.gif");
      Util.wallPaper(this, g, bg);
  }
  public boolean mouseDown(Event event, int x, int y) {
      if(running()) stop ();
      else          start();
      return true;
  }
  public void spriteCollision(Sprite sprite, Sprite sprite2) {
      // Nothing to do:  only 1 sprite!
  }
  public void edgeCollision(Sprite       sprite,
                            Orientation orientation) {
      if(orientation == Orientation.RIGHT ||
         orientation == Orientation.LEFT)
          sprite.reverseX();
      else
          sprite.reverseY();
  }
  private void makeSequencesAndSprites() {
```

```
String  file;
Point   startLoc   = new Point(10, 10);
Image[] spinImages = new Image[19];

for(int i=0; i < spinImages.length; ++i) {
    file = "gifs/spin";

    if(i < 10) file += "0" + i + ".gif";
    else       file += i + ".gif";

    spinImages[i] = applet.getImage(cb, file);
}
spinSequence = new Sequence(this, spinImages);
javaDrinker  = new Sprite(this, spinSequence, startLoc);

javaDrinker.setMoveVector(new Point(2,2));
addSprite(javaDrinker);
    }
}
```

Notice that `SimplePlayfield` implements an animation that can be stopped and started with a mouse down, complete with collision detection, in a mere 50 lines of code. All that was necessary on our part was to:

1.   Subclass `Playfield`.

2.   Implement a method for painting the background.

3.   Create instances of `Sequence` and `Sprite` objects.

4.   Define the behavior of collisions.

5.   Add the `Sprite` objects to the `Playfield`.

Bump Animation

Now let's add some more behavior to our `javaDrinker` when he bumps into the boundaries of the `Playfield`. We will create another sequence that `javaDrinker` will play when he bumps into a wall. Just to make things a little more interesting, we will have our `javaDrinker` cycle through the *bump* sequence once for collisions with the left wall and twice for collisions with the right wall. We will also slow down the rate at which `javaDrinker` cycles through its images. You can see a picture of the bump sequence in Figure 17-8.

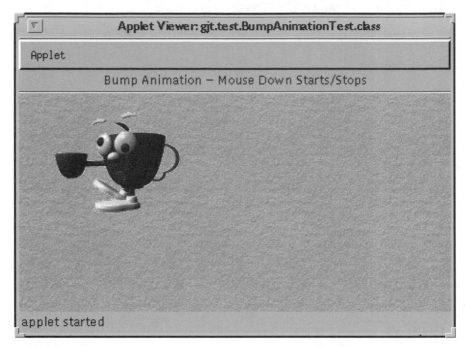

Figure 17-8 Bump Animation Unit Test
This sprite goes through a bump sequence after bumping into a
wall.

Our applet in Example 17-9 looks exactly the same as the one in Example 17-8,
except the names of the classes have changed. Pay attention to the differences
between `BumpPlayfield` and `SimplePlayfield` on page 506. In
`BumpPlayfield`, we create a second sequence, `bumpSequence`, and set the
advance interval for the spin sequence to 100 milliseconds and the advance
interval for the bump sequence to 200 milliseconds.

We've modified the `edgeCollision()` method so that a bump into the right or
left walls causes `javaDrinker` to play the bump sequence the appropriate
number of times. When the orientation is `RIGHT`, our `javaDrinker` has run into
the left wall, and vice versa. The orientation specifies the side of the `Sprite` that
hits the edges of the `Playfield`.

Example 17-9 gjt.test.BumpAnimationTest **Class Source Code**

```
package gjt.test;

import java.net.URL;
import java.applet.Applet;
import java.awt.*;

import gjt.Util;
import gjt.Orientation;
import gjt.animation.*;

public class BumpAnimationTest extends UnitTest {
  public String title() {
      return "Bump Animation - Mouse Down Starts/Stops";
  }
  public Panel centerPanel() {
      return new BumpAnimationTestPanel(this);
  }
}

class BumpAnimationTestPanel extends Panel {
  public BumpAnimationTestPanel(Applet applet) {
      setLayout(new BorderLayout());
      add("Center", new BumpPlayfield(applet));
  }
}

class BumpPlayfield extends Playfield {
  private Applet    applet;
  private URL       cb;
  private Sprite    javaDrinker;
  private Sequence  spinSequence, bumpSequence;

  public BumpPlayfield(Applet applet) {
      this.applet = applet;
      cb          = applet.getCodeBase();
      makeSequencesAndSprites();
  }
```

```java
public void paintBackground(Graphics g) {
    Image bg = applet.getImage(cb, "gifs/background.gif");
    Util.wallPaper(this, g, bg);
}
public boolean mouseDown(Event event, int x, int y) {
    if(running()) stop ();
    else          start();
    return true;
}
public void spriteCollision(Sprite sprite, Sprite sprite2) {
    // Nothing to do:  only 1 sprite!
}
public void edgeCollision(Sprite       sprite,
                          Orientation orientation) {
    if(orientation == Orientation.RIGHT ||
       orientation == Orientation.LEFT) {
       if(sprite.getSequence() != bumpSequence) {
           sprite.reverseX();

           if(orientation == Orientation.RIGHT)
               sprite.play(bumpSequence, 1);
           else
               sprite.play(bumpSequence, 2);
       }
    }
    else
        sprite.reverseY();
}
private void makeSequencesAndSprites() {
    String  file;
    Point   startLoc    = new Point(10, 10);
    Image[] spinImages = new Image[19];
    Image[] bumpImages = new Image[6];
```

```
for(int i=0; i < spinImages.length; ++i) {
    file = "gifs/spin";

    if(i < 10) file += "0" + i + ".gif";
    else       file += i + ".gif";

    spinImages[i] = applet.getImage(cb, file);
}
for(int i=0; i < bumpImages.length; ++i) {
    file = "gifs/bump0" + i + ".gif";
    bumpImages[i] = applet.getImage(cb, file);
}
spinSequence = new Sequence(this, spinImages);
bumpSequence = new Sequence(this, bumpImages);
javaDrinker  = new Sprite(this, spinSequence, startLoc);

spinSequence.setAdvanceInterval(100);
bumpSequence.setAdvanceInterval(200);

javaDrinker.setMoveVector(new Point(2,2));
addSprite(javaDrinker);
    }
}
```

Now, let's make one final iteration over our unit test to illustrate sprite-on-sprite collisions.

Two-Sprite Collision

This unit test adds another javaDrinker to the Playfield. We'll have one of the javaDrinker objects spin fast and move slow, while the other will spin slow and move fast. We will also create two bump sequences, one fast and the other slow. When the two javaDrinker objects collide, we'll have one of them play the slow bump sequence and the other the fast bump sequence. In Figure 17-9 you can see the disoriented look on the sprites after colliding.

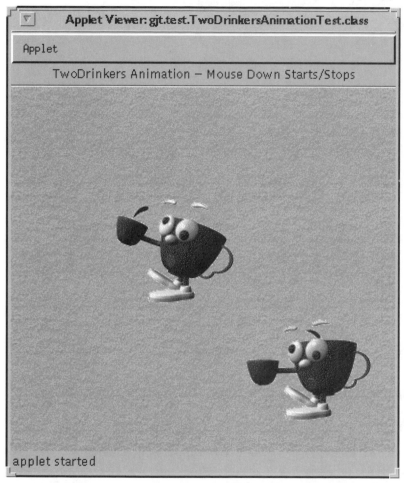

Figure 17-9 Two Sprite Collision Animation Unit Test
The sprites each go through their individual bump sequences when they collide.

Example 17-10 shows the unit test with two sprites colliding. It is identical to the previous animation tests, except that this one creates a `TwoDrinkersPlayfield`. This time around, we will just show you the code without any accompanying commentary; it should be apparent what we're up to with the `TwoDrinkersPlayfield`.

Example 17-10 `gjt.test.TwoDrinkersAnimationTest` **Class Source Code**

```java
package gjt.test;

import java.net.URL;
import java.applet.Applet;
import java.awt.*;
import java.awt.Panel;

import gjt.Util;
import gjt.Orientation;
import gjt.animation.*;

public class TwoDrinkersAnimationTest extends UnitTest {
    public String title() {
        return
            "TwoDrinkers Animation - Mouse Down Starts/Stops";
    }
    public Panel centerPanel() {
        return new TwoDrinkersAnimationTestPanel(this);
    }
}

class TwoDrinkersAnimationTestPanel extends Panel {
    public TwoDrinkersAnimationTestPanel(Applet applet) {
        setLayout(new BorderLayout());
        add("Center", new TwoDrinkersPlayfield(applet));
    }
}

class TwoDrinkersPlayfield extends Playfield {
    private Applet    applet;
    private URL       cb;
    private Sprite    moveFastSpinSlow, moveSlowSpinFast;
    private Sequence  fastSpinSequence,
                      slowSpinSequence,
                      fastBumpSequence,
                      slowBumpSequence;
```

```java
    public TwoDrinkersPlayfield(Applet applet) {
        this.applet = applet;
        cb           = applet.getCodeBase();
        makeSequencesAndSprites();
    }
    public void paintBackground(Graphics g) {
        Image bg = applet.getImage(cb, "gifs/background.gif");
        Util.wallPaper(this, g, bg);
    }
    public boolean mouseDown(Event event, int x, int y) {
        if(running()) stop ();
        else          start();
        return true;
    }
    public void spriteCollision(Sprite sprite, Sprite sprite2) {
        if(moveSlowSpinFast.getSequence() != fastBumpSequence) {
            sprite.reverse();
            sprite2.reverse();

            moveSlowSpinFast.play(fastBumpSequence, 3);
            moveFastSpinSlow.play(slowBumpSequence, 3);
        }
    }
    public void edgeCollision(Sprite     sprite,
                              Orientation orientation) {
        if(orientation == Orientation.RIGHT ||
           orientation == Orientation.LEFT)
            sprite.reverseX();
        else
            sprite.reverseY();
    }
    private void makeSequencesAndSprites() {
        String  file;
        Image[] spinImages = new Image[19];
        Image[] bumpImages = new Image[6];
        Image[] volleyball = new Image[4];

        for(int i=0; i < spinImages.length; ++i) {
            file = "gifs/spin";

            if(i < 10) file += "0" + i + ".gif";
            else       file += i + ".gif";
```

```
            spinImages[i] = applet.getImage(cb, file);
    }
    for(int i=0; i < bumpImages.length; ++i) {
        file = "gifs/bump0" + i + ".gif";
        bumpImages[i] = applet.getImage(cb, file);
    }
    fastSpinSequence = new Sequence(this, spinImages);
    slowSpinSequence = new Sequence(this, spinImages);

    fastBumpSequence = new Sequence(this, bumpImages);
    slowBumpSequence = new Sequence(this, bumpImages);

    moveFastSpinSlow =
        new Sprite(this,
            slowSpinSequence, new Point(25, 75));

    moveSlowSpinFast =
        new Sprite(this,
            fastSpinSequence, new Point(250,250));

    fastSpinSequence.setAdvanceInterval(50);
    slowSpinSequence.setAdvanceInterval(300);

    fastBumpSequence.setAdvanceInterval(25);
    slowBumpSequence.setAdvanceInterval(200);

    moveFastSpinSlow.setMoveVector(new Point(2,3));
    moveSlowSpinFast.setMoveVector(new Point(-1,-1));

    moveSlowSpinFast.setMoveInterval(100);

    addSprite(moveFastSpinSlow);
    addSprite(moveSlowSpinFast);
    }
}
```

Summary

By introducing the gjt.animation package, we have covered a number of
animation-related topics, such as creating sprites, playfields, animation
sequences, and using a technique for double buffering.

By studying the series of unit tests presented in this chapter, it should be apparent
how to go about creating your own animations, using the Graphic Java Toolkit.
The first unit test presented is simple enough that it should be a good starting
point for developing your own animations.

Appendixes

PART THREE

APPENDIX A

AWT Class
Diagrams

Imagine a world where architects write volumes of prose describing their buildings instead of drawing blueprints. While such a scenario would certainly be absurd, many software engineers are quick to eschew the software developer's equivalent of blueprints: the class diagram.

Class diagrams are to software development what blueprints are to the world of architecture. Class diagrams are essential for succinctly communicating one's design to others; as a result *Graphic Java* uses class diagrams extensively for documenting the classes from the Graphic Java Toolkit and the Abstract Window Toolkit.

This appendix includes class diagrams for all of the classes in the AWT, including java.awt.image—in all over 50 class diagrams. We think that you will find the diagrams in this chapter useful for understanding the relationships between classes in the AWT.

The class diagrams in this appendix and throughout *Graphic Java* are of the *Booch* variety.[1] For those of you unfamiliar with Booch diagrams, we show a legend on the next page and then we discuss a simple, yet fairly complete class diagram.

---

1. See Booch, Grady. *Object-Oriented Analysis And Design*. Benjamin/Cummings.

Legend

The following is a legend of the elements used in our class diagrams.

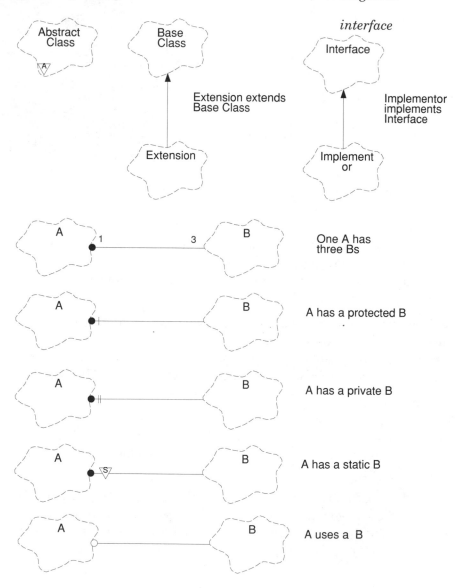

A Look At An Example Class Diagram

The class diagram below is for the `java.awt.Component` class.

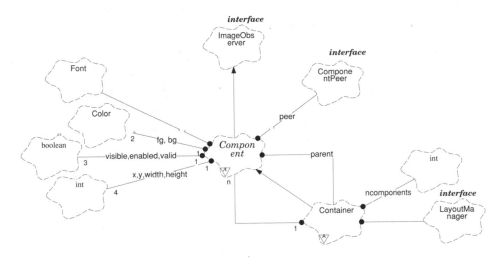

Container extends Component. Both Container and Component are abstract classes, meaning they have either declared or inherited abstract methods that they have not implemented. Component, on the other hand implements the ImageObserver interface[2], and maintains an association with a ComponentPeer. Each Component has:

- 4 integer values, named x, y, width and height

- 3 boolean values, named visible, enabled and valid

- 2 colors, fg and bg, and one Font

Note that the relationship between Component and Font is not labeled—we do not label relationships unless the name of the object adds some value. We choose to label the int, boolean and Color relationships because the roles of those particular objects are not apparent without a label. Also note that int and boolean are not really objects; they are intrinsic types. We denote intrinsic types by changing the font of their "class" names.

One Container has potentially many Components. A Container also maintains a relationship with a LayoutManager, and keeps track of the number of components it currently contains with an integer named ncomponents.

---

2. We denote interfaces by adorning them with an "interface" label. There is currently no notation in the Booch method for depicting interfaces.

AWT Component Classes:

Button
Canvas
Checkbox/CheckboxGroup
Choice
Component
Container
Label
List
Menu/MenuItem
MenuBar
Scrollbar
TextArea
TextComponent
TextField

Component Overview

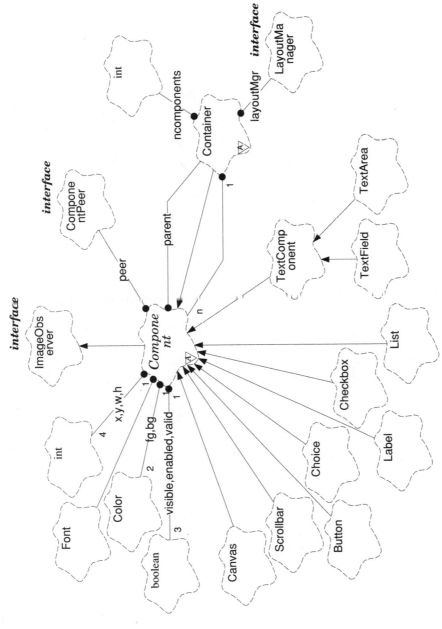

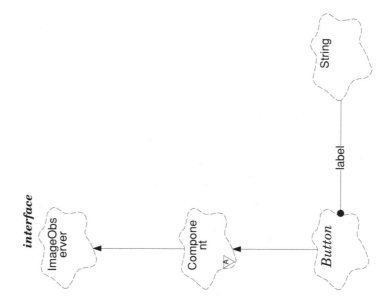

java.awt.Button

java.awt.Canvas

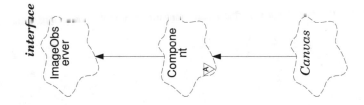

interface

ImageObs
erver

Compone
nt

Canvas

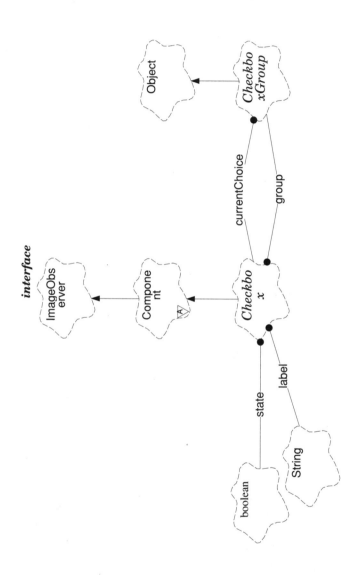

java.awt.Checkbox
java.awt.CheckboxGroup

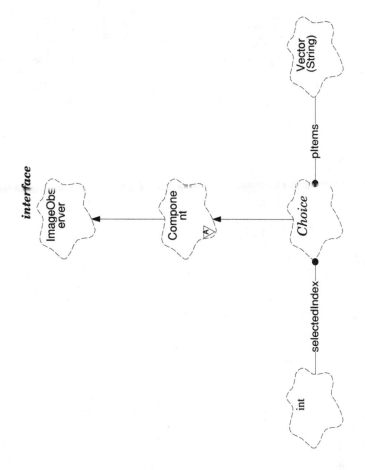

java.awt.Choice

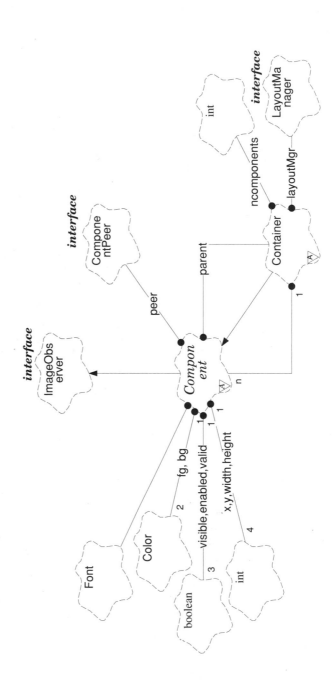

java.awt.Component

java.awt.Container

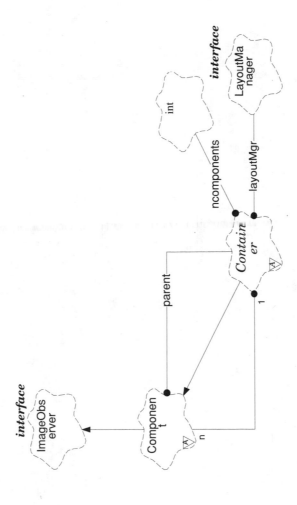

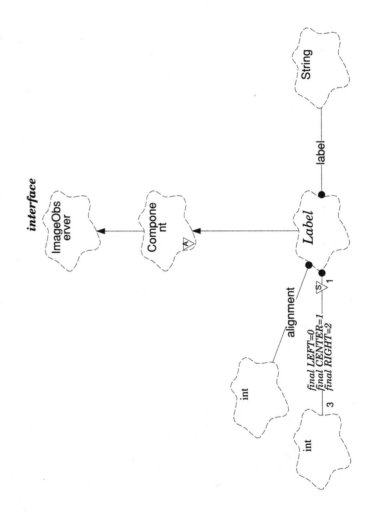

java.awt.Label

java.awt.List

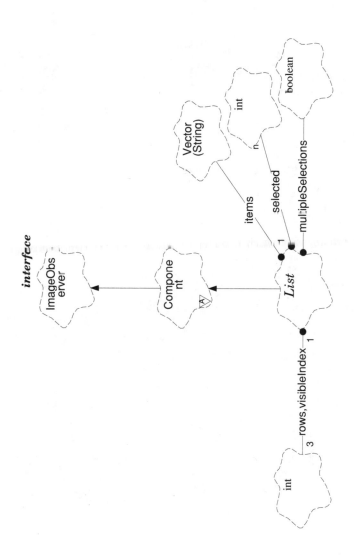

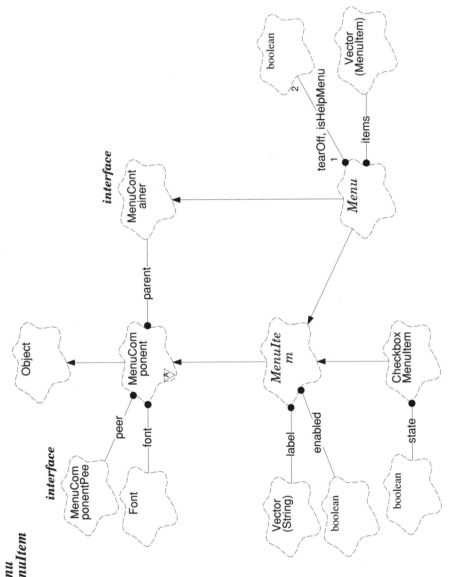

java.awt.Menu
java.awt.MenuItem

java.awt.MenuBar

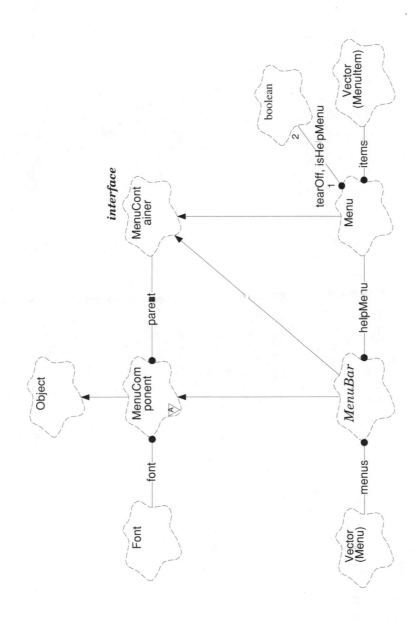

java.awt.Scrollbar

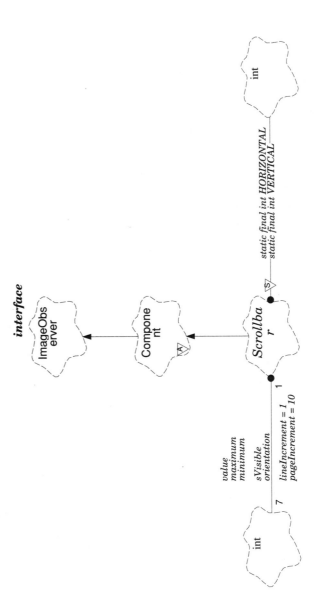

interface

ImageObserver

Component

Scrollbar

int

static final int HORIZONTAL
static final int VERTICAL

int

value
maximum
minimum

sVisible
orientation

lineIncrement = 1
pageIncrement = 10

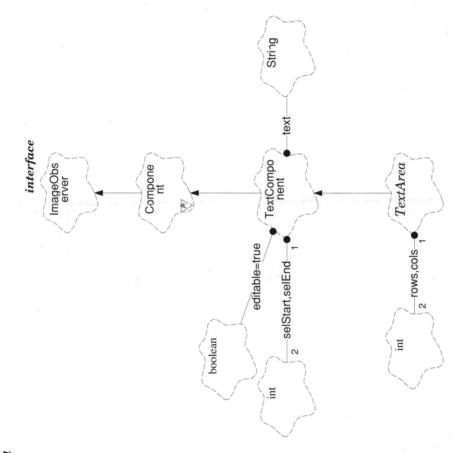

java.awt.TextArea

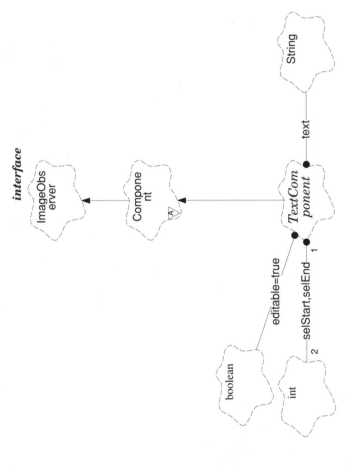

java.awt.TextComponent

java.awt.TextField

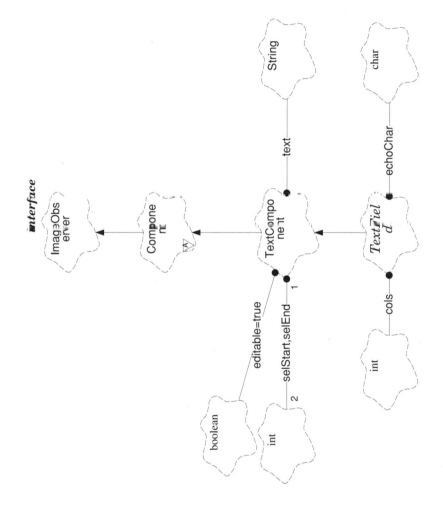

AWT Container Classes:

Dialog
FileDialog
Frame
Panel
Window

Container Overview

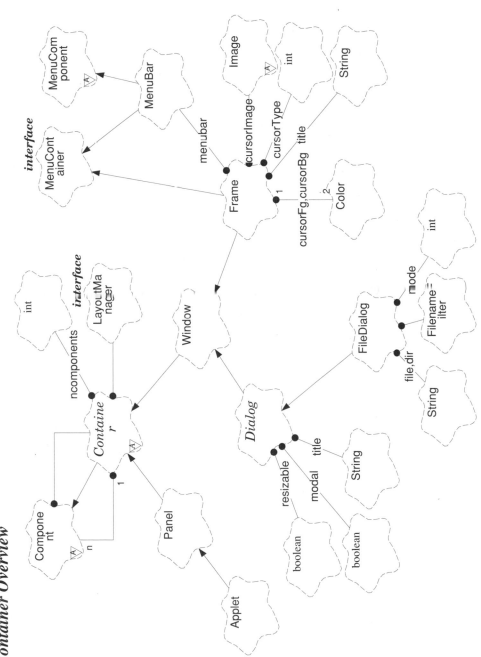

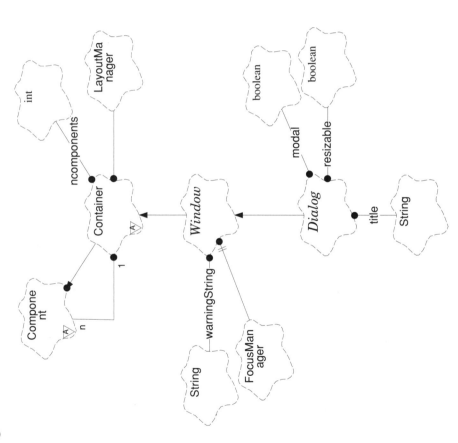

java.awt.Dialog

java.awt.FileDialog

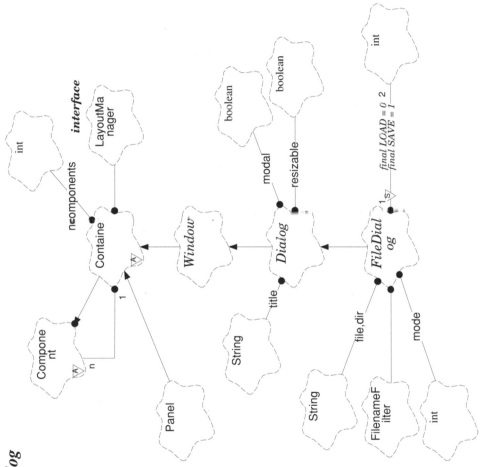

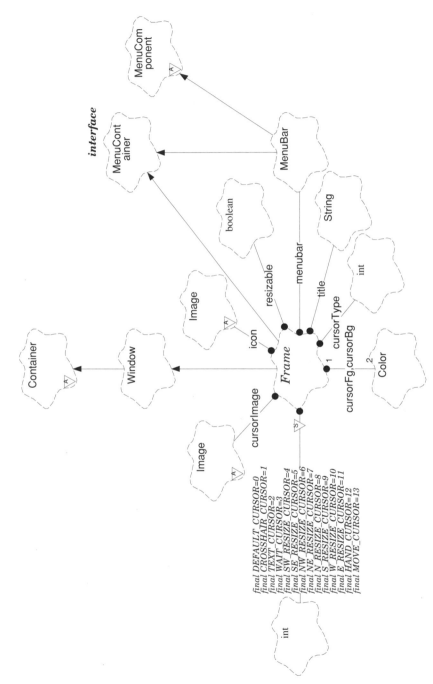

java.awt.Frame

java.awt.Panel

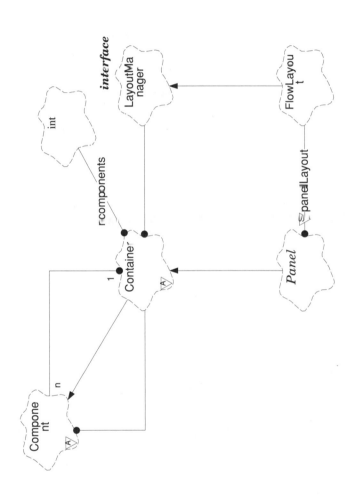

java.awt.Window

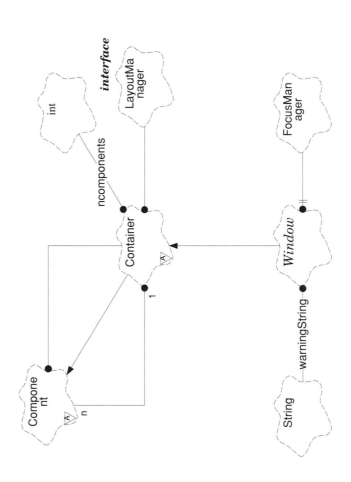

java.awt.image Classes:

ColorModel
CropImageFilter
DirectColorModel
FilteredImageSource
ImageFilter
IndexColorModel
MemoryImageSource
PixelGrabber
RGBImageFilter

java.awt.image Overview

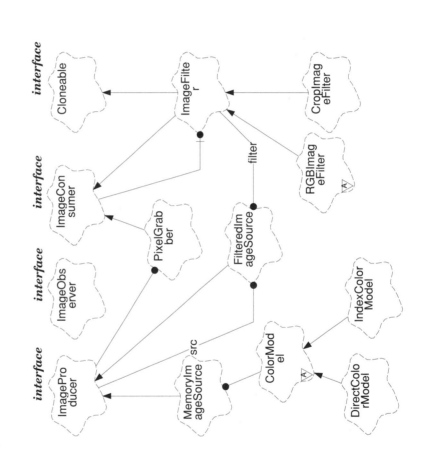

java.awt.image.ColorModel

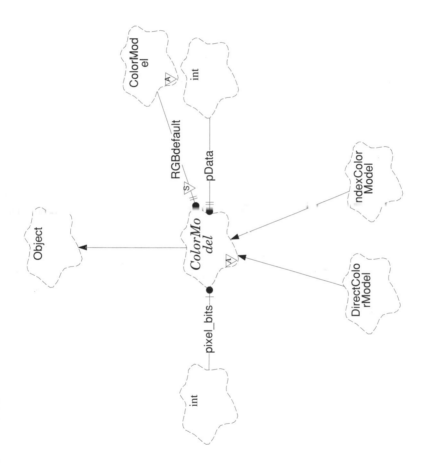

java.awt.image.CropImageFilter

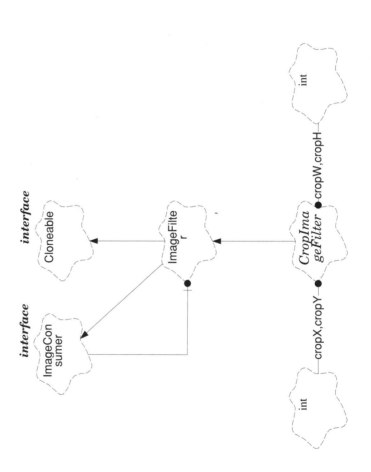

java.awt.image.DirectColorModel

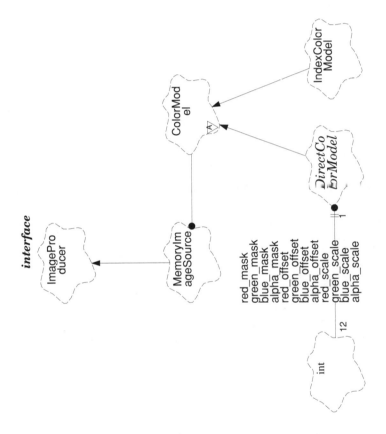

java.awt.image.FilteredImageSource

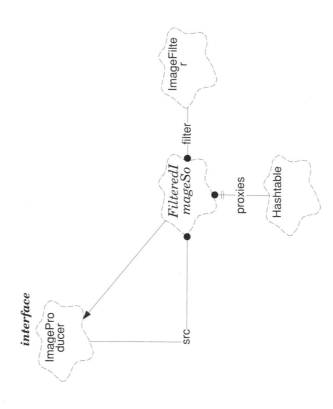

interface

ImagePro
ducer

src

*FilteredI
mageSo*

filter

ImageFilte
r

proxies

Hashtable

java.awt.image.ImageFilter

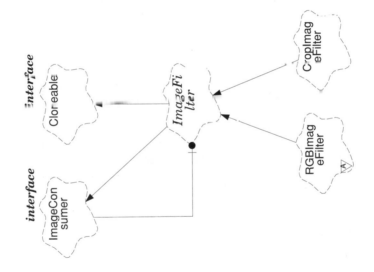

java.awt.image.IndexColorModel

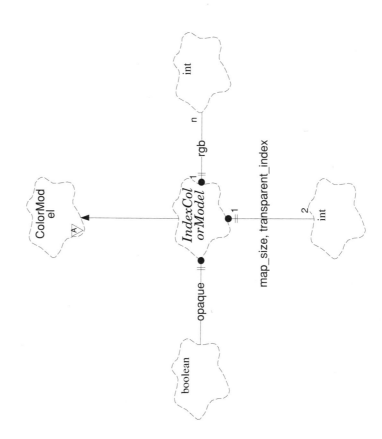

java.awt.image.MemoryImageSource

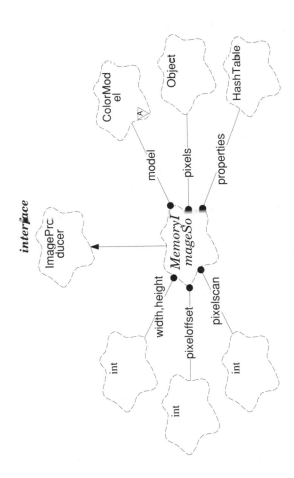

java.awt.image.PixelGrabber

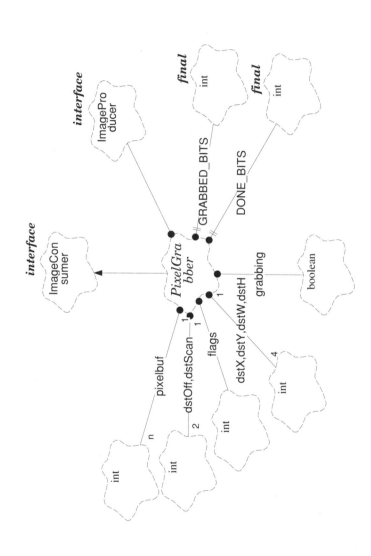

java.awt.image.RGBImageFilter

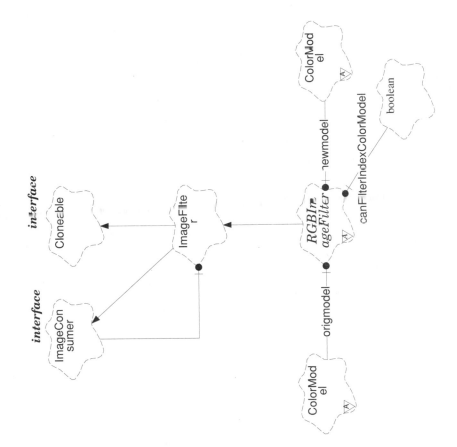

AWT LayoutManager Classes:

BorderLayout
CardLayout
FlowLayout
GridBagLayout
GridLayout

LayoutManager Overview

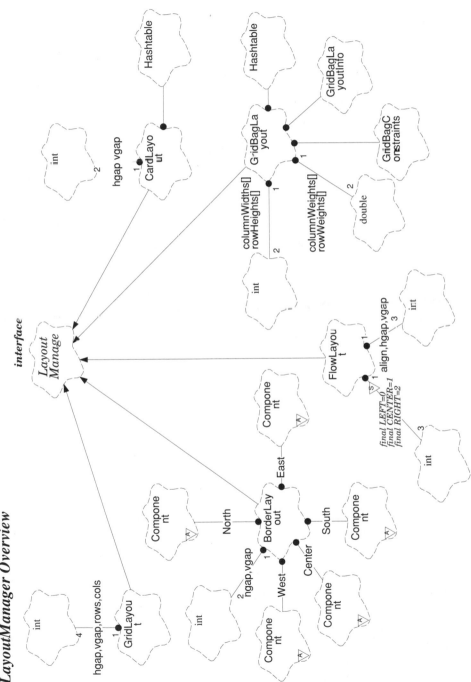

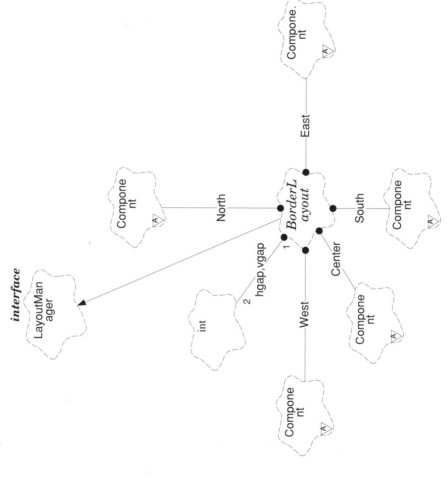

java.awt.BorderLayout

java.awt.CardLayout

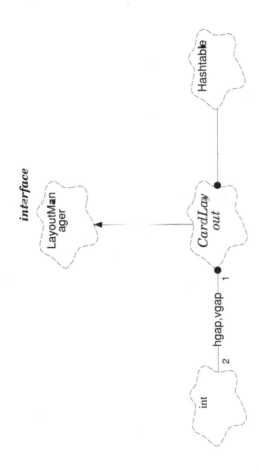

java.awt.FlowLayout

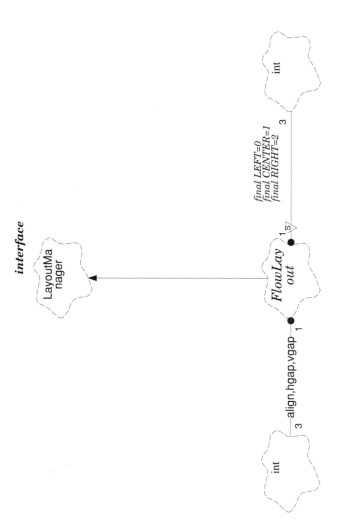

java.awt.GridBagLayout

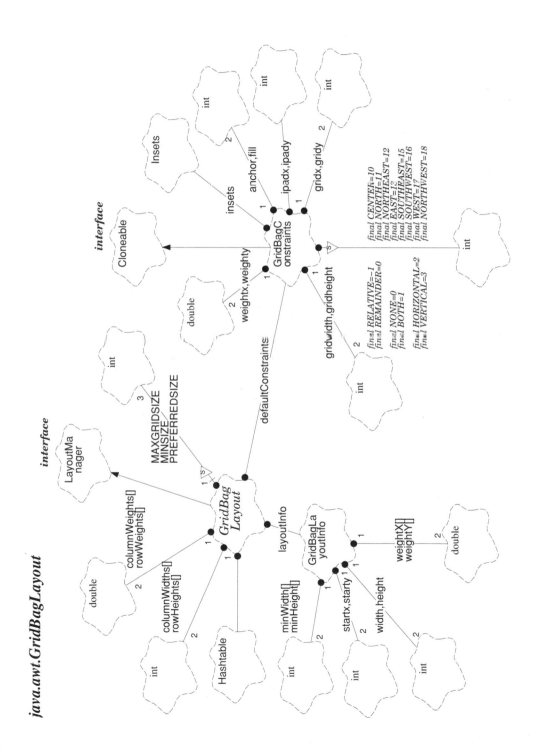

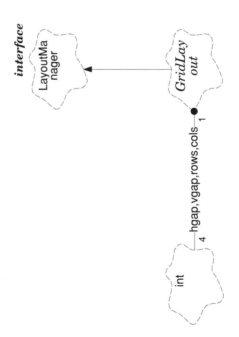

interface

LayoutMa
nager

*GridLay
out*

hgap,vgap,rows,cols

1

4

int

java.awt.GridLayout

Miscellaneous AWT Classes:

Color
Dimension
Error/Exception
Event
Font
FontMetrics
Graphics
Insets
Point
Polygon
MediaTracker
Rectangle
Toolkit

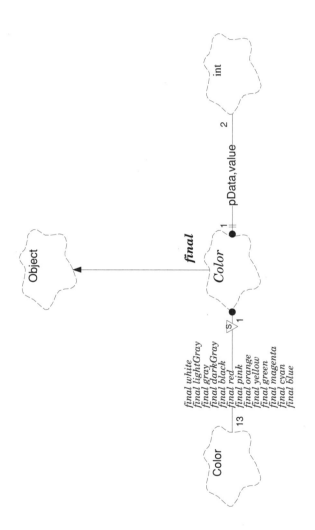

java.awt.Color

java.awt.Dimension

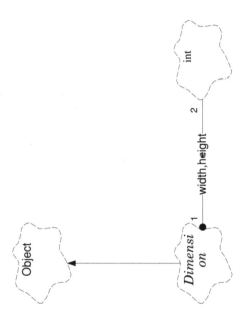

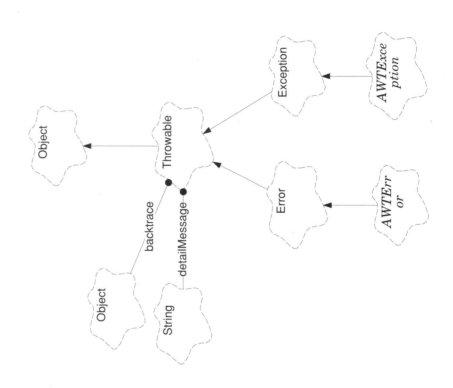

java.awt.Error
java.awt.Exception

java.awt.Event

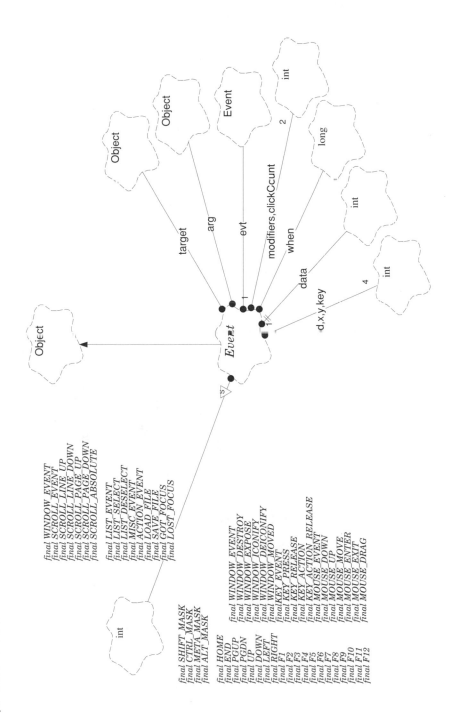

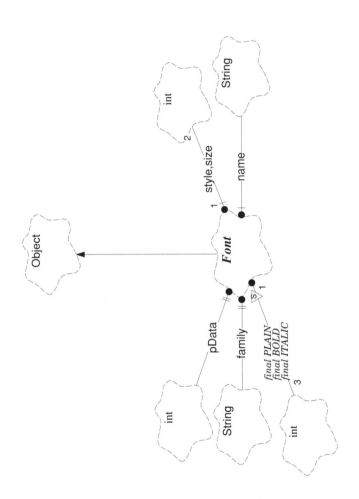

java.awt.Font

java.awt.FontMetrics

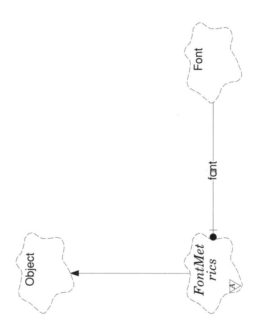

java.awt.Graphics

java.awt.Insets

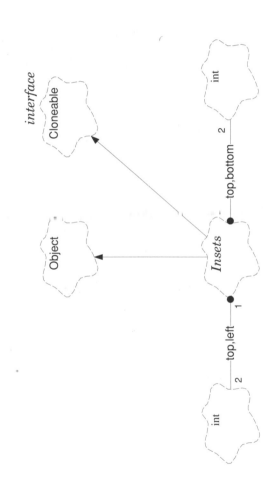

java.awt.MediaTracker

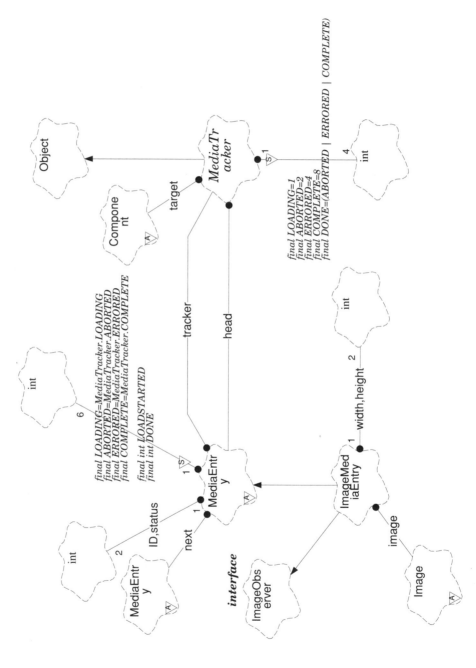

java.awt.Point

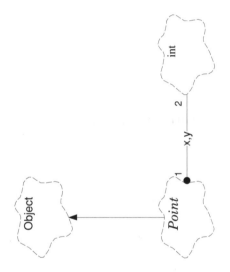

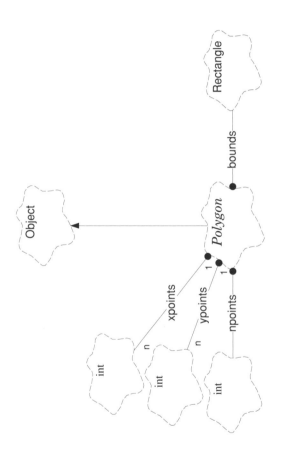

java.awt.Polygon

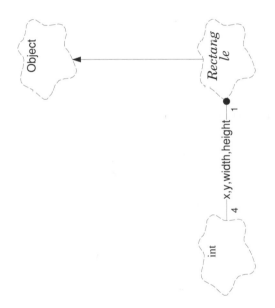

java.awt.Rectangle

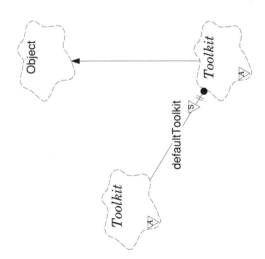

java.awt.Toolkit

APPENDIX B

- Using the CD-ROM on Windows 95 and Windows NT

- Using the CD-ROM on Solaris 2

The Graphic Java CD-ROM

The Graphic Java CD-ROM contains all of the sample code from the book and the complete Graphic Java Toolkit (GJT). The CD also contains the Java Developer's Kit (Release 1.0.2) for Solaris 2.x, Windows 95, and Windows NT.

Using the CD-ROM on Windows 95 and Windows NT

In addition to the JDK and the GJT, the Windows directory contains a Java Work-Shop presentation, Symantec's Café Lite and shareware versions of WinEdit and WinZip. **This CD-ROM does not support Windows 3.1.**

The Windows directory structure is as follows:

Directory/File	Contents
Grfxjava.zip	Contains the complete Graphics Java Toolkit
Cafelite.exe	The installation program for Café Lite
jdk_x86.zip	The 1.0.2 release of the JDK
Winedit	Contains the installation program for WinEdit
Winzip95.exe	The installation program for WinZip95
Workshop.zip	Contains the Java Workshop html files

BEFORE ATTEMPTING TO UNZIP ANY OF THE .ZIP FILES, YOU MUST INSTALL WINZIP95.

To install WinZip95:

1. Click the Start button and choose Run. (Windows NT users, Select Run from the Program Manager File menu.)

2. Type **D:\Windows\Winzip95.exe** and click the OK button.
(If your CD-ROM drive is not drive D, substitute the appropriate letter.)

3. The setup program will display a dialog box first prompting you to proceed with set up and then asking you where to install WinZip95.

4. Follow on-screen installation instructions.

To install the JDK (Release 1.0.2):

1. Double click on the file **jdk_x86.zip** found in the Windows folder.

2. If you have not previously installed WinZip95, you should do so now. See install instructions above. After completing the WinZip95 installation, the WinZip Wizard program will prompt you to select the file or folder you wish to unzip.

3. Using WinZip, select the drive and directory you want to use. [You will probably want to unzip the file **jdk_x86.zip** in the root directory of the C drive to create C:\java].There should not be any copies of previous versions of the JDK on your computer.

4. The unzipped files will take up just over 5.5MB

5. If you are installing the JDK for the first time, you will have to update your system's environment variables. You should add the java\bin directory to your Path and update the CLASSPATH environment variable to point to classes.zip. For example:

   > set CLASSPATH=.;C:\java\lib\classes.zip

   This will make sure that you are using the correct classes for the JDK1.0.2 release.

 Do not unzip the **classes.zip** file.

To install the Java WorkShop Presentation

1. Double click on the file **Workshop.zip**.

2. If you have not previously installed WinZip95, you should do so now. See install instructions above. After completing the WinZip95 installation, the WinZip Wizard program will prompt you to select the file or folder you wish to unzip.

3. Using WinZip select the drive and directory you want to use for each of the files you select. Click "Unzip Now" to unzip the selected file or folder.

4. To view the Java WorkShop presentation, use a web browser and enter the following URL:

file://<*location of unzipped files*>**/Workshop/index.html**

For best results, we recommend that you use Java enabled Netscape Navigator 2.X. With Navigator 2.x you will see a "live" version of the Java WorkShop demo and tutorial.

To install Café Lite:

Café Lite is a trial version of Symantec Café, the Integrated Java Development Environment. A coupon for an upgrade to the full version of Symantec Café is included at the back of this book. Please note that the Café Lite installation program also installs a copy of the JDK (Release 1.0) on your system.

1. Click the Start button and choose Run. (Windows NT users, Select Run from the Program Manager File menu.)

2. Type **D:\Windows\Cafelite.exe** and click the OK button. (If your CD-ROM drive is not drive D, substitute the appropriate letter.)

To install WinEdit:

1. Click the Start button and choose Run. (Windows NT users, Select Run from the Program Manager File menu.)

2. Type **D:\Windows\Winedit\Setup.exe** and click the OK button. (If your CD-ROM drive is not drive D, substitute the appropriate letter.)

The installation program adds the directory you specified for installing WinEdit to the PATH statement in your AUTOEXEC.BAT file.

To customize WinEdit for Java Programming:

If you would like to customize WinEdit to make Java programming easier, the SunSoft Press book, *Core Java* describes useful modifications to the standard WinEdit configuration (See Chapter 2). This CD-ROM contains a batch file named Wepatch.bat that you can run to make these modifications.

Wepatch.bat and the other files needed to modify WinEdit are on the CD-ROM in a subdirectory of Winedit named Winedita.

To run Wepatch.bat:

1. Install WinEdit as described above.

2. Change to the Winedita directory.

3. **Run Wepatch** <*WinEdit directory*> <*Windows directory*>

For example, if you installed WinEdit in a directory on your hard drive named C:\Programs\WinEdit and your Windows directory is C:\Windows, at the system prompt you would type:

Wepatch C:\Programs\WinEdit C:\Windows

Using the CD-ROM on Solaris 2.x

Because this CD-ROM is a standard ISO-9660 disk that does not support long file names and other UNIX extensions, the Java Developer's Kit (JDK) for Solaris 2.x, the Java WorkShop presentation, and the Graphic Java Toolkit (GJT) are stored as tar archives. Use the *more* command or *vi* to read the **readme.txt** file.

The Unix directory structure is as follows:

jdk_102.tar	Solaris 2.x JDK (Release 1.0.2)
Workshop	Contains the Java Workshop html files
Grfxjava.tar	The Graphic Java Toolkit(GJT)
readme.txt	Installation notes for Solaris users

To install the Graphic Java Toolkit (GJT):

1. Make a directory on your UNIX filesystem and change to that directory. Then copy the file **grfxjava.tar** from the CD-ROM to that directory.

2. Use the command *tar -xvf* to unarchive the file. For example:

    tar -xvf grfxjava.tar

To install the Java Developer's Kit (Solaris 2.3 or later):

1. Make a directory on your UNIX filesystem and change to that directory. Then copy the file **sparc.tar** or **x86.tar** from the CD-ROM to that directory.

2. Use the command *tar -xvf* to unarchive the file. For example:

    tar -xvf sparc.tar

3. Add or modify the appropriate variables in your .cshrc (or whatever initialization file is appropriate for the shell you use) to put the Java bin directory in your path and to set a CLASSPATH environment variable to point to the Java runtime library, which is in the lib directory under the JDK. For example:

    setenv CLASSPATH "where-you-put-java"/lib/classes.zip.

4. Logout and login again so the new variables take effect.

 Do not unzip the **classes.zip** file.

To install the Java WorkShop Presentation:

1.   Make a directory on your UNIX filesystem and change to that directory. Then copy the file **workshop.tar** from the CD-ROM to that directory.

2.   Use the command tar -xvf to unarchive the file. For example:

tar -xvf workshop.tar

3.   To view the Java WorkShop presentation, use a web browser and enter the following URL:

file://<*location of unarchived files*>**/workshop/index.html**

For best results, we recommend that you use Java enabled Netscape Navigator 2.X. With Navigator 2.x you will see a "live" version of the Java WorkShop demo and tutorial.

Index

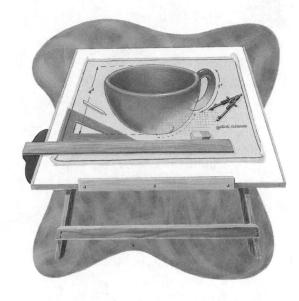

Numerics

3-D effect
    See also ThreeDRectangle
    borders 46
    rectangle 42–47
    shading 46

A

action event, constants 71
action() method
    converting string to orientation
        constant, example 222
    extracting integer value 198
    identifying triggering button 87
    propagated 72
    routed events 83
    RowLayoutApplet example 222
    what argument values 85
ACTIVATE, image button event state
    315

add() method
    adding image to
        ImageButtonPanel 333
    Toolbar 331, 336, 338
addLayoutComponent() method 160
addNotify() method, overriding 419
ALLBITS constant, determining image
    filled 130
ALT_MASK, Event constant 77
anchor
    described 179
    setting, example 185
anchor() method, for rubberband
    operation 353
animation
    advanced behavior, example 507
    bump sequence example 511
    creating 502, 507
    flicker-free 495
    package description 238
    paint() and run() methods 495
    simple applet example 503–507
    starting 492

animation package
    classes 241
    described 238
applet
    ActionEventApplet 83
    ColumnLayoutApplet 230
    DoubleClickApplet 81
    EventMonitorApplet 78
    GridLabApplet 200–204
    HTML file 14
    HTML tag 14
    MouseSensorApplet 76
    nested layout 73
    scrollbar implementation 432
    TenPixelBorderTestApplet 165
    unit test for custom components
        246
    viewing 14
    vs. Java application 18, 127, 162
appletviewer 13
ARM, image button event state 315
Assert class, methods 243
AWT
    bug
        box repainting 416
        calculating size of Choice
            objects in Motif 290
        consuming resources in
            bargauge test 269
        dialog positioning 382
        incorrect repainting after
            resize 459
        mouse events not propagated
            54
        mouse up in Windows 95 77
        Playfield reshaping 493
        progress dialog updates
            incorrectly in Motif
            399
        propagated events in
            Windows 95 80
        resize GTJ dialogs 374

    setting menu font in
        Windows 95 119
    updating menu item's label
        119
    font model 53
    image interfaces 124
    layout managers 168
    mouse button handling 78
    peers classes 4
AWT class
    Dialog 373
    Event 75
    Font 52
    FontMetrics 54
    Label 54, 244
    MediaTracker 133
    Rectangle 27
    Toolkit 128
awt.Button 299, 307, 312

B

background, handling for animation
    495
bargauge
    associations 262
    fill color 262
    height/width determination 264
    painting border 264
    in ProgressDialog 380, 396
Bargauge class
    creating vertical/horizontal
        gauges, example 270
    fulfilling its contract, example 243
    resizing example 267
    source code 265
blitImage() method 150
blitting
    background 496
    example 150
    meaning 147
    to screen 498
Booch class diagram, described 242

border
    classes 277
    construction example 465
    etched, creating 283
    raised or inset 282
    scrolled components 465
    thickness, specifying 281
Border class
    extending for 3-D 282
    methods 278
    source code 279
    variables 278
BorderLayout
    Bargauge example 272
    borderMe component 164
    described 159, 168
    DialogButtonPanel example 383
    font layout 409
    in gjt.test package 247
    nested layout 170
    RowLayoutApplet example 219
    scrollbar example 432
    Toolbar 330, 337
    when to use 169
BorderLayoutApplet 170
Box class
    constructor example 182
    methods 181
    source code 181
    unit test example 186
brighter() method 32
browser, Java-enabled, how it works 14
BulletinLayout custom layout manager
    described 205
    source code 205
button
    labelling 412
    labels and internationalization 87
    layout example 195
    preview 413
    springy/sticky, grid setting 318
Button object, in dialog 384

C

CardLayout
    controlling component display 173
    description 168, 171
    methods 173
    output 172
    when to use 169
CheckboxMenuItem class 111
class
    See also *AWT class, Component class,
        Container class*
    acting as type-checked constants
        244
    Color 26
    Component 18
    DrawnRectangle 27
    Graphics 25
    layout managers implemented 168
    Orientation 222
    relationship with clients 242
clear() method, DrawnRectangle 30
clickCount, advancing 82
clip bounds 482
clip rectangle
    bounds 497
    setting/resetting 498
collision detection
    handling aftermath 499
    in Playfield 489
    Sprite objects 500
CollisionArena interface 499
CollisionDetector
    described 474
    source code 500
    subclasses 500
color
    background 31
    constants provided 49
    etched effect, achieving 255
    inverting foreground &
        background 60

color (continued)
  making brighter/darker 32
  shading 32
Color class
  constants 49
  shading methods 32
ColumnLayout custom layout
    manager
  ColumnLayoutApplet source code
    230
  methods 225
  source code 226
  unit test 228
component
  adding to scroller 438
  in Component class 7, 9
  controlling display of 173
  custom
    constants for event generation
      88
    creating/delivering events 91
    extending Event class 89
    painting 163
  graphic objects 7
  grid layout 176
  grid layout variables 179
  identifying by label, problems 86,
    87
  identifying by reference 87
  laying out 156, 212
  layout manager interaction 166
  painting 163
  positioning in a row 209
  positioning in columns 225
  propagated event choices 74
  role in image loading 480
  space specification (ipadx, ipady)
    179
  surrounded 185
Component class
  described 5
  instance information 9

subclasses
    action event activation 82
component() method, described 29
ComponentScroller
  methods, implementation 455
  source code 454
  use 435
ComponentScrollerTest
  source code 466–470
composite design pattern 191
constructor, default 455
container
  card-deck display 171
  forcing a layout 200
  insets 161, 162
  invalidating 200
  LayoutManager, invoking 157
  nested 191
  painting components 163
  setting insets 161
Container class
  Applet
    methods 15
  default layout manager 169
  described 5
  Dialog 374
  inset defaults 162
  Panel
    in java.applet 15
  Window, default layout manager
    169
createImage() method 140

D

darker() method 32
deliverEvent() method, with custom
    component 91
destroy() method 16
dialog
  centering in frame 382
  classes 379

client, changing 382
dismissing 376, 382, 384
disposing of 391
modal/non-modal 375
notification to dismiss, methods
    375
positioning 382
setting title 375
showing & program execution 375
Dialog class
    constructing with Frame 375
    Window extension 375
Dialog, default layout manager 169
DialogButtonPanel
    methods of adding buttons 383
    source code 382
DialogClient interface
    implementing 376
dialogDismissed() method 376
Dimension
    column layout 225
    row layout 210
    values for ProgressDialog
        bargauge 396
disable() method, described 300
DISARM, image button event state 315
dispose() method, use for dialogs 391
DissolveFilter class
    public instance methods 145
double buffering 493, 496
DrawnRectangle class
    constructors 28
    description 27
    innerBounds() method 37
    member objects 30
    public methods 29, 30
    source code 34–37
    use by Border class 277
drawString() method 53

E

edge collisions
    edgeCollision() method 502, 508
    EdgeCollisionDetector, source
        code 501
enable() method
    described 300
    mouse events 299
EtchedBorder class 283
EtchedRectangle class
    drawing borders 37
    methods 38
etching
    changing state 40
    creating effect 41
    rectangle 37
    style in Separator 253
event
    action, subclasses 82
    generating for custom component
        88
    handling with AWT 68
    mouse double-clicked 81
    overriding 68
    propagated
        component's handling choices
            74
        example 80
        halting 73
        handling choices 72
    return values 73
    sifter 447
Event class
    constants 70, 77
    extending for custom component
        89
    id field 87
    modifier constants 75
    sensing double-click 81
event handler, calling superclass
        version of method 68

ExclusiveImageButtonPanel
    adding image button 341
    creating new instance, example 345

F

fadeIn() method
    described 147
    ImageDissolver example 149
fadeOut() method, described 147
fill instance variable
    described 179
    set to BOTH 185
fill() method
    bargauge 264
    bargauge rectangle 263
    DrawnRectangle 30, 33
filterRGB() method 141
FlowLayout
    "hidden" component after resizing
        209
    default layout manager 169
    described 159, 168
    in Panel 158
    layout manager implementation
        159
    in Panel 15
    positioning components after
        resizing 174
    responsibilities 160
    when to use 176
focus, requesting 384, 392, 413, 424
font
    available, listing 412
    centering by height/ascent 58
    default sizes, listing 412
    dimensions 57
    displaying current selection 415
    list of names, styles, sizes 413
    mapping from Java 52
    model, AWT 53
    previewing 424

    selection enabling 414
    style determination 415
Font class, font style constants 52
FontButtonsPanel
    button focus 424
    implementation 422
FontDialog
    dismissal notification 411
    inheritance 406
    layout manager 409
    methods 412
    source code 410
    unit test 426
FontDialog class
    methods 406
FontMetrics class, accessing 57
FontPanel
    construction 414
    layout 409
FontPickerPanel
    code 420–422
    layout 419
    lists contained 413
FontPreviewPanel 414
FontSelectionPanel 418
Frame
    default layout manager 169
    insets 162
    method for returning 375
frame, centering dialog 382
Frame.setMenuBar() method 99

G

getFontNames() method 412
getImage() method 128
gjt package
    classes 239
    described 238
GJTDialog class
    FontDialog 406
    role 381
    source code 381

Graphic Java Toolkit (GJT)
   animation package 474
   Assert class 243
   Bargauge class 262
   Border class 277
   Box class 180, 415
   CD directory structure xxxiv
   components used in
      GridLabApplet 200
   contents 238
   dialog classes 379
   DrawnRectangle 27
   EtchedRectangle 37
   FontDialog 405
   gjt.rubberband package 352
   image button 297
   image button controller hierarchy
      307
   image package 238, 241
   image scrolling 462
   ImageButtonController,
      derivations 299
   Orientation class 222
   package structure xxxv
   packages 238
   scroller classes 435
   Separator class 252
   ThreeDRectangle 42
   Toolbar 329
   Util class 246
Graphic Java web site xxxv
Graphics class
   described 5
   filling methods 33
   overview 26
Graphics methods
   drawLine() method 46
   drawRect(), used with
      drawString() 53
   getBackground() 31, 32
   getFontMetrics() 57
   getGraphics() 31, 47
   getImage() 125
   overview 26
Graphics object
   accessing 31
   in component 26
   FontMetrics affiliation 57
   usage example 150
grid
   component position variables 179
   layout managers 168
   setting gap, rows, columns 176
   specifying position parameters 178
GridBagConstraints
   Box constructor example 182
   controlling resize effects, example
      188
   ImageButton example 318
   insets 185
   instance variables/values 179
   Separator example 261
   specifying constraints for multiple
      components 186
GridBagLayout
   Box layout manager 183
   described 168, 178
   example
      purchase form button layout
         465
      with BoxTest class 180, 186
      with font picker panel 419
      with GridBagConstraints 182
      with ImageButtonTest 317
   setting constraints 178, 186
   when to use 169
GridLabApplet
   button layout 195
   custom components from GJT 200
   overview 191
   source code 201–204
   updating ButtonPanel 198
GridLayout
   creating anew 199

GridLayout (continued)
    described 168, 176
    GridLayoutApplet source code 177
    when to use 169, 176
gridwidth, specification as
        REMAINDER 183, 188

H

handleEvent() method
    convenience methods invoked 71
    default behavior, Component 72
    FontDialog class 407
    with hand-delivered events 91
    implementations invoked from
        Scroller 450
    managing menu events 100
    overriding 80
    Scroller 447
hardcoding
    button labels 87
    component layout 205
    orientation 338, 345
    sizes 413
HTML file
    applet 14
    for GJT classes, location 242

I

id field
    custom component event 90
    described 87
IllegalArgumentException 243, 244
image
    adding to container 457
    asynchronous methods 126
    color manipulation 141
    creating off-screen 495
    displaying
        simple example 125
    fading in/out 147
    interfaces 124

requirements for Sprite class 487
    scrolling 459, 462
image button
    controllers 308
    event states 315
    mouse events, decoupled 307
    overview 297
Image object
    determining when filled 130
    monitoring its loading 133
image package
    classes 241
    described 238
ImageButton class
    associating object with controller
        342
    delivering events 92
    enabling/disabling 299
    ensuring only one painted inset
        338, 340
    methods 299
    relationships 298
    source code 303
    variables 300
ImageButtonController
    derivations 299
    objects 310
ImageButtonPanel
    adding an image 333
    adding space 334
    constructors 338
    controller 332
    described 331
    methods 331
    null controller 333
    overriding default constructor 333
    setting orientation 333
    source code 334
    variables 332
ImageButtonPanelController
    mouse event control 339
    source code 339

ImageCanvas 457
ImageDissolver class
    constructors 148
    fadeIn() method 149
    image fade in/out 147
    source code 147
ImageObserver interface
    asynchronous image display 126
    constants 130
    ImageProducer relationship 124
ImageProducer interface 124, 129
ImageScroller
    source code 457
    use 435
ImageScrollerTest 461
imageUpdate() method 124, 126, 128
init() method
    in RowLayout example 219
    for applet 22
    described 16
    in UnitTest 248
inset() method
    border drawing style 282
    ThreeDRectangle 43
insets
    default value 163
    defaults for Container extension
        162
    in Java application Frame object
        162
insets instance variable, described 179
insets() method
    Border 279
    Toolbar 331
internationalization 86, 87
isModal() method, for dialog 375

J

Java
    font mapping 52
    mouse button 78
java interpreter 18

Java mail alias xxxv
Java newsgroup xxxv
Java web site xxxv
javaDrinker 504

K

Key, event constants 70

L

LabelCanvas class
    event hand-delivery example 91
    handleEvent() example 90
    select/deselect event example 88
    source code 60
    unit test 92
layout manager
    Bargauge example 271
    BorderLayout 169
    CardLayout 171
    choosing which to use 169
    constraints 179
    for container 158
    custom
        BulletinLayout 205
        ColumnLayout 225
        RowLayout 209
        when to use 207
    default for Container extension
        classes 169
    default for Panel 15
    FlowLayout 174
    GridBagLayout 178
    GridLayout 176
    invoking addLayoutComponent
        160
    layering example 259
    non-null implementation 160
    no-op implementation 160
    null 204
    RowLayout 209–223
    ScrollerLayout 436

layout manager (continued)
  setConstraints() 184
  sizing a separator 253
  sizing component 167
layout, forcing 415
layoutContainer() method
  BorderLayout vs. FlowLayout 160
  implementation 212, 439
  invoking variables 441
  reshaping/resizing BulletinLayout
    components 205
LayoutManager interface
  classes 10
  definition 204
  described 5
  methods to be defined 158
  sizing methods 166
list, event constants 71

M

main() method
  in applet 14
  in Java application 19
MediaTracker
  encapsulation in Util 135, 148
  image loading 133
menu
  adding items 99
  cascading 114
  checkbox 111
  file 97
  general printing utility 103
  handling events 99
  help 108
  help in Motif 108
  help in Windows 95 108
  limitations creating pop-up 95
  Menu.add(String) and 101
  modifying items dynamically 116
  Motif tear-off 101
  printing status 103

radio button 112
Menu, relationship with other menu
    classes 97
Menu.add() method
  how used 99
  MenuItem version 101
  String version 101
menubar
  printing 103
  relationship to Frame 95
  setting a frame's 99
  steps for adding 104
MenuBar, relationship with other
    menu classes 97
MenuBar.setHelpMenu() method 108
MenuBarPrinter class, menu print
    utility 103
MenuItem, relationship with other
    menu classes 97
MessageDialog
  client access 388
  constructor
    arguments 386
    implementation 386
  dismissal implementation 377
  dismissing dialog 384
  Ok button focus 384
  reusing 387
  source code 384
  static members 387
  viewer's option 379
META_MASK, Event constant 77
Meyer, Bertrand 242
minimumLayoutSize() 211
minimumSize() method
  Bargauge 263
  Border class 279
  Component interaction with layout
    manager 166
  ImageButton 300
  LabelCanvas 56
  minimumLayoutSize() 211

overriding 167
Separator 252
use in scroller layout 439
modifier field
    mouse event handling 78
    use 75
mouse button
    double-clicked 81
    event handling 309
    event modifiers 75
    event monitoring 78
    last down 341
    types 78
mouse event constants 71
MouseController interface, for image
        button controllers 309
mouseDown() method
    event handler 72
    hand-delivered event example 91
    ImageButton 300
    LabelCanvas 56
    overriding 49, 76, 504
    setting variable 60
    Toolbar 332
mouseDrag() method
    event handler 72
    ImageButton 300
    overriding 76
    Toolbar 332
mouseUp() method
    AWT 78
    event handler 72
    ImageButton 300
    overriding 76
    rubberband example 366
    Toolbar 332

N

nested layout 73, 170
nested panels 196
null checking 47
null pointer exception 455

O

Object-Oriented Software Construction
        242
Ok button
    in MessageDialog 385
    requesting focus 384, 392
Orientation class 222
orientation, hardcoding 345

P

pack() method, described 374
pack() method, sizing window/dialog
        413
paint() method
    animation 495
    Bargauge 263
    Border class 279
    Box 181
    described 18
    double buffering 495
    DrawnRectangle 30
    eliminating flashing, example 448
    etched borders 38
    EtchedRectangle 38
    ImageButton 300, 302
    LabelCanvas 56
    overriding in custom components
        68
    scrolling example 448
    Separator 252, 254, 255
    Sequence 480
    setting state for 282, 283
    ThreeDRectangle 43
paintBackground() method 495
paintSprite() method 497
Panel
    vs. Canvas 83
    default layout manager 169
    extending (example) 48
    invalidating (example) 199
    layout manager, default 158

Panel (continued)
    orientation, hardcoding 345
    panelLayout 159
paramString() method
    Border class 279
    custom components 267
    DrawnRectangle 30
    EtchedRectangle 38
    ThreeDRectangle 43
pause() method 150
peer
    advancing clickCount 82
    definition 4
    ensuring creation 419
    example 4
    font selection 418
    inset values 162
    Menu 4
percent() method, described 141
Playfield class
    collision detectors 493
    described 474
    double buffering 493
    extending 502
    how it works 488
    implementation example 504
    interfaces 488
    methods 492
    source code 490
pop-up menus 95
preferredLayoutSize() method 210
preferredSize() method
    Bargauge 263
    Component 166
    ImageButton 300, 302
    LabelCanvas 56
    overriding by Bargauge 264
    overriding by ProgressDialog 396
    Separator 252
    use in scroller layout 439
preview, enabling 413

ProgressDialog
    dismissing 380
    example 380
    source code 396

Q

QuestionDialog
    described 380
    source code 392

R

RadioImageButtonPanelController
    how it works 340, 341
    source code 340
raise() method
    controlling border drawing style
        282
    ThreeDRectangle 43
rectangle
    clip, in animation 497
    constructing with DrawnRectangle
        class 28–31
    creating etched effect 255
    etching 37–42
    filling 33
    shadowing borders 46
    three-dimensional 42
Rectangle class 27
refactoring 366
REMAINDER, component positioning
    183
repaint() method
    described 18
    image display example 131
reshape() method
    animation implementation 493
    Bargauge 263
    Border class 279
    Box 181
    ImageButton 300
    LabelCanvas 56

overriding in custom components
68
repositioning 57
resize() method
Bargauge 263
Border class 279
Box 181
ImageButton 300
LabelCanvas 56
overriding 68
overriding in custom components
68
retrofitPreviewPanel() method, forcing
layout 416
RowLayout custom layout manager
constructors 213
methods 209
positioning components 212
positioning image buttons 222
sizing 210
source code 213
rubberband
drawing lines 358
drawing rectangles/ellipses 359
supplying with component 356
use examples 363
uses 351
Rubberband class
events occurring 352
methods 353
source code 354
stretch() method 357
variables 353
rubberband package
classes 241
described 238
RubberbandPanel, source code 360
run() method
animation 492, 495

S

scrollbar
creation 446
event constants 71
line/page increments 433, 450
management 448, 449
reshape methods 441
setting initial values 459
setting values 433, 450
setting values, example 432
Windows 95/Motif comparison
433
scroller
adding/removing components 437
eliminating flashing 448
keeping track of 459
maintaining references 437
managing scrollbars 441
updating 459
Scroller class
components 436
constructor 446
extensions
described 435
responsibilities 446
layout manager 437
methods 445, 449, 454
overriding methods 451
source code 451–454
ScrollerLayout
assertion protections 438
component checking 446
source code 437
scrolling
See also Scroller *class*
classes for handling 435
component 454–457
image 459
protected methods 451
scrollTo() method
calling 448, 450

scrollTo() method (continued)
    described 455
    null pointer exception 455
    overriding 459
select() method, for LabelCanvas 56
SelectionEvent class
    source code 89
    use of instanceof operator 90
separator
    in DialogButtonPanel 383
    etched effect 255
    sizing 253
    thickness 253
Separator class
    Canvas relationship 252
    private variables 253
    source code 256
Sequence class
    animation, described 474
    construction 480
    how it works 475
    methods 480
    painting/repainting 480
    source code 477
setConstraints() method 184, 186
setImage() method, described 459
setInsets() method, for LabelCanvas 56
setLayout() method
    in GridBagLayout 183
    for Panel 199
    in RowLayout 221
setTitle(String) method, for dialog 375
show() method
    dialog display 375
    ensuring dialog centering 384
    overriding by GJTDialog 382
    overriding by QuestionDialog 392
    sizing dialog 412
    window display 374
singleton pattern
    described 388
    FontDialog, why unused 412

ProgressDialog 395
    QuestionDialog, why unused 391
someMethod() 375
SpringyImageButtonController
    default for ImageButton 301
    described 299
    source code 311, 314
sprite
    changing sequence 481
    functions 475
    painting into workplace buffer 497
    painting with paintSprites() 496
Sprite class
    clip bounds 482
    construction 487
    described 474
    determining direction 481, 504
    image size requirements 487
    methods 487
    relationship to sequence 480
    role in double buffering 498
    sequences 481
    source code 483
Sprite object
    adding to, example 504
    collision detection 500
    responsibilities 475
    tracking by Playfield 489
start() method
    for applet 22
    animation 492
    described 16
    in UnitTest 248
StateButton
    controller 323
    source code 322
    unit test 326
StateButtonController
    described 299
    source code 324
StickyImageButtonController
    described 299

source code 312
use 307
use example 320, 466
stop() method 16, 492
stopwatch, of sprite 481
strategy pattern 158, 204
stretch() method, for rubberbanding
        354, 357
string
    calculating location 57
    determining baseline 53
super.addNotify() method 419
super.reshape() method, when
        overriding reshape 264
superclass, processing an event 70

T

TenPixelBorder
    GridLayout example 196
    RowButtonPanel example 221
    source code 163
    test applet 165
    unit test 164–166
test package
    classes 241, 246
    described 238
ThreeDBorderStyle class 244
ThreeDRectangle class
    border thicknesses 42
    methods 43
    raised/inset borders 46
    source code 43
    specifying border style 245
Tips
    Canvas vs. Panel, when to use 278
    custom component package
        inclusions 242
    designing classes 309
    DrawnRectangle defaults,
        overriding 32
    DrawnRectangle methods 34, 37

expanding grid cell and
        component 319
forcing container to be laid out 200
Frame object inset 104, 106, 162
hardcoding orientation 254
hardcoding shading colors 254
identifying component by
        reference 87
insets values 185
overriding addNotify() 419
overriding size for Canvas
        extension 167
propagating unhandled events 75
reshape(), overriding 264
resizing grid cell vs. resizing
        component 189
returning false from handleEvent()
        70
unit test uses 242
using paramString() for custom
        components 267
TitledPanel 247
toolbar
    described 329
    overview 329
Toolbar class
    creation example 345
    relationships 329
    source code 337
    unit test, source code 344
Toolkit class 128
toString() method
    DrawnRectangle 30
    printing values of constants 245
type-checked constants 244

U

unit test
    Bargauge 270
    Border class 284
    Box class 186

unit test (continued)
- custom components 242
- DrawnRectangle 49
- FontDialog 426
- GJT dialogs 397–399
- ImageButton 317
- infrastructure classes 246
- LabelCanvas 92
- LabelCanvas source code 62
- MessageDialog 377
- RowLayout 223
- Rubberband 361
- Separator 258–261
- sprite-on-sprite collision 511
- StateButton 326
- Toolbar 342
- UnitTest class 247
- uses 242

UnitTest class
- described 247
- setting cursor 248

update() method 18
- overriding for scrolling 448, 459
- overriding in custom components 68

URL, for images 128

Util class
- methods 246
- returning Frame associated with Component 375

V

validate() method
- example 199

validate() method, forcing layout 416

viewport
- creation 446
- described 436
- reshaping 441

W

wallPaper() method 504

web browser, Java-enabled 13

web page, with applet 14

whichMouseButton() method 78

Window
- default layout manager 169
- event constants 70
- methods 374

X

XOR mode, for painting 357

Y

YesNoDialog
- example 380

SUNSOFT PRESS

Prentice Hall PTR is pleased to publish SunSoft Press books. This year's SunSoft catalog has unprecedented breadth and depth, covering not only the inner workings of Sun operating systems, but also guides to multiprocessing, internationalization of software, networking, and other topics important to anyone working with these technologies.

These and other Prentice Hall PTR books are available at your local Magnet Store. To locate the store nearest you fax (201) 236-7123 or visit our web site at:

http://www.prenhall.com

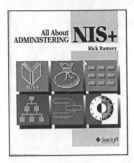

ALL ABOUT ADMINISTERING NIS+, Second Edition
Rick Ramsey

Updated and revised for Solaris™ 2.3, this book is ideal for network administrators who want to know more about NIS+: its capabilities, requirements, how it works, and how to get the most out of it. Includes planning guidelines for both new installations and for transitions from NIS; detailed descriptions of the structure of NIS+ objects and security; and setup instructions for both standard NIS+ comands and NIS+ shell scripts. Presents modular, fully-tested, step-by-step instructions and many illustrations, examples, and tips.

1995, 480 pp., Paper, 0-13-309576-2 (30957-5)

AUTOMATING SOLARIS INSTALLATIONS
Paul Anthony Kasper and Alan L. McClellan

If you want to minimize the time you spend installing the Solaris environment on SPARC™ or x86 systems, this book is for you! It describes how to set up "hands-off" Solaris installations for hundreds of SPARC or x86 systems. It explains in detail how to configure your site so that when you install Solaris, you simply boot a system and walk away - the software installs automatically! Topics covered include setting up network booting, enabling automatic system configuration, setting up custom JumpStart files, booting and installing, debugging and troubleshooting. A diskette containing working shell scripts that automate pre- and post-installation tasks is provided.

1995, 320 pp., Paper, 0-13-312505-X (31250-4) Book/Diskette

CONFIGURATION AND CAPACITY PLANNING FOR SOLARIS SERVERS
Brian L. Wong

Written for MIS staff, this book provides information on planning and configuring Solaris servers for use in NFS™, DBMS, and timesharing environments. The material concentrates on applied computer architecture, case studies and experimentally-based, real-world results rather than on queueing models.

1996, 300 pp., Paper. 0-13-349952-9 (34995-1)

ALSO AVAILABLE FROM SUNSOFT PRESS...

DESIGNING VISUAL INTERFACES:
Communication Oriented Techniques
Kevin Mullet and Darrell K. Sano

Useful to anyone responsible for designing, specifying, implementing, documenting, or managing the visual appearance of computer-based information displays, this book applies the fundamentals of graphic design, industrial design, interior design, and architecture to solve the human computer interface problems experienced in commercial software development. It describes basic design principles (the what and why), common errors, and practical techniques (the how). Readers will gain a new perspective on product development as well as an appreciation for the contribution visual design can offer to their products and users. Six major areas: Elegance and Simplicity; Scale, Contrast, and Proportion; Organization and Visual Structure; Module and Programme; Image and Representation; and Style.

1995, 304 pp., Paper, 0-13-303389-9 (30338-8) (includes 4-color plates)

DEVELOPING VISUAL APPLICATIONS OPENXIL:
An Imaging Foundation Library
William K. Pratt

A practical introduction to imaging into new, innovative applications for desktop computing. For applications in the technical, commercial, and consumer environments, imaging should be considered as basic as putting text or user interface elements into an application. This book breaks down the barriers that developers may have in integrating imaging into their applications. It acquaints developers with the basics of image processing, compression, and algorithm implementation by providing clear, real-world examples of how they can be applied using OpenXIL, a cross-platform imaging foundation library. This book acquaints knowledgeable imaging developers with the architectural features and capabilities of OpenXIL. It can also serve as a primer for new OpenXIL programmers.

1996, 400 pp., Paper, 0-13-461948-X (46194-7)

HTML FOR FUN AND PROFIT Gold Signature Ed.
Mary E. S. Morris

This book is about writing HTML pages for the World Wide Web. Written in a step-by-step, hands on, tutorial style, it presents all the information needed by an aspiring web page author. Platforms are also discussed. Includes:

- Setting up your server
- Learning HTML formatting basics, including lists and special characters
- Integrating multimedia into web pages
- Formatting tables in HTML
- Creating interactive HTML documents with CGI scripting
- Customizing HTML pages with Server Includes
- Designing effective web page layouts
- Appendices on installing and using Xmosaic, WinMosaic, and MacMosaic browsers are included.
- A CD-ROM containing shareware and extensive examples of sample HTML pages and sample perl scripts is also provided.

This book also includes a chapter on Netscape with HTML examples on the CD-ROM. The CD-ROM includes a web server for Microsoft Windows 3.1, NT, Macintosh and UNIX.

1996, 330 pp., Paper, 0-13-242488-6 (24248-7) Book/CD-ROM

EXPERT C PROGRAMMING:
Deep C Secrets
Peter van der Linden

Known as "the butt-ugly fish book" because of the coelacanth on the cover, this is a very different book on the C language! In an easy, conversational style, *it* reveals coding techniques used by the best C programmers. It relates C to other languages and includes an introduction to C++ that can be understood by any programmer without weeks of mind-bending study. Covering both the IBM PC and UNIX systems, this book is a *must read* for anyone who wants to learn more about the implementation, practical use, and folk lore of C!

1994, 384 pp., Paper, 0-13-177429-8 (17742-8)

MANAGING THE NEW ENTERPRISE:

The Proof, Not The Hype
Harris Kern, Randy Johnson, Andrew Law, and Michael Hawkins with William Kennedy

In this follow-up to the best selling *Rightsizing the New Enterprise*, the authors discuss how to build and manage a heterogeneous client/ server environment. *Managing the New Enterprise* describes in detail the key technology support infrastructures, including networking, data centers, and system administration, as well as how Information Technology must change in order to manage the New Enterprise. This is an indispensable reference for anyone within Information Technology who is facing the challenges of building and managing client/server computing.

*1996, 240 pp., Cloth,
0-13-231184-4 (23118-3)*

INTERACTIVE UNIX OPERATING SYSTEM:

A Guide for System Administrators
Marty C. Stewart

Written for first-time system administrators and end users, this practical guide describes the common system administration menus and commands of the INTERACTIVE UNIX System V/386 Release 3.2, Version 4.0 and SVR 3.2 UNIX in general. Loaded with step-by-step instructions and examples, it discusses how to install and configure the INTERACTIVE UNIX system, including the hardware requirements. It describes the unique CUI menu interface, basic OS commands, administration of new user accounts, configuration of customized kernels, and working with the INTERACTIVE UNIX system as an end user.

*1996, 320 pp., Paper,
0-13-161613-7 (16161-2)*

PC HARDWARE CONFIGURATION GUIDE:

For DOS and Solaris
Ron Ledesma

This book eliminates trial-and-error methodology by presenting a simple, structured approach to PC hardware configuration. The author's time-tested approach is to configure your system in stages, verify and test at each stage, and troubleshoot and fix problems before going on to the next stage. Covers both standalone and networked machines. Discusses how to determine x86 hardware configuration requirements, how to configure hardware components (MCA, ISA, and EISA), partitioning hard disks for DOS and UNIX, and installing DOS and/or UNIX (Solaris x86). Includes configuration instructions, checklists, worksheets, diagrams of popular SCSI host bus, network, and video adapters, and basic installation troubleshooting.

1995, 352 pp., Paper, 0-13-124678-X (12467-7)

MULTIPROCESSOR SYSTEM ARCHITECTURES:

A Technical Survey of Multiprocessor / Multithreaded Systems Using SPARC, Multi-level Bus Architectures and Solaris (SunOS)
Ben Catanzaro

Written for engineers seeking to understand the problems and solutions of multiprocessor system design, this hands-on guide is the first comprehensive description of the elements involved in the design and development of Sun's multiprocessor systems. Topics covered include SPARC processor design and its implementations, an introduction to multilevel bus architectures including MBus and XBus/XDBus, an overview of the Solaris/SunOS™ multithreaded architecture and programming, and an MBus Interface Specification and Design Guide. This book can serve as a reference text for design engineers as well as a hands-on design guide to MP systems for hardware/software engineers.

1994, 528 pp., Paper, 0-13-089137-1 (08913-6)

ALSO AVAILABLE FROM SUNSOFT PRESS...

PANIC! UNIX System Crash Dump Analysis
Chris Drake and Kimberley Brown

PANIC! is the first book to discuss in detail UNIX system panics, crashes and hangs, their causes, what to do when they occur, how to collect information about them, how to analyze that information, and how to get the problem resolved. PANIC! presents this highly technical and intricate subject in a friendly, easy style which even the novice UNIX system administrator will find readable, educational and enjoyable. It is written for systems and network administrators and technical support engineers who are responsible for maintaining and supporting UNIX computer systems and networks. Includes a CD-ROM containing several useful analysis tools, such as adb macros and C tags output from the source trees of two different UNIX systems.

1995, 496 pp., Paper, 0-13-149386-8 (14938-5) Book/CD-ROM

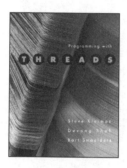

NEW!

PROGRAMMING WITH THREADS
Steve Kleiman, Devang Shah, and Bart Smaalders

Written by senior threads engineers at Sun Microsystems, Inc., this book is the definitive guide to programming with threads. It is intended for both novice and more sophisticated threads programmers, and for developers multithreading existing programs as well as for those writing new multithreaded programs. The book provides structured techniques for mastering the complexity of threads programming with an emphasis on performance issues. Included are detailed examples using the new POSIX threads (Pthreads) standard interfaces. The book also covers the other UNIX threads interface defined by UNIX International.

1996, 250 pp., Paper, 0-13-172389-8 (17238-9)

RIGHTSIZING THE NEW ENTERPRISE:
THE PROOF, NOT THE HYPE
Harris Kern and Randy Johnson

A detailed account of how Sun Microsystems implemented its rightsizing strategy going from a mainframe data center to a heterogeneous client/server distributed environment. This book covers the key infrastructures of an IT organization (the network, data center, and system administration), the rightsizing/management tools, and the training/resource issues involved in transitioning from mainframe to UNIX support. The facts contained in this book provide you with the PROOF that 'rightsizing' can be done.and has been done.

1995, 352 pp., Cloth, 0-13-490384-6 (49038-3)

NEW!

READ ME FIRST!
A Style Guide for the Computer Industry
Sun Technical Publications

A comprehensive look at documenting computer products, from style pointers to legal guidelines, from working with an editor to building a publications department — in both hard copy and electronic copy with an on line viewer, FrameMaker templates for instant page design, and a detailed guide to establishing a documentation department and its processes. Based on an internationally award-winning Sun Microsystems style guide (Award of Excellence in the STC International Technical Publications Competition, 1994)

1996, 300 pp., Paper, 0-13-455347-0 (45534-6)

Book/CD-ROM

RIGHTSIZING FOR CORPORATE SURVIVAL:
An IS Manager's Guide
Robert Massoudi, Astrid Julienne, Bob Millradt, and Reed Hornberger

This book provides IS managers with 'hands-on' guidance for developing a rightsizing strategy and plan. Based upon research conducted through customer visits with multinational corporations, it details the experiences and insights gained by IS professionals that have implemented systems in distributed, client-server environments. Topics covered include:

- Why rightsize?
- What business results can rightsizing produce?
- Key technologies critical to rightsizing
- Good starting points for rightsizing
- What is the process to rightsize an information system?
- Cost considerations and return on investment (ROI) analysis
- How to manage the transition

Throughout the book, case studies and `lessons learned' reinforce the discussion and document best practices associated with rightsizing.

1995, 272 pp., Paper,
0-13-123120-X (12312-5)

SOLARIS IMPLEMENTATION:
A Guide for System Administrators
George Becker, Mary E. S. Morris and Kathy Slattery

Written by three expert Sun system administrators, this book discusses real world, day-to-day Solaris 2 system administration for both new installations and for those migrating an installed Solaris 1 base. It presents tested procedures to help system administrators to improve and customize their networks by eliminating trial-and-error methodologies. Also includes advice for managing heterogeneous Solaris environments and provides autoinstall sample scripts and disk partitioning schemes (with recommended sizes) used at Sun. *1995, 368 pp., Paper, 0-13-353350-6 (35335- 9)*

SOLARIS INTERNATIONAL DEVELOPER'S GUIDE, Second Edtion
Bill Tuthill and David Smallberg

Written for software developers and business managers interested in creating global applications for the Solaris environment (SPARC and x86), this 2nd edition expands on the 1st edition and has updated information on international markets, standards organizations, and writing international documents. New topics in the 2nd edition include CDE/Motif, NEO (formerly project DOE)/ OpenStep, Universal codesets, global internet applications, code examples, and success stories.

1990, 250 pp., Paper,
0-13-494493-3 (49449-2)

SOLARIS PORTING GUIDE, Second Edition
SunSoft Developer Engineering

Ideal for application programmers and software developers, the Solaris Porting Guide, Second Edition, provides a comprehensive technical overview of the Solaris 2.x operating environment and its related migration strategy. The second edition is current through Solaris 2.4 (both the SPARC and x86 platforms) and provides all the information necessary to migrate from Solaris 1 (SunOS 4.x) to Solaris 2 (SunOS 5.x). Other additions include a discussion of emerging technologies such as the Common Desktop Environment (CDE), hints for application performance tuning, and extensive pointers to further information, including Internet sources.

1995, 752 pp., Paper,
0-13-443672-5 (44367-1)

SUN PERFORMANCE AND TUNING:
SPARC and Solaris
Adrian Cockcroft

An indispensable reference for anyone working with Sun workstations running the Solaris environment, this book provides detailed performance and configuration information on all SPARC machines and peripherals, as well as on all operating system releases from SunOS 4.1 through Solaris 2.4. It includes hard-to-find tuning information and offers insights that cannot be found elsewhere. This book is written for developers who want to design for performance and for system administrators who have a system running applications on which they want to improve performance.

1995, 288 pp., Paper,
0-13-149642-5 (14964-1)

ALSO AVAILABLE FROM SUNSOFT PRESS...

NEW!

THREADS PRIMER:
A Guide to Solaris Multithreaded Programming
Bil Lewis and Daniel J. Berg

Written for developers interested in MT programming, this primer overviews the concepts involved in multithreaded development. Based on the Solaris multithreaded architecture, the primer delivers threading concepts that can be applied to almost any multithreaded platform. The book covers the design and implementation of multithreaded programs as well as the business and technical benefits of threads. Both the Solaris and the POSIX threads API are used as the interface needed to develop applications. Extensive examples highlight the use of threads in real-world applications. This book is a must read for developers interested in MT technology!

1996, 352 pp., Paper,
0-13-443698-9 (44369-7)

NEW!

WABI 2: Opening Windows
Scott Fordin and Susan Nolin

Wabi™ 2 is here and now you can run Microsoft and Windows 3.1 applications on UNIX-based computers! Written for both users and system administrators of Wabi software, this book covers everything you wanted to know about Wabi 2, including: Wabi technical history, how Wabi works, UNIX for Microsoft Windows users, Microsoft Windows for UNIX users, X Window terminology and interface objects, additional sources of information on Wabi, sample settings in which Wabi is used, and common questions asked by users.

1996, 400 pp., Paper,
0-13-461617-0 (46161-6)

NEW!

VERILOG HDL:
A Guide to Digital Design and Synthesis
Samir Palnitkar

Everything you always wanted to know about Verilog HDL, from fundamentals such as gate, RTL and behavioral modeling to advanced concepts such as timing simulation, switch level modeling, PLI and logic synthesis. This book approaches Verilog HDL from a practical design perspective rather than from a language standpoint. Includes over 300 illustrations, examples, and exercises, and a Verilog Internet reference resource list. Learning objectives and summaries are provided for each chapter. The CD-ROM contains a verilog simulator with a graphical user interface and the source code for the examples in the book. This book is of value to new and experienced Verilog HDL users, both in industry and at universities (logic design courses).

1996, 400 pp., Cloth, 0-13-451675-3 (45167-4) Book/CD-ROM

TOOLTALK AND OPEN PROTOCOLS:
Interapplication Communication
Astrid M. Julienne and Brian Holtz

This book discusses how to design, write, and implement open protocols and includes examples using the ToolTalk™ messaging service. Both procedural and object-oriented protocols are covered in detail. While the ToolTalk service is used as a point of reference throughout, the information provided conforms to the standardization efforts currently in progress for inter-application communication. A valuable resource for the developer writing applications for both the common desktop environment (CDE) and SunSoft's Project DOE system (now known as NEO™).

1994, 384 pp., Paper, 0-13-031055-7 (03105-4)

NEW!

WEB PAGE DESIGN:
A Different Multimedia
Mary E. S. Morris and Randy J. Hinrichs

Everything you always wanted to know about practical Web page design from the best-selling author of *HTML for Fun and Profit*. Written for Web page authors, this hands on guide covers the key aspects of designing a successful web site including cognitive design, content design, audience consideration, interactivity, organization, navigational pathways, and graphical elements. Includes designing for VRML and Java sites as well as designing with templates, style sheets, and Netscape Frames. Also contains many examples of successful Web pages, including 16 color plates.

1996, 200 pp., Paper, 0-13-239880-X (23988-9)

...ALSO AVAILABLE FROM SUNSOFT PRESS

INSTANT JAVA   NEW!

John A. Pew

The easy, practical way to add Java applets to your Web pages!

Now programmers and nonprogrammers alike can instantly create sizzling Web pages filled with sound, animation, and interactivity using this Java cookbook. The book provides a variety of applets and shows users how to easily plug them into existing Web pages. The applets in this book are designed to be as flexible as possible. You can customize as few or as many settings as you wish. With very little effort you can create applets that are both personal and unique. The following are among the 60+ applets included in the book:

* Audio
* Multiple Simultaneous Animations
* Image maps
* Ticker tapes
* And more...

The book provides detailed, step-by-step instructions on how to customize the applets on the accompanying CD-ROM to suit specific needs. The CD-ROM also includes the source code for all the applets in the book and the Java Developer's Kit, as well as HTML sample pages that show exactly how to embed the applets into your Web page. Instant Java is an invaluable reference that offers well-organized instructions for easily adding Java special effects to any HTML document.

Other Java books focus on history, theory, or technical details. Instant Java lets you use your text, your images, and your sound on your Web pages right now.

1996, 340pp, Paper
0-13-565821-7 (56582-0)

Book/CD-ROM

SunSoft Press

JAVA BY EXAMPLE   NEW!

Jerry R. Jackson and Alan L. McClellan

There is no better way to learn Java than by example...

Learn Java from proven examples written by experts. Written for intermediate and experienced programmers, Java By Example presents the Java language through examples, developing Java applets and applications from simple to complex. By reviewing real, working code, you will learn the right way to develop Java code that is elegant, readable, and easy to maintain. The book's carefully annotated code is designed to help programmers start developing with Java immediately. The book is divided into two main parts:

Working with the Java Language
* Memory and constructors
* Input/Output
* Threads
* Exception handling
* Interfacing with C programs

Writing Java Applets
* Threads in applets
* Interactive applets
* Forms and components
* Animation in applets

The accompanying CD-ROM includes example code from the book ready to run on Solaris™, Windows® 95 and Windows NT™ systems, as well as the complete 1.0 release of the Java Developer's Kit (JDK), Symantec's Café™ Lite, and more.

1996, 368pp, Paper
0-13-565763-6 (56576-2)

Book/CD-ROM

ALSO AVAILABLE FROM SUNSOFT PRESS...

JUST JAVA

Peter van der Linden

A unique introduction to Java and Object-Oriented Programming.

Learn Java with Peter van der Linden's straight talk, interesting examples, and unique style. Written by the author of the bestselling Expert C Programming: Deep C Secrets, this book conveys a sense of the enjoyment that lies in computer programming. The author strongly believes that programming should be challenging, exciting, and enjoyable, and that books about programming should be too. Topics discussed include:

- The Story of O—
  Object-Oriented Programming
- The Robot Ping-Pong Player
- GIGO—Garbage In, Gospel Out
- Associativity and the
  "Coffeepot Property"

Also included are more traditionally titled topics such as:

- Applications versus Applets
- Identifiers, Comments, Keywords, and Operators
- Packages, Classes, and Interfaces
- Arrays, Exceptions, and Threads
- Java Libraries—Networking and Windowing

Just Java is practical, understandable, and fun. Its CD-ROM includes Java sample code and applications, an anagram program, images, and the complete 1.0 release of the Java Developer's Kit (JDK) for Solaris™, Windows® 95 and Windows NT™.

1996, 354pp, Paper
0-13-565839-X (56583-8)
Book/CD-ROM

SunSoft
Press

CORE JAVA

**Gary Cornell and
Cay S. Horstmann**

Get quickly to the heart of Java.

With Core Java, experienced programmers can get to the heart of Java quickly and easily. You'll start with the fundamentals and move quickly to the most advanced topics. Core Java provides comprehensive coverage of all Java features including numerous tips and tricks as well as Visual Basic and C/C++ notes that compare and contrast features of Java to those languages. Among the many topics covered in depth are:

- Classes
- Inheritance
- Graphics programming with AWT
- Interface design with AWT
- Exception handling
- Debugging
- Data structures
- Networking
- And much more

Core Java introduces the new Java development environments for both Solaris™, and Windows® 95. It presents detailed coverage of Java's AWT system for graphics programming and interface design. Then it walks you through the construction, and debugging of numerous real-world Java programs.

1996, 622pp, Paper
0-13-565755-5 (56575-4)
Book/CD-ROM

Get Café 1.0 at a Special Price

The full version of Symantec Café contains the latest Java Development Kit and many exciting new features and tools:

✔ Debug your Java applets with the Café Visual Java Debugger

✔ Design your forms and menus with the Café Studio

✔ Navigate and edit your classes and methods with the Hierarchy Editor and Class Editor

✔ Compile your Java applets and applications 20 times faster with the Café native compiler

✔ Double the speed of your Java applications with the Café native Java virtual machine

SYMANTEC.

http://www.Café.Symantec.com

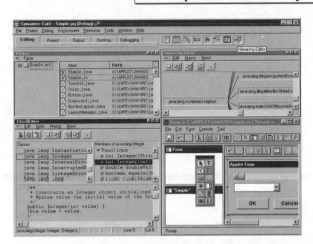

Symantec Café includes all the components found in Café Lite, plus a 2-way hierarchy editor, a class editor, a GUI multi-thread debugger, a visual menu and form designer, a native compiler which compiles the .class files up to 20 times faster, a new Java virtual machine for Windows which doubles the speed of your applications, 85 samples, a tutorial, and the API docs in help.

Get more information on Café automatically sent to you via e-mail. Send an email to **info@bedford.symantec.com** with no subject line, and an overview document will be sent to you along with a description of the other documents available and how to get them.

Yes! I want the most advanced Java development tool for Windows NT and Windows 95. Please rush me Symantec Café 1.0 at this special discount offer!
Available in U.S. only. Offer expires 12/31/96.

(Please print neatly)

Name: _____

Company: _____

Title:_____

Address: _____

_____

City:_____

State/Province: _____

Country (if not USA): _____

Phone: _____

E-mail: _____

You can receive updates on new developments regarding Symantec Café approximately once per month via e-mail. Do you wish to be added to our information bulletin list?

❏ Yes ❏ No

Upgrade from Cafe Lite to Café 1.0 Product Code: FULLCAFE	**$ 129.95**
Number of Units Requested:	$ _____
Applicable sales tax:	$ _____
Shipping $8.00 for each product shipped in USA/Canada	$ _____
PAYMENT TOTAL:	$ _____

Payment Method: ❏ Check ❏ Money Order ❏ Visa

(Please do not send cash*)* ❏ American Express ❏ MasterCard

Name on card: _____

Expiration date: _____

Signature (required) :_____

Mail to: Cafe Lite Upgrade
P.O. Box 10849
Eugene, OR 97440-9711
Call 1-800-240-2275 24hrs. / 7 days
or fax your order to 800-800-1438
Product code: FULLCAFE

State Sales/Use Tax

In the following states, add sales/use tax: CO-3%; GA, LA, NY-4%; VA-4.5%; KS-4.9%; AZ, IA, IN, MA, MD, OH, SC, WI-5%; CT, FL, ME, MI, NC, NJ, PA, TN-6%; CA, IL, TX-6.25%; MN, WA-6.5%;DC-5.75%.

Please add local tax for AZ, CA, FL, GA, MO, NY, OH, SC, TN, TX, WA, WI.

Order Information:

- Please allow 2-4 weeks for processing your order.
- Please attach the order form with your payment.
- No P.O. boxes and no C.O.D.s accepted.
- Order form good in the U.S. only.
- If you are tax exempt, please include exemption certificate or letter with tax-exempt number.
- Resellers not eligible.
- Offer not valid with any other promotion.
- One copy per product, per order.

THE ARCHIVE UTILITY FOR WINDOWS

Windows 95 FEATURES INCLUDE long filename support and the ability to zip and unzip files without leaving the Explorer

WINZIP®
Nico Mak Computing, Inc.

KEY FEATURES

- Brings the convenience of Windows to Zipping
- Built-in PKZIP-compatible ZIP & UNZIP (PKZIP & PKUNZIP are not required)
- Built-in support for popular Internet file compression formats TAR, gzip, and Unix compress
- Full drag and drop support
- Works with ARJ, ARC, and LZH files
- Optional virus scanning support

Have you ever used the Internet, a BBS, or CompuServe? If so, you've probably encountered .ZIP, .TAR, .GZ, and .Z files. Are you a Windows user? If so, WinZip is the way to handle these archived files.

WinZip brings the convenience of Windows to the use of ZIP files without requiring PKZIP and PKUNZIP. It features an intuitive point-and-click drag-and-drop interface for viewing, running, extracting, adding, deleting, and testing files in ZIP, LZH, ARJ, and ARC files. Optional virus scanning support is included. Windows and Windows 95 versions are included in the same package.

Shareware evaluation versions of WinZip are available on better bulletin boards and online services everywhere. Be sure to get version 6.0 or later.

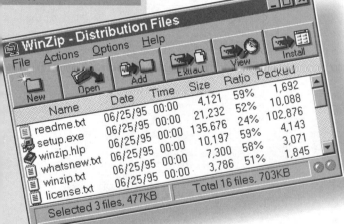

"These days everyone needs a good unzipping utility. This is the best."
PC Computing, 12/95

"Recommended download"
Windows Magazine, 9/95

"Cadillac of unzippers"
PC Magazine, 3/95

Voted "Best Utility"
1994 Annual Shareware Industry Awards

SPECIAL OFFER!

SAVE $5 OFF THE $29 PRICE (includes shipping) with this coupon.

- -

Offer good only when paying by check to Nico Mak Computing, Inc., P.O. Box 919, Bristol, CT 06011-0919. Connecticut residents please add 6% sales tax.

NAME: _____

COMPANY: _____

ADDRESS:_____

CITY _____ STATE _____ ZIP: _____

COUNTRY: _____

Payment must be in US funds. Offer expires April 1997. Original coupons only. Price subject to change without notice. This coupon in not valid in France or French speaking territories.

LICENSE AGREEMENT AND LIMITED WARRANTY

READ THE FOLLOWING TERMS AND CONDITIONS CAREFULLY BEFORE OPENING THIS DISK PACKAGE. THIS LEGAL DOCUMENT IS AN AGREEMENT BETWEEN YOU AND PRENTICE-HALL, INC. (THE "COMPANY"). BY OPENING THIS SEALED DISK PACKAGE, YOU ARE AGREEING TO BE BOUND BY THESE TERMS AND CONDITIONS. IF YOU DO NOT AGREE WITH THESE TERMS AND CONDITIONS, DO NOT OPEN THE DISK PACKAGE. PROMPTLY RETURN THE UNOPENED DISK PACKAGE AND ALL ACCOMPANYING ITEMS TO THE PLACE YOU OBTAINED THEM FOR A FULL REFUND OF ANY SUMS YOU HAVE PAID.

1.   **GRANT OF LICENSE:** In consideration of your payment of the license fee, which is part of the price you paid for this product, and your agreement to abide by the terms and conditions of this Agreement, the Company grants to you a nonexclusive right to use and display the copy of the enclosed software program (hereinafter the "SOFTWARE") on a single computer (i.e., with a single CPU) at a single location so long as you comply with the terms of this Agreement. The Company reserves all rights not expressly granted to you under this Agreement.

2.   **OWNERSHIP OF SOFTWARE:** You own only the magnetic or physical media (the enclosed disks) on which the SOFTWARE is recorded or fixed, but the Company retains all the rights, title, and ownership to the SOFTWARE recorded on the original disk copy(ies) and all subsequent copies of the SOFTWARE, regardless of the form or media on which the original or other copies may exist. This license is not a sale of the original SOFTWARE or any copy to you.

3.   **COPY RESTRICTIONS:** This SOFTWARE and the accompanying printed materials and user manual (the "Documentation") are the subject of copyright. You may not copy the Documentation or the SOFTWARE, except that you may make a single copy of the SOFTWARE for backup or archival purposes only. You may be held legally responsible for any copying or copyright infringement which is caused or encouraged by your failure to abide by the terms of this restriction.

4.   **USE RESTRICTIONS:** You may not network the SOFTWARE or otherwise use it on more than one computer or computer terminal at the same time. You may physically transfer the SOFTWARE from one computer to another provided that the SOFTWARE is used on only one computer at a time. You may not distribute copies of the SOFTWARE or Documentation to others. You may not reverse engineer, disassemble, decompile, modify, adapt, translate, or create derivative works based on the SOFTWARE or the Documentation without the prior written consent of the Company.

5.   **TRANSFER RESTRICTIONS:** The enclosed SOFTWARE is licensed only to you and may not be transferred to any one else without the prior written consent of the Company. Any unauthorized transfer of the SOFTWARE shall result in the immediate termination of this Agreement.

6.   **TERMINATION:** This license is effective until terminated. This license will terminate automatically without notice from the Company and become null and void if you fail to comply with any provisions or limitations of this license. Upon termination, you shall destroy the Documentation and all copies of the SOFTWARE. All provisions of this Agreement as to warranties, limitation of liability, remedies or damages, and our ownership rights shall survive termination.

7.   **MISCELLANEOUS:** This Agreement shall be construed in accordance with the laws of the United States of America and the State of New York and shall benefit the Company, its affiliates, and assignees.

8.   **LIMITED WARRANTY AND DISCLAIMER OF WARRANTY:** The Company warrants that the SOFTWARE, when properly used in accordance with the Documentation, will operate in substantial conformity with the description of the SOFTWARE set forth in the Documentation. The Company does not warrant that the SOFTWARE will meet your requirements or that the operation of the SOFTWARE will be uninterrupted or error-free. The Company warrants that the media on which the SOFTWARE is delivered shall be free from defects in materials and workmanship under normal use for a period of thirty (30) days from the date of your purchase. Your only remedy and the Company's only obligation under these limited warranties is, at the Company's option, return of the warranted item for a refund of any amounts paid by you or replacement of the item. Any replacement of SOFTWARE or media under the warranties shall not extend the original warranty period. The limited warranty set forth above shall not apply to any SOFT-WARE which the Company determines in good faith has been subject to misuse, neglect, improper installation, repair, alteration, or damage by you. EXCEPT FOR THE EXPRESSED WARRANTIES SET FORTH ABOVE, THE COMPANY DISCLAIMS ALL WARRANTIES, EXPRESS OR IMPLIED, INCLUDING WITHOUT LIMITATION, THE IMPLIED WARRANTIES OF MERCHANTABILITY AND FITNESS FOR A PARTICULAR PURPOSE. EXCEPT FOR THE EXPRESS WARRANTY SET FORTH ABOVE, THE COMPANY DOES NOT WARRANT, GUARANTEE, OR MAKE ANY REPRESENTATION REGARDING THE USE OR THE RESULTS OF THE USE OF THE SOFTWARE IN TERMS OF ITS CORRECTNESS, ACCURACY, RELIABILITY, CURRENTNESS, OR OTHERWISE.

IN NO EVENT, SHALL THE COMPANY OR ITS EMPLOYEES, AGENTS, SUPPLIERS, OR CONTRACTORS BE LIABLE FOR ANY INCIDENTAL, INDIRECT, SPECIAL, OR CONSEQUENTIAL DAMAGES ARISING OUT OF OR IN CONNECTION WITH THE LICENSE GRANTED UNDER THIS AGREEMENT, OR FOR LOSS OF USE, LOSS OF DATA, LOSS OF INCOME OR PROFIT, OR OTHER LOSSES, SUSTAINED AS A RESULT OF INJURY TO ANY PERSON, OR LOSS OF OR DAMAGE TO PROPERTY, OR CLAIMS OF THIRD PARTIES, EVEN IF THE COMPANY OR AN AUTHORIZED REPRESENTATIVE OF THE COMPANY HAS BEEN ADVISED OF THE POSSIBILITY OF SUCH DAMAGES. IN NO EVENT SHALL LIABILITY OF THE COMPANY FOR DAMAGES WITH RESPECT TO THE SOFT-WARE EXCEED THE AMOUNTS ACTUALLY PAID BY YOU, IF ANY, FOR THE SOFTWARE.

SOME JURISDICTIONS DO NOT ALLOW THE LIMITATION OF IMPLIED WARRANTIES OR LIABILITY FOR INCIDENTAL, INDIRECT, SPECIAL, OR CONSEQUENTIAL DAMAGES, SO THE ABOVE LIMITATIONS MAY NOT ALWAYS APPLY. THE WARRANTIES IN THIS AGREEMENT GIVE YOU SPECIFIC LEGAL RIGHTS AND YOU MAY ALSO HAVE OTHER RIGHTS WHICH VARY IN ACCORDANCE WITH LOCAL LAW.

ACKNOWLEDGMENT

YOU ACKNOWLEDGE THAT YOU HAVE READ THIS AGREEMENT, UNDERSTAND IT, AND AGREE TO BE BOUND BY ITS TERMS AND CONDITIONS. YOU ALSO AGREE THAT THIS AGREEMENT IS THE COMPLETE AND EXCLUSIVE STATEMENT OF THE AGREEMENT BETWEEN YOU AND THE COMPANY AND SUPERSEDES ALL PROPOSALS OR PRIOR AGREEMENTS, ORAL, OR WRITTEN, AND ANY OTHER COMMUNICATIONS BETWEEN YOU AND THE COMPANY OR ANY REPRESENTATIVE OF THE COMPANY RELATING TO THE SUBJECT MATTER OF THIS AGREEMENT.

Should you have any questions concerning this Agreement or if you wish to contact the Company for any reason, please contact in writing at the address below.

Robin Short
Prentice Hall PTR
One Lake Street
Upper Saddle River, New Jersey 07458

Read before opening CD package!

LICENSE AGREEMENT
AND LIMITED WARRANTY

BY OPENING THIS SEALED SOFTWARE CD PACKAGE, YOU ACCEPT AND AGREE TO THE TERMS AND CONDITIONS PRINTED BELOW AND IN THE FULL AGREEMENT PRINTED ON THE PAGES FOLLOWING THE INDEX. IF YOU DO NOT AGREE, DO NOT OPEN THE PACKAGE.

The software is distributed on an "AS IS" basis, without warranty. Neither the authors, the software developers nor Prentice Hall make any representation, or warranty, either express or implied, with respect to the software programs, their quality, accuracy, or fitness for a specific purpose. Therefore, neither the authors, the software developers, nor Prentice Hall shall have any liability to you or any other person or entity with respect to any liability, loss, or damage caused or alleged to have been caused directly or indirectly by the programs contained on the CD. This includes, but is not limited to, interruption of service, loss of data, loss of classroom time, loss of consulting or anticipatory profits, or consequential damages from the use of these programs. If the CD medium is defective, you may return it for a replacement CD.

The SunSoft Press Java Series CD-ROM is a standard ISO-9660 disc. Software on this CD-ROM requires Windows 95, Windows NT, Solaris 2 or Macintosh (System 7.5).

Windows 3.1 IS NOT SUPPORTED